Skip·Beat!

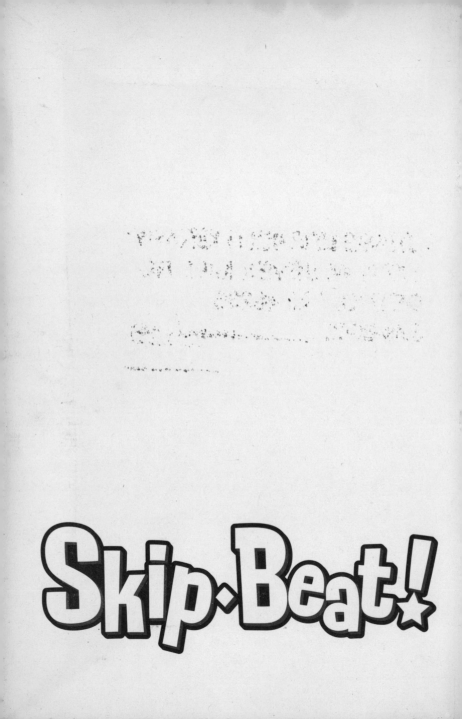

Shojo Beat

Skip·Beat!

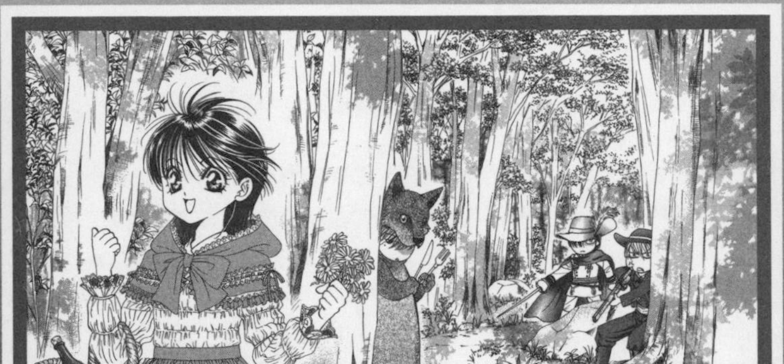

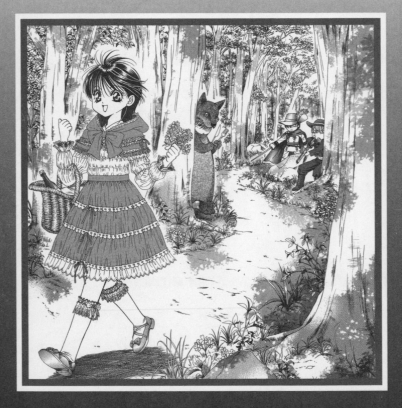

15

Story & Art by Yoshiki Nakamura

Skip·Beat!

Volume 15

CONTENTS

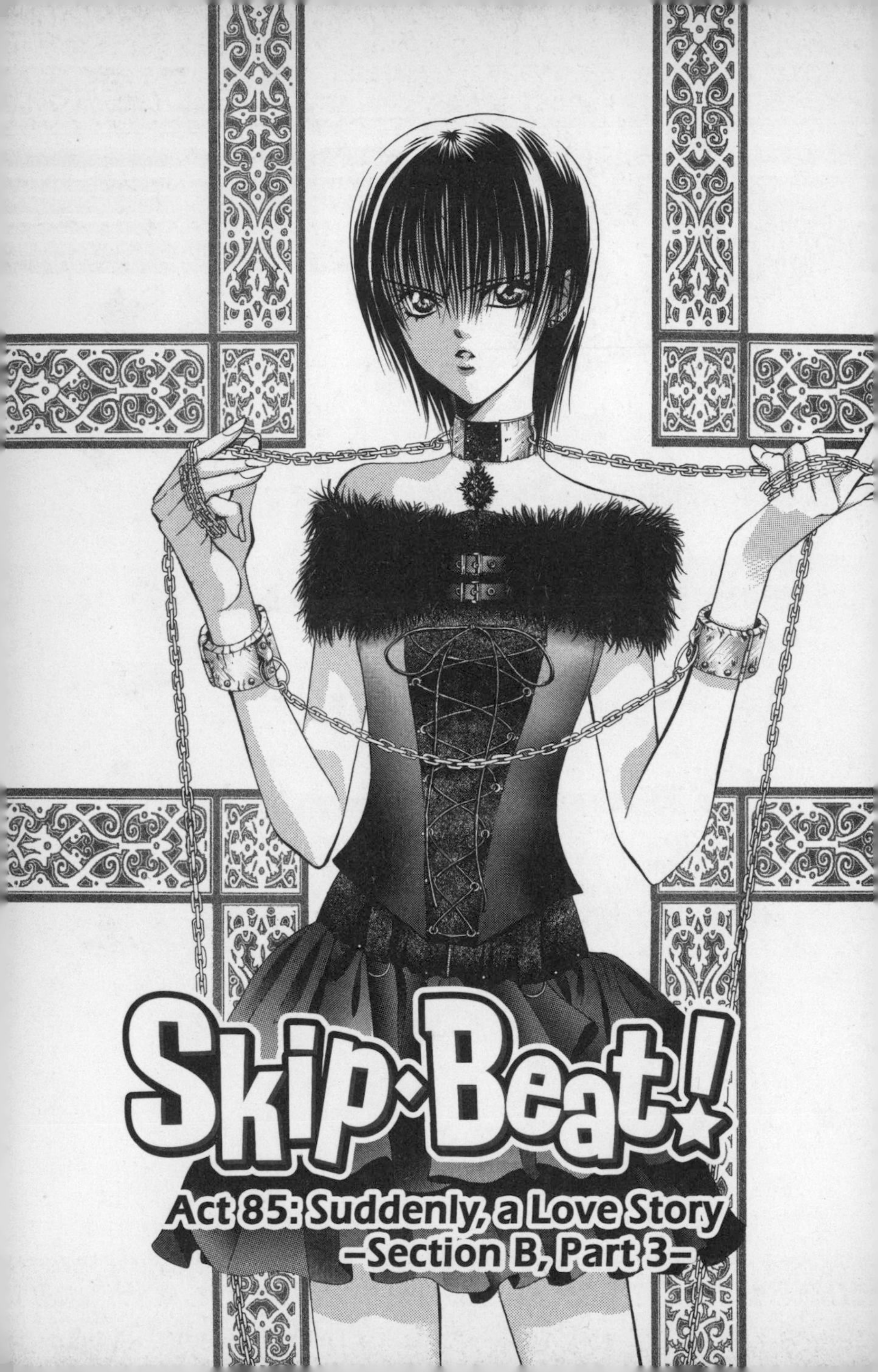
Skip·Beat!
Act 85: Suddenly, a Love Story
–Section B, Part 3–

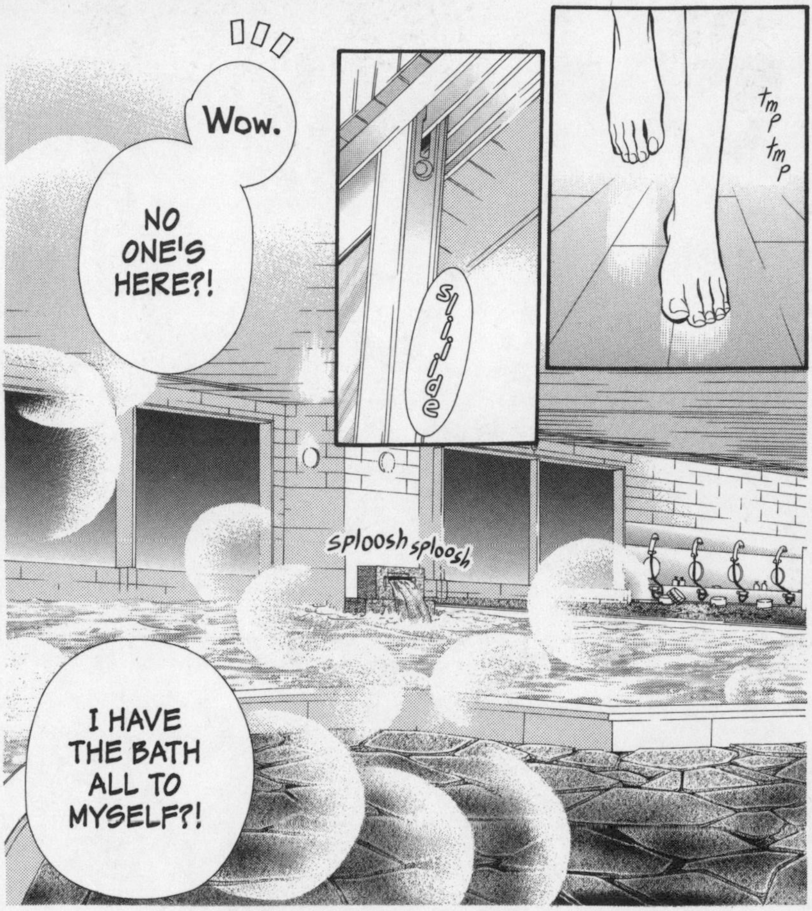
tmp tmp
sliiide
Wow.
NO ONE'S HERE?!
sploosh sploosh
I HAVE THE BATH ALL TO MYSELF?!

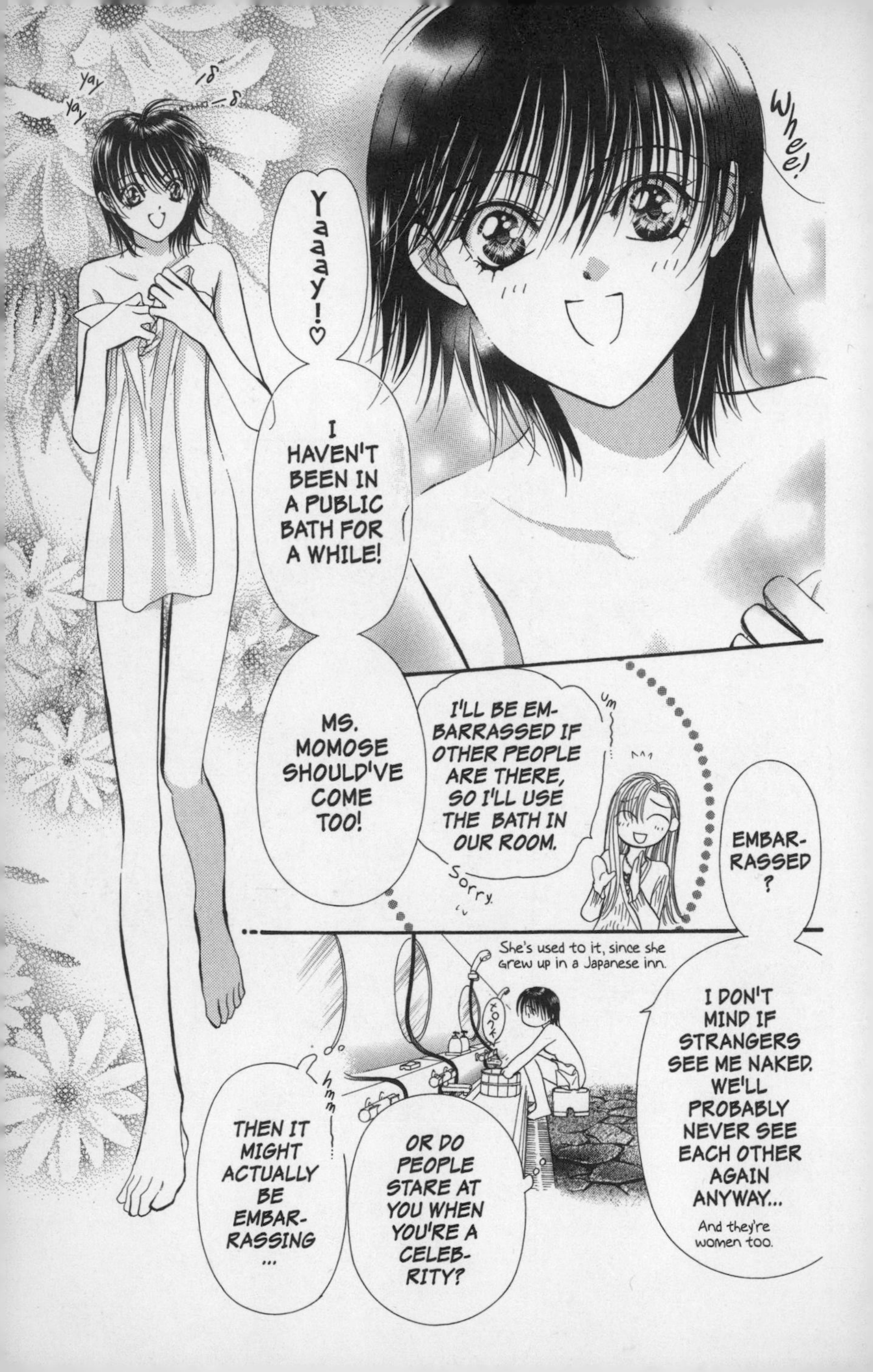
Whee!
yay yay
Yaaay!♡
I HAVEN'T BEEN IN A PUBLIC BATH FOR A WHILE!
MS. MOMOSE SHOULD'VE COME TOO!
um...
I'LL BE EMBARRASSED IF OTHER PEOPLE ARE THERE, SO I'LL USE THE BATH IN OUR ROOM.
Sorry.
EMBARRASSED?
I DON'T MIND IF STRANGERS SEE ME NAKED. WE'LL PROBABLY NEVER SEE EACH OTHER AGAIN ANYWAY...
And they're women too.
She's used to it, since she grew up in a Japanese inn.
OR DO PEOPLE STARE AT YOU WHEN YOU'RE A CELEBRITY?
hmm...
THEN IT MIGHT ACTUALLY BE EMBARRASSING...

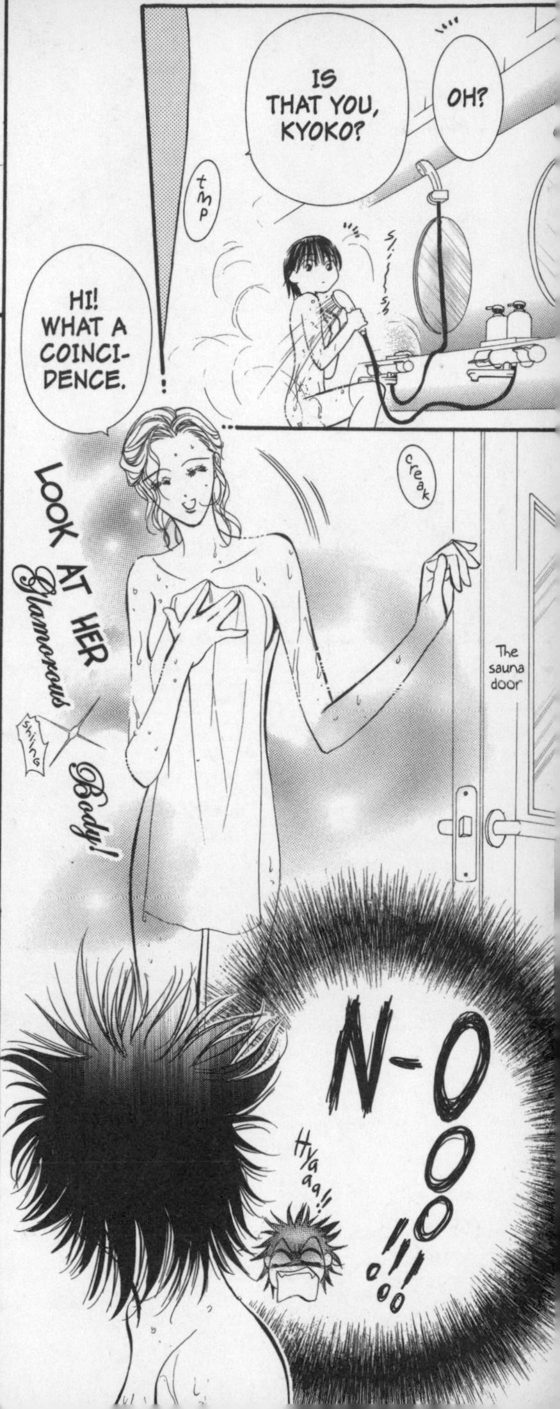

...
OH?
IS THAT YOU, KYOKO?
tmp
HI! WHAT A COINCIDENCE.
creak
The sauna door
LOOK AT HER Glamorous Body!
shining
N-OOOO!!!
Hyaaa!!

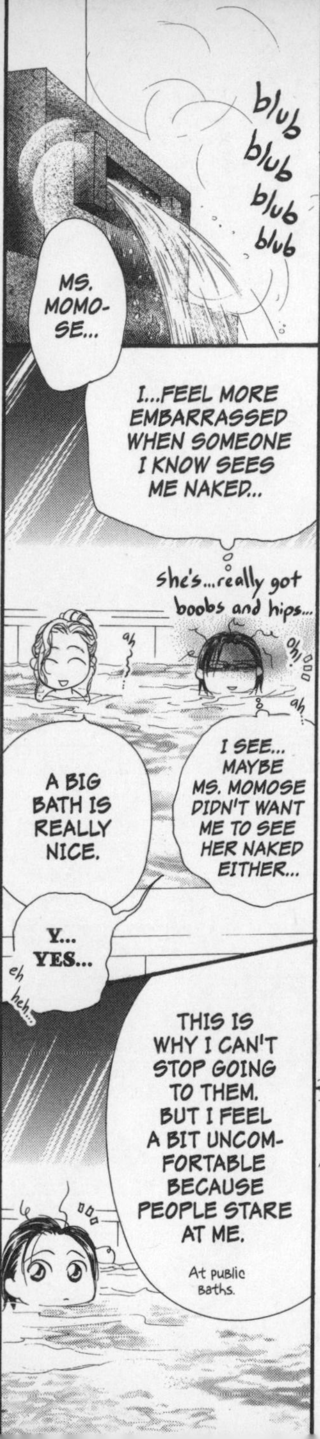

blub blub blub blub
MS. MOMOSE...
I...FEEL MORE EMBARRASSED WHEN SOMEONE I KNOW SEES ME NAKED...
she's...really got boobs and hips...
ah
oh!
ah...
I SEE... MAYBE MS. MOMOSE DIDN'T WANT ME TO SEE HER NAKED EITHER...
A BIG BATH IS REALLY NICE.
Y... YES...
eh heh...
THIS IS WHY I CAN'T STOP GOING TO THEM. BUT I FEEL A BIT UNCOMFORTABLE BECAUSE PEOPLE STARE AT ME.
At public baths.

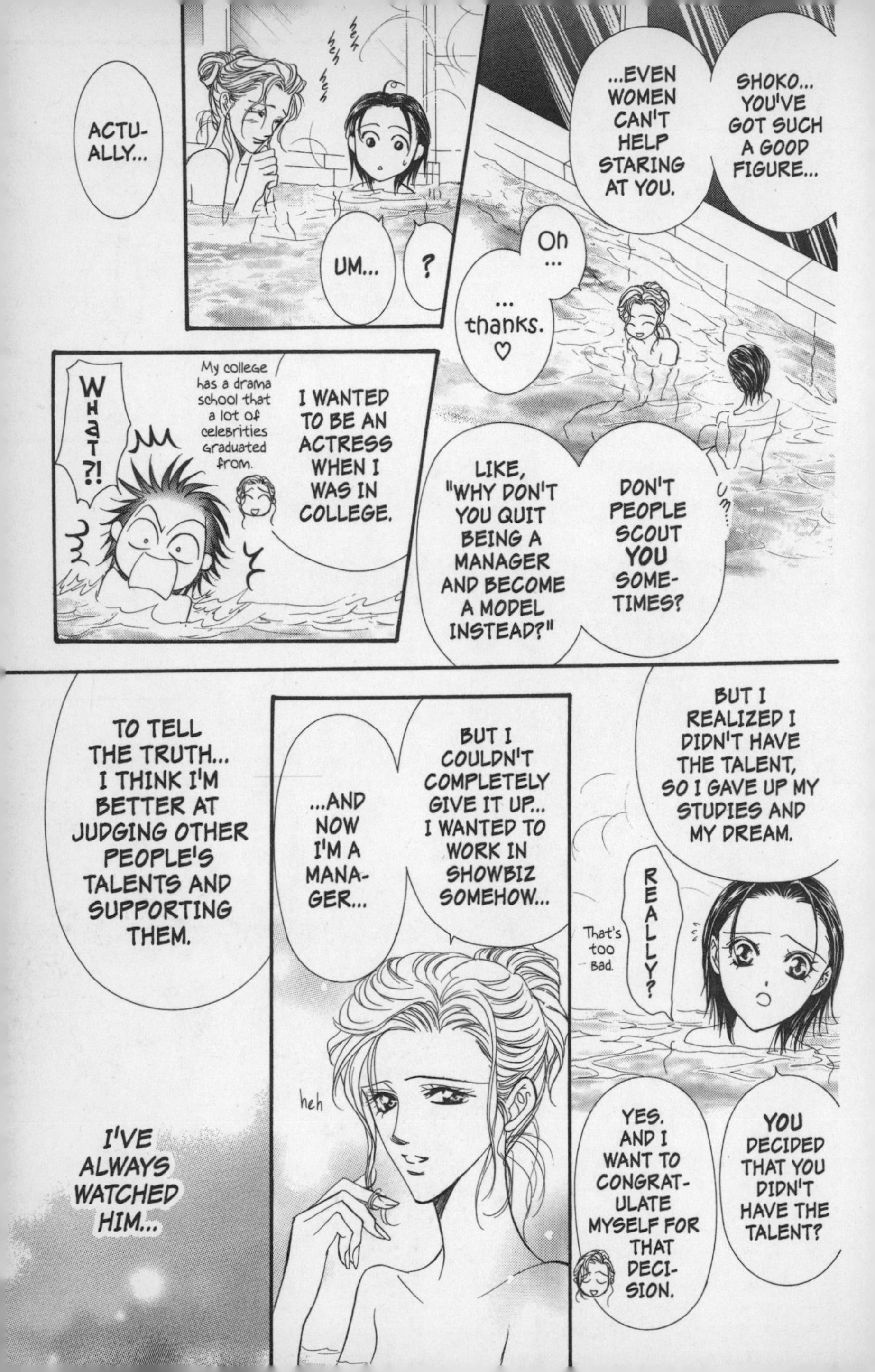
SHOKO... YOU'VE GOT SUCH A GOOD FIGURE...
...EVEN WOMEN CAN'T HELP STARING AT YOU.
Oh ... ... thanks. ♡
Um...
DON'T PEOPLE SCOUT YOU SOMETIMES?
LIKE, "WHY DON'T YOU QUIT BEING A MANAGER AND BECOME A MODEL INSTEAD?"
heh heh heh
?
UM...
ACTU-ALLY...
I WANTED TO BE AN ACTRESS WHEN I WAS IN COLLEGE.
My college has a drama school that a lot of celebrities graduated from.
WHAT?!
BUT I REALIZED I DIDN'T HAVE THE TALENT, SO I GAVE UP MY STUDIES AND MY DREAM.
REALLY?
That's too bad.
BUT I COULDN'T COMPLETELY GIVE IT UP... I WANTED TO WORK IN SHOWBIZ SOMEHOW...
...AND NOW I'M A MANA-GER...
heh
TO TELL THE TRUTH... I THINK I'M BETTER AT JUDGING OTHER PEOPLE'S TALENTS AND SUPPORTING THEM.
YOU DECIDED THAT YOU DIDN'T HAVE THE TALENT?
YES. AND I WANT TO CONGRAT-ULATE MYSELF FOR THAT DECI-SION.
I'VE ALWAYS WATCHED HIM...

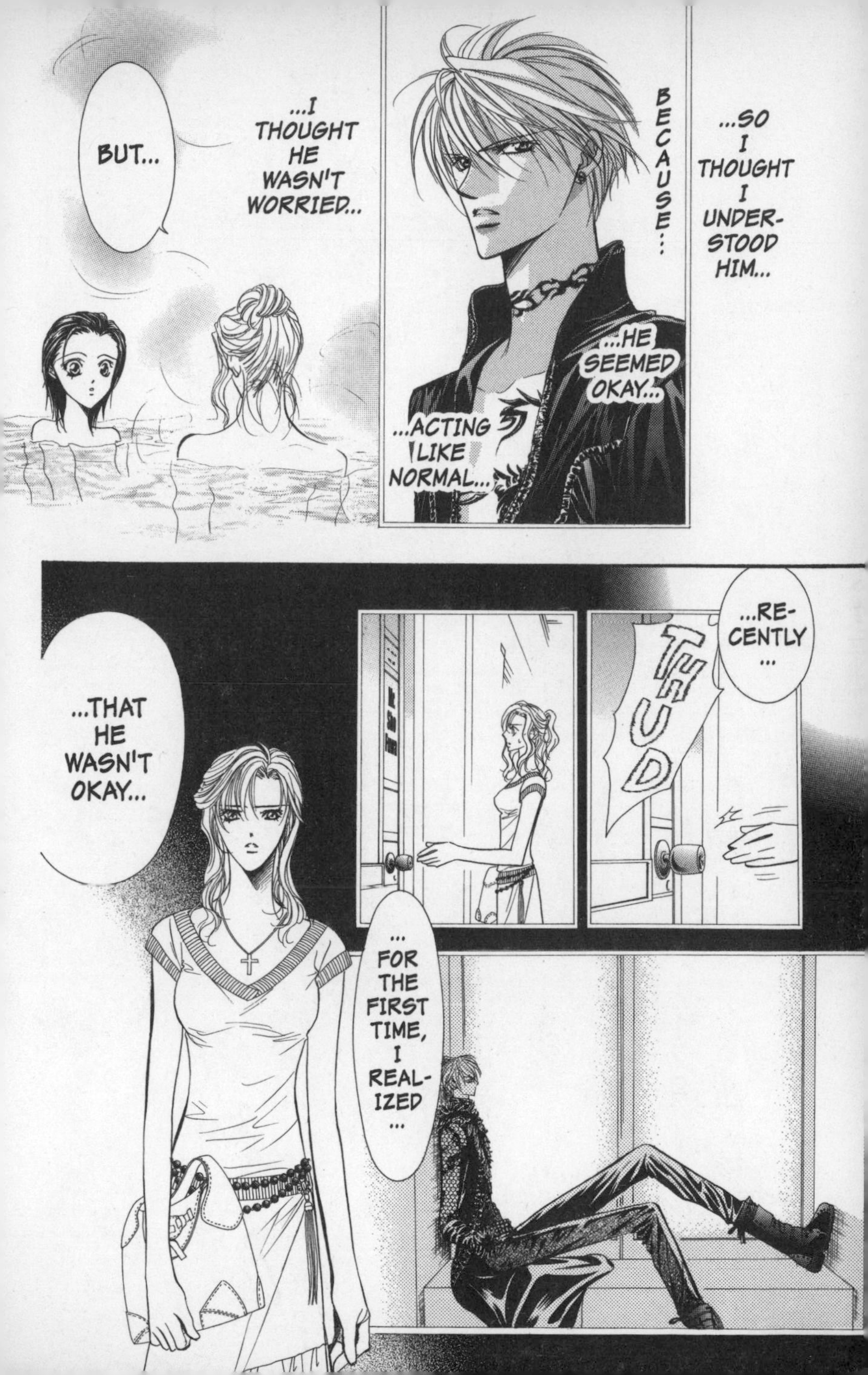
...SO I THOUGHT I UNDERSTOOD HIM...
BECAUSE...
...HE SEEMED OKAY...
...ACTING LIKE NORMAL...
...I THOUGHT HE WASN'T WORRIED...
BUT...
...RE-CENTLY...
THUD
...FOR THE FIRST TIME, I REAL-IZED...
...THAT HE WASN'T OKAY...

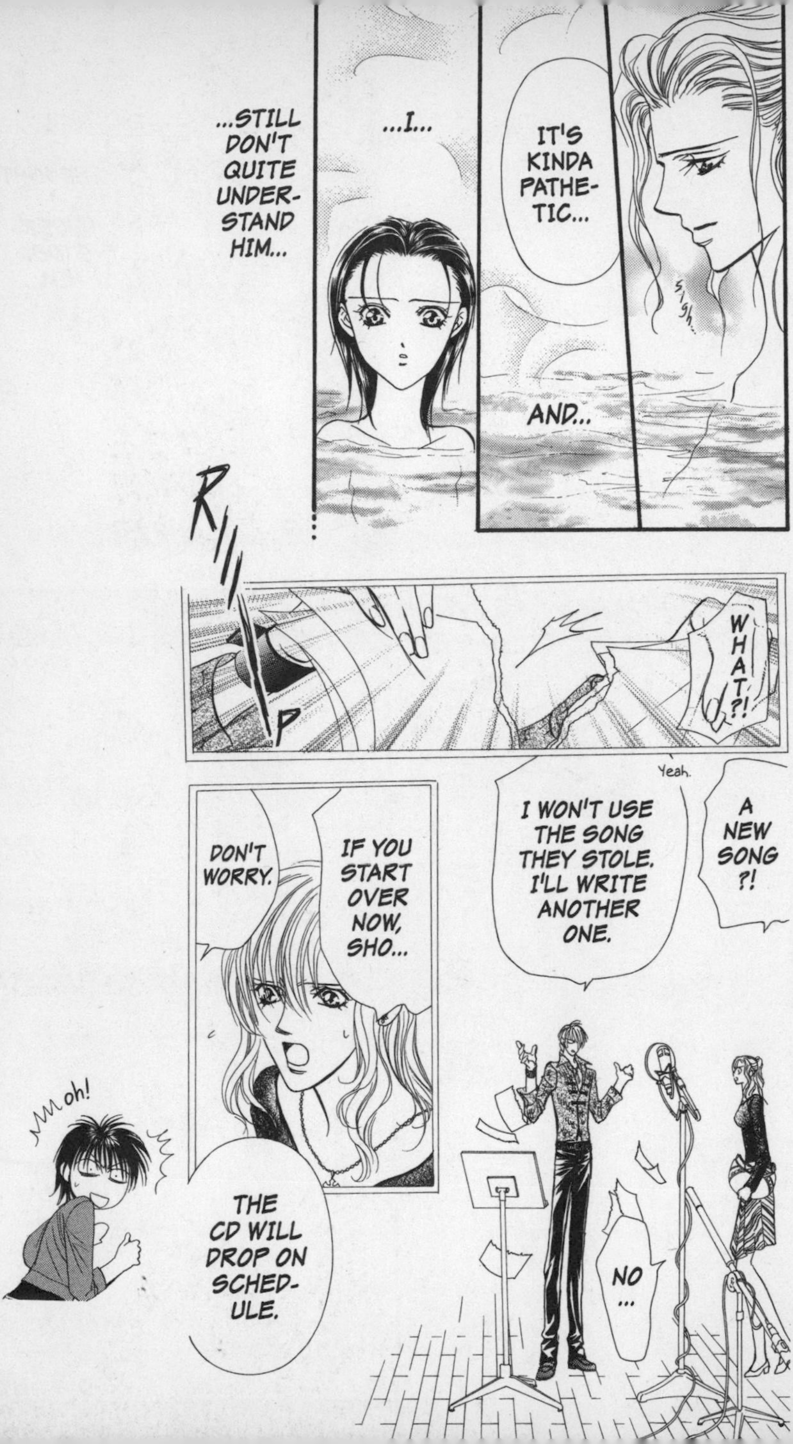
sigh...
IT'S KINDA PATHETIC...
AND...
...I...
...STILL DON'T QUITE UNDERSTAND HIM...
RIIIP
WHAT?!
A NEW SONG?!
Yeah.
I WON'T USE THE SONG THEY STOLE. I'LL WRITE ANOTHER ONE.
NO ...
IF YOU START OVER NOW, SHO...
DON'T WORRY.
THE CD WILL DROP ON SCHEDULE.
oh!

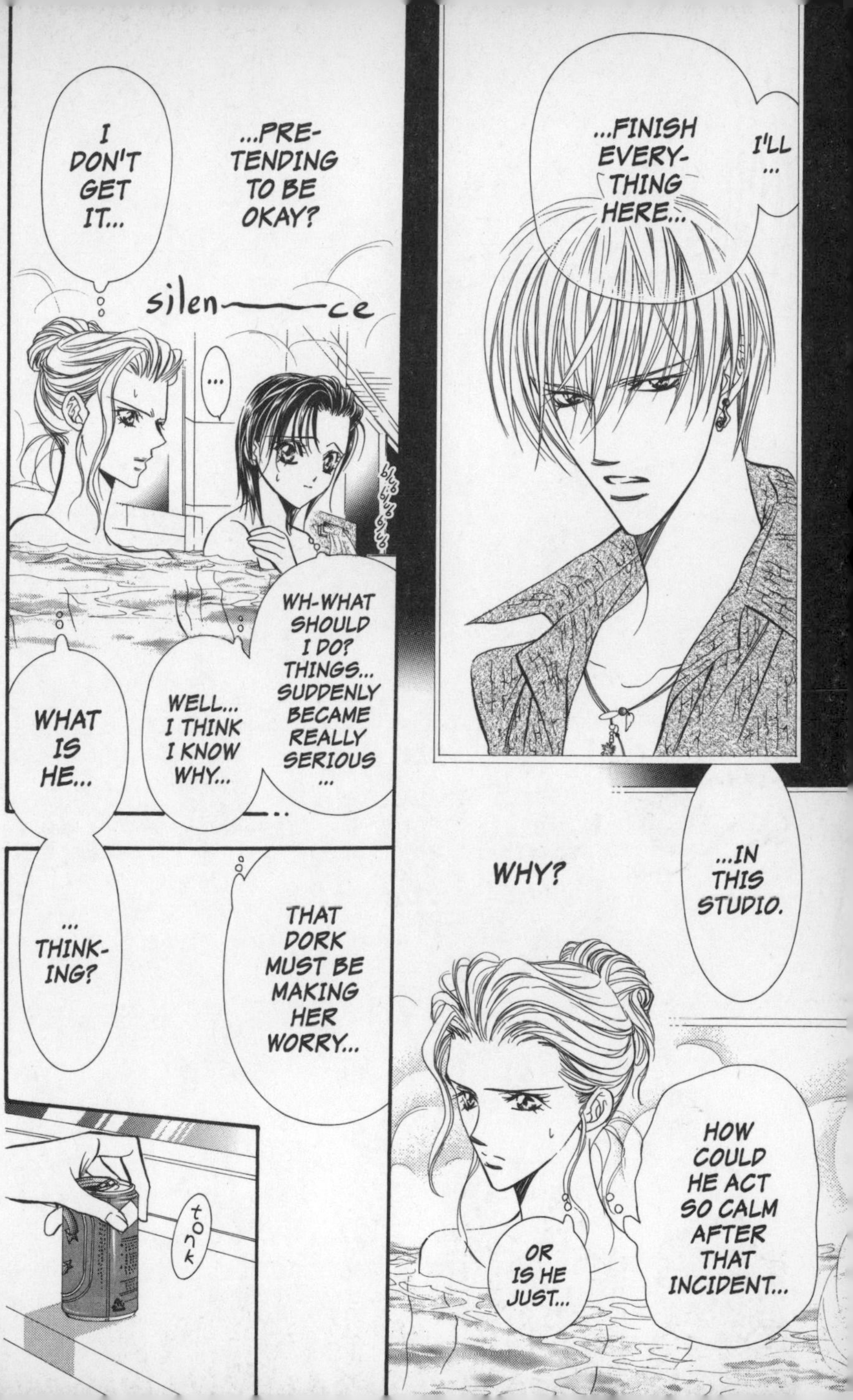
I'LL ...
...FINISH EVERY-THING HERE...
...IN THIS STUDIO.
WHY?
HOW COULD HE ACT SO CALM AFTER THAT INCIDENT...
OR IS HE JUST...
...PRE-TENDING TO BE OKAY?
I DON'T GET IT...
silen——ce
...
blub blub blub
WH-WHAT SHOULD I DO? THINGS... SUDDENLY BECAME REALLY SERIOUS ...
WELL... I THINK I KNOW WHY...
WHAT IS HE...
THAT DORK MUST BE MAKING HER WORRY...
... THINKING-ING?
tonk

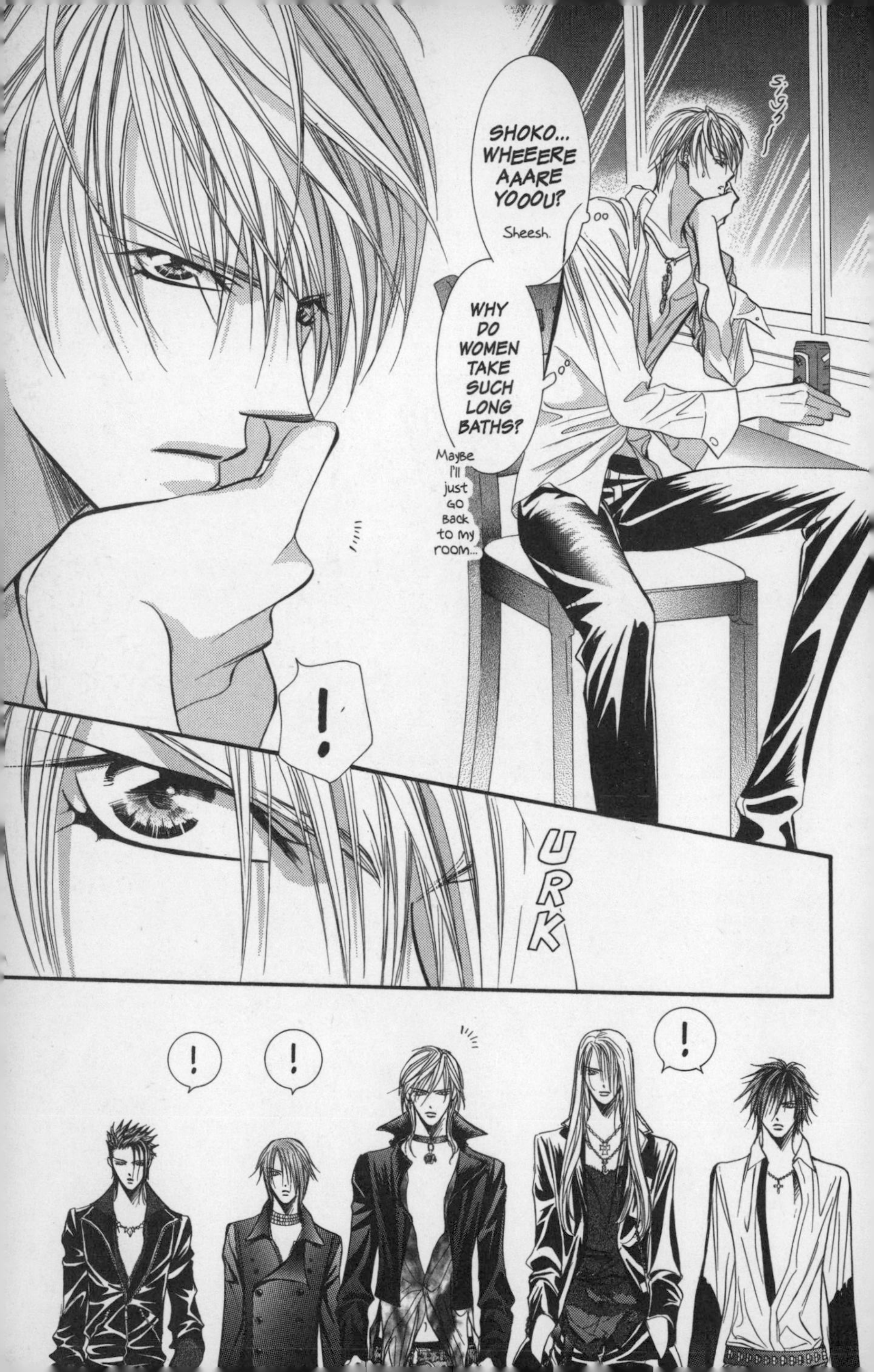
SHOKO... WHEEERE AAARE YOOOU?
Sheesh.
WHY DO WOMEN TAKE SUCH LONG BATHS?
Maybe I'll just go back to my room...
!
URK
!
!
!

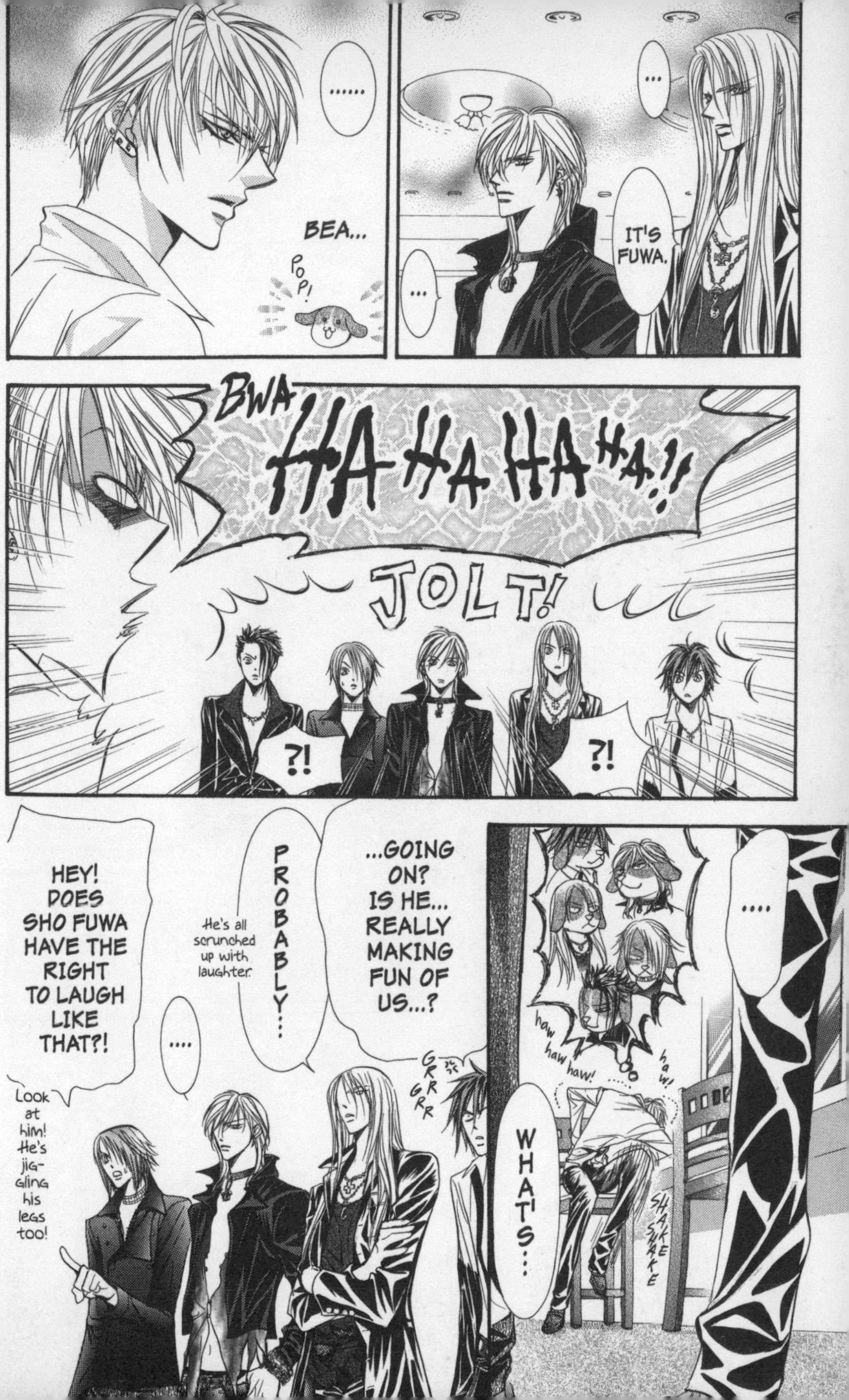
...
IT'S FUWA.
...
......
BEA...
POP!
BWA HA HA HA HA!!
JOLT!
?!
?!
....
haw haw haw!
haw!
SHAKE SHAKE
WHAT'S...
...GOING ON? IS HE... REALLY MAKING FUN OF US...?
GRR GRR
PROBABLY...
He's all scrunched up with laughter.
HEY! DOES SHO FUWA HAVE THE RIGHT TO LAUGH LIKE THAT?!
....
Look at him! He's jig-gling his legs too!

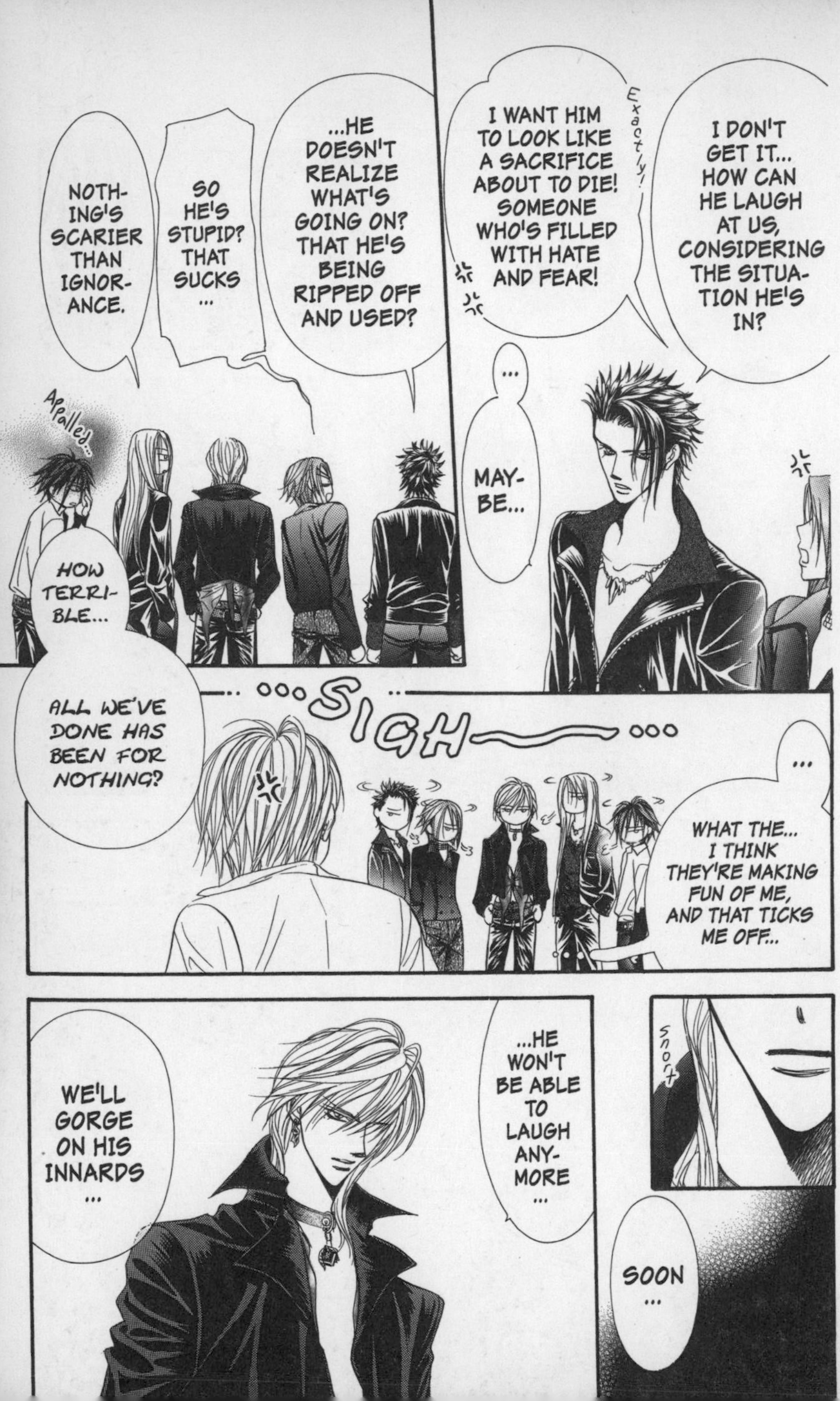
I DON'T GET IT... HOW CAN HE LAUGH AT US, CONSIDERING THE SITUATION HE'S IN?
Exactly!
I WANT HIM TO LOOK LIKE A SACRIFICE ABOUT TO DIE! SOMEONE WHO'S FILLED WITH HATE AND FEAR!
...
MAY-BE...
...HE DOESN'T REALIZE WHAT'S GOING ON? THAT HE'S BEING RIPPED OFF AND USED?
SO HE'S STUPID? THAT SUCKS...
NOTH-ING'S SCARIER THAN IGNOR-ANCE.
Appalled...
HOW TERRI-BLE...
ALL WE'VE DONE HAS BEEN FOR NOTHING?
...ooo SIGH——ooo
...
WHAT THE... I THINK THEY'RE MAKING FUN OF ME, AND THAT TICKS ME OFF...
Snort
SOON...
...HE WON'T BE ABLE TO LAUGH ANY-MORE...
WE'LL GORGE ON HIS INNARDS...

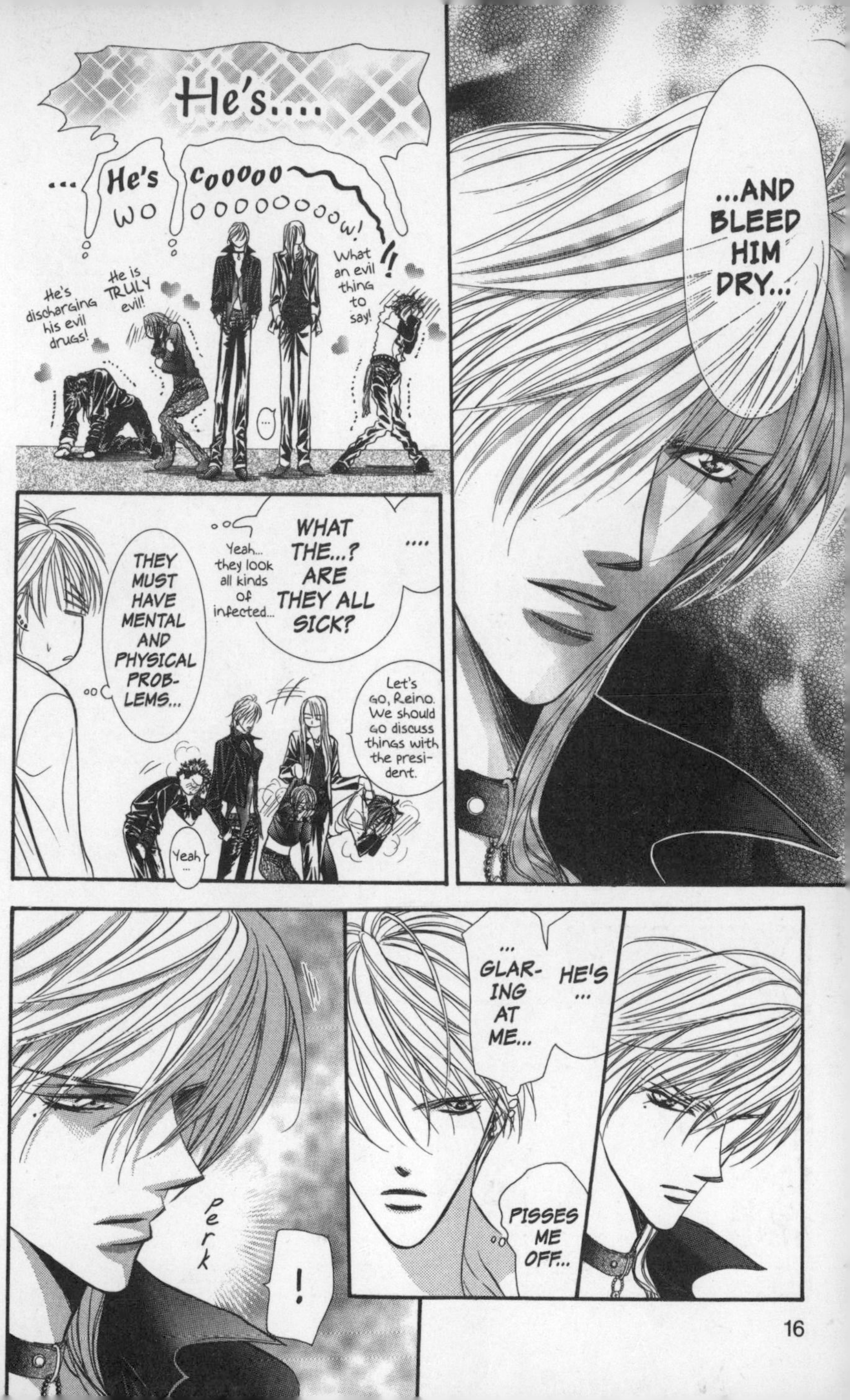
...AND BLEED HIM DRY...
He's....
...He's cooooo~ wo oooooooooow!
What an evil thing to say!
He is TRULY evil!
He's discharging his evil drugs!
...
....
WHAT THE...? ARE THEY ALL SICK?
Yeah... they look all kinds of infected...
THEY MUST HAVE MENTAL AND PHYSICAL PROB-LEMS...
Let's go, Reino. We should go discuss things with the president.
Yeah...
HE'S...
...GLARING AT ME...
PISSES ME OFF...
Perk
!

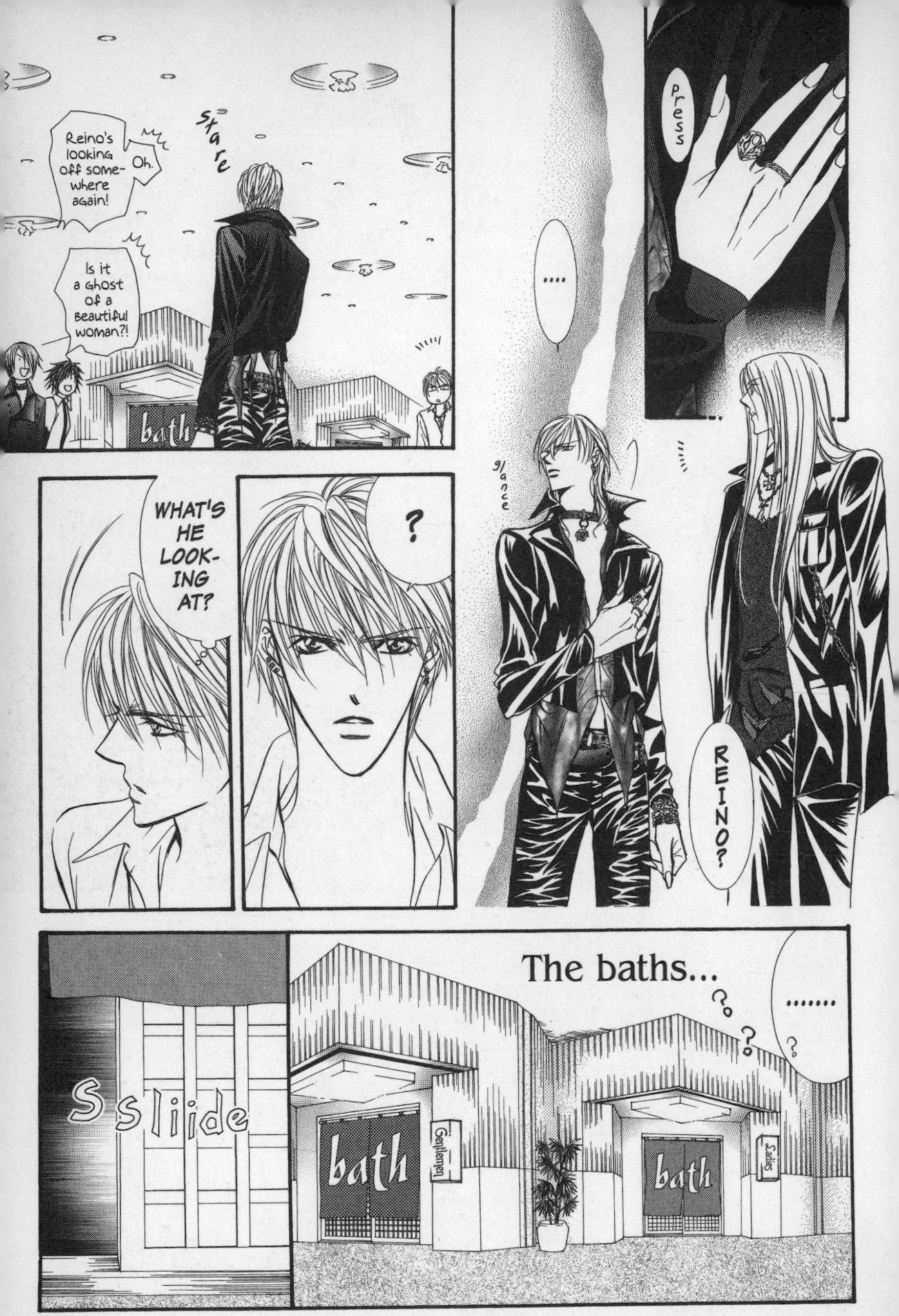
Press
....
glance
REINO?
Stare
Reino's looking off somewhere again!
Oh.
Is it a Ghost of a Beautiful woman?!
?
WHAT'S HE LOOKING AT?
The baths...
....
?
Sslide

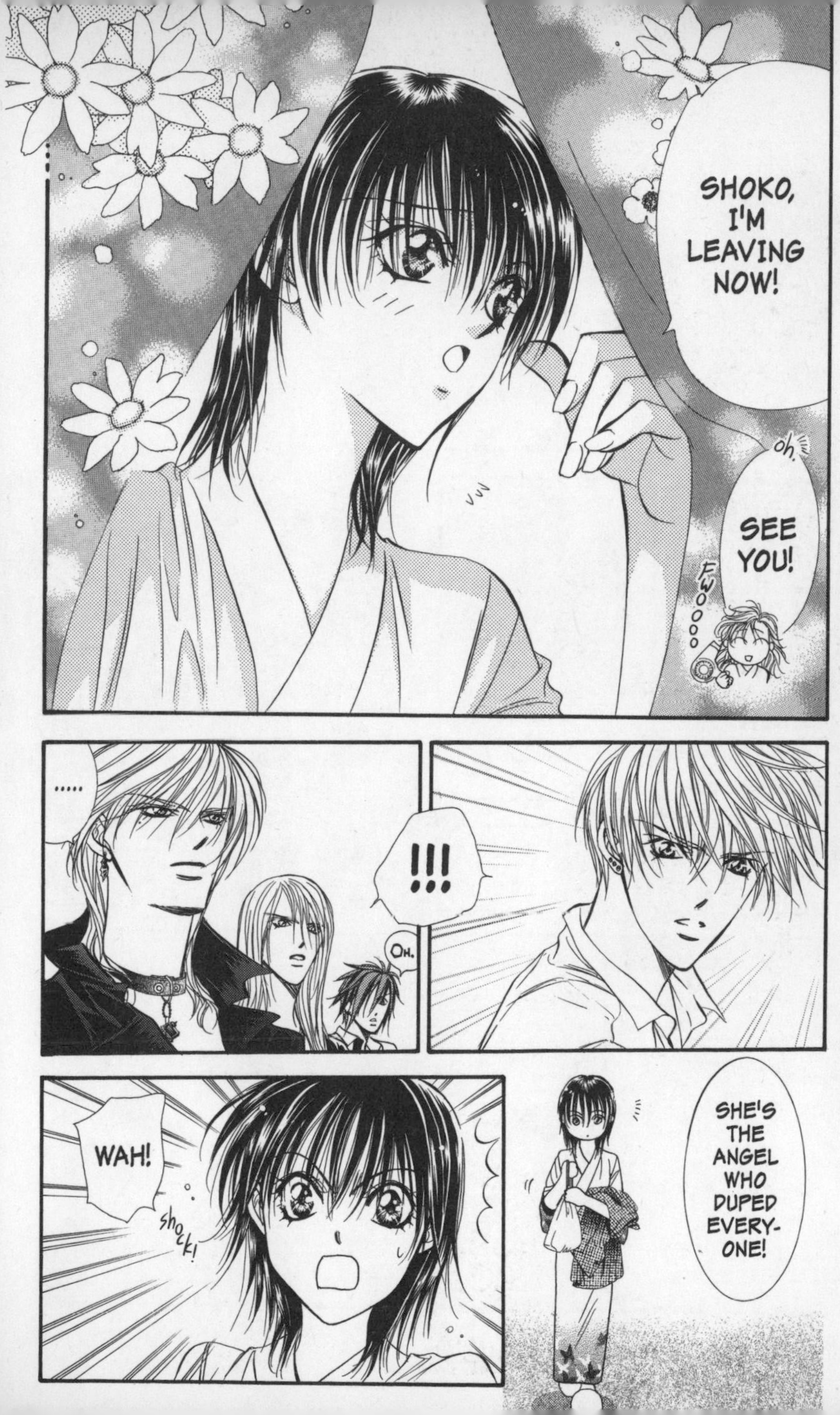
SHOKO, I'M LEAVING NOW!
oh.
SEE YOU!
FWOOOOO
......
!!!
OH.
SHE'S THE ANGEL WHO DUPED EVERY-ONE!
WAH!
shock!

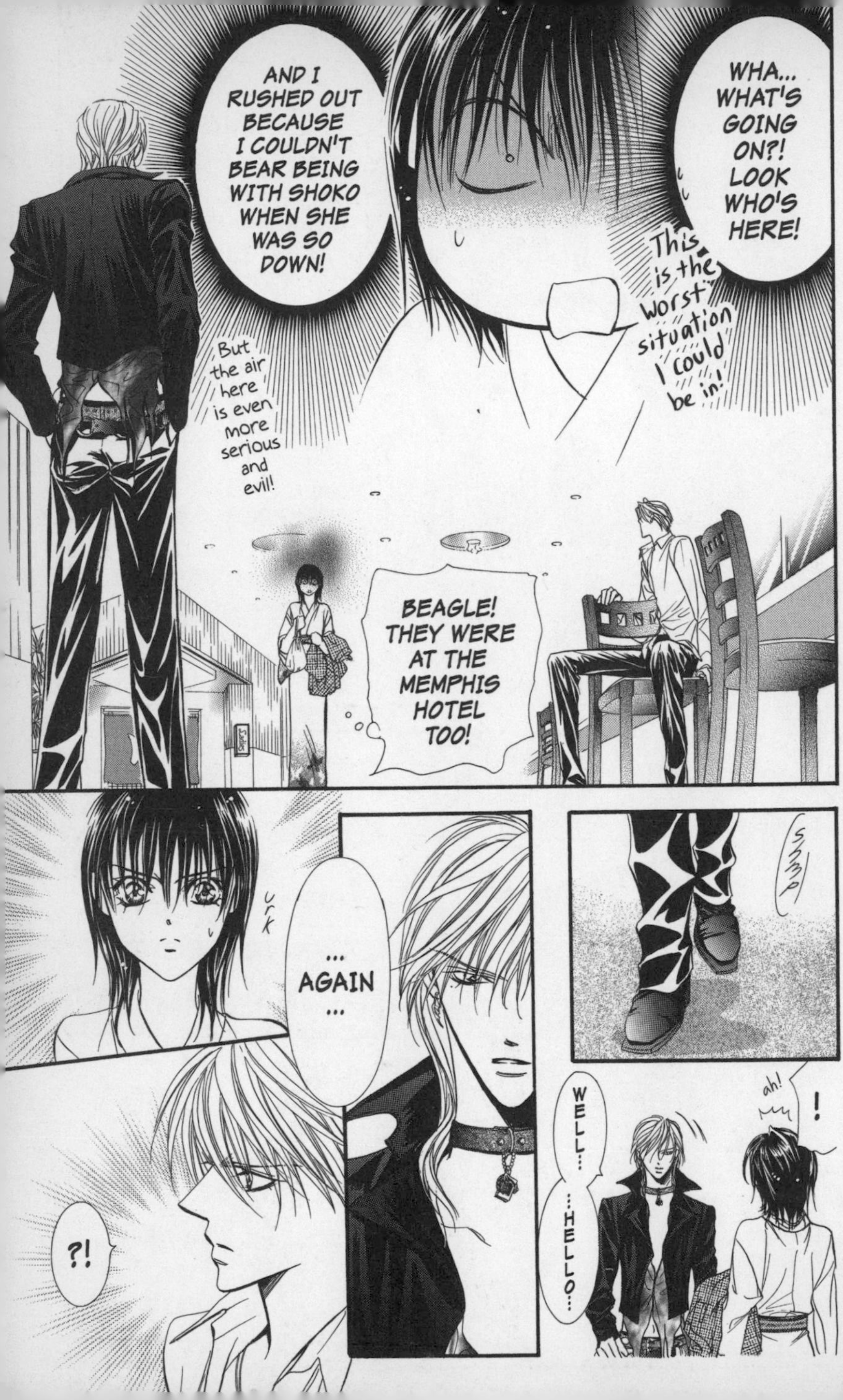
WHA... WHAT'S GOING ON?! LOOK WHO'S HERE!
This is the worst situation I could be in!
AND I RUSHED OUT BECAUSE I COULDN'T BEAR BEING WITH SHOKO WHEN SHE WAS SO DOWN!
But the air here is even more serious and evil!
BEAGLE! THEY WERE AT THE MEMPHIS HOTEL TOO!
SHMP
... AGAIN ...
urk
ah!
!
WELL... ...HELLO...
?!

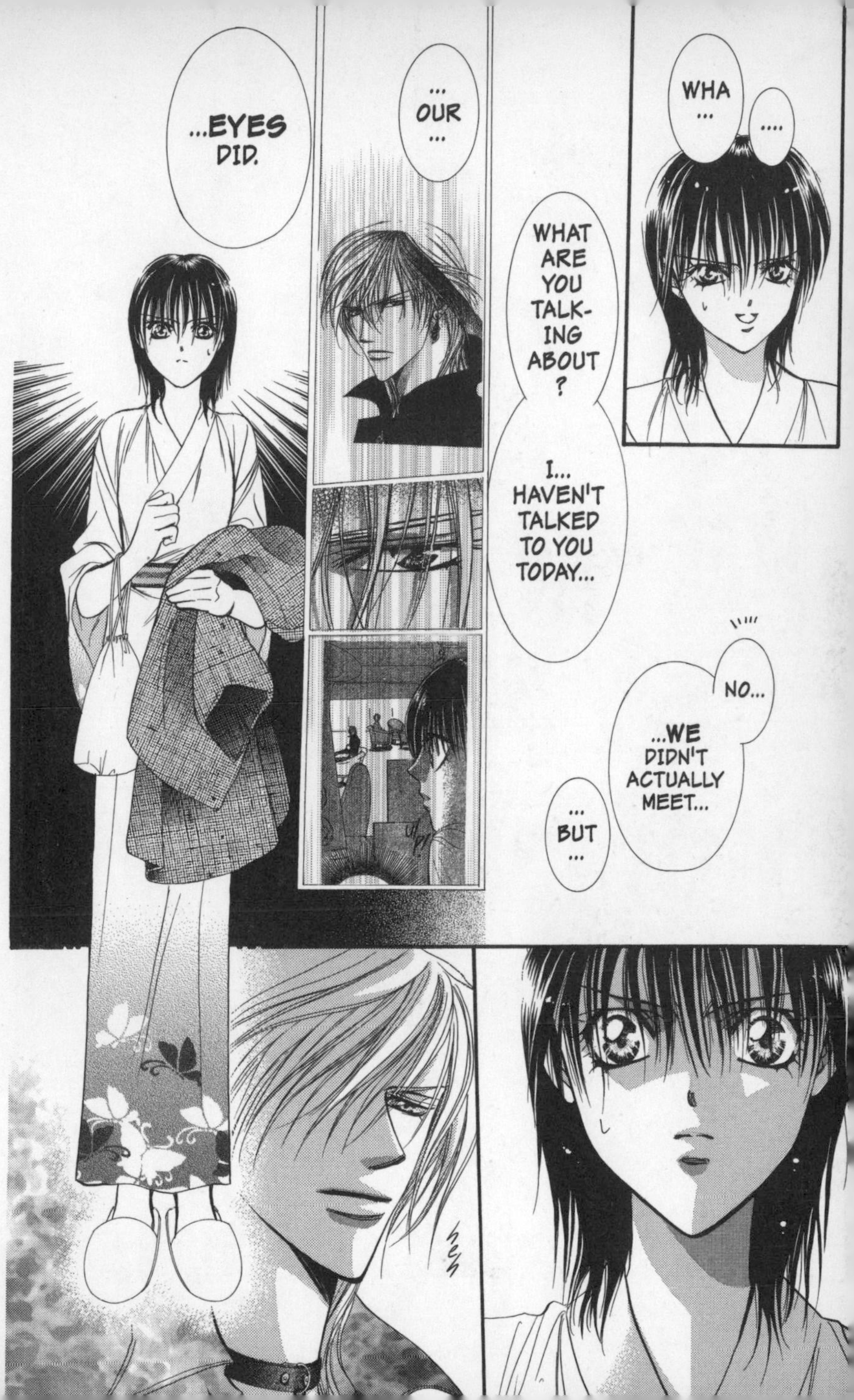
WHA ...
....
WHAT ARE YOU TALKING ABOUT ?
I... HAVEN'T TALKED TO YOU TODAY...
NO...
...WE DIDN'T ACTUALLY MEET...
... BUT ...
... OUR ...
...EYES DID.

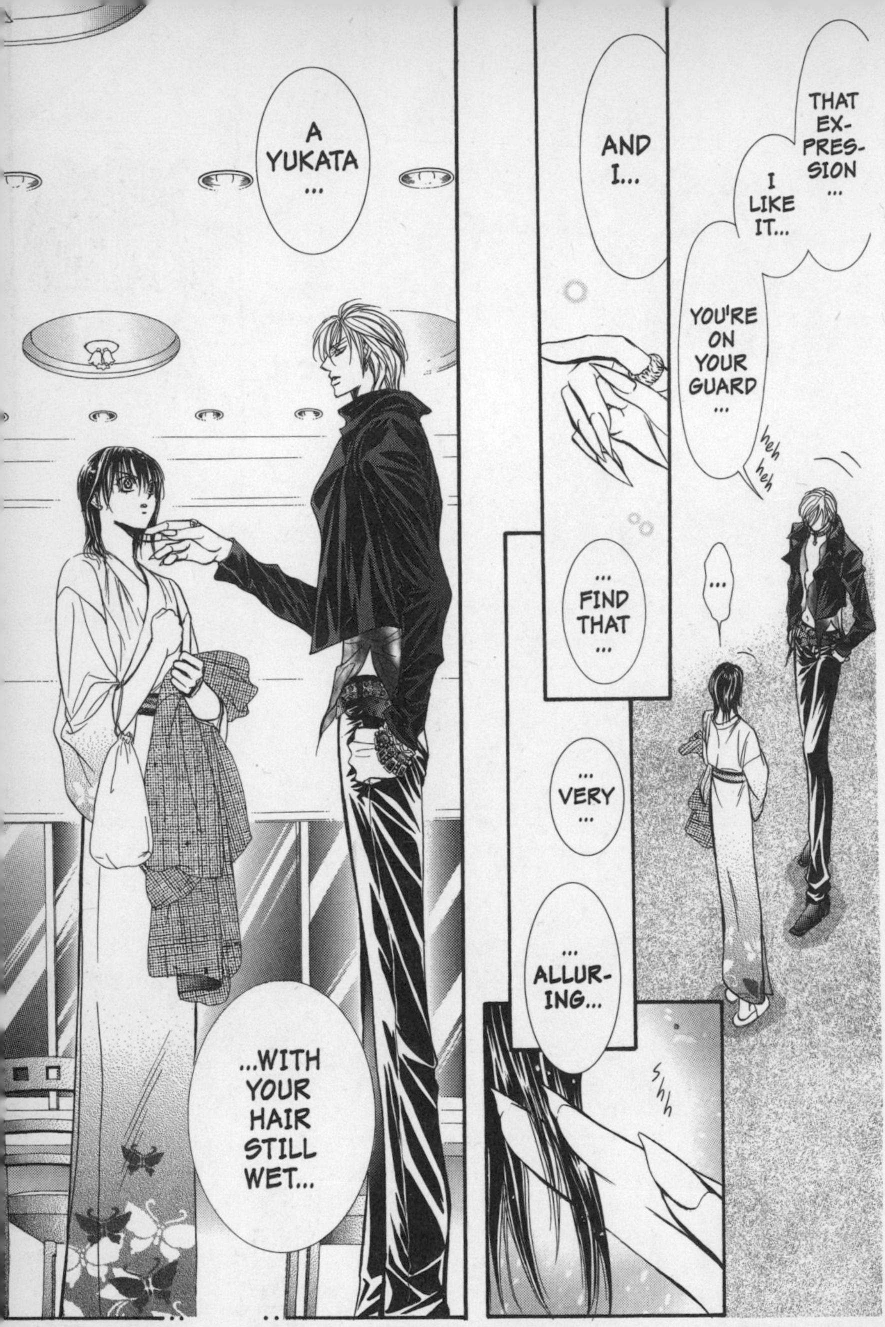
THAT EX-PRES-SION ...
I LIKE IT...
YOU'RE ON YOUR GUARD ...
heh heh
...
AND I...
... FIND THAT ...
... VERY ...
... ALLUR-ING...
shh
A YUKATA ...
...WITH YOUR HAIR STILL WET...

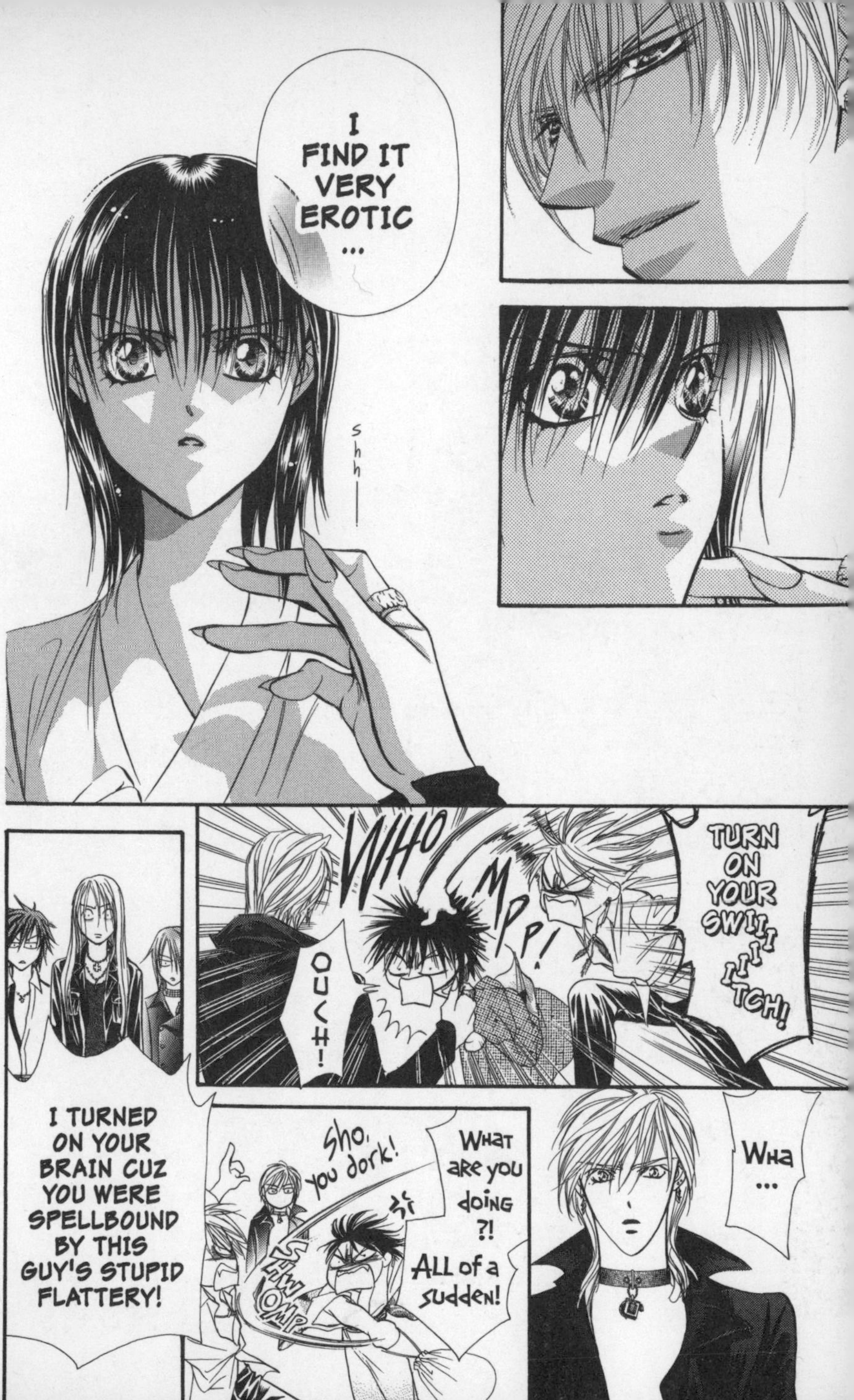
I FIND IT VERY EROTIC ...
shh—
TURN ON YOUR SWIIIIIIITCH!
WHOMP!
OUCH!
Wha ...
What are you doing?! All of a sudden!
Sho, you dork!
SHWOMP
I TURNED ON YOUR BRAIN CUZ YOU WERE SPELLBOUND BY THIS GUY'S STUPID FLATTERY!

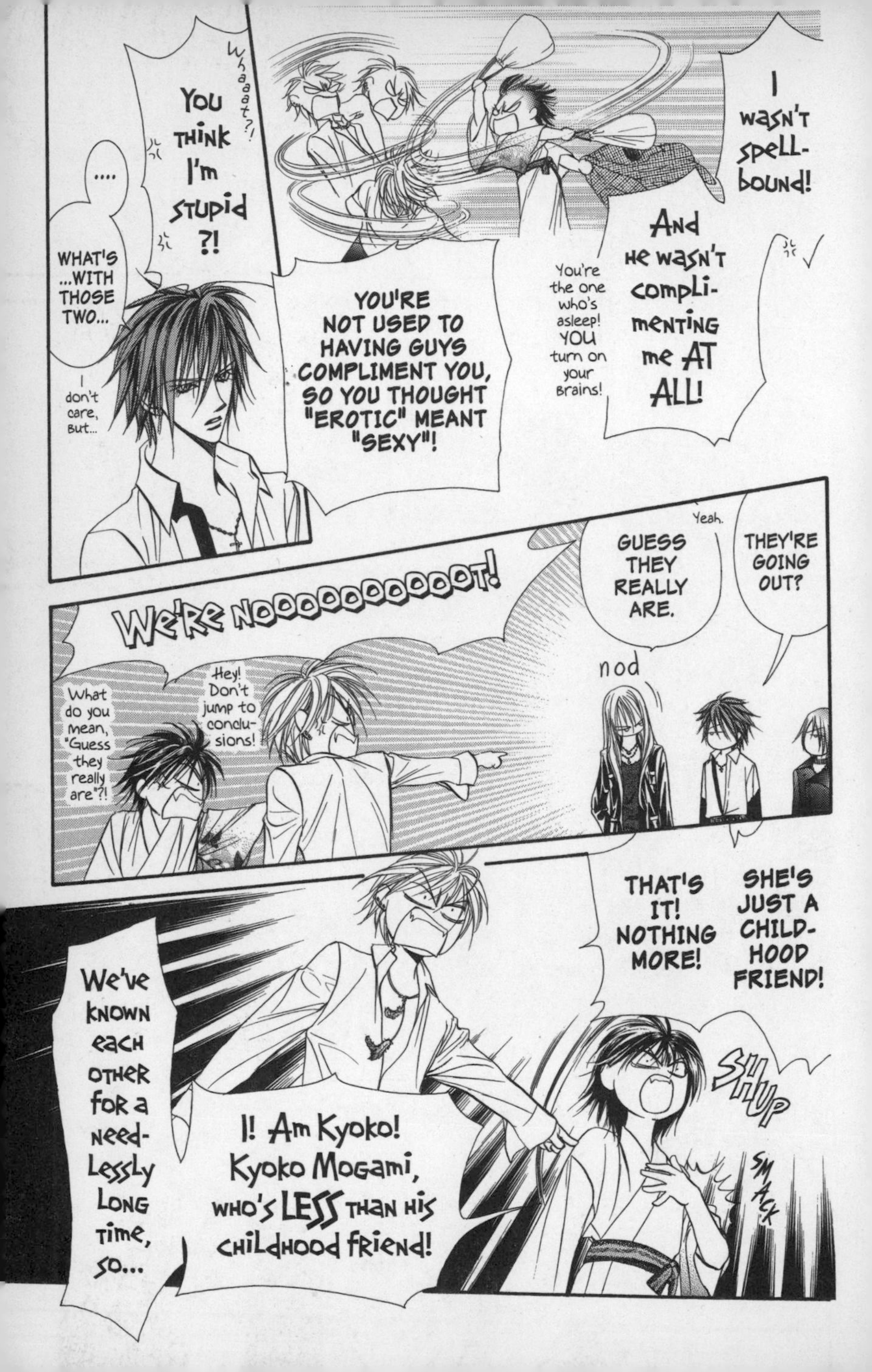
I wasn't spell-bound!
And he wasn't compli-menting me AT ALL!
You're the one who's asleep! YOU turn on your Brains!
YOU'RE NOT USED TO HAVING GUYS COMPLIMENT YOU, SO YOU THOUGHT "EROTIC" MEANT "SEXY"!
Whaaaat?!
YOU THINK I'm stupid?!
....
WHAT'S ...WITH THOSE TWO...
I don't care, but...
THEY'RE GOING OUT?
Yeah.
GUESS THEY REALLY ARE.
nod
We're NOOOOOOOOOOOOT!
Hey! Don't jump to conclusions!
What do you mean, "Guess they really are"?!
SHE'S JUST A CHILD-HOOD FRIEND!
THAT'S IT! NOTHING MORE!
We've known each other for a need-lessly long time, so...
SHUP
SMACK
I! Am Kyoko! Kyoko Mogami, who's LESS than his childhood friend!

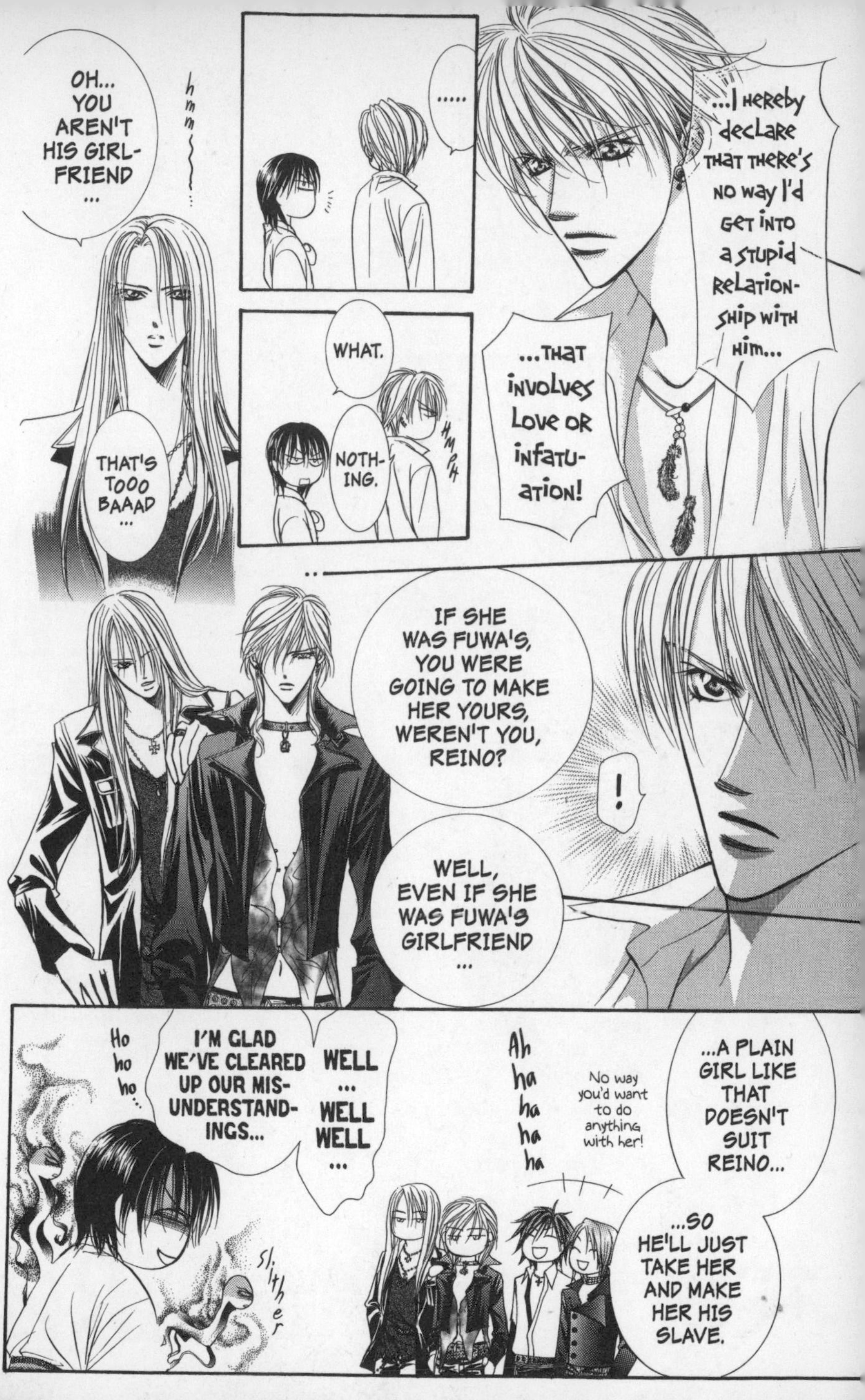
...I hereby declare that there's no way I'd get into a stupid relation-ship with him...
...that involves love or infatu-ation!
.....
WHAT.
NOTHING.
HMPH
OH... YOU AREN'T HIS GIRL-FRIEND...
hmm~~~...
THAT'S TOOO BAAAD...
..
IF SHE WAS FUWA'S, YOU WERE GOING TO MAKE HER YOURS, WEREN'T YOU, REINO?
!
WELL, EVEN IF SHE WAS FUWA'S GIRLFRIEND...
...A PLAIN GIRL LIKE THAT DOESN'T SUIT REINO...
...SO HE'LL JUST TAKE HER AND MAKE HER HIS SLAVE.
Ah ha ha ha ha
No way you'd want to do anything with her!
WELL ... WELL WELL ...
I'M GLAD WE'VE CLEARED UP OUR MIS-UNDERSTAND-INGS...
Ho ho ho...
slither

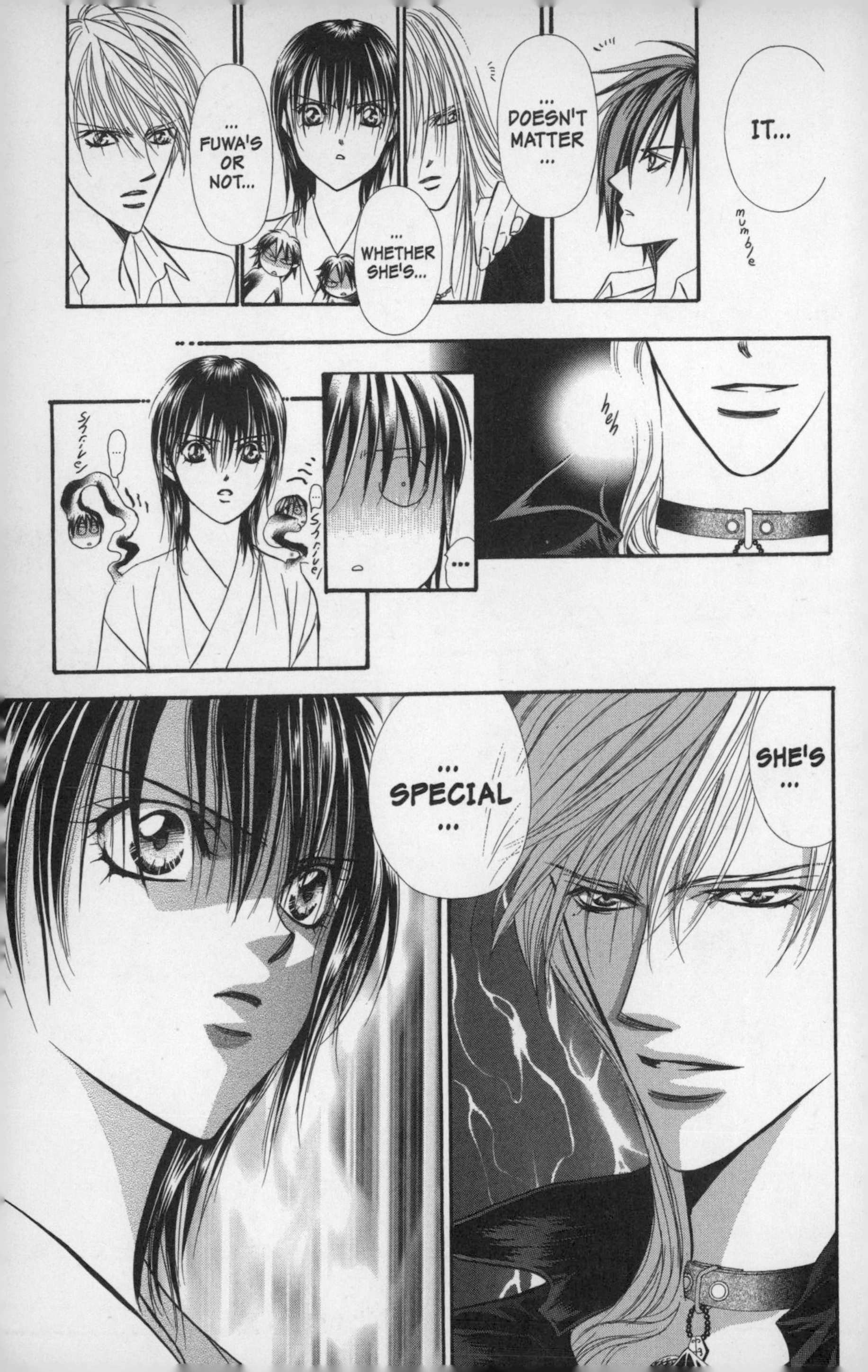
IT...
mumble
... DOESN'T MATTER ...
... WHETHER SHE'S...
... FUWA'S OR NOT...
heh
...
...
...
shrivel
...
shrivel
SHE'S ...
... SPECIAL ...

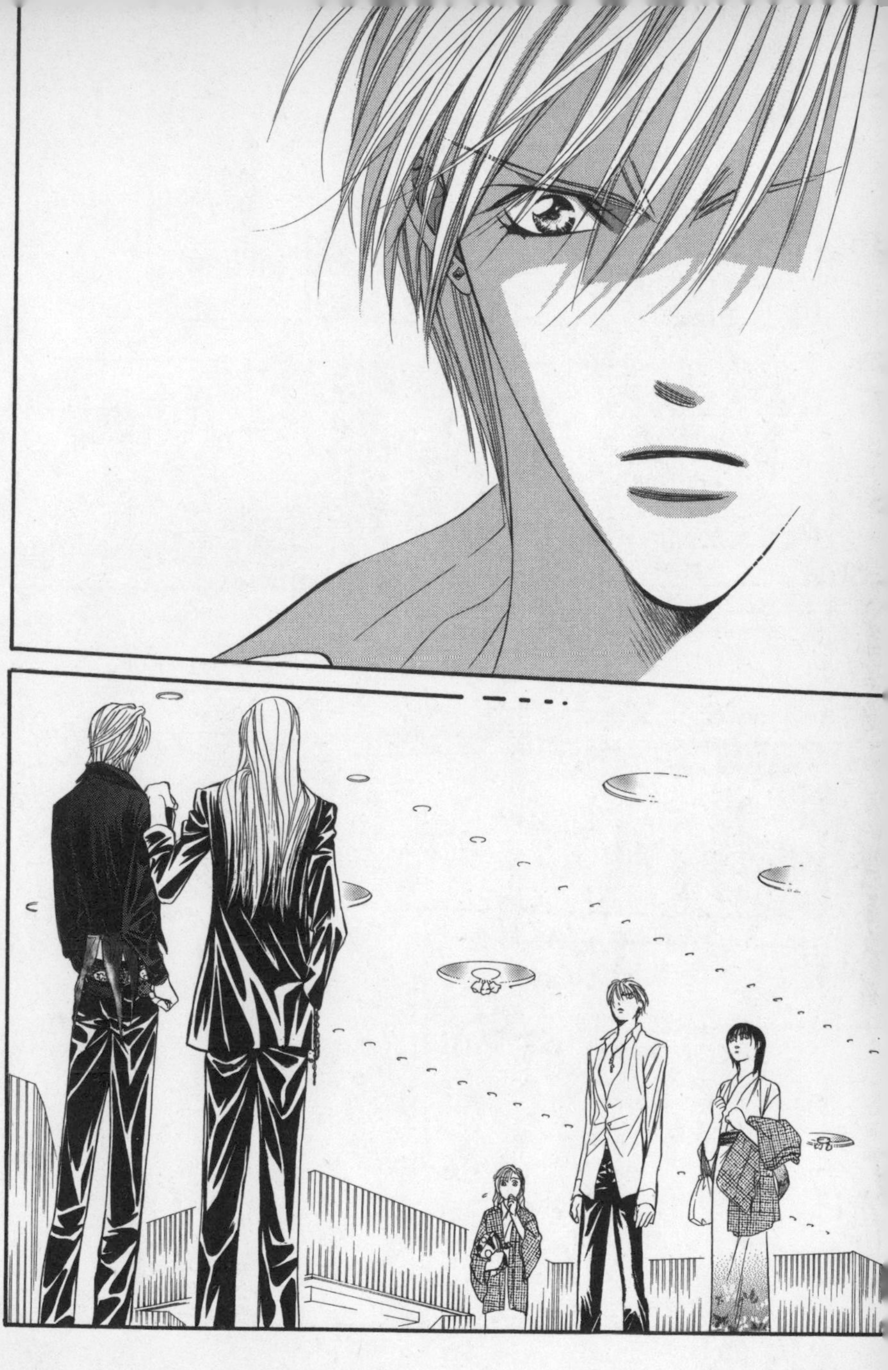

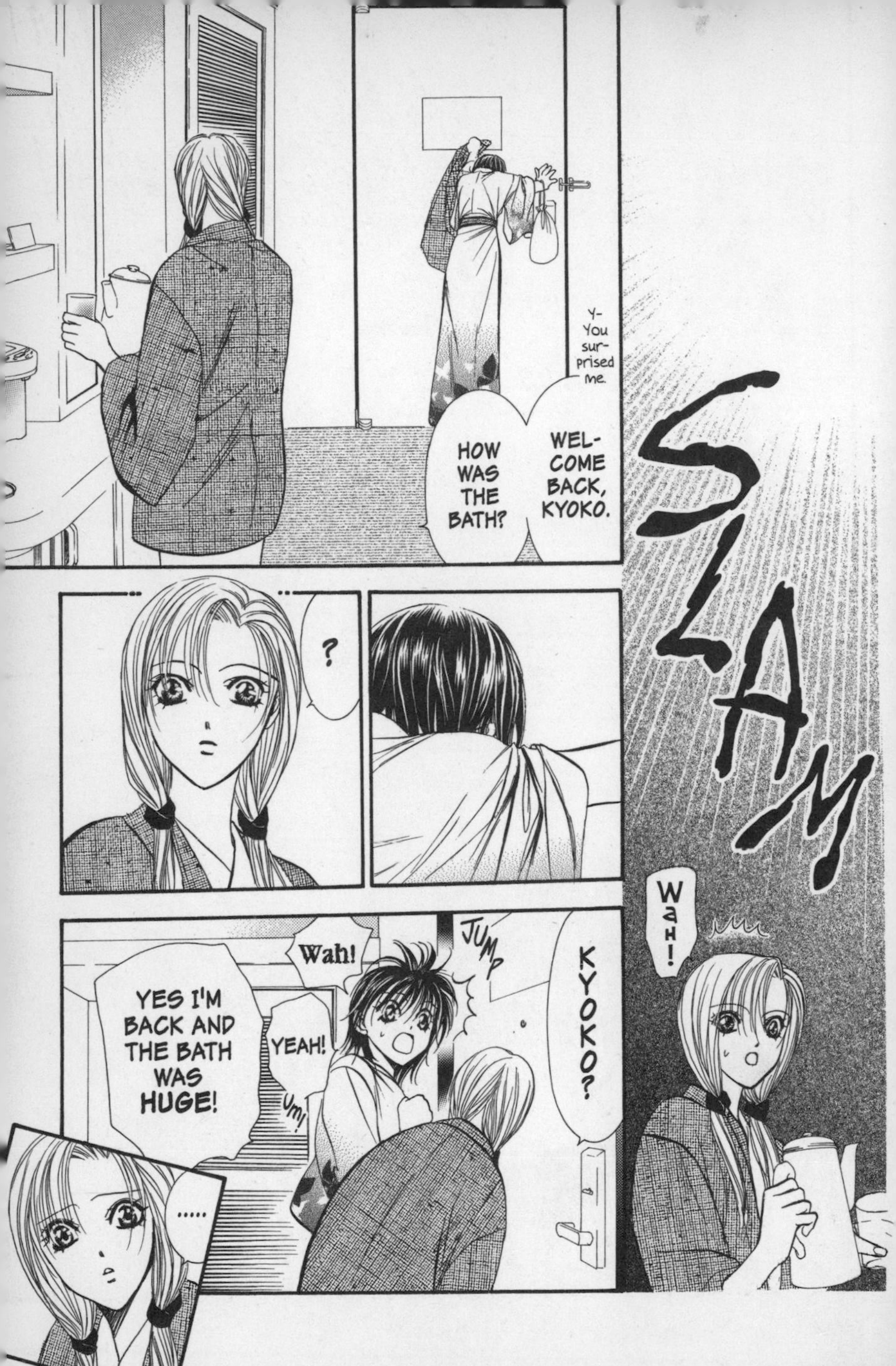
SLAM
Wah!
WEL-COME BACK, KYOKO.
Y-You sur-prised me.
HOW WAS THE BATH?
?
KYOKO?
JUMP
Wah!
YEAH!
YES I'M BACK AND THE BATH WAS HUGE!
Um!
.....

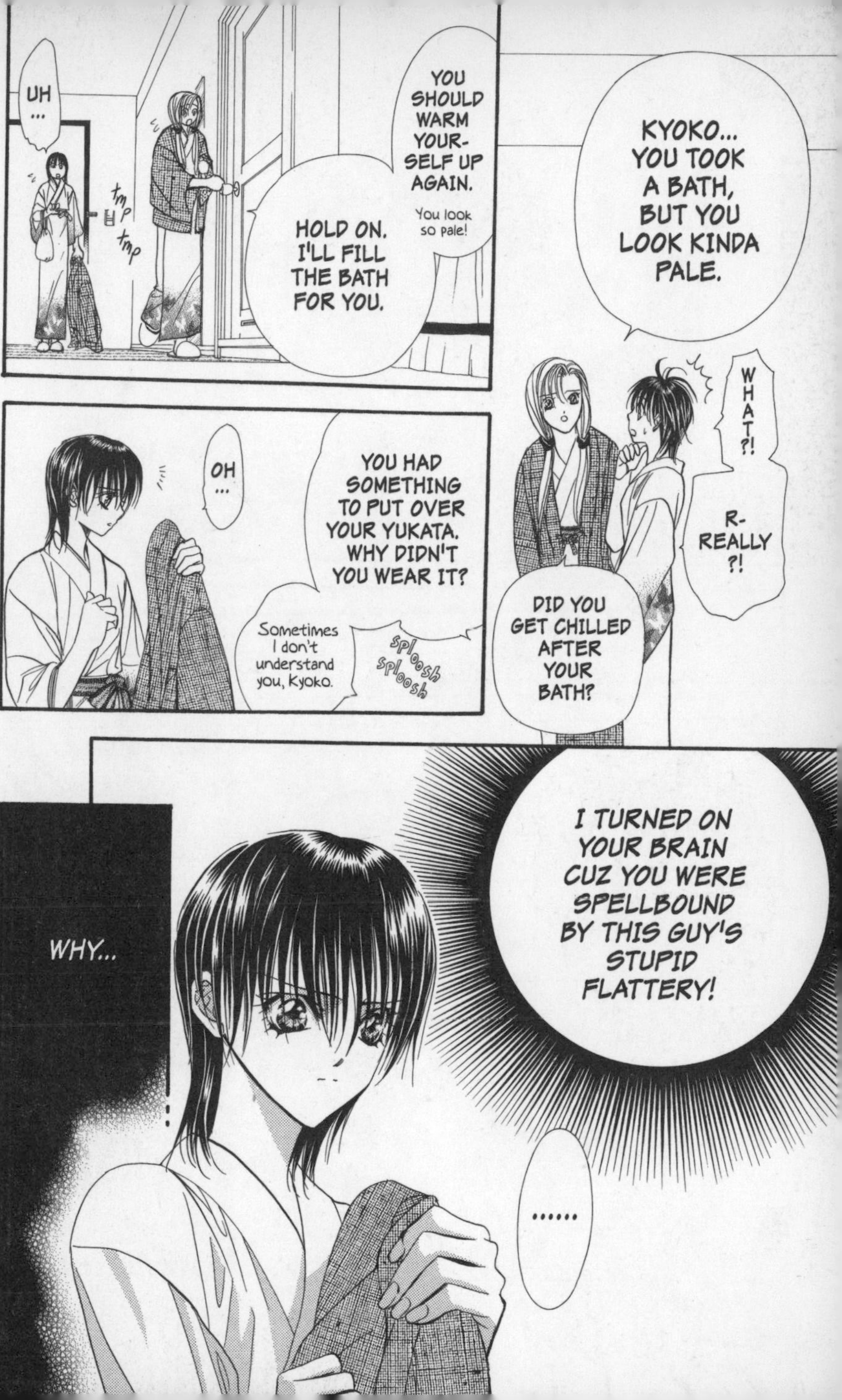
KYOKO... YOU TOOK A BATH, BUT YOU LOOK KINDA PALE.
WHAT?!
R-REALLY?!
DID YOU GET CHILLED AFTER YOUR BATH?
YOU SHOULD WARM YOUR-SELF UP AGAIN.
You look so pale!
HOLD ON. I'LL FILL THE BATH FOR YOU.
UH...
tmp tmp
YOU HAD SOMETHING TO PUT OVER YOUR YUKATA. WHY DIDN'T YOU WEAR IT?
Sometimes I don't understand you, Kyoko.
sploosh sploosh
OH...
I TURNED ON YOUR BRAIN CUZ YOU WERE SPELLBOUND BY THIS GUY'S STUPID FLATTERY!
......
WHY...

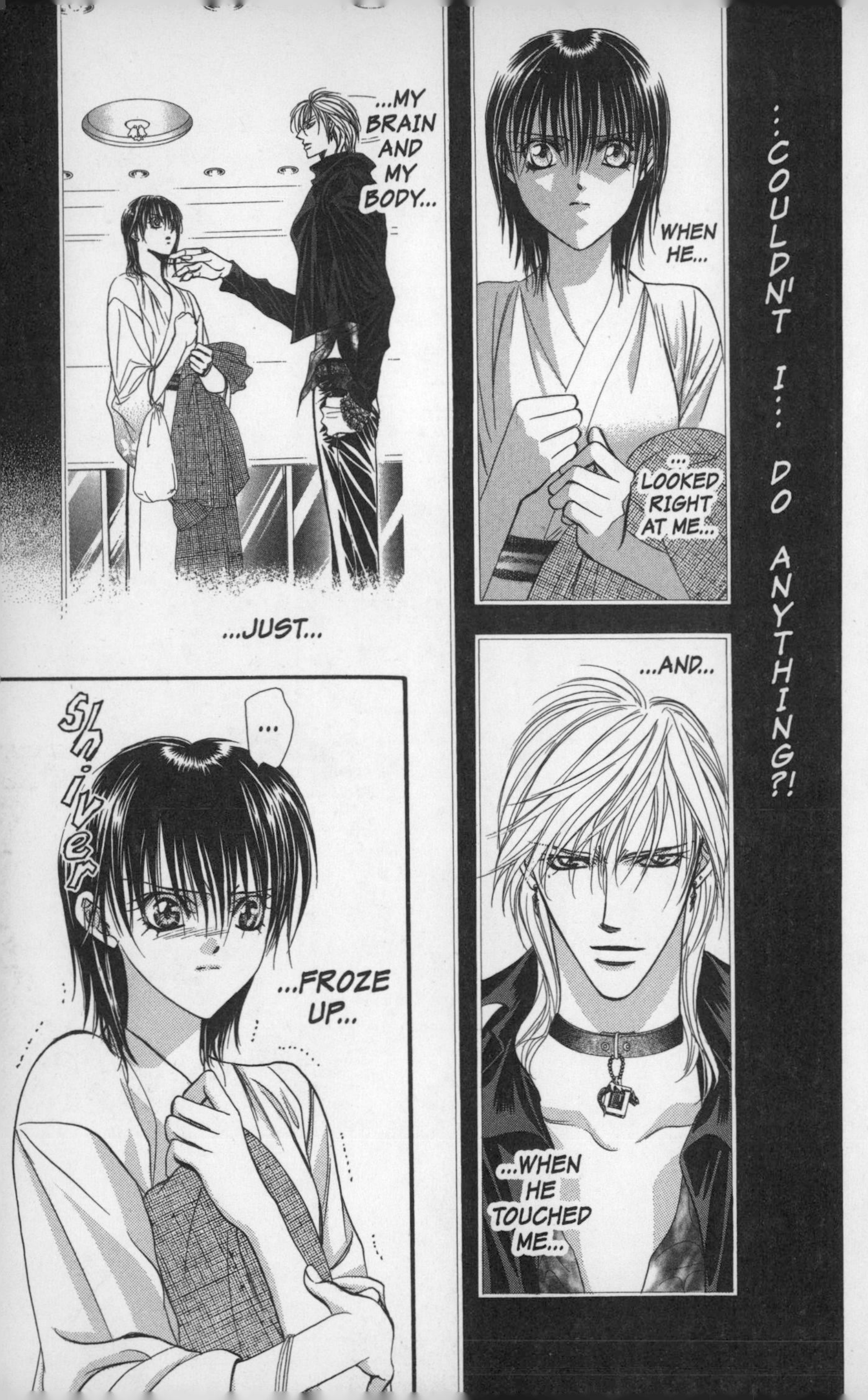
...COULDN'T I... DO ANYTHING?!
WHEN HE...
...LOOKED RIGHT AT ME...
...AND...
...WHEN HE TOUCHED ME...
...MY BRAIN AND MY BODY...
...JUST...
...
Shiver
...FROZE UP...

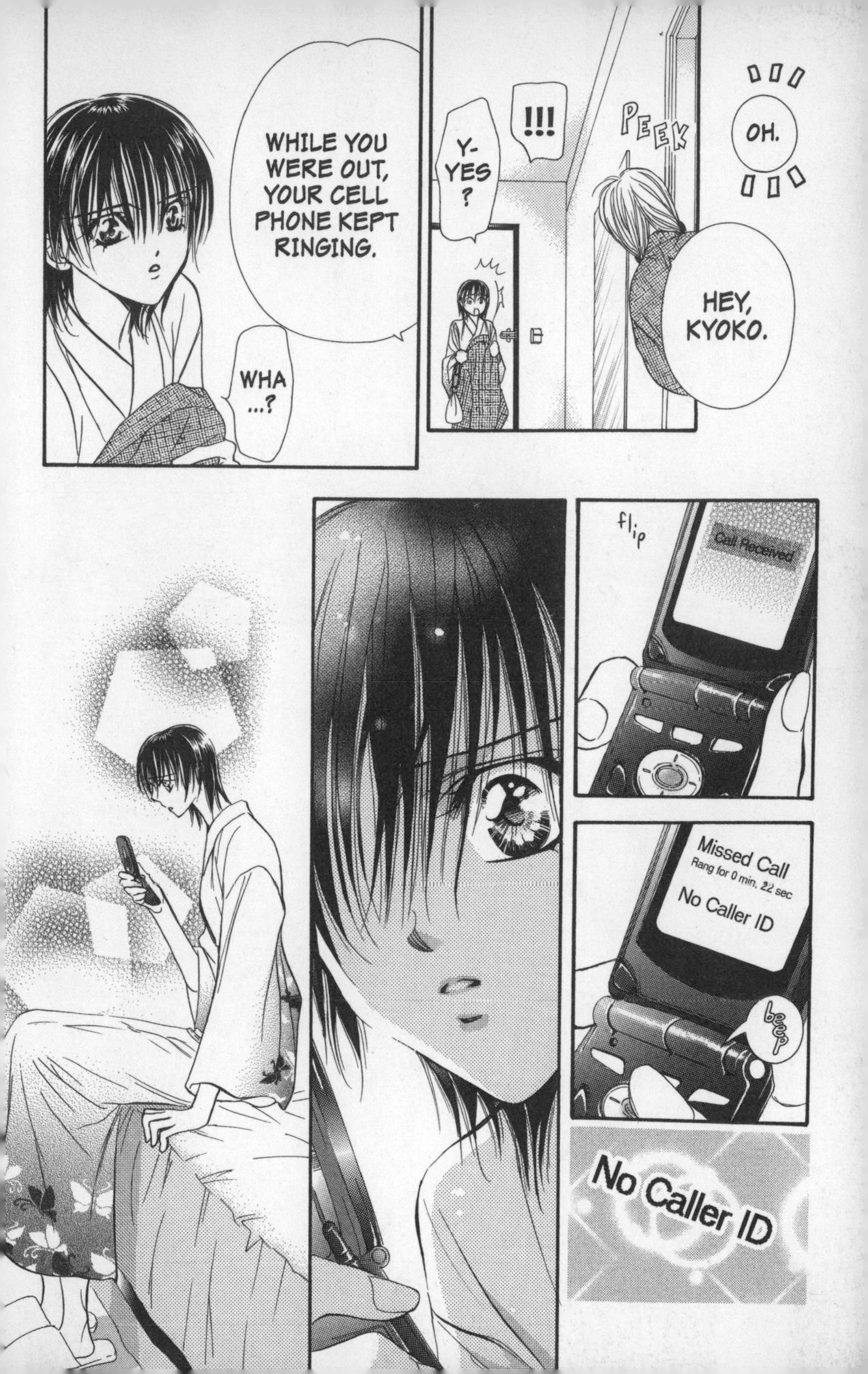
OH.
PEEK
HEY, KYOKO.
!!!
Y-YES?
WHILE YOU WERE OUT, YOUR CELL PHONE KEPT RINGING.
WHA...?
flip
Call Received
Missed Call
Rang for 0 min. 22 sec
No Caller ID
beep
No Caller ID

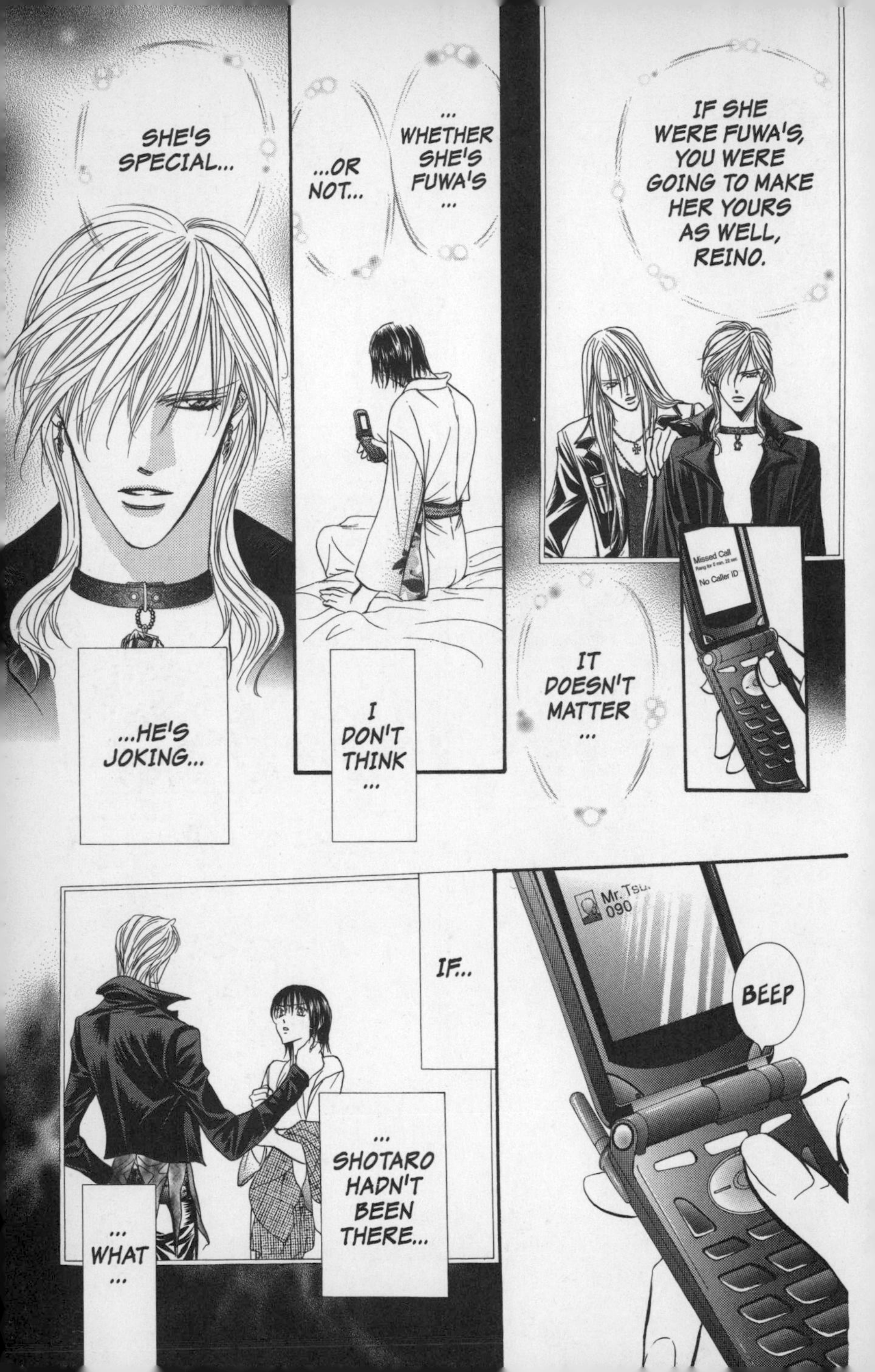
IF SHE WERE FUWA'S, YOU WERE GOING TO MAKE HER YOURS AS WELL, REINO.
Missed Call
No Caller ID
IT DOESN'T MATTER ...
... WHETHER SHE'S FUWA'S ...
...OR NOT...
I DON'T THINK ...
SHE'S SPECIAL...
...HE'S JOKING...
Mr. Tsu.
090
BEEP
IF...
... SHOTARO HADN'T BEEN THERE...
... WHAT ...

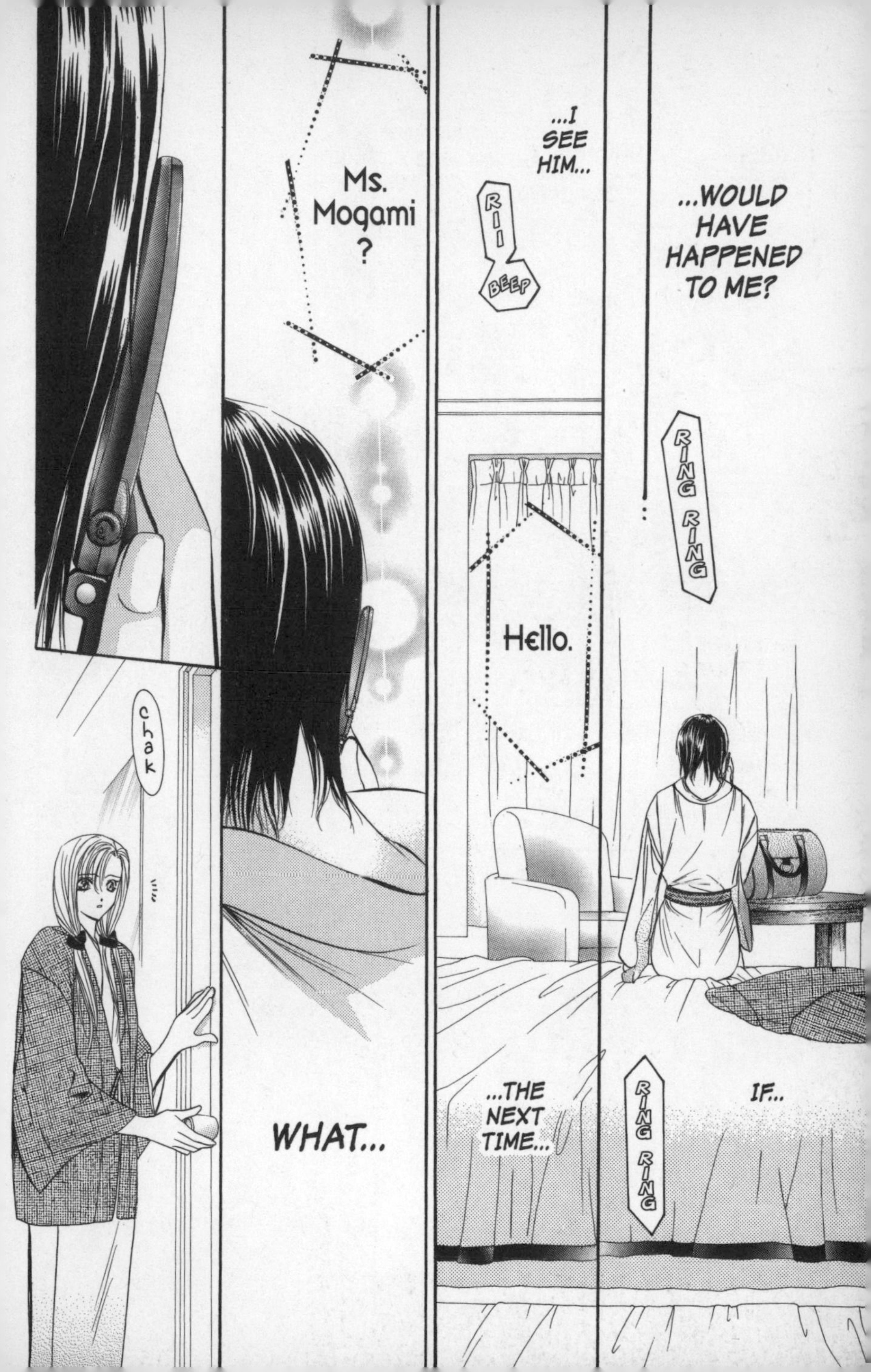
...WOULD HAVE HAPPENED TO ME?
RING RING
IF...
RING RING
...I SEE HIM...
RII BEEP
Hello.
...THE NEXT TIME...
Ms. Mogami ?
WHAT...
Chak

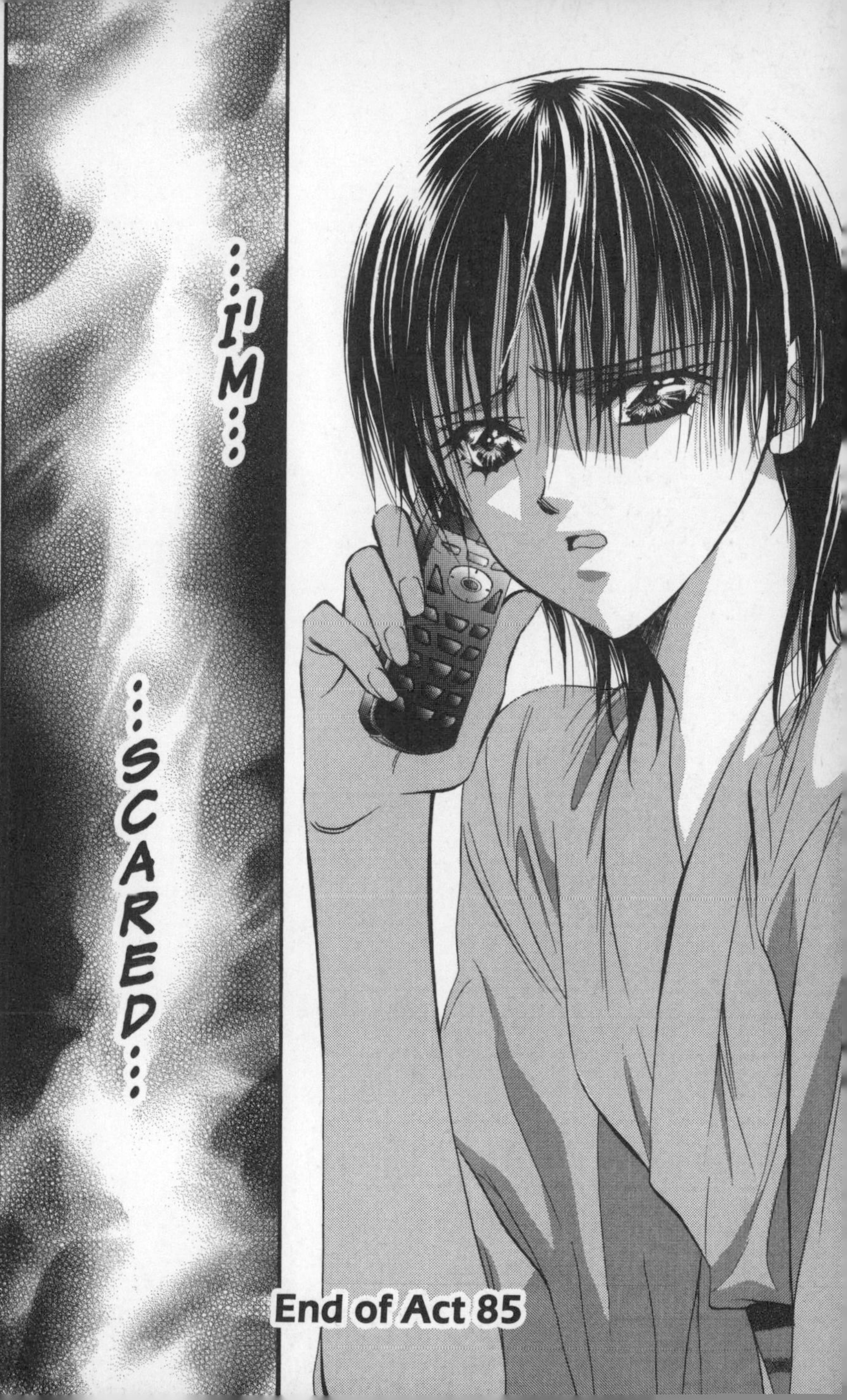
...I'M...
...SCARED...
End of Act 85

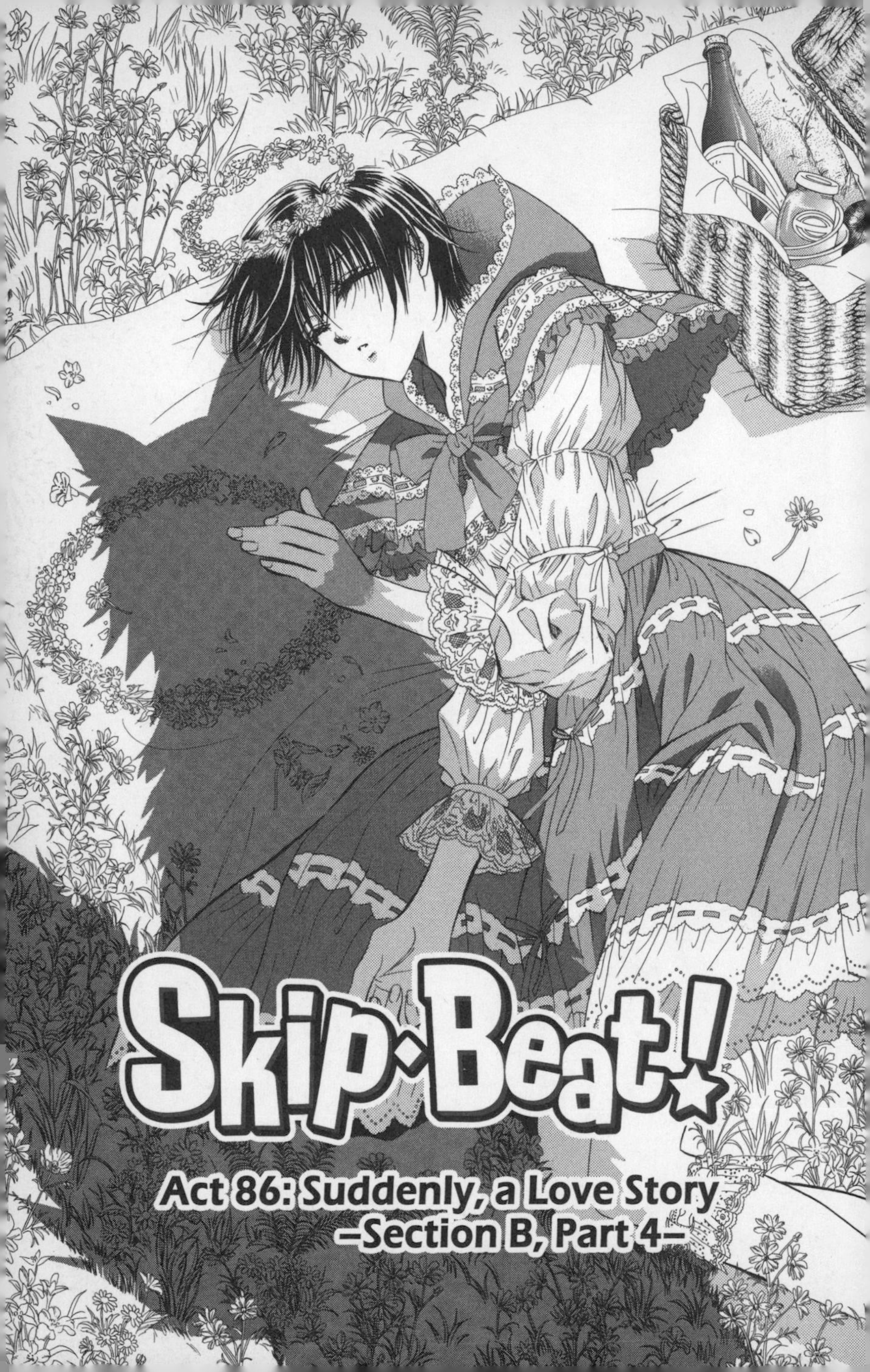
Skip·Beat!
Act 86: Suddenly, a Love Story
–Section B, Part 4–

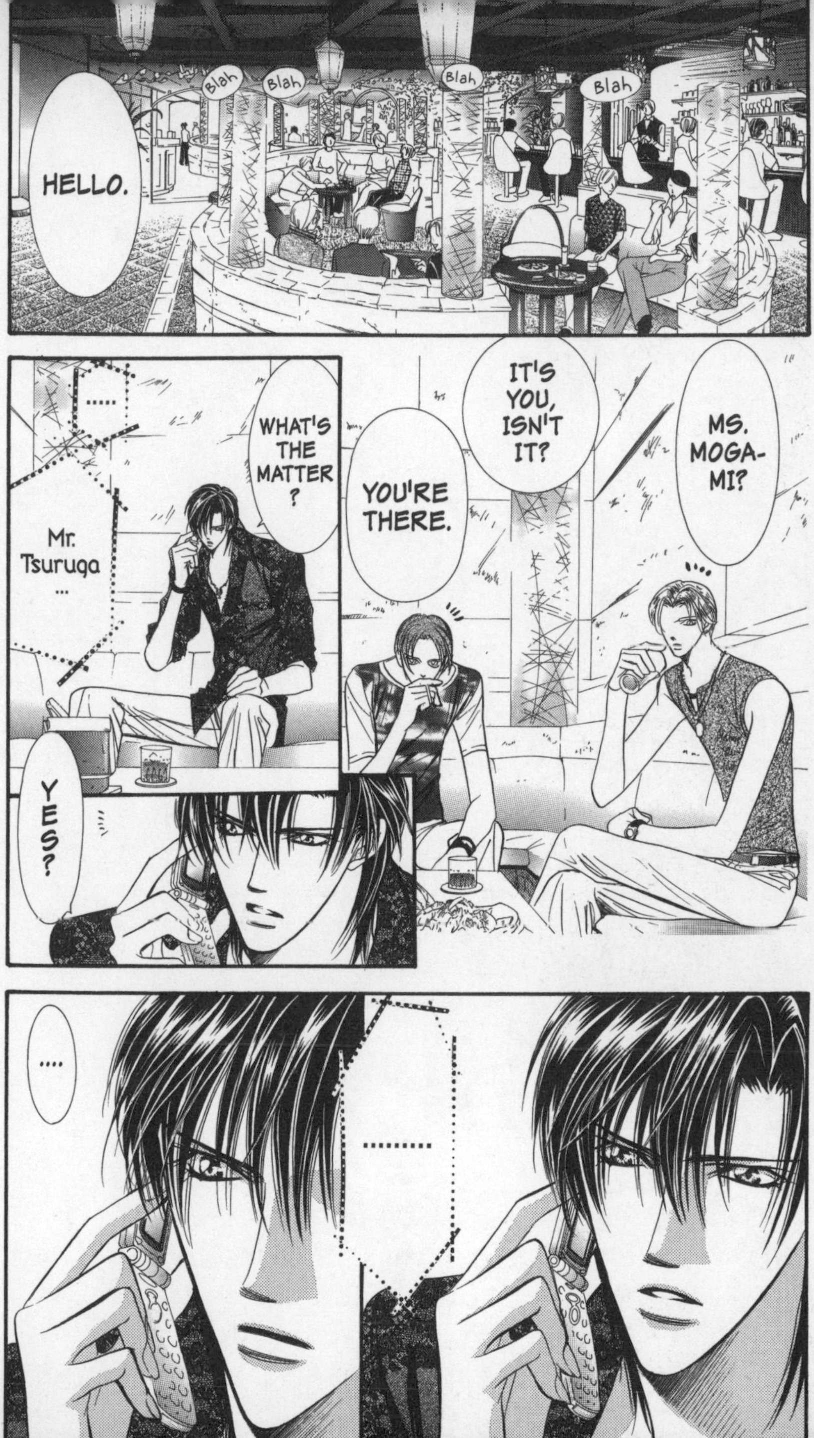

Blah
Blah
Blah
Blah
HELLO.
MS. MOGA-MI?
IT'S YOU, ISN'T IT?
YOU'RE THERE.
WHAT'S THE MATTER?
.....
Mr. Tsuruga ...
YES?
....
....

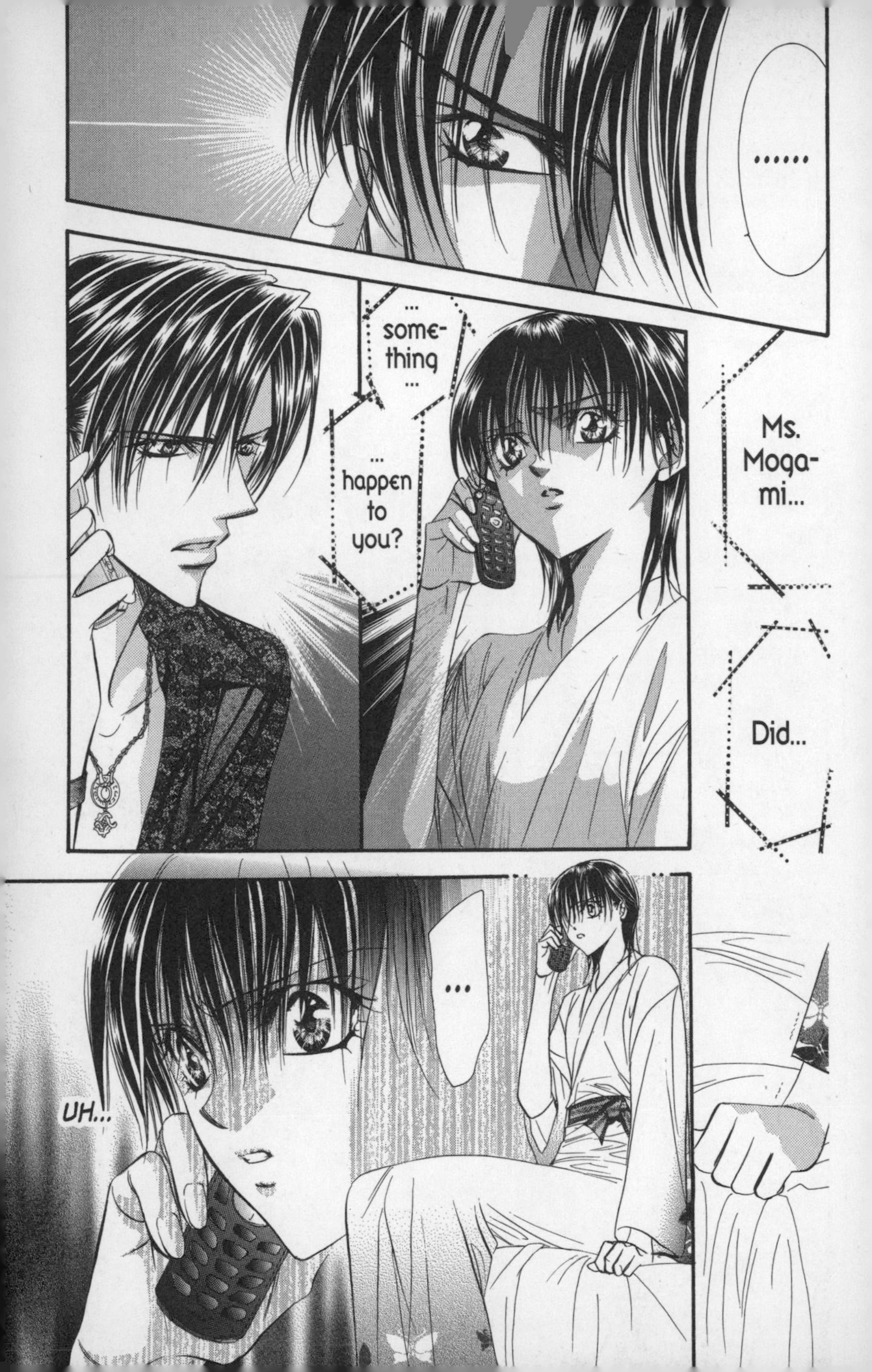
......
Ms. Mogami...
Did...
... something ...
... happen to you?
...
UH...

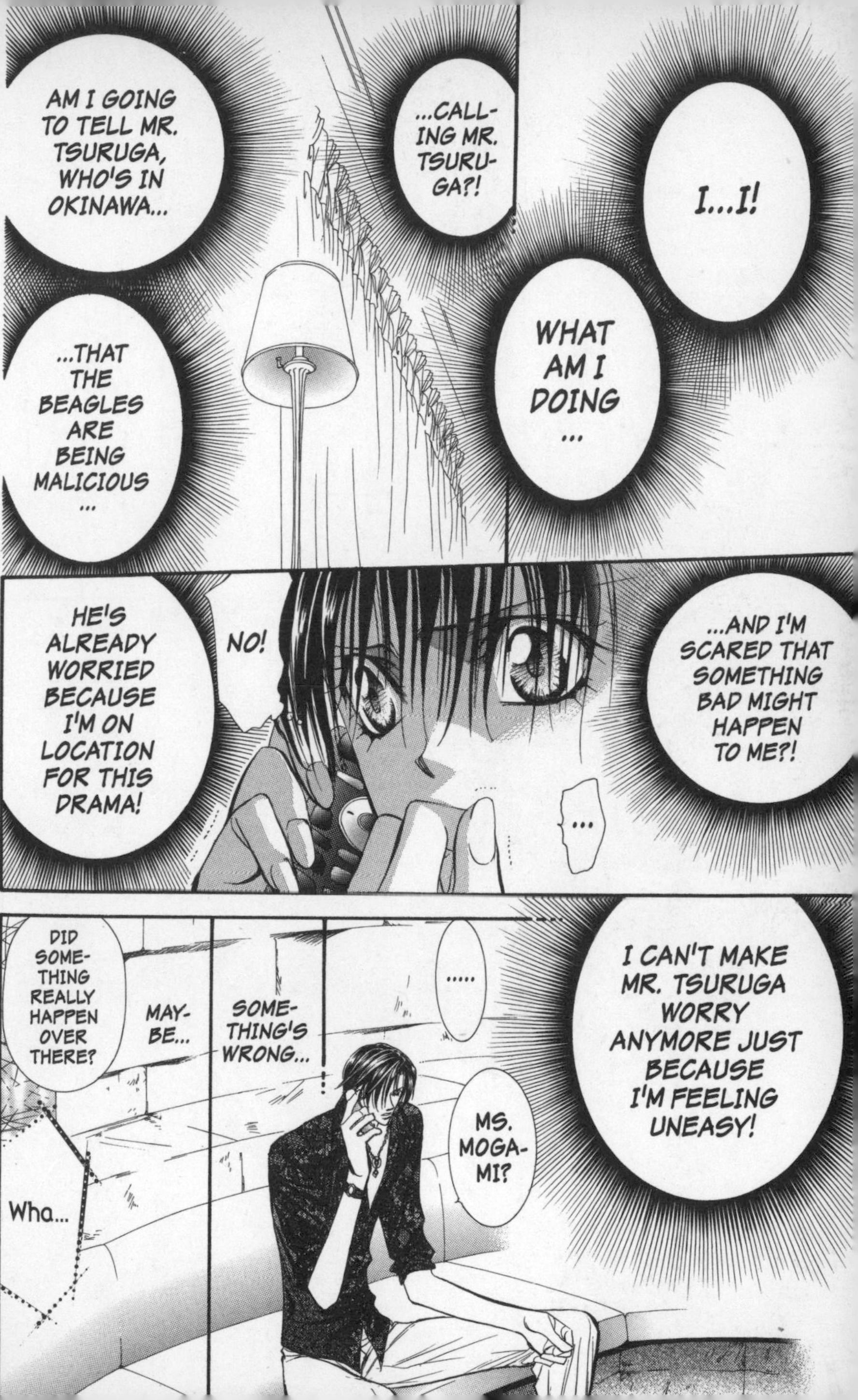
I...I!
WHAT AM I DOING ...
...CALLING MR. TSURUGA?!
AM I GOING TO TELL MR. TSURUGA, WHO'S IN OKINAWA...
...THAT THE BEAGLES ARE BEING MALICIOUS ...
...AND I'M SCARED THAT SOMETHING BAD MIGHT HAPPEN TO ME?!
...
NO!
HE'S ALREADY WORRIED BECAUSE I'M ON LOCATION FOR THIS DRAMA!
I CAN'T MAKE MR. TSURUGA WORRY ANYMORE JUST BECAUSE I'M FEELING UNEASY!
.....
MS. MOGAMI?
SOMETHING'S WRONG...
MAYBE...
DID SOMETHING REALLY HAPPEN OVER THERE?
Wha...

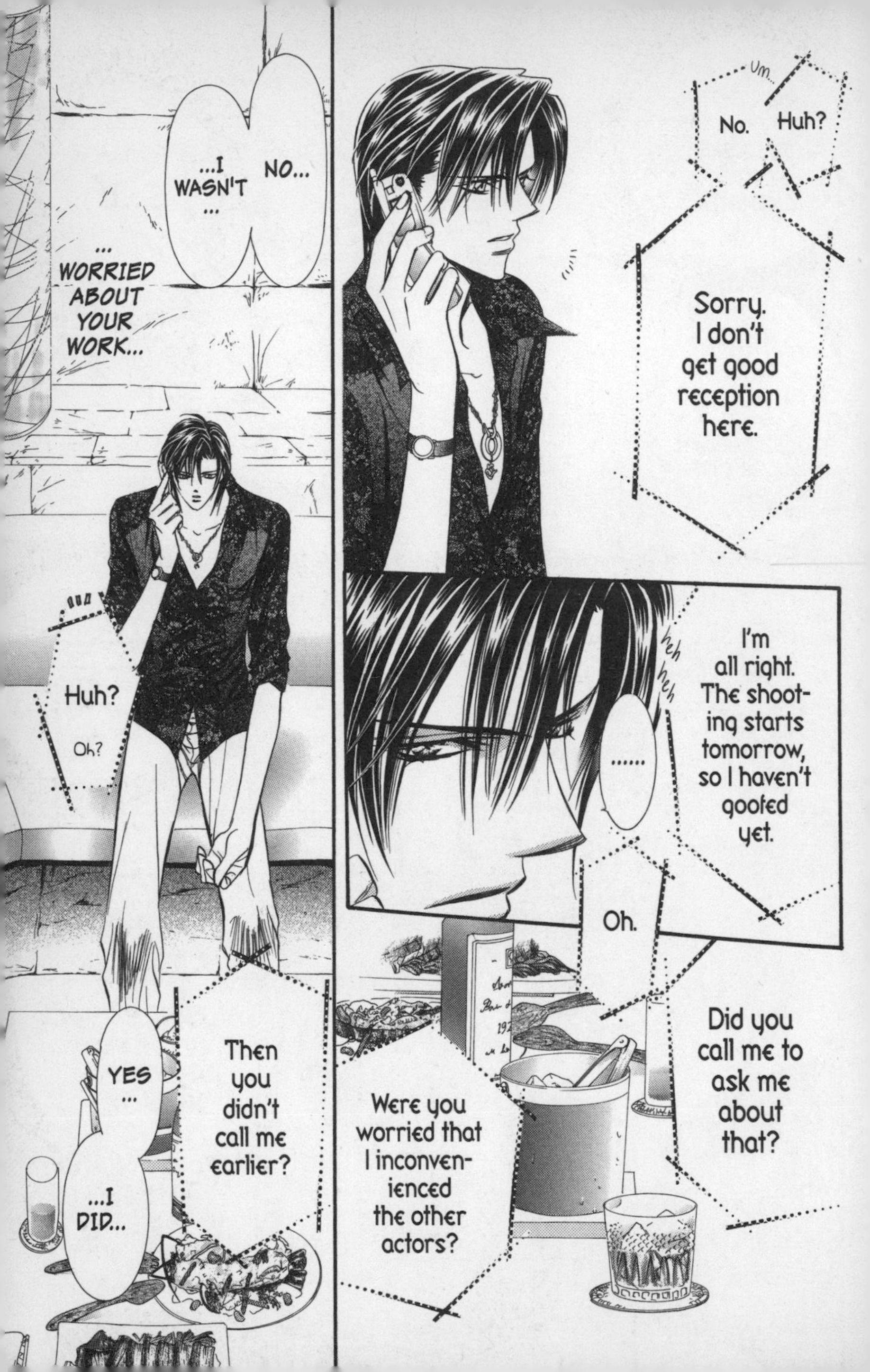
Um...
Huh?
No.
Sorry. I don't get good reception here.
heh heh
I'm all right. The shooting starts tomorrow, so I haven't goofed yet.
......
Oh.
Did you call me to ask me about that?
Were you worried that I inconvenienced the other actors?
NO...
...I WASN'T ...
... WORRIED ABOUT YOUR WORK...
Huh?
Oh?
Then you didn't call me earlier?
YES ...
...I DID...

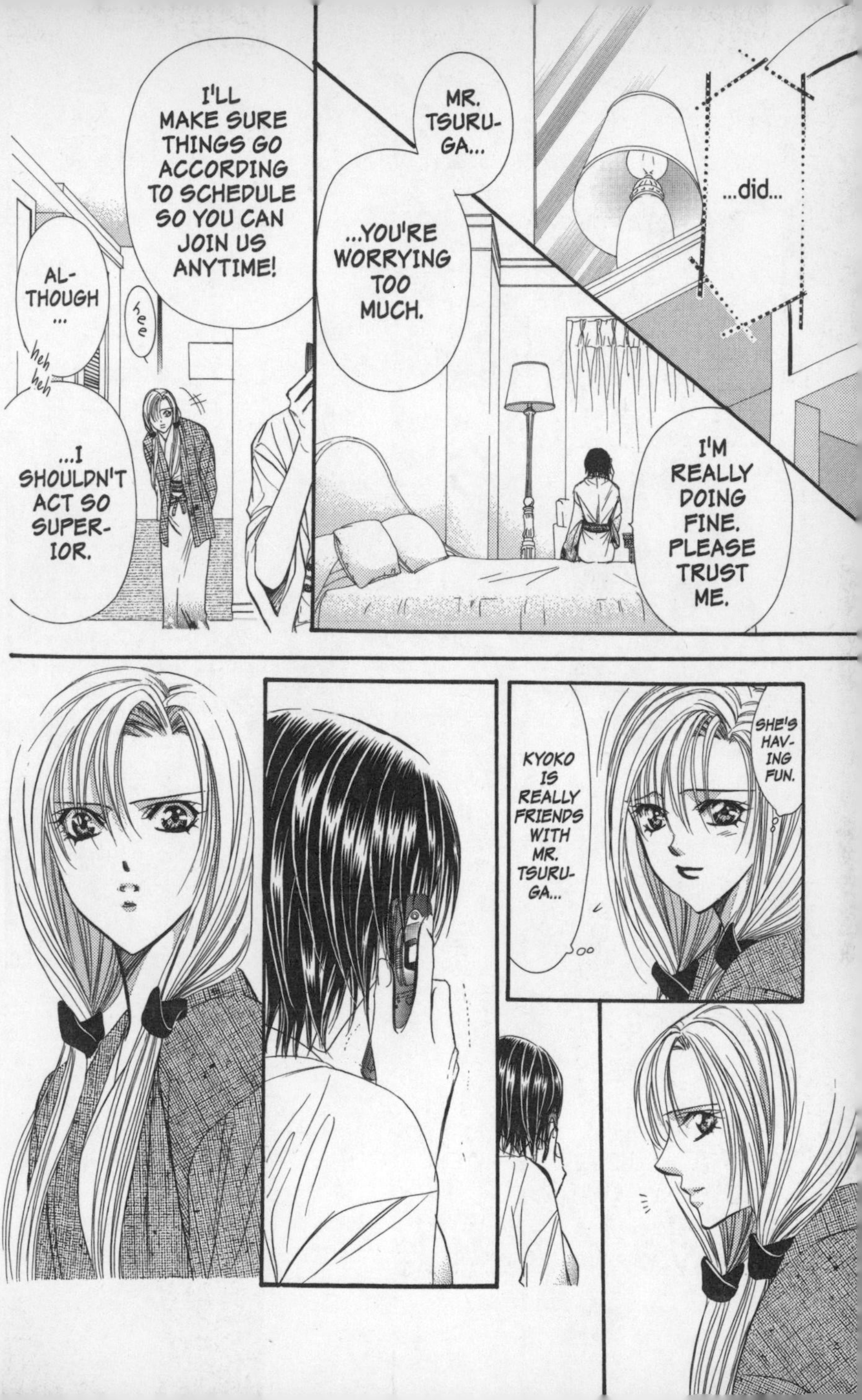
...did...
MR. TSURU-GA...
...YOU'RE WORRYING TOO MUCH.
I'M REALLY DOING FINE. PLEASE TRUST ME.
I'LL MAKE SURE THINGS GO ACCORDING TO SCHEDULE SO YOU CAN JOIN US ANYTIME!
hee
AL-THOUGH ...
heh heh
...I SHOULDN'T ACT SO SUPER-IOR.
SHE'S HAV-ING FUN.
KYOKO IS REALLY FRIENDS WITH MR. TSURU-GA...

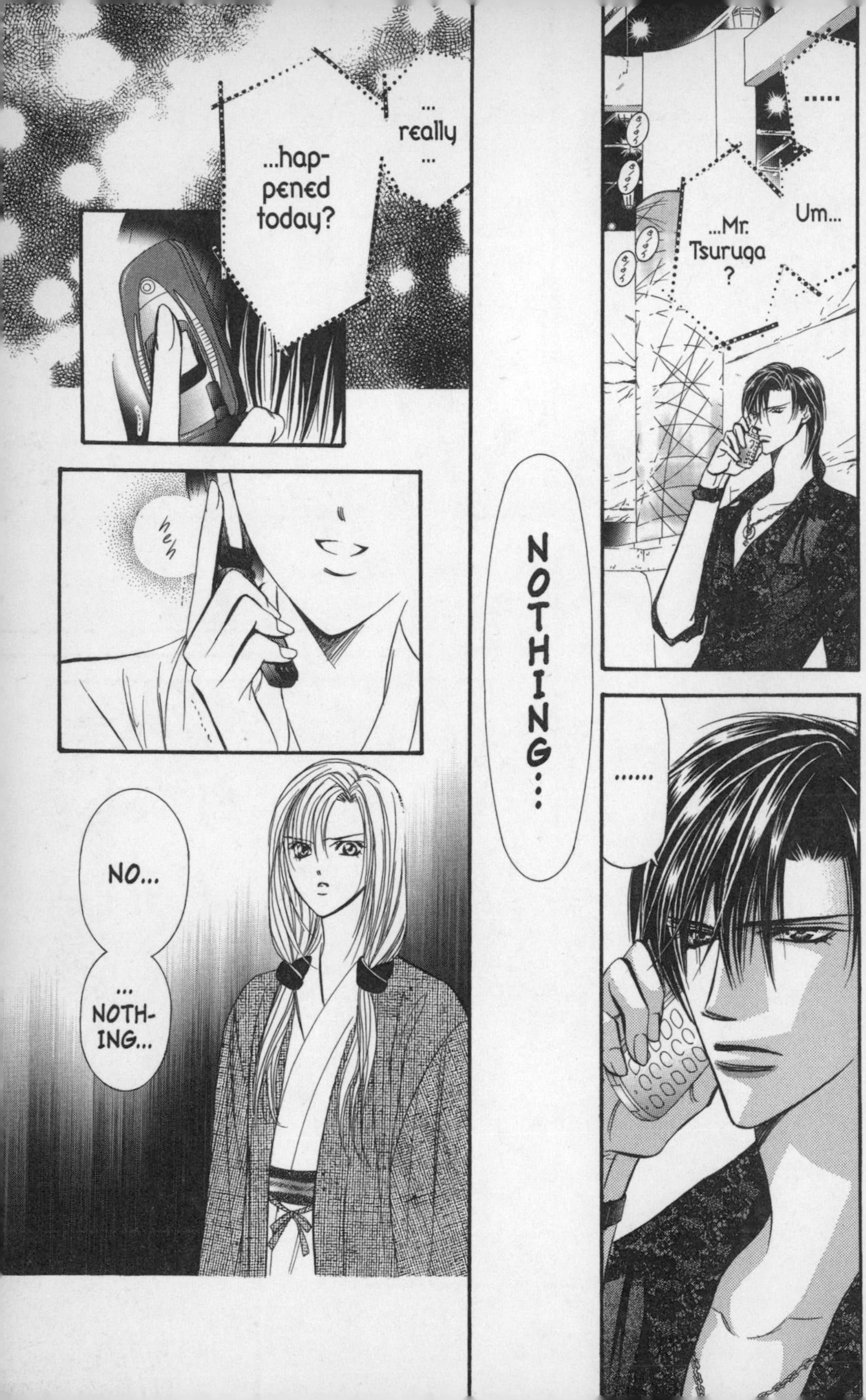
.....
Um...
...Mr. Tsuruga ?
NOTHING...
......
... really ...
...hap-pened today?
heh
NO...
... NOTH-ING...

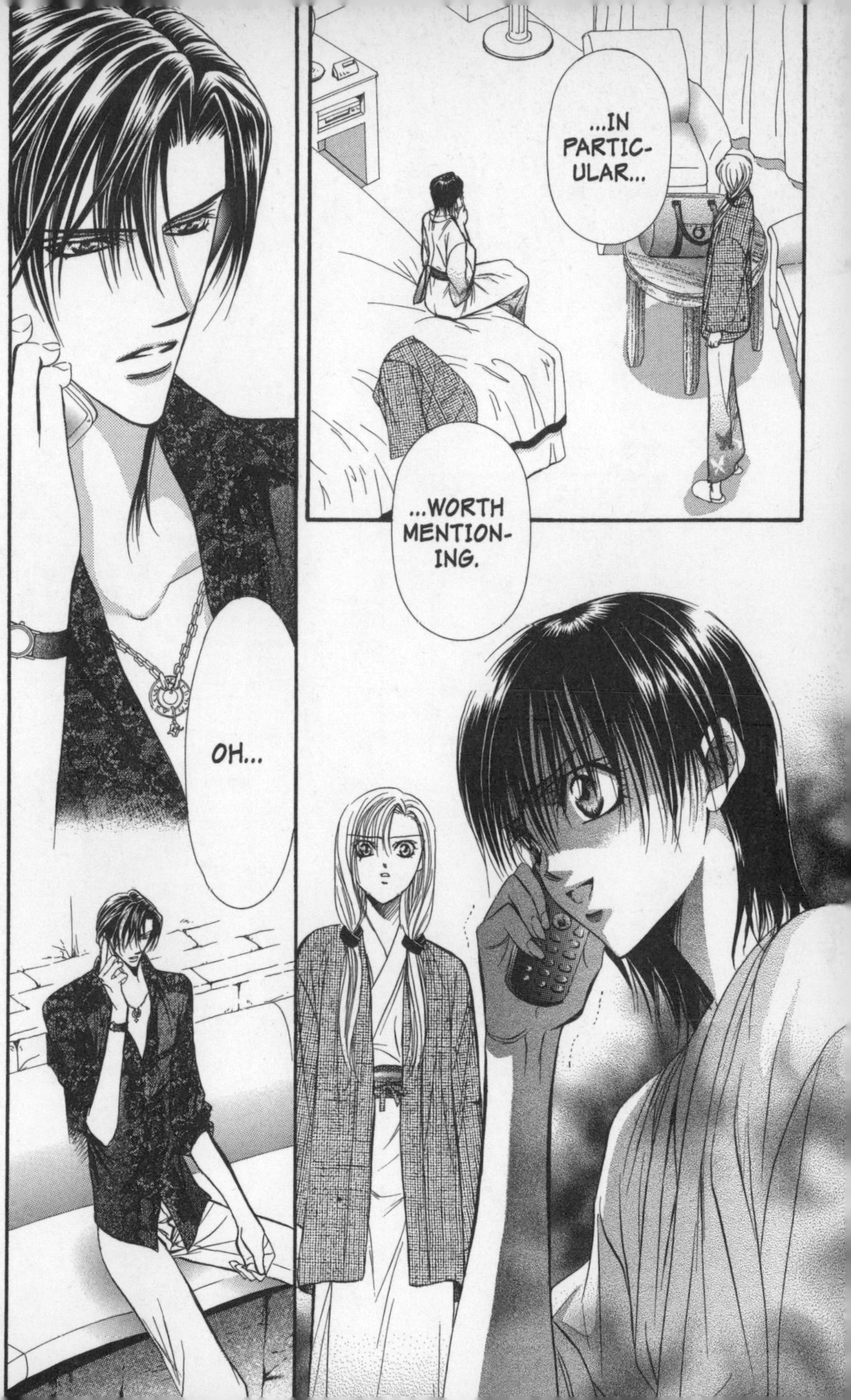
...IN PARTIC-ULAR...
...WORTH MENTION-ING.
OH...

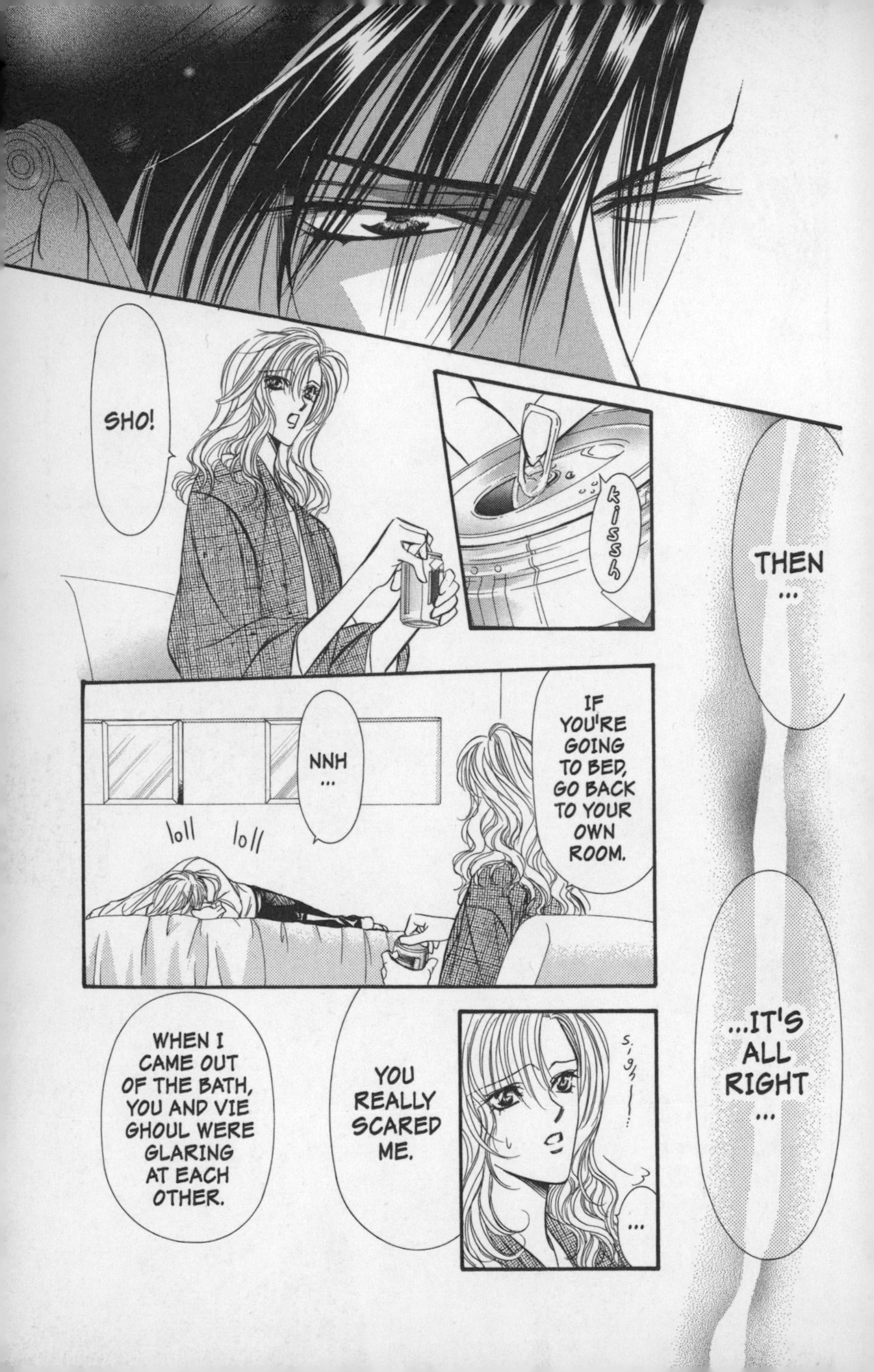
THEN ...
...IT'S ALL RIGHT ...
kissh
SHO!
IF YOU'RE GOING TO BED, GO BACK TO YOUR OWN ROOM.
NNH ...
loll
loll
sigh
...
YOU REALLY SCARED ME.
WHEN I CAME OUT OF THE BATH, YOU AND VIE GHOUL WERE GLARING AT EACH OTHER.

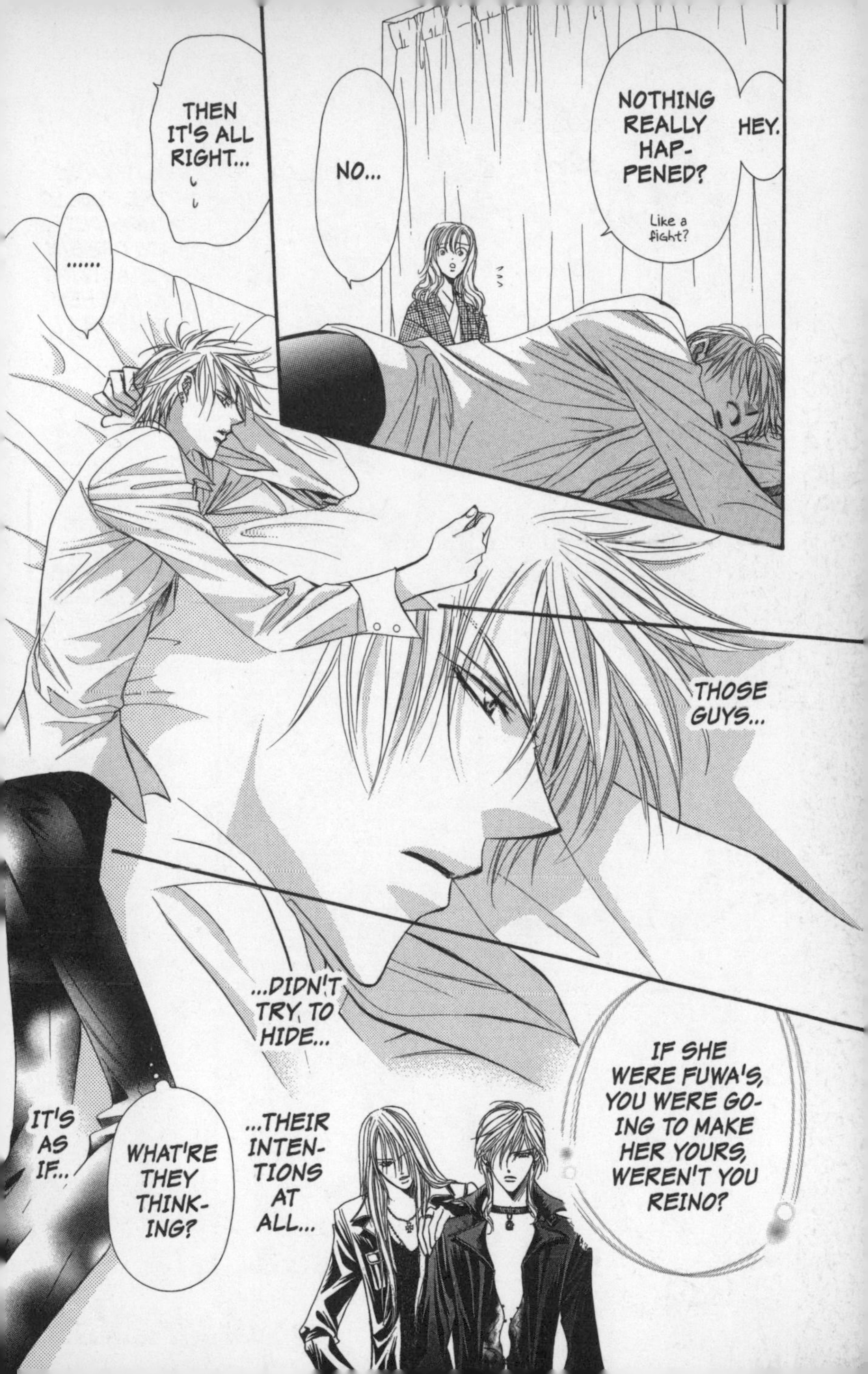
HEY.
NOTHING REALLY HAP-PENED?
Like a fight?
NO...
THEN IT'S ALL RIGHT...
......
THOSE GUYS...
...DIDN'T TRY TO HIDE...
IF SHE WERE FUWA'S, YOU WERE GO-ING TO MAKE HER YOURS, WEREN'T YOU REINO?
...THEIR INTEN-TIONS AT ALL...
WHAT'RE THEY THINK-ING?
IT'S AS IF...

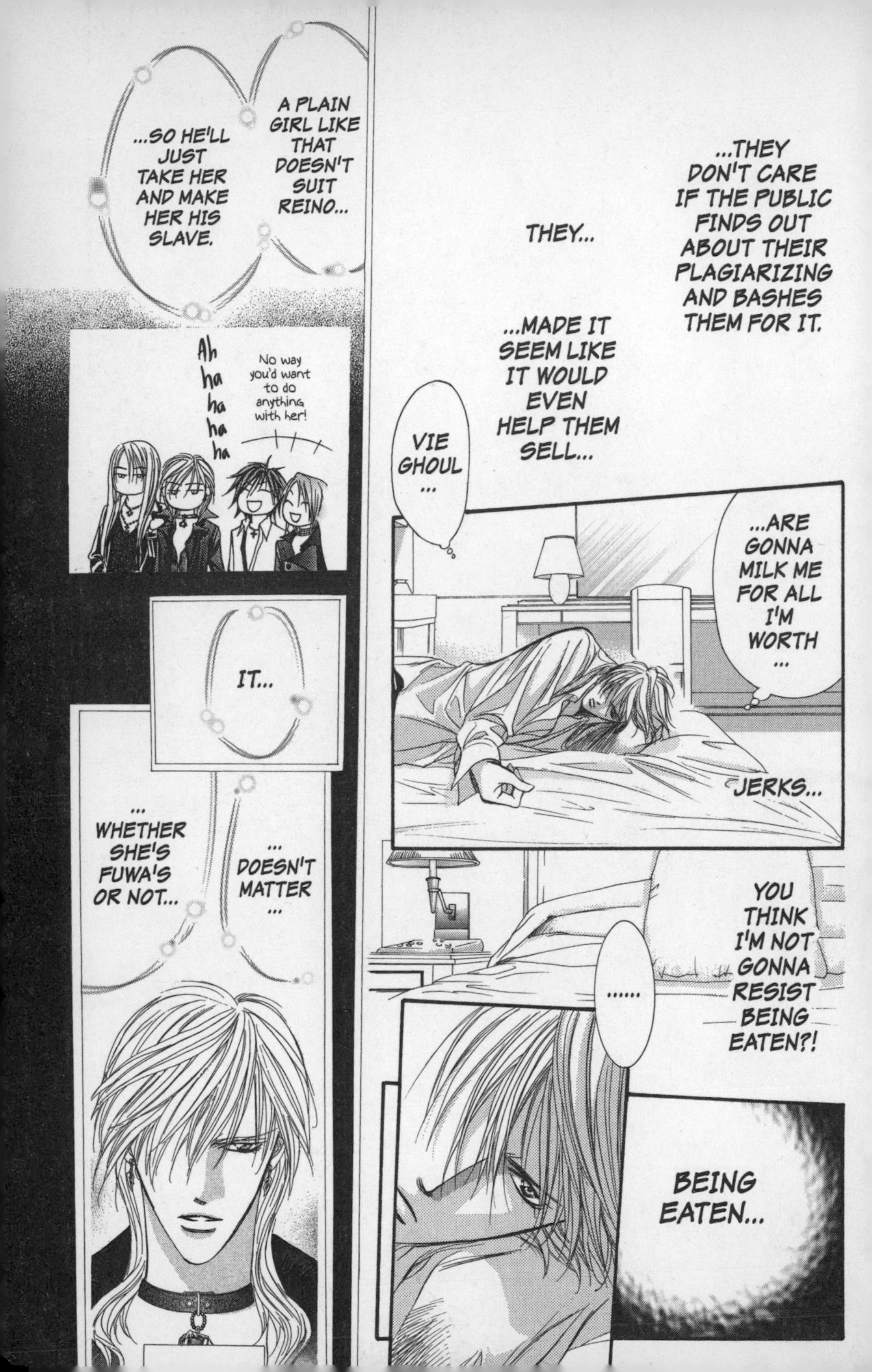
...THEY DON'T CARE IF THE PUBLIC FINDS OUT ABOUT THEIR PLAGIARIZING AND BASHES THEM FOR IT.
THEY...
...MADE IT SEEM LIKE IT WOULD EVEN HELP THEM SELL...
VIE GHOUL...
...ARE GONNA MILK ME FOR ALL I'M WORTH...
JERKS...
YOU THINK I'M NOT GONNA RESIST BEING EATEN?!
......
BEING EATEN...
A PLAIN GIRL LIKE THAT DOESN'T SUIT REINO...
...SO HE'LL JUST TAKE HER AND MAKE HER HIS SLAVE.
No way you'd want to do anything with her!
Ah ha ha ha ha
IT...
...DOESN'T MATTER...
...WHETHER SHE'S FUWA'S OR NOT...

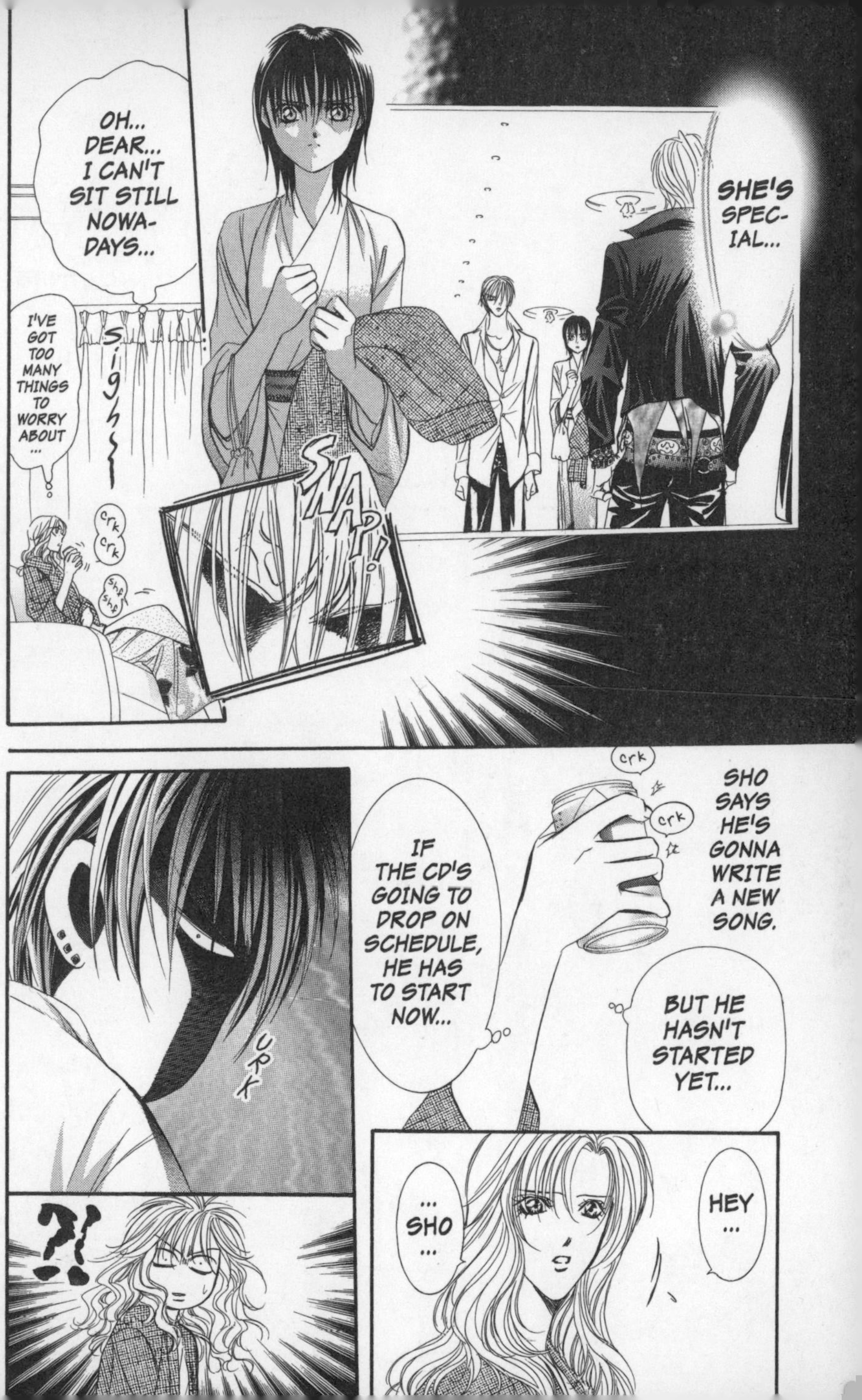
SHE'S SPECIAL...
OH... DEAR... I CAN'T SIT STILL NOWADAYS...
I'VE GOT TOO MANY THINGS TO WORRY ABOUT...
Sigh~
SNAP!!
crk crk
shf shf
crk
crk
SHO SAYS HE'S GONNA WRITE A NEW SONG.
IF THE CD'S GOING TO DROP ON SCHEDULE, HE HAS TO START NOW...
BUT HE HASN'T STARTED YET...
HEY...
...SHO...
URK
?!

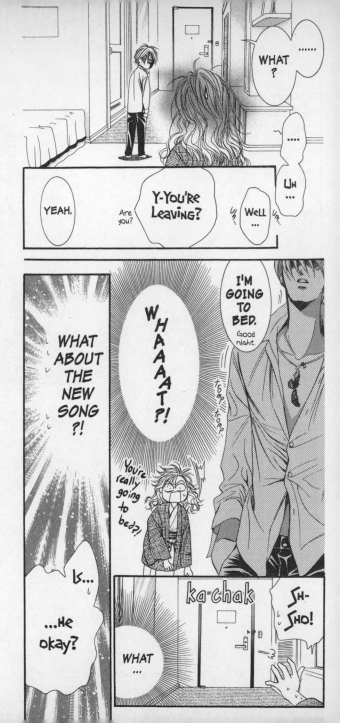

......
WHAT?
....
UH ...
Well ...
Y-You're Leaving?
Are you?
YEAH.
I'M GOING TO BED.
Good night.
WHAAAAT?!
tromp tromp
You're really going to bed?!
SH-SHO!
ka-chak
WHAT ...
WHAT ABOUT THE NEW SONG?!
Is...
...he okay?

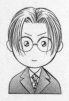

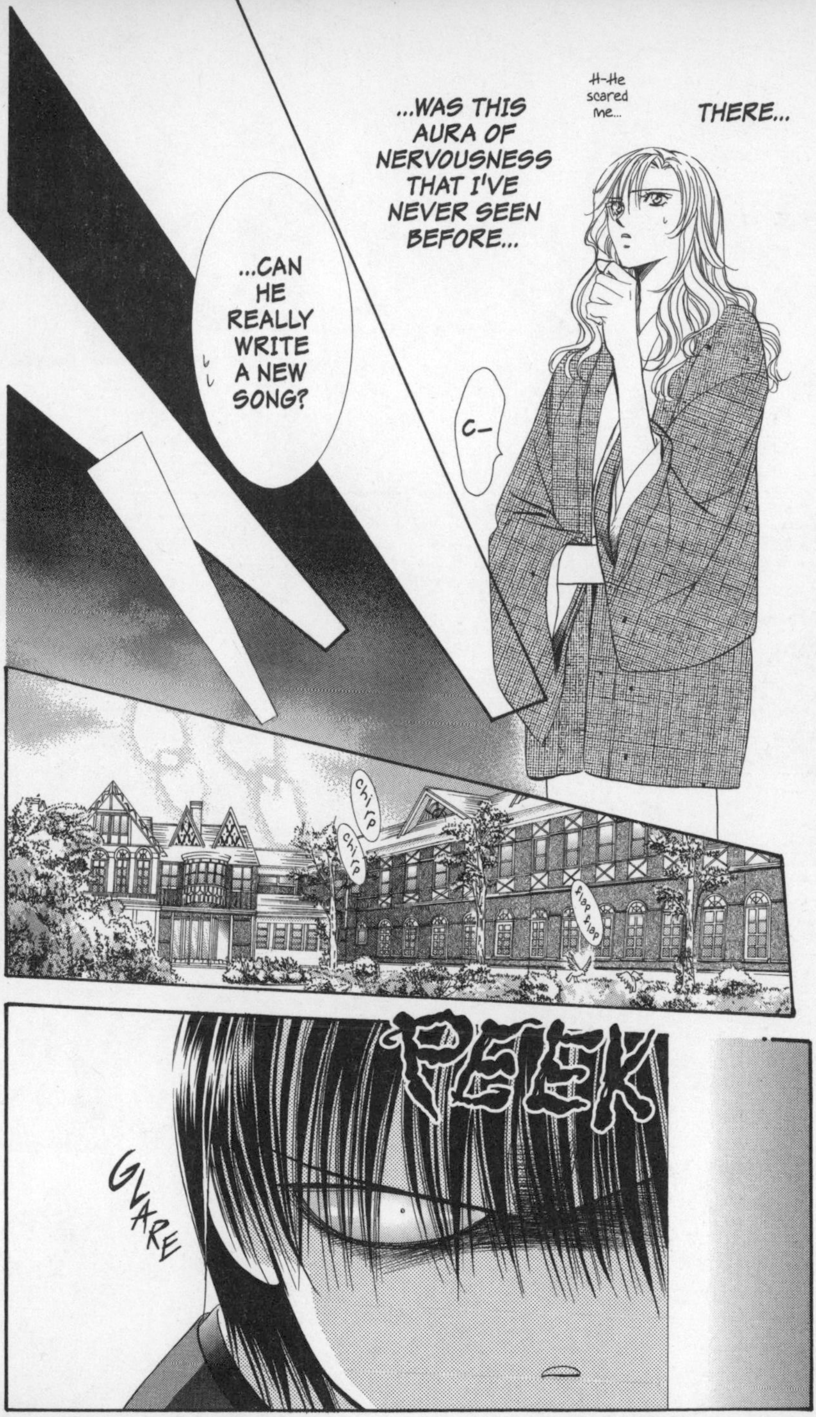
THERE...
H-He scared me...
...WAS THIS AURA OF NERVOUSNESS THAT I'VE NEVER SEEN BEFORE...
C–
...CAN HE REALLY WRITE A NEW SONG?
chirp
chirp
flap flap
PEEK
GLARE

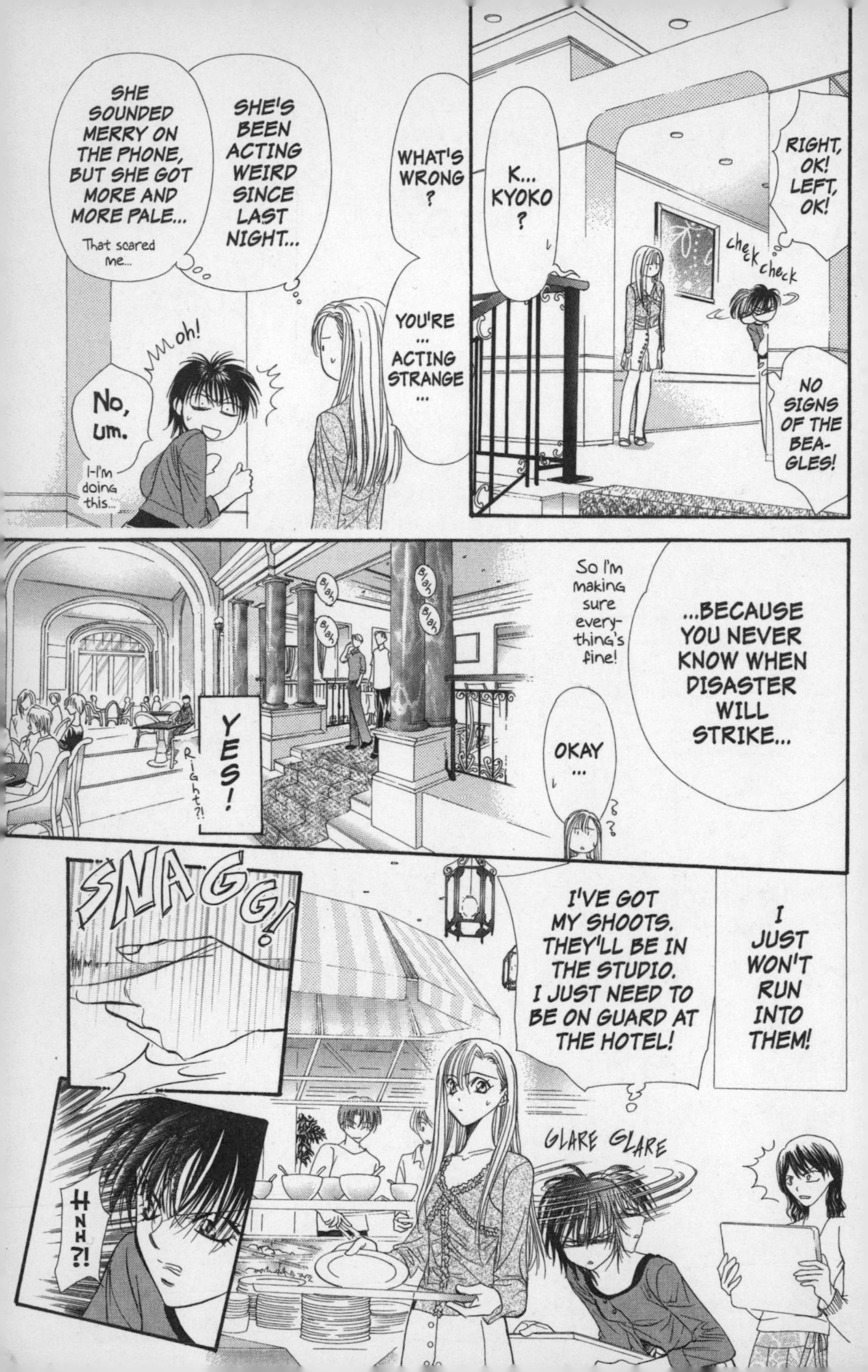
RIGHT, OK! LEFT, OK!
check check
NO SIGNS OF THE BEAGLES!
K... KYOKO?
WHAT'S WRONG?
YOU'RE ... ACTING STRANGE ...
SHE'S BEEN ACTING WEIRD SINCE LAST NIGHT...
SHE SOUNDED MERRY ON THE PHONE, BUT SHE GOT MORE AND MORE PALE...
That scared me...
oh!
No, um.
I-I'm doing this...
...BECAUSE YOU NEVER KNOW WHEN DISASTER WILL STRIKE...
So I'm making sure every-thing's fine!
OKAY ...
YES!
Right?!
Blah
Blah
Blah
Blah
I JUST WON'T RUN INTO THEM!
I'VE GOT MY SHOOTS. THEY'LL BE IN THE STUDIO. I JUST NEED TO BE ON GUARD AT THE HOTEL!
GLARE GLARE
SNAGG!
HNH?!

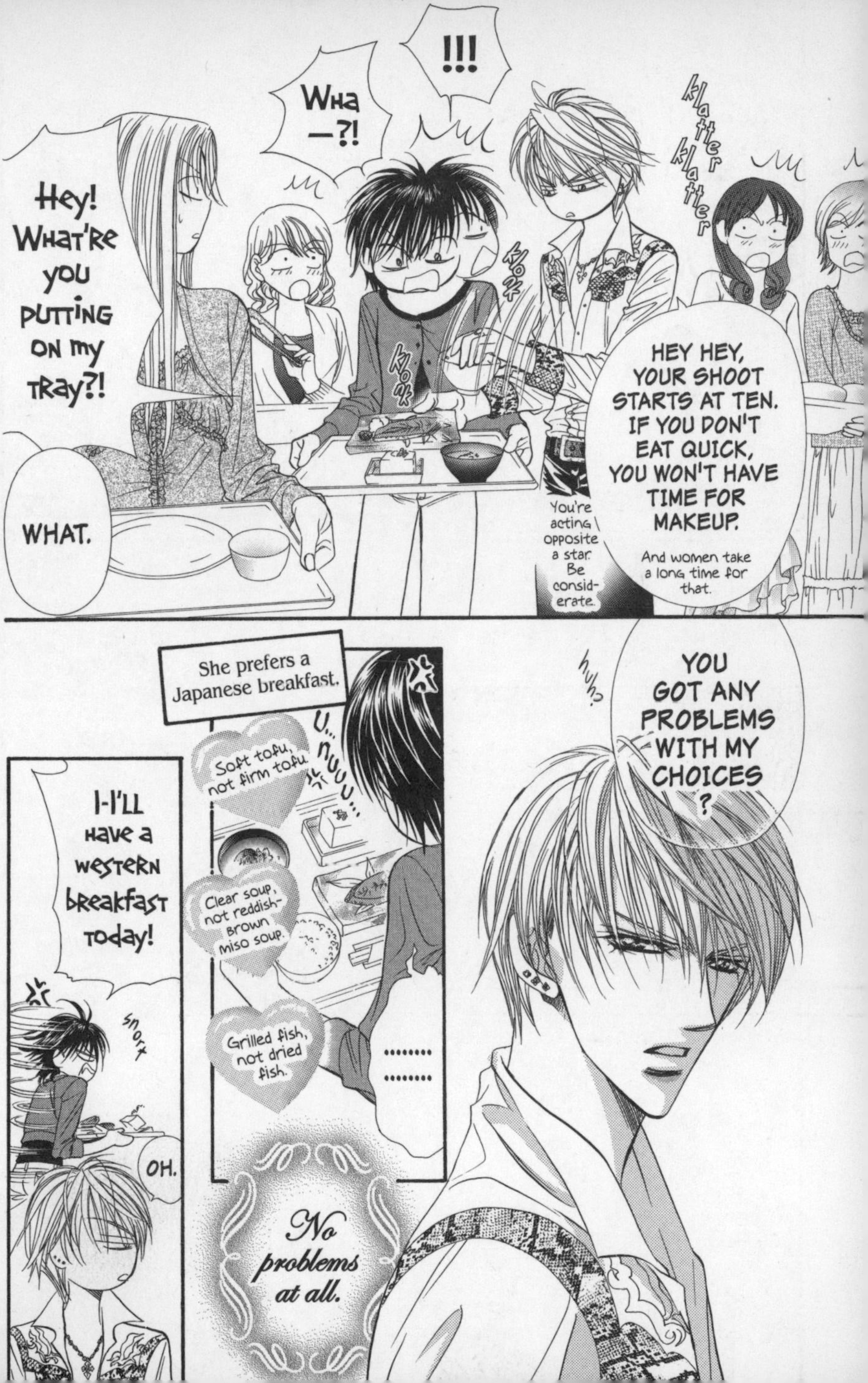
klatter klatter
!!!
Wha—?!
HEY HEY, YOUR SHOOT STARTS AT TEN. IF YOU DON'T EAT QUICK, YOU WON'T HAVE TIME FOR MAKEUP.
And women take a long time for that.
You're acting opposite a star. Be consid-erate.
klok
klok
Hey! What're you putting on my tray?!
WHAT.
huh?
YOU GOT ANY PROBLEMS WITH MY CHOICES?
She prefers a Japanese breakfast.
U... nuuuu...
Soft tofu, not firm tofu.
Clear soup, not reddish-brown miso soup.
Grilled fish, not dried fish.
....
....
No problems at all.
I-I'll have a western breakfast today!
snort
OH.

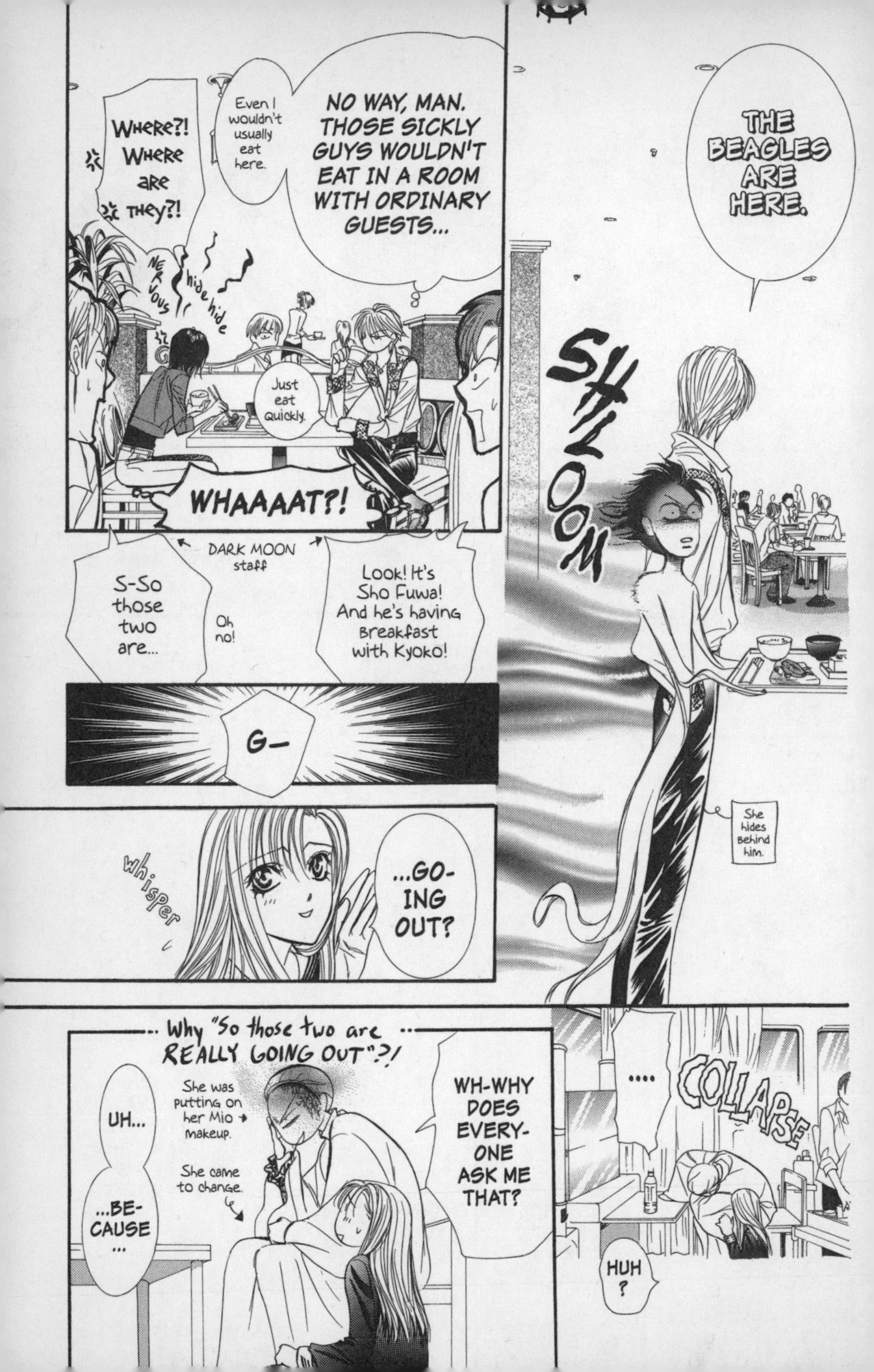
THE BEAGLES ARE HERE.
SHLOOM
She hides behind him.
NO WAY, MAN. THOSE SICKLY GUYS WOULDN'T EAT IN A ROOM WITH ORDINARY GUESTS...
Even I wouldn't usually eat here.
Where?! Where are they?!
NERVOUS
hide hide
Just eat quickly.
WHAAAAT?!
Look! It's Sho Fuwa! And he's having breakfast with Kyoko!
DARK MOON staff
Oh no!
S-So those two are...
G—
...GO-ING OUT?
whisper
COLLAPSE
....
HUH?
Why "So those two are REALLY GOING OUT"?!
WH-WHY DOES EVERYONE ASK ME THAT?
She was putting on her Mio makeup.
She came to change.
UH...
...BE-CAUSE...

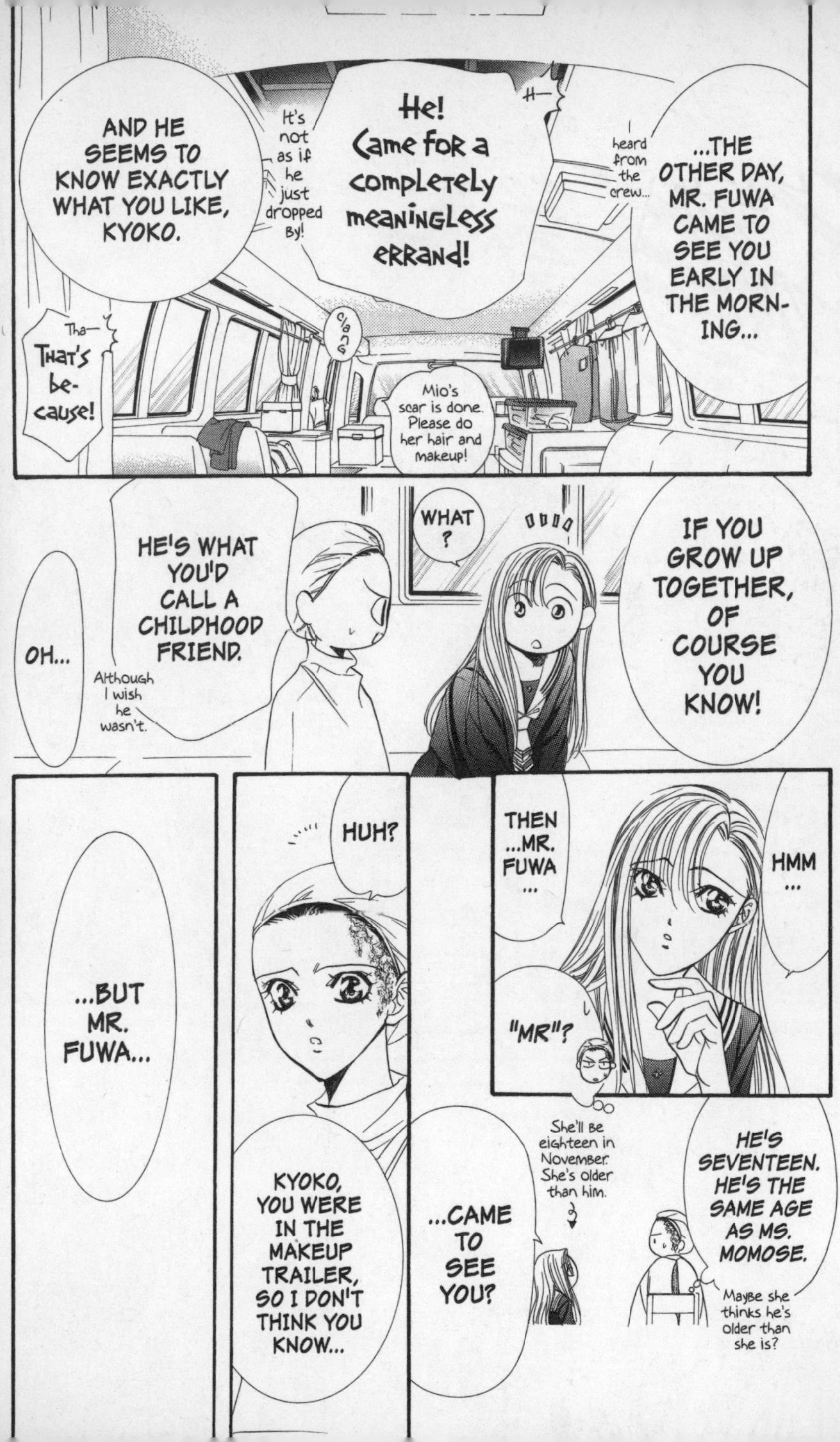
...THE OTHER DAY, MR. FUWA CAME TO SEE YOU EARLY IN THE MORNING...
I heard from the crew...
H—
He! Came for a completely meaningless errand!
It's not as if he just dropped By!
AND HE SEEMS TO KNOW EXACTLY WHAT YOU LIKE, KYOKO.
Tha— That's be-cause!
clang
Mio's scar is done. Please do her hair and makeup!
IF YOU GROW UP TOGETHER, OF COURSE YOU KNOW!
WHAT?
HE'S WHAT YOU'D CALL A CHILDHOOD FRIEND.
Although I wish he wasn't.
OH...
HMM...
THEN ...MR. FUWA...
"MR"?
HE'S SEVENTEEN. HE'S THE SAME AGE AS MS. MOMOSE.
Maybe she thinks he's older than she is?
She'll be eighteen in November. She's older than him.
HUH?
...CAME TO SEE YOU?
KYOKO, YOU WERE IN THE MAKEUP TRAILER, SO I DON'T THINK YOU KNOW...
...BUT MR. FUWA...

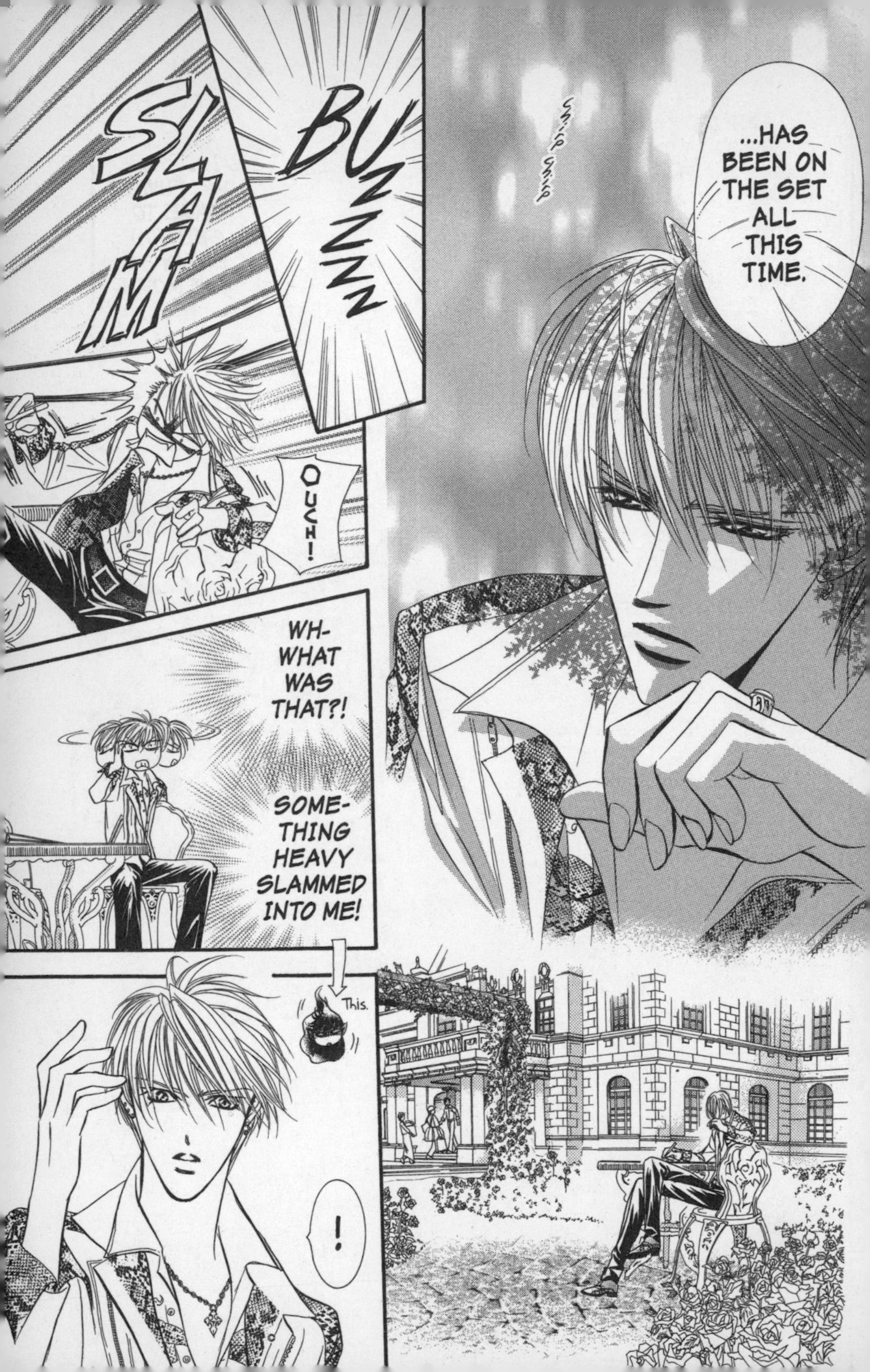
chirp chirp
...HAS BEEN ON THE SET ALL THIS TIME.
SLAM
BUZZZZZ
OUCH!
WH-WHAT WAS THAT?!
SOMETHING HEAVY SLAMMED INTO ME!
This.
!

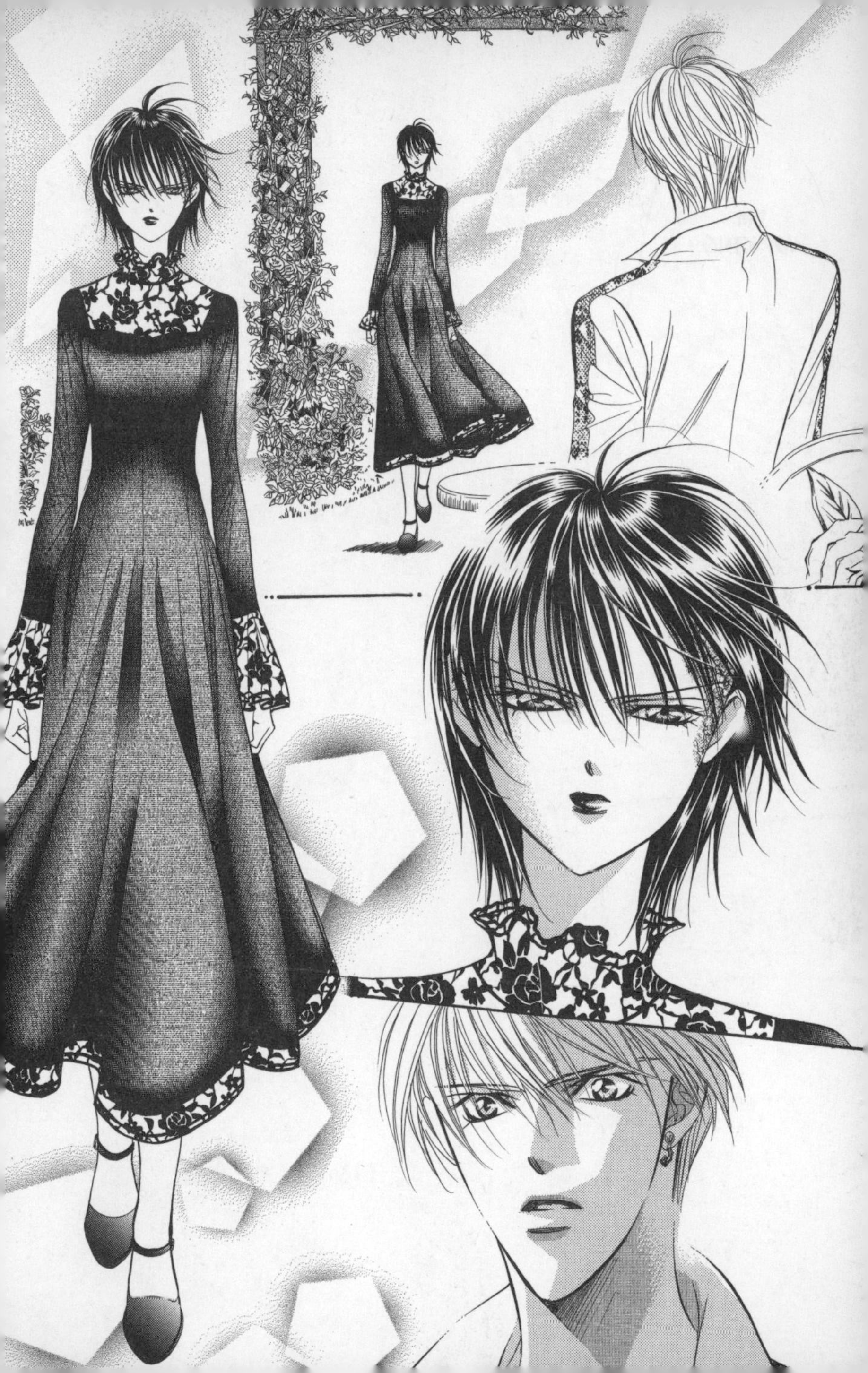

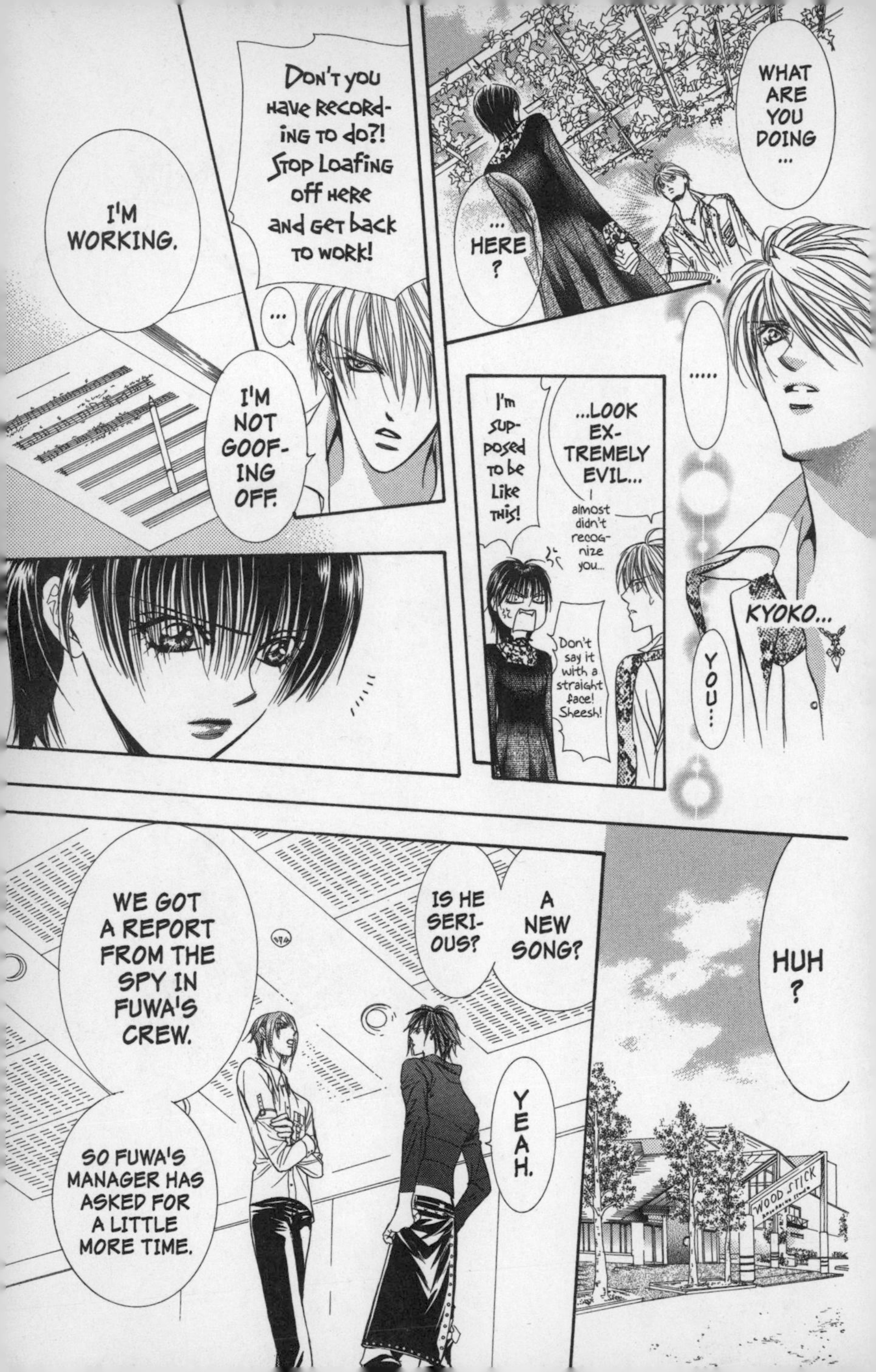
WHAT ARE YOU DOING ...
... HERE ?
I'M WORKING.
DON'T YOU HAVE RECORDING TO DO?! STOP LOAFING OFF HERE AND GET BACK TO WORK!
...
I'M NOT GOOFING OFF.
.....
KYOKO...
YOU...
...LOOK EXTREMELY EVIL...
I almost didn't recognize you...
I'm supposed to be like this!
Don't say it with a straight face! Sheesh!
HUH ?
WOOD STICK
A NEW SONG?
IS HE SERIOUS?
YEAH.
WE GOT A REPORT FROM THE SPY IN FUWA'S CREW.
SO FUWA'S MANAGER HAS ASKED FOR A LITTLE MORE TIME.

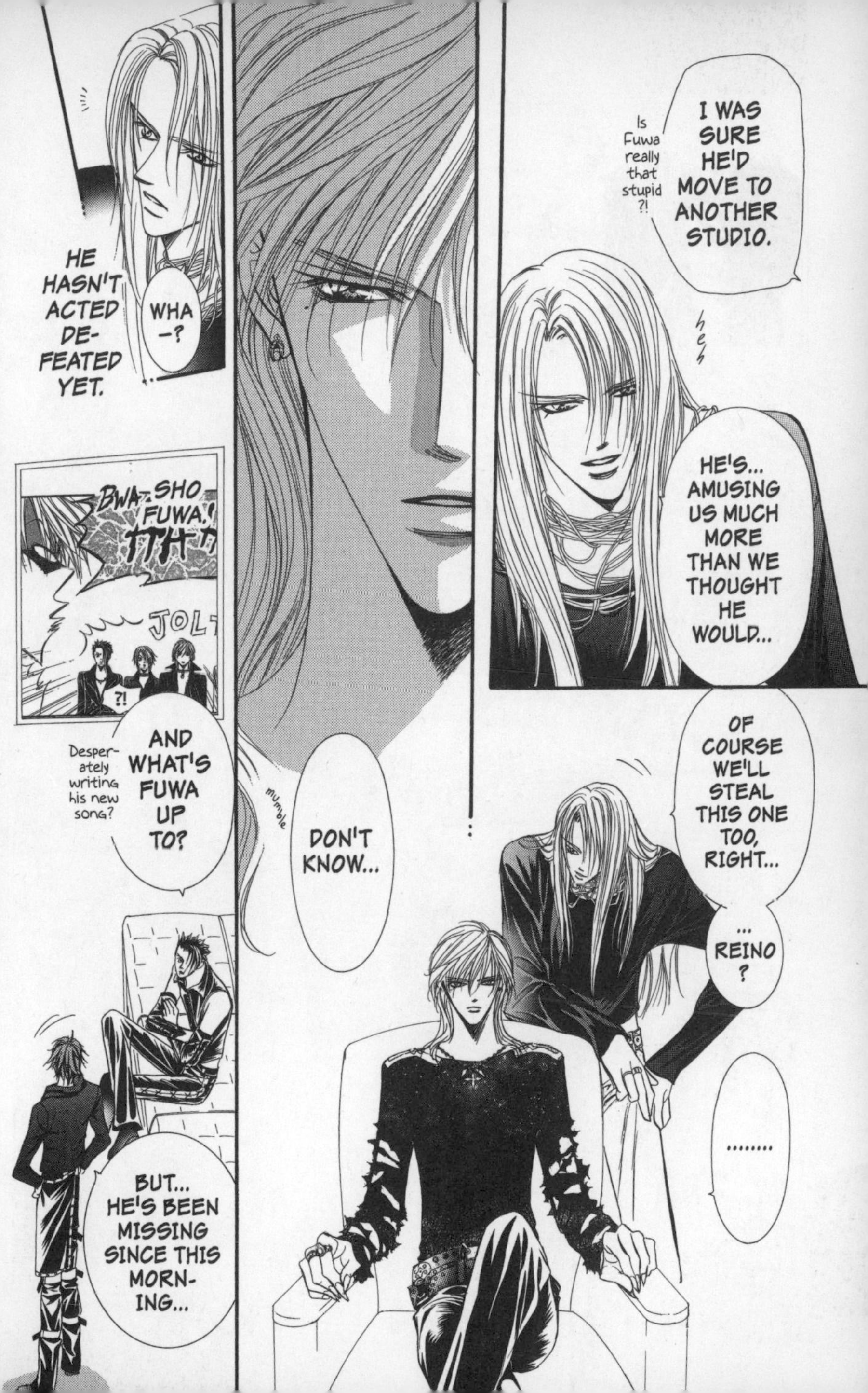
I WAS SURE HE'D MOVE TO ANOTHER STUDIO.
Is Fuwa really that stupid ?!
heh
HE'S... AMUSING US MUCH MORE THAN WE THOUGHT HE WOULD...
OF COURSE WE'LL STEAL THIS ONE TOO, RIGHT...
... REINO ?
....
mumble
DON'T KNOW...
HE HASN'T ACTED DE-FEATED YET.
WHA-?
BWA-SHO FUWA!
JOLT
?!
AND WHAT'S FUWA UP TO?
Desper-ately writing his new song?
BUT... HE'S BEEN MISSING SINCE THIS MORN-ING...

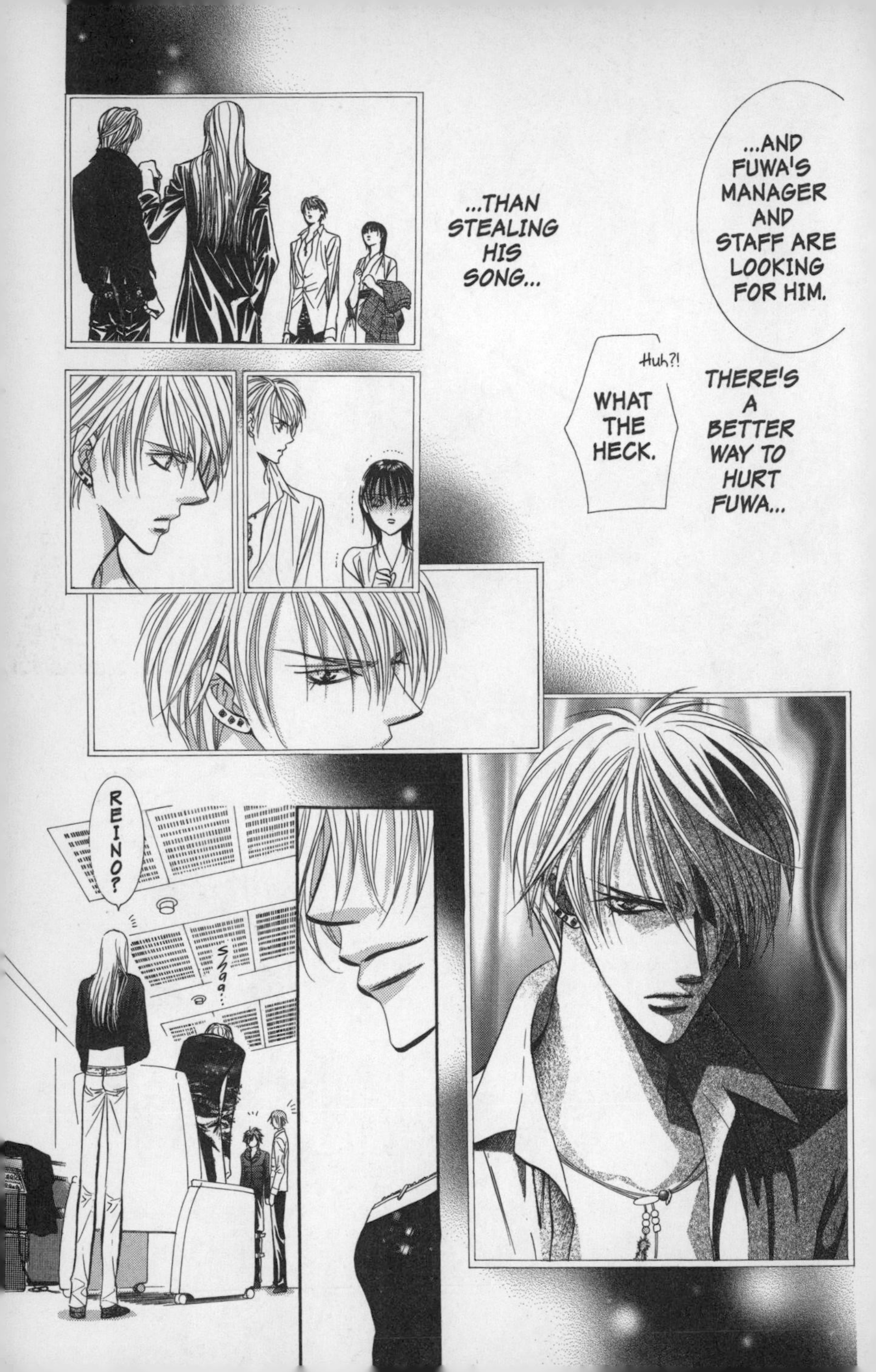
...AND FUWA'S MANAGER AND STAFF ARE LOOKING FOR HIM.
...THAN STEALING HIS SONG...
THERE'S A BETTER WAY TO HURT FUWA...
Huh?!
WHAT THE HECK.
REINO?
Shagg...

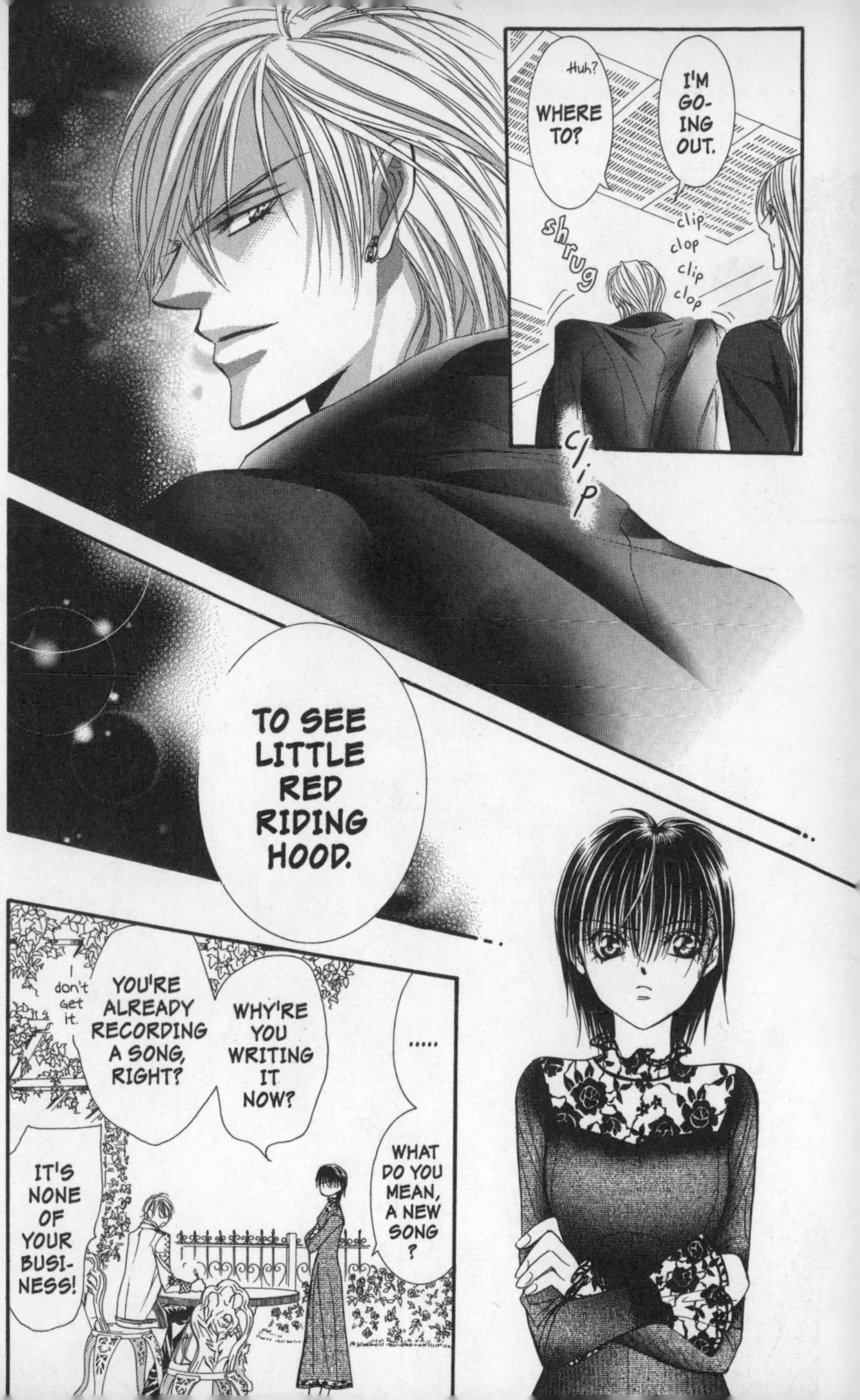
I'M GO-ING OUT.
Huh?
WHERE TO?
shrug
clip clop clip clop
clip
TO SEE LITTLE RED RIDING HOOD.
.....
WHAT DO YOU MEAN, A NEW SONG?
WHY'RE YOU WRITING IT NOW?
YOU'RE ALREADY RECORDING A SONG, RIGHT?
I don't get it.
IT'S NONE OF YOUR BUSI-NESS!

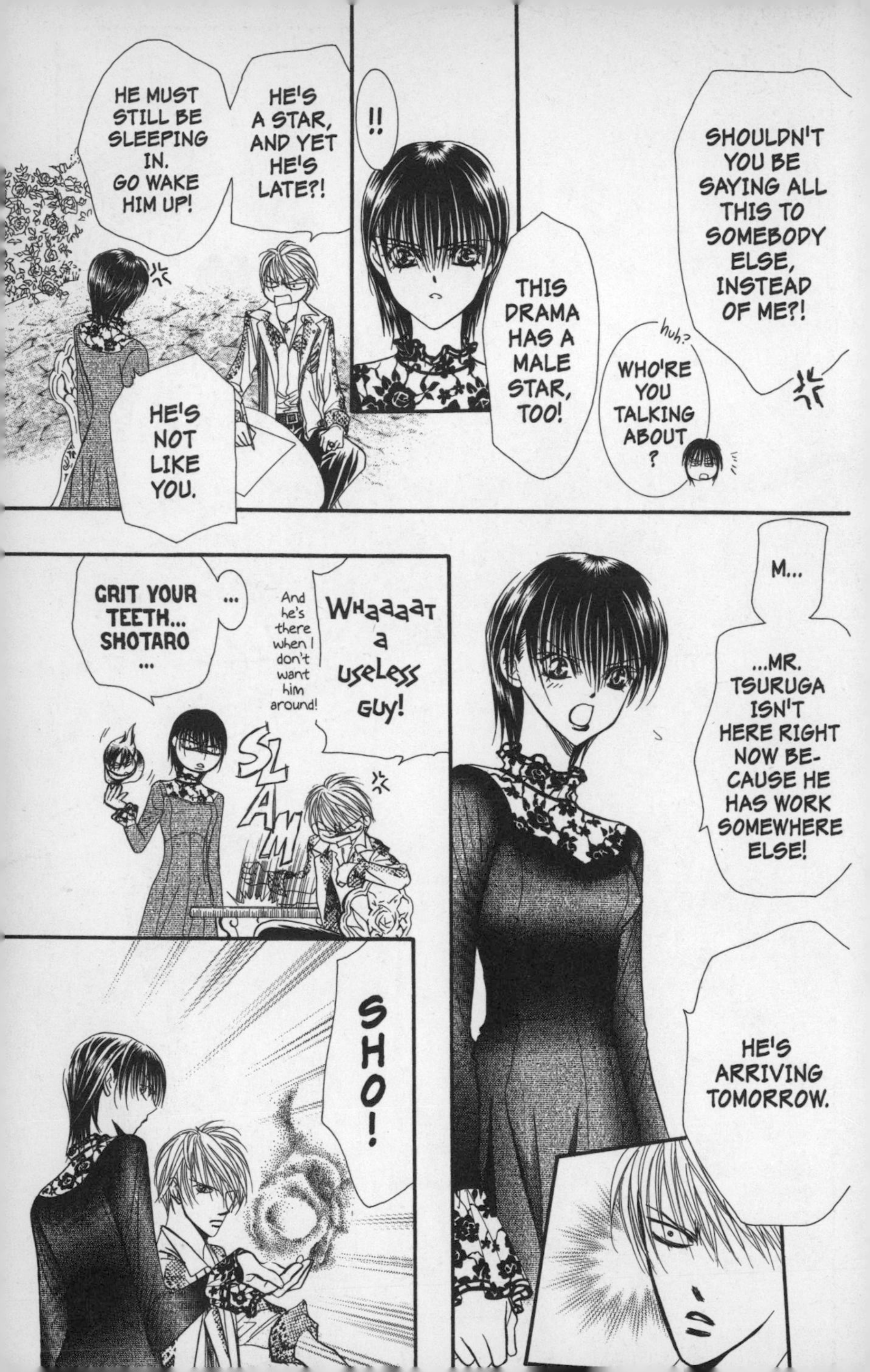
SHOULDN'T YOU BE SAYING ALL THIS TO SOMEBODY ELSE, INSTEAD OF ME?!
huh?
WHO'RE YOU TALKING ABOUT ?
!!
THIS DRAMA HAS A MALE STAR, TOO!
HE'S A STAR, AND YET HE'S LATE?!
HE MUST STILL BE SLEEPING IN. GO WAKE HIM UP!
HE'S NOT LIKE YOU.
M...
...MR. TSURUGA ISN'T HERE RIGHT NOW BE-CAUSE HE HAS WORK SOMEWHERE ELSE!
HE'S ARRIVING TOMORROW.
WHAAAAT a USELESS GUY!
And he's there when I don't want him around!
...
GRIT YOUR TEETH... SHOTARO ...
SLAM
SHO!

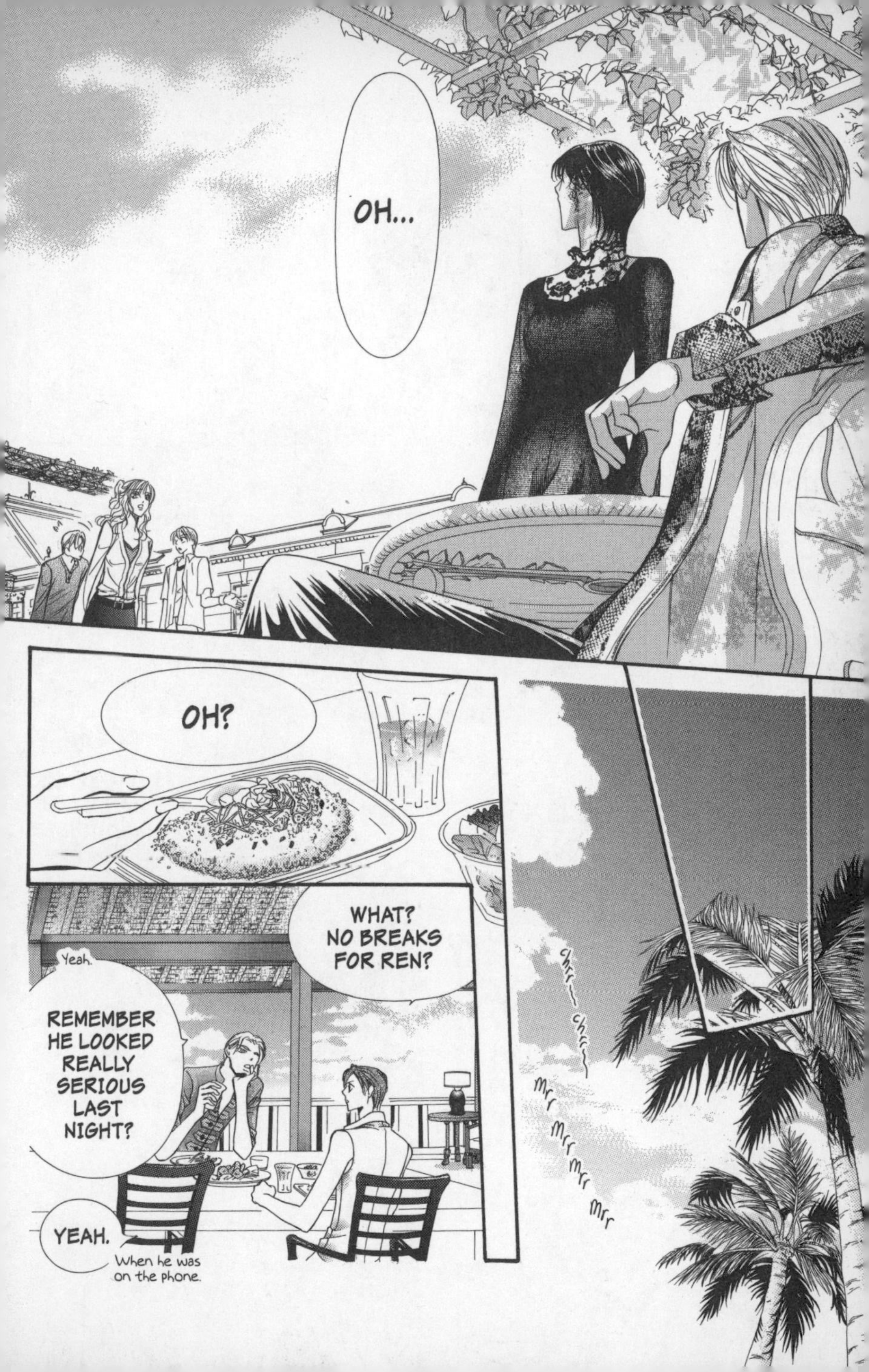
OH...
chrr chrr
mrr mrr mrr mrr mrr
OH?
WHAT? NO BREAKS FOR REN?
Yeah.
REMEMBER HE LOOKED REALLY SERIOUS LAST NIGHT?
YEAH.
When he was on the phone.

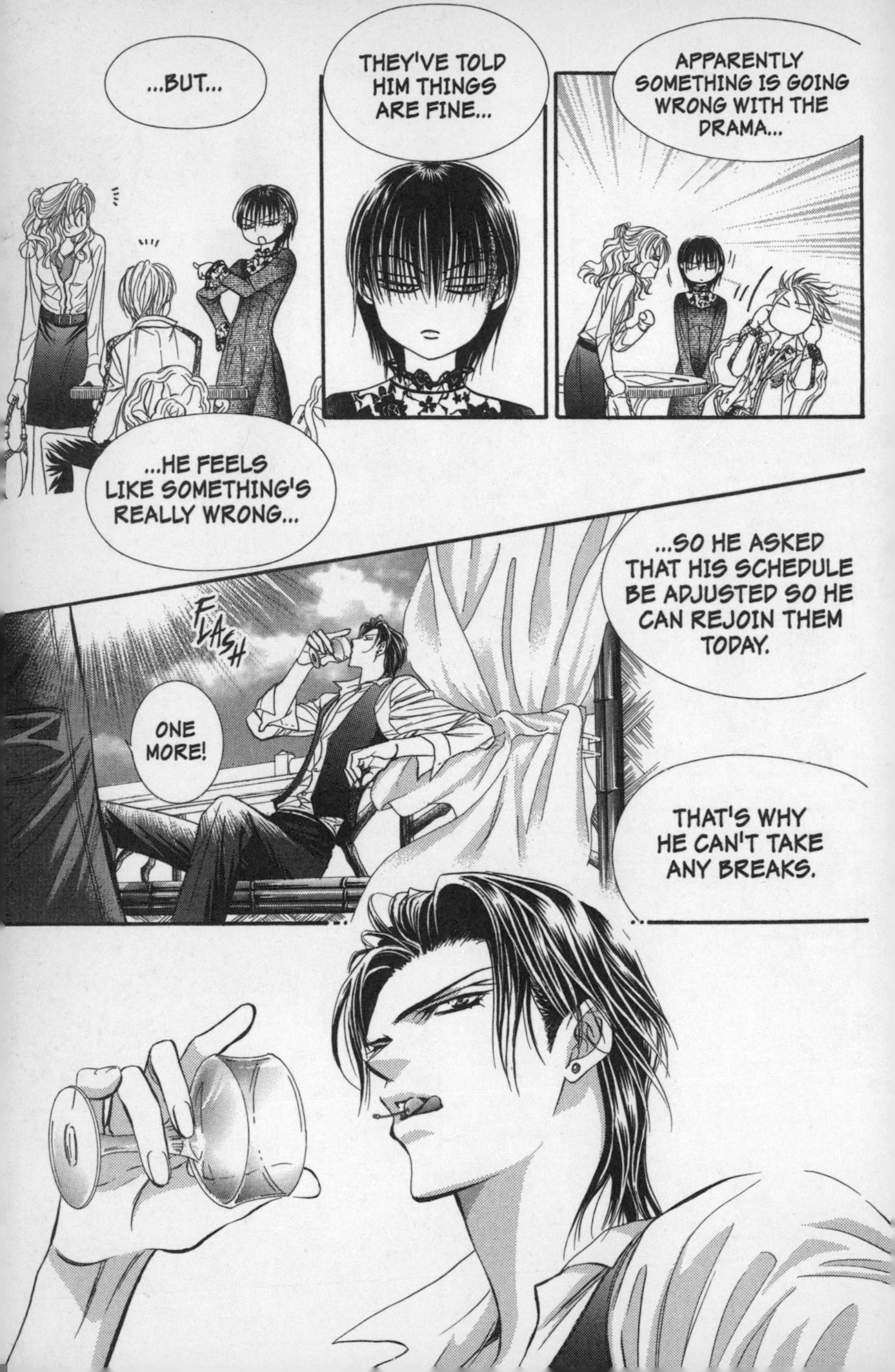
APPARENTLY SOMETHING IS GOING WRONG WITH THE DRAMA...
THEY'VE TOLD HIM THINGS ARE FINE...
...BUT...
...HE FEELS LIKE SOMETHING'S REALLY WRONG...
...SO HE ASKED THAT HIS SCHEDULE BE ADJUSTED SO HE CAN REJOIN THEM TODAY.
FLASH
ONE MORE!
THAT'S WHY HE CAN'T TAKE ANY BREAKS.

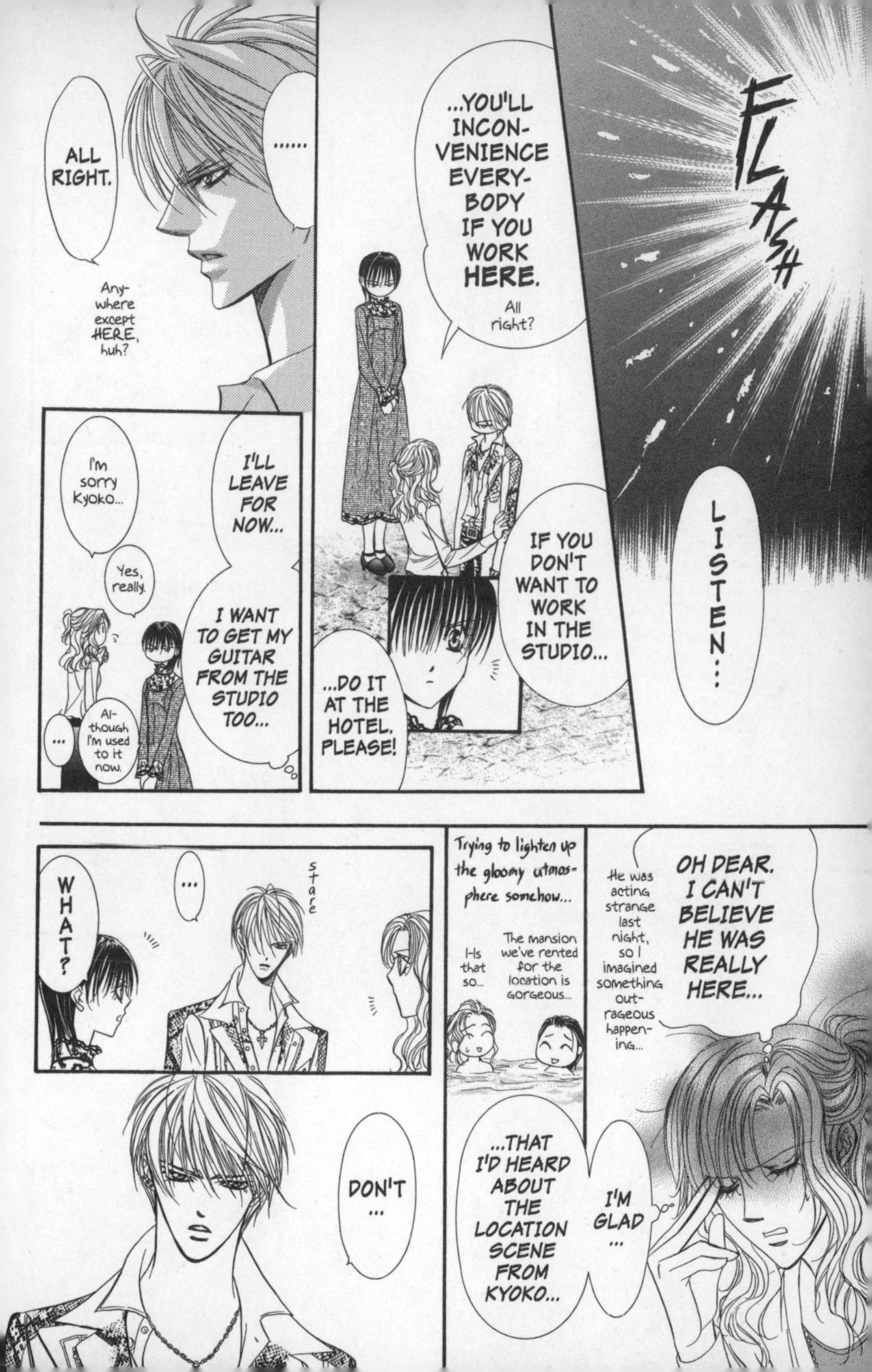
FLASH
LISTEN...
...YOU'LL INCONVENIENCE EVERYBODY IF YOU WORK HERE.
All right?
IF YOU DON'T WANT TO WORK IN THE STUDIO...
...DO IT AT THE HOTEL, PLEASE!
......
ALL RIGHT.
Anywhere except HERE, huh?
I'LL LEAVE FOR NOW...
I WANT TO GET MY GUITAR FROM THE STUDIO TOO...
I'm sorry Kyoko...
Yes, really.
...
Although I'm used to it now.
OH DEAR. I CAN'T BELIEVE HE WAS REALLY HERE...
He was acting strange last night, so I imagined something outrageous happening...
I'M GLAD...
...THAT I'D HEARD ABOUT THE LOCATION SCENE FROM KYOKO...
Trying to lighten up the gloomy atmosphere somehow...
The mansion we've rented for the location is gorgeous...
I-Is that so...
stare
...
WHAT?
DON'T ...

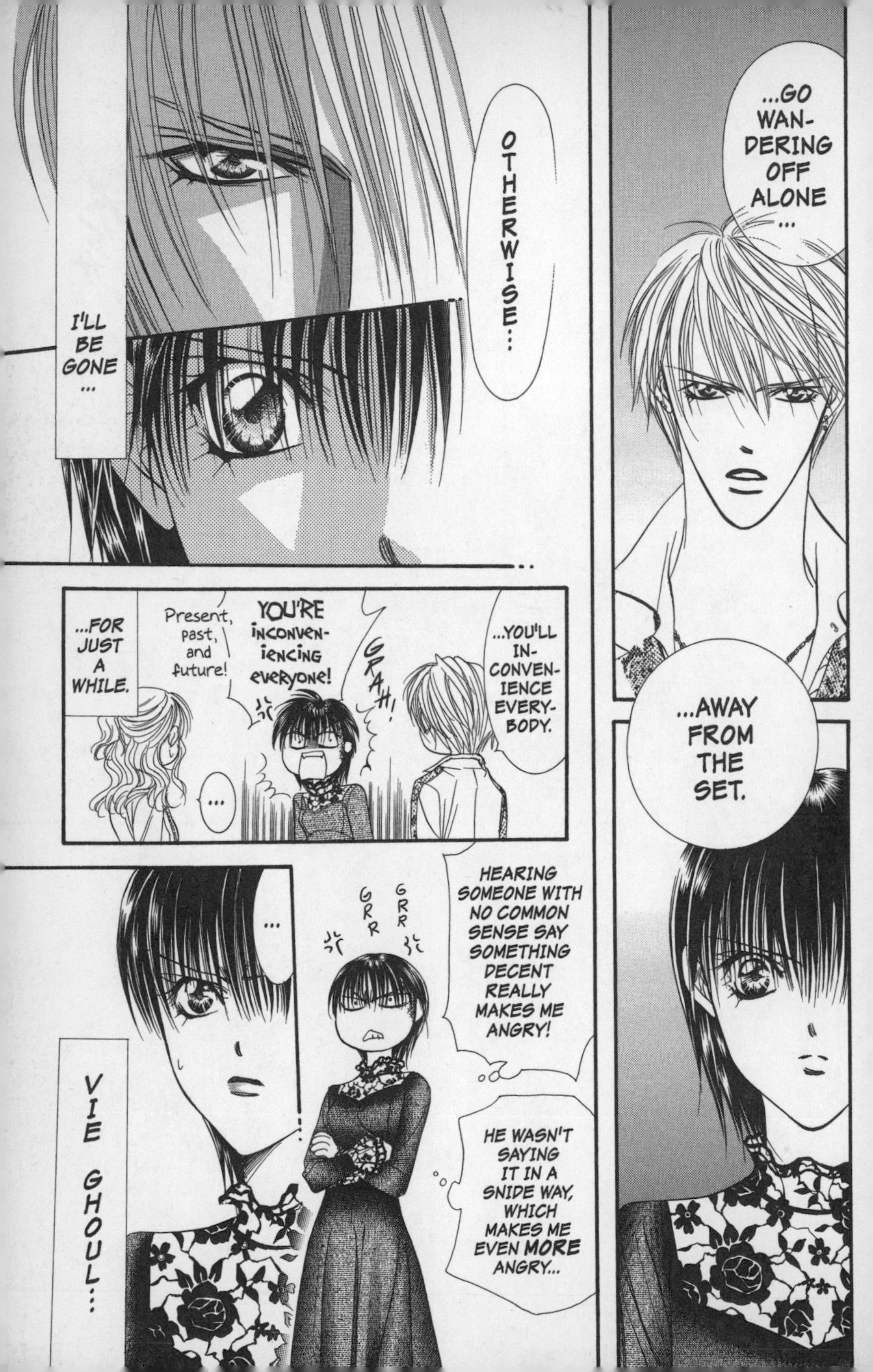
...GO WANDERING OFF ALONE...
...AWAY FROM THE SET.
OTHERWISE...
I'LL BE GONE...
...YOU'LL INCONVENIENCE EVERYBODY.
GRAH!
YOU'RE INCONVENIENCING EVERYONE!
Present, past, and future!
...
...FOR JUST A WHILE.
HEARING SOMEONE WITH NO COMMON SENSE SAY SOMETHING DECENT REALLY MAKES ME ANGRY!
HE WASN'T SAYING IT IN A SNIDE WAY, WHICH MAKES ME EVEN MORE ANGRY...
GRR GRR
...
VIE GHOUL...

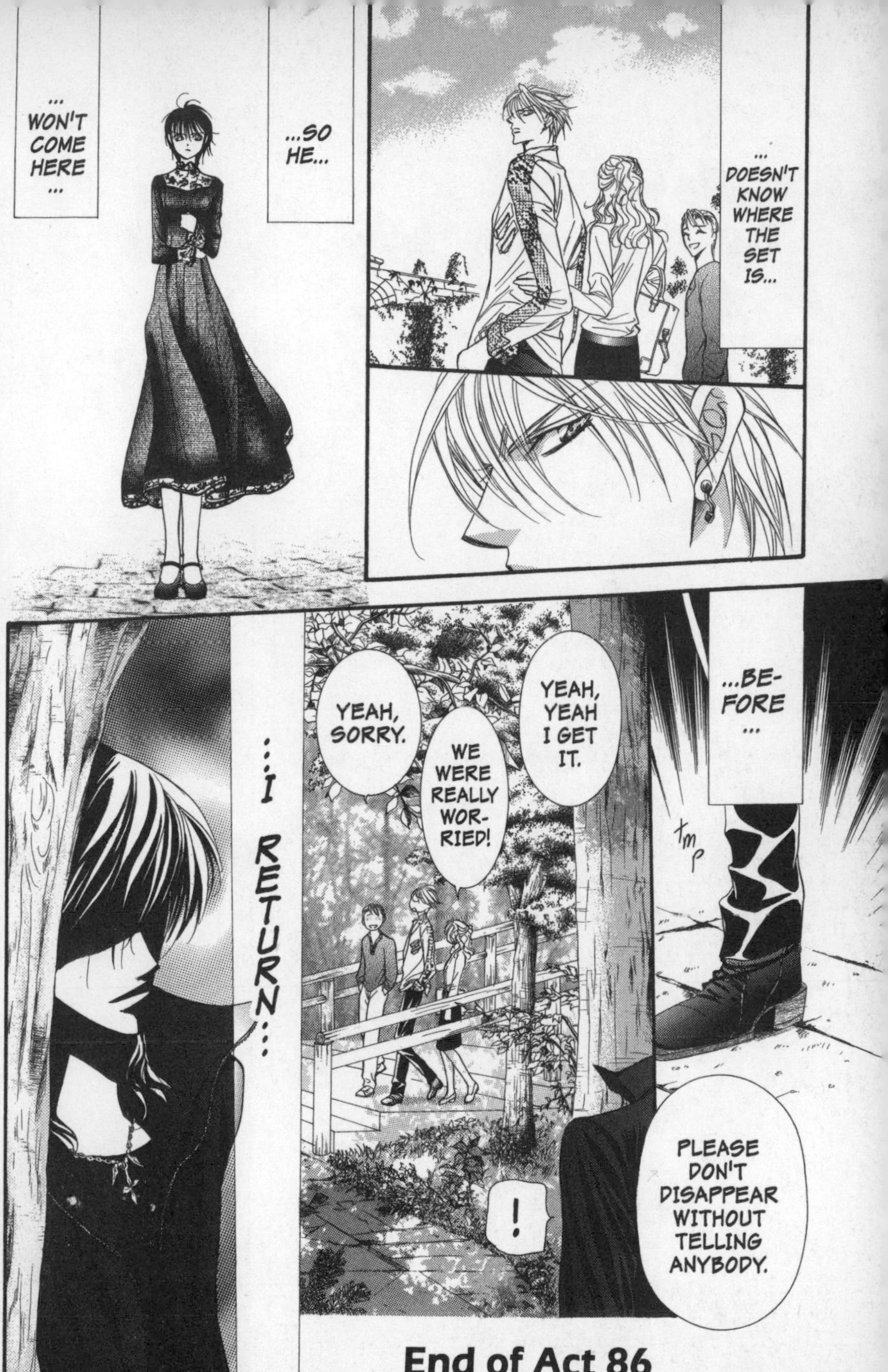

...DOESN'T KNOW WHERE THE SET IS...
...SO HE...
...WON'T COME HERE...
...BE-FORE...
tmp
PLEASE DON'T DISAPPEAR WITHOUT TELLING ANYBODY.
!
YEAH, YEAH I GET IT.
WE WERE REALLY WOR-RIED!
YEAH, SORRY.
...I RETURN...

End of Act 86

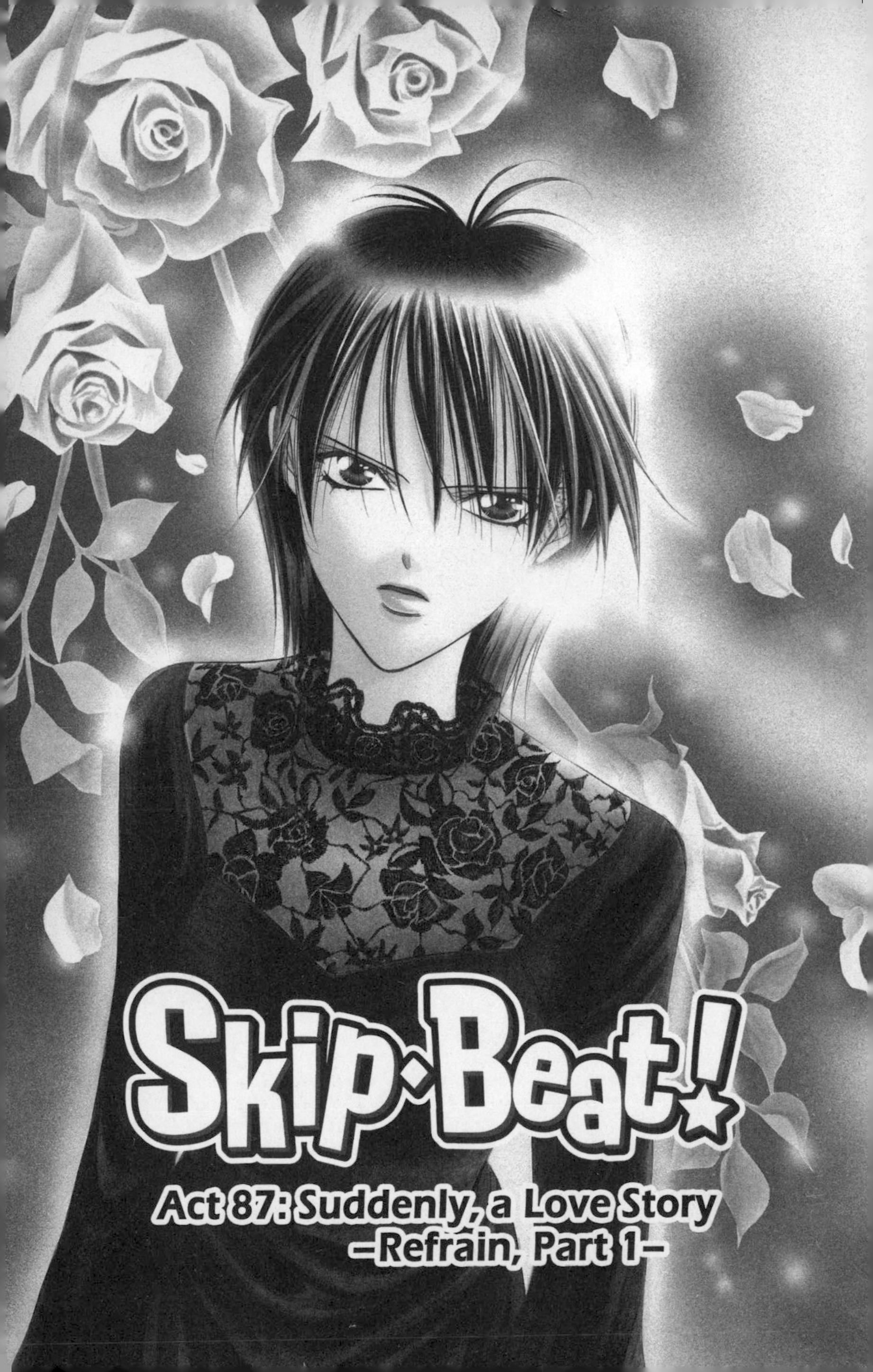
Skip·Beat!
Act 87: Suddenly, a Love Story
-Refrain, Part 1-

For all the Ren fans...an extra...♡

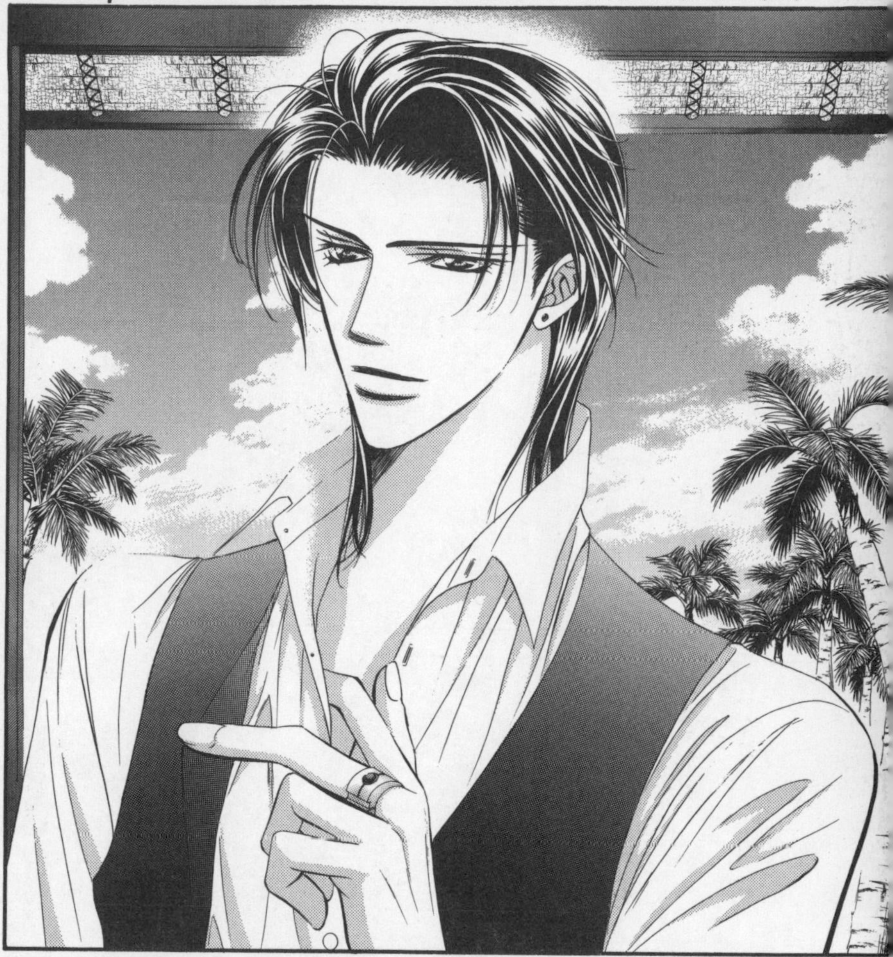

Thank you for reading this volume of *Skip•Beat* this time around, too. I'm saying hello here because...I couldn't fill the sidebars...(*tears*) And the reason is that I was drawing the cover and back flap illustrations, which the Ren x Kyoko readers don't care at all about...(*sweat*) Ugh... 💧💧 'Cuz...I wanted to draw it...!! 💧💧 In color...! Vampire Hunter Sho...!! And Reino's official portrait...!...When *Hana to Yume* magazine held a character contest for *Skip•Beat*, I drew a pic of Reino, but back then, I hadn't decided what color Reino's hair was. I hesitated, hesitated, hesitated, and in the end, didn't like what I drew...(*wry smile*)...so...I wanted to officially publicize it after I decided to go with my initial image...well well...for people who are fans of Ren or Sho, they probably don't care about this guy at all...

I just went with what I wanted to draw for this volume cover.

To all the Ren fans...I'm sorry (humble apology).

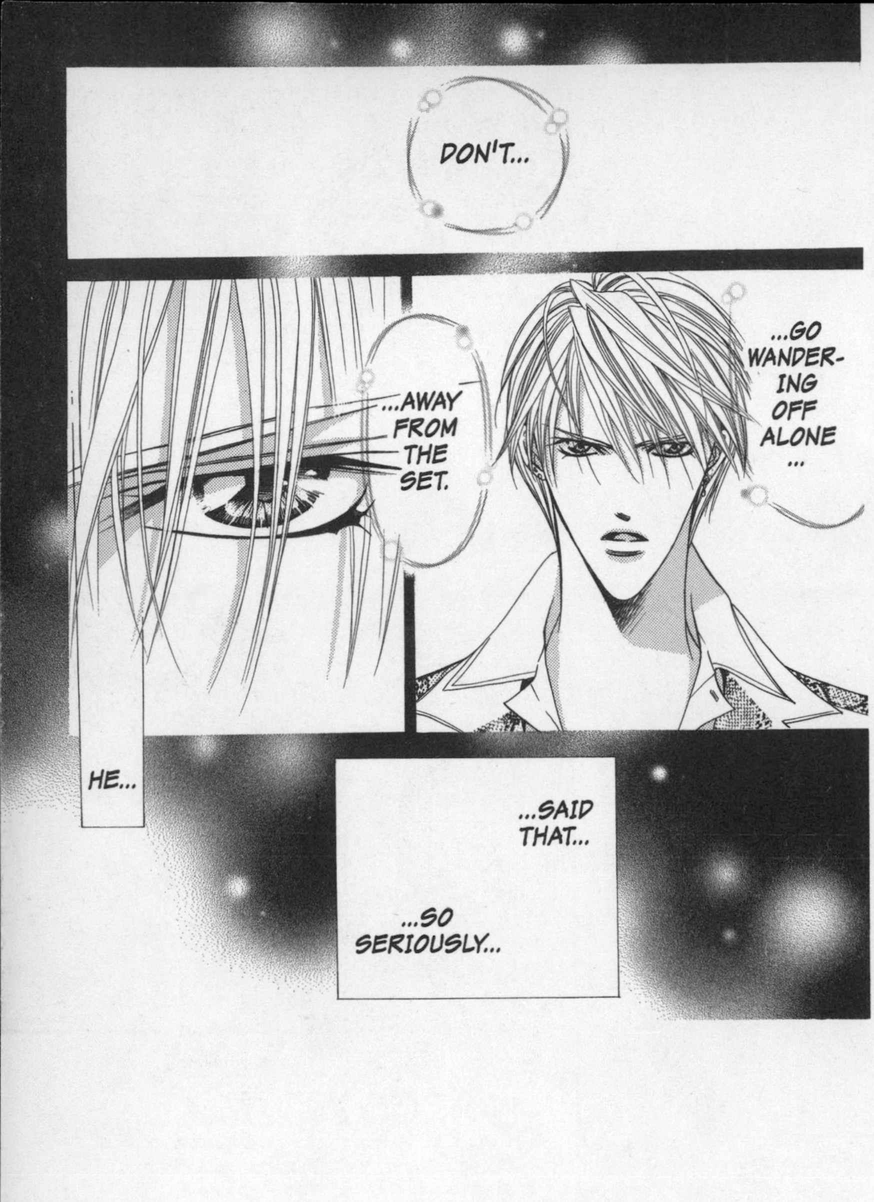
DON'T...
...GO WANDERING OFF ALONE ...
...AWAY FROM THE SET.
HE...
...SAID THAT...
...SO SERIOUSLY...

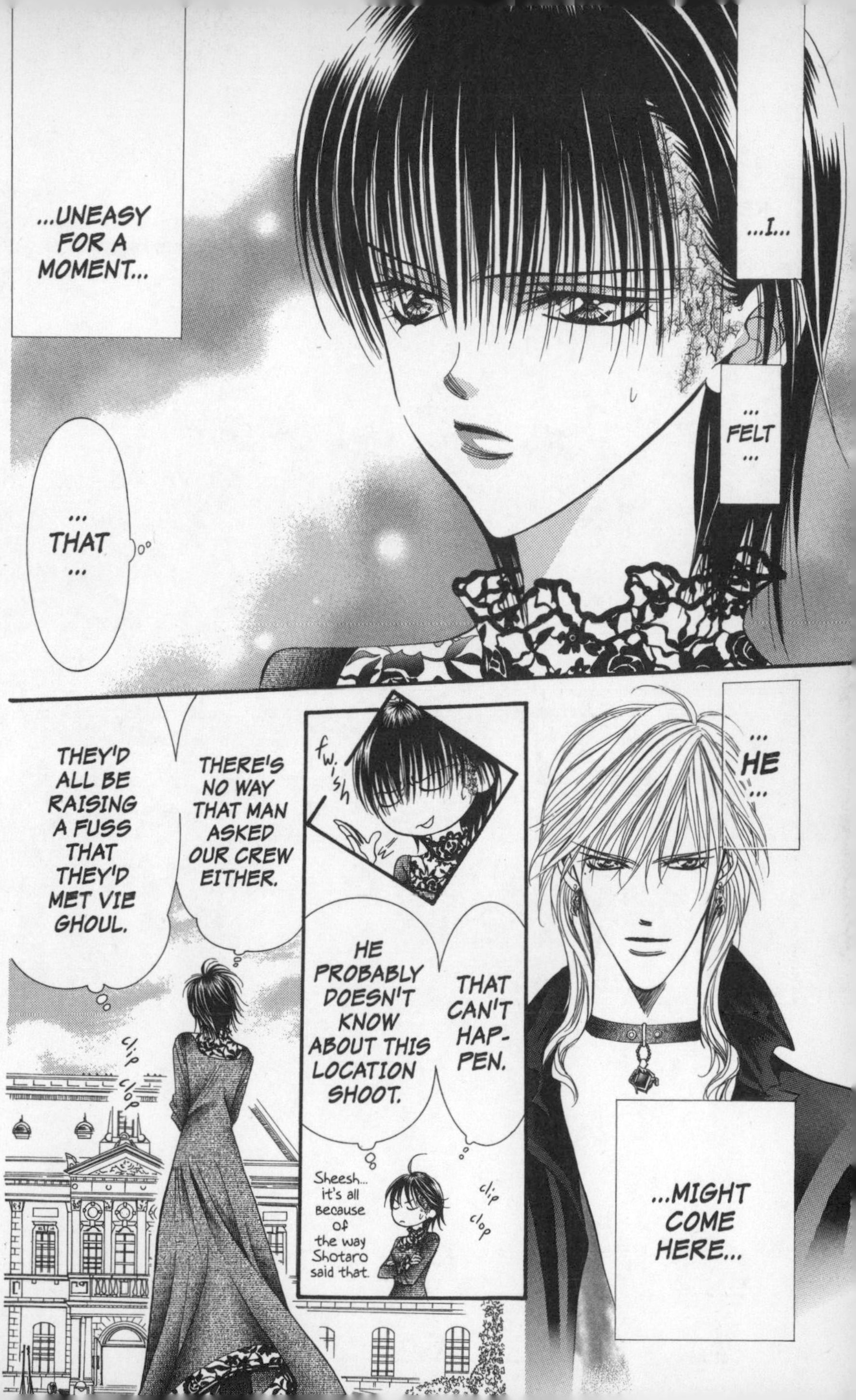
...I...
...FELT...
...UNEASY FOR A MOMENT...
...THAT...
...HE...
...MIGHT COME HERE...
fwish
THAT CAN'T HAP-PEN.
HE PROBABLY DOESN'T KNOW ABOUT THIS LOCATION SHOOT.
clip clop
Sheesh... it's all because of the way Shotaro said that.
THERE'S NO WAY THAT MAN ASKED OUR CREW EITHER.
THEY'D ALL BE RAISING A FUSS THAT THEY'D MET VIE GHOUL.
clip clop

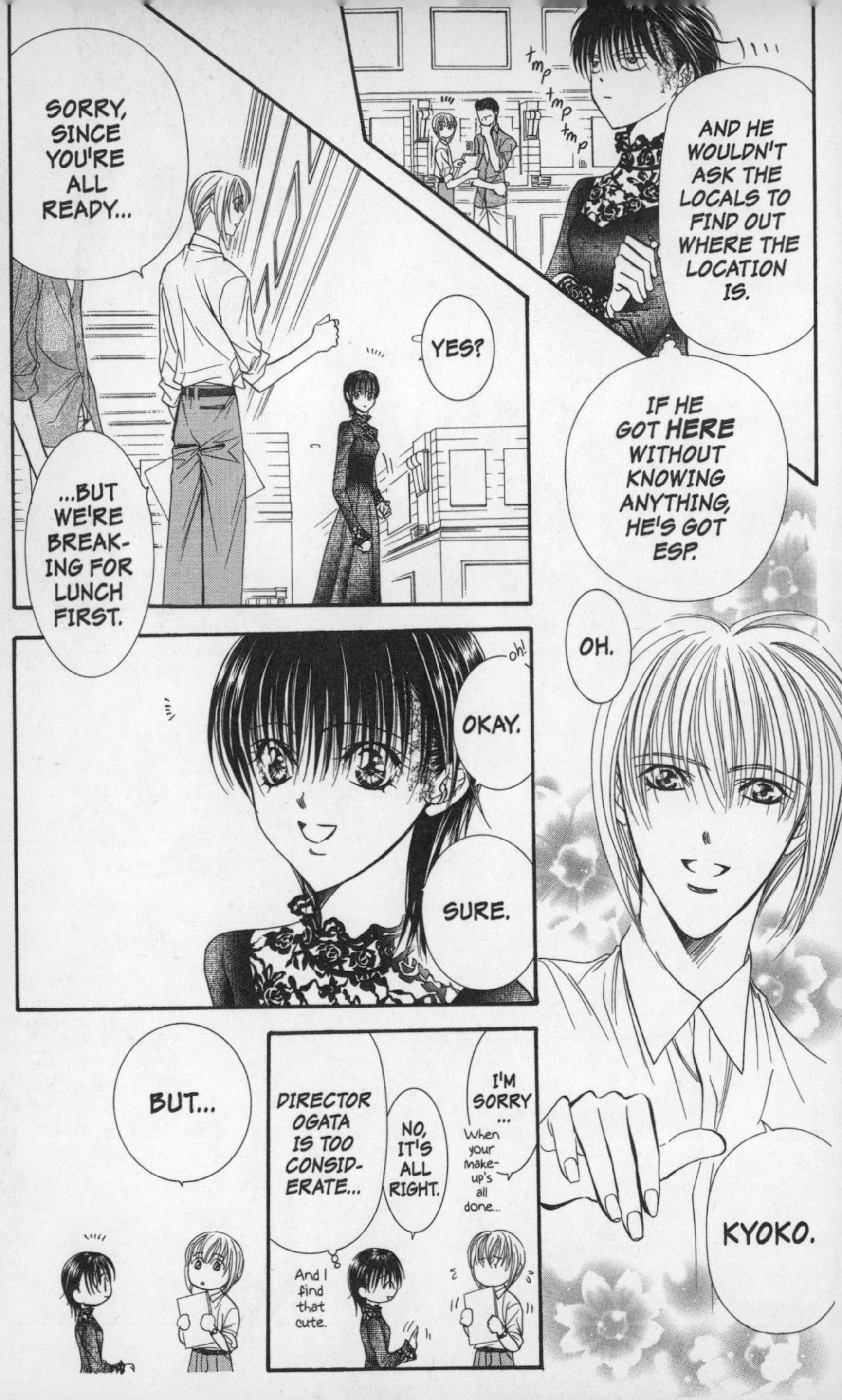
tmp tmp tmp
AND HE WOULDN'T ASK THE LOCALS TO FIND OUT WHERE THE LOCATION IS.
IF HE GOT HERE WITHOUT KNOWING ANYTHING, HE'S GOT ESP.
SORRY, SINCE YOU'RE ALL READY...
YES?
...BUT WE'RE BREAKING FOR LUNCH FIRST.
OH.
KYOKO.
oh!
OKAY.
SURE.
I'M SORRY ...
When your make-up's all done...
NO, IT'S ALL RIGHT.
DIRECTOR OGATA IS TOO CONSIDERATE...
And I find that cute.
BUT...

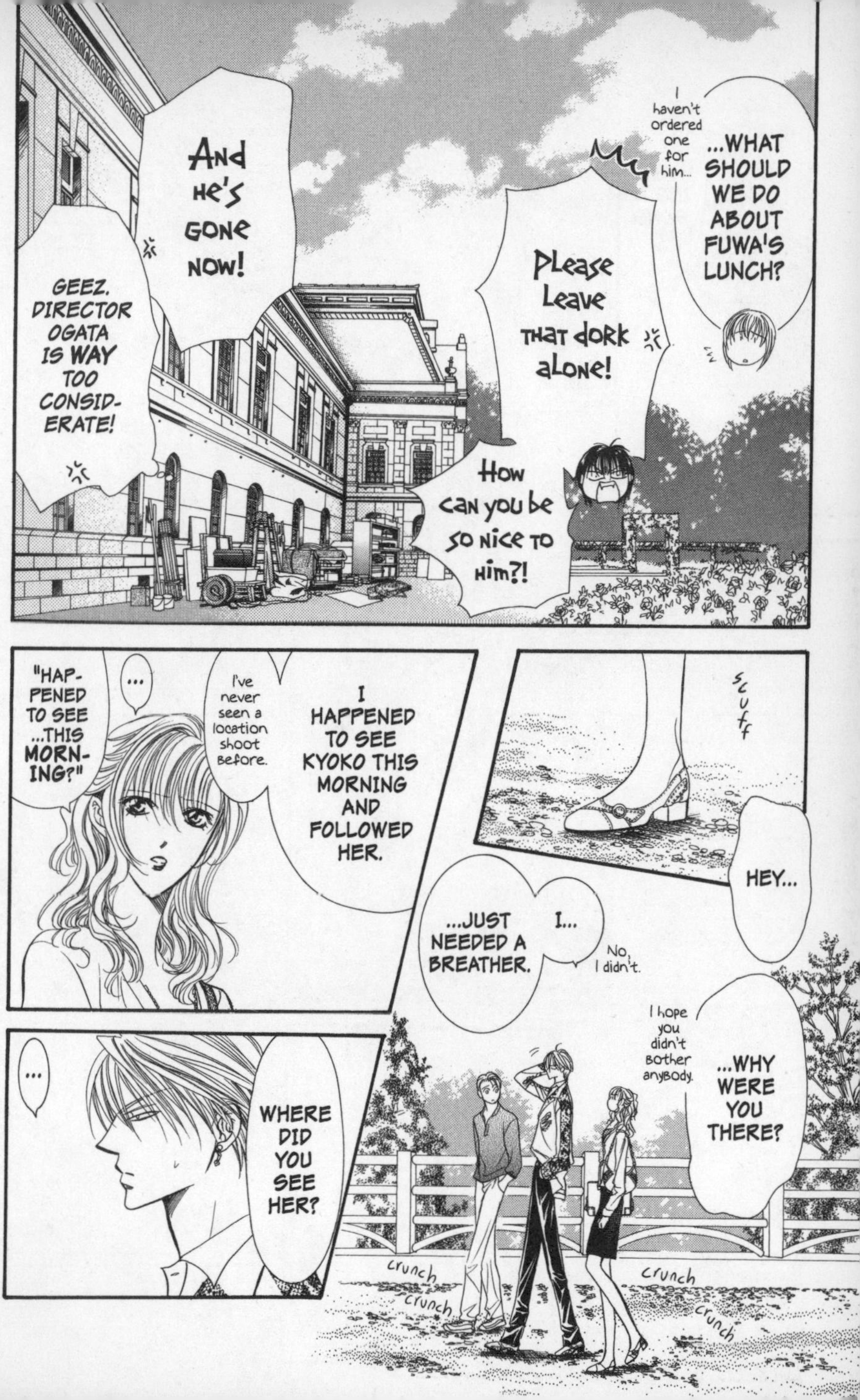
I haven't ordered one for him...
...WHAT SHOULD WE DO ABOUT FUWA'S LUNCH?
Please Leave that dork alone!
How can you be so nice to him?!
And he's gone now!
GEEZ. DIRECTOR OGATA IS WAY TOO CONSID-ERATE!
scuff
HEY...
I...
No, I didn't.
...JUST NEEDED A BREATHER.
I HAPPENED TO SEE KYOKO THIS MORNING AND FOLLOWED HER.
I've never seen a location shoot before.
...
"HAP-PENED TO SEE ...THIS MORN-ING?"
...WHY WERE YOU THERE?
I hope you didn't bother anybody.
crunch
crunch
crunch
crunch
WHERE DID YOU SEE HER?
...

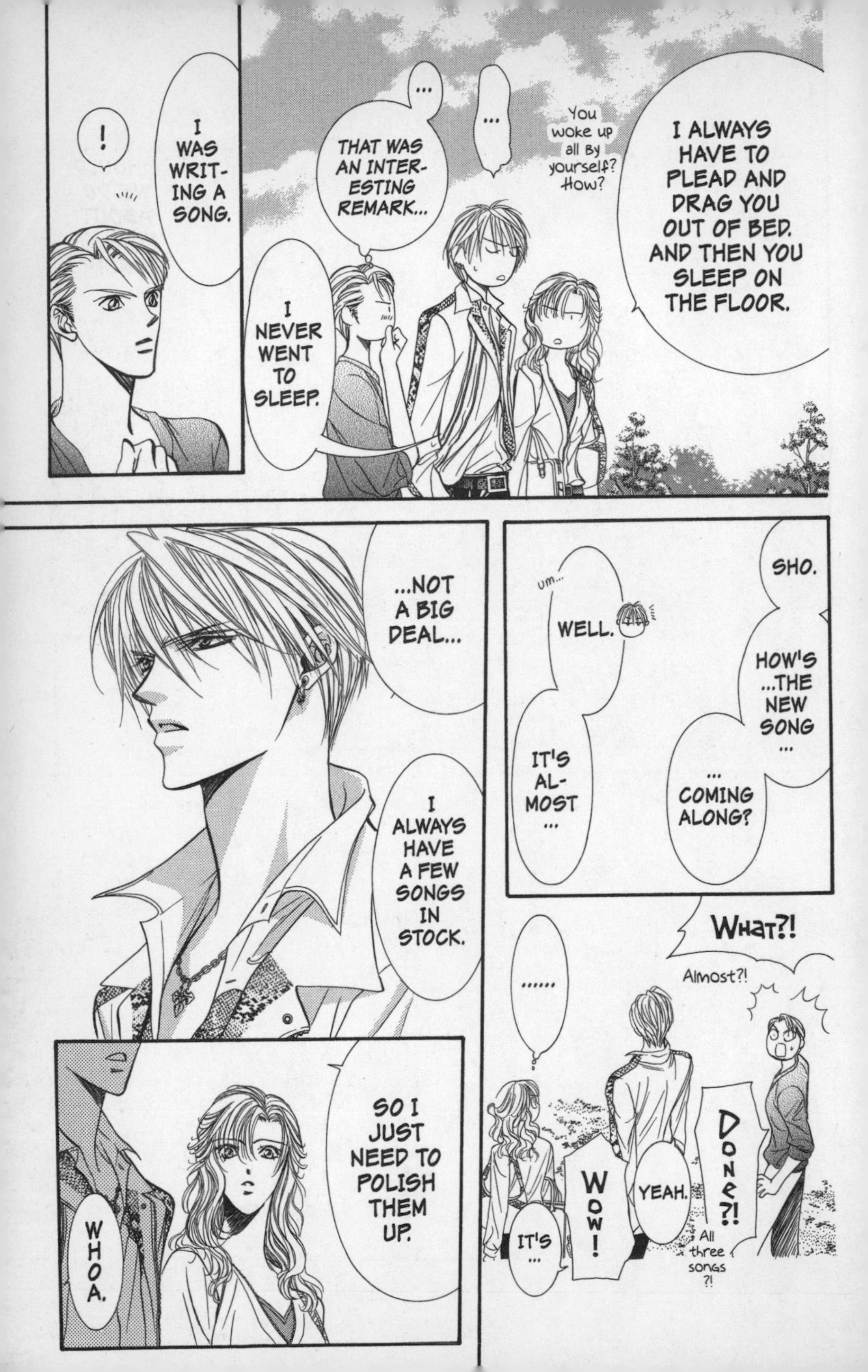
I ALWAYS HAVE TO PLEAD AND DRAG YOU OUT OF BED. AND THEN YOU SLEEP ON THE FLOOR.
You woke up all by yourself? How?
...
...
THAT WAS AN INTERESTING REMARK...
I NEVER WENT TO SLEEP.
I WAS WRITING A SONG.
!
SHO.
HOW'S ...THE NEW SONG ...
... COMING ALONG?
um...
WELL.
IT'S ALMOST ...
WHAT?!
Almost?!
......
DONE?!
All three songs?!
YEAH.
WOW!
IT'S ...
...NOT A BIG DEAL...
I ALWAYS HAVE A FEW SONGS IN STOCK.
SO I JUST NEED TO POLISH THEM UP.
WHOA.

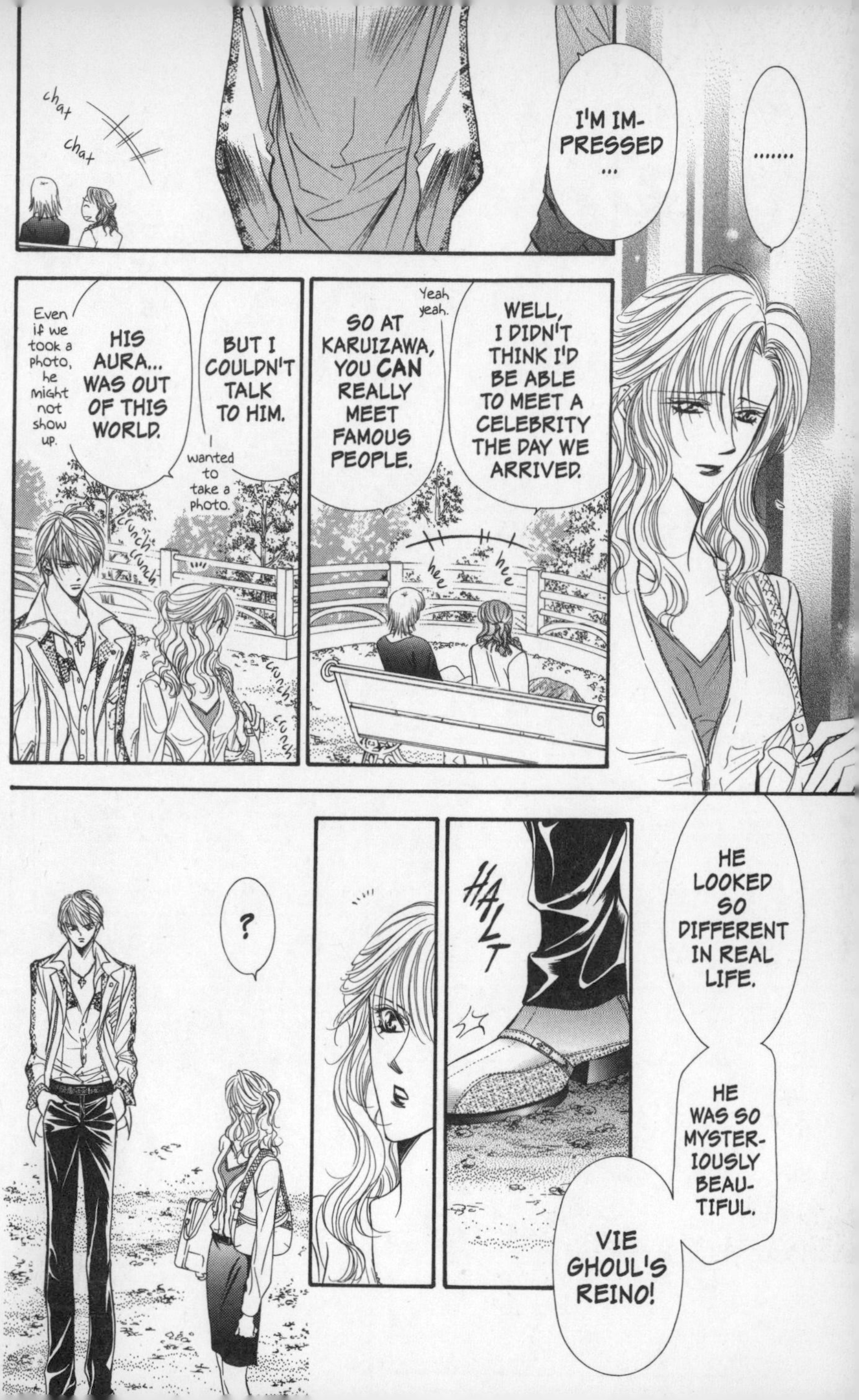
....
I'M IM-PRESSED ...
chat chat
WELL, I DIDN'T THINK I'D BE ABLE TO MEET A CELEBRITY THE DAY WE ARRIVED.
Yeah yeah.
hee hee
SO AT KARUIZAWA, YOU CAN REALLY MEET FAMOUS PEOPLE.
BUT I COULDN'T TALK TO HIM.
I wanted to take a photo.
HIS AURA... WAS OUT OF THIS WORLD.
Even if we took a photo, he might not show up.
crunch crunch
crunch crunch
HE LOOKED SO DIFFERENT IN REAL LIFE.
HE WAS SO MYSTERIOUSLY BEAUTIFUL.
VIE GHOUL'S REINO!
HALT
?

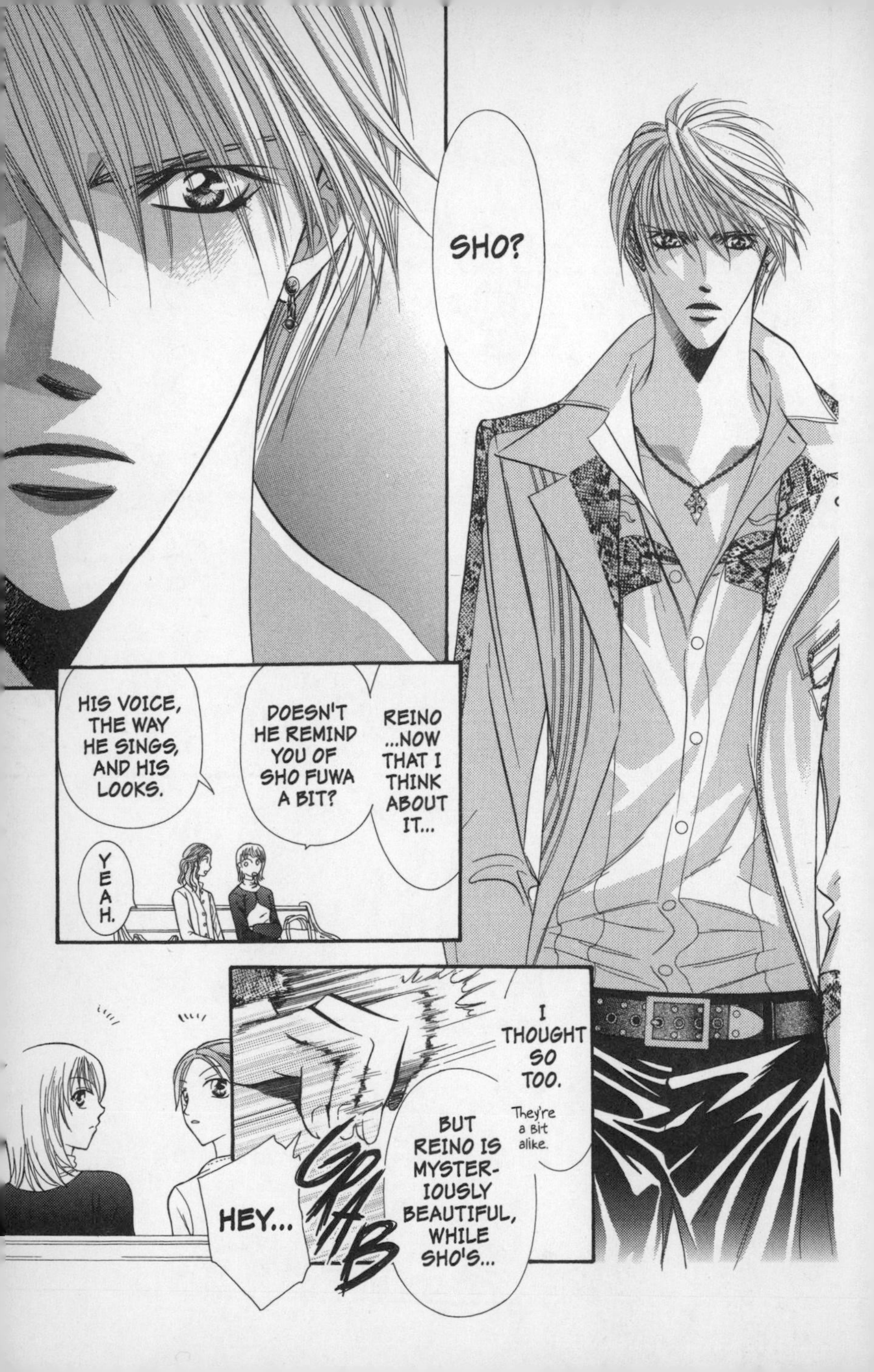
SHO?
REINO ...NOW THAT I THINK ABOUT IT...
DOESN'T HE REMIND YOU OF SHO FUWA A BIT?
HIS VOICE, THE WAY HE SINGS, AND HIS LOOKS.
YEAH.
I THOUGHT SO TOO.
They're a bit alike.
BUT REINO IS MYSTERIOUSLY BEAUTIFUL, WHILE SHO'S...
GRAB
HEY...

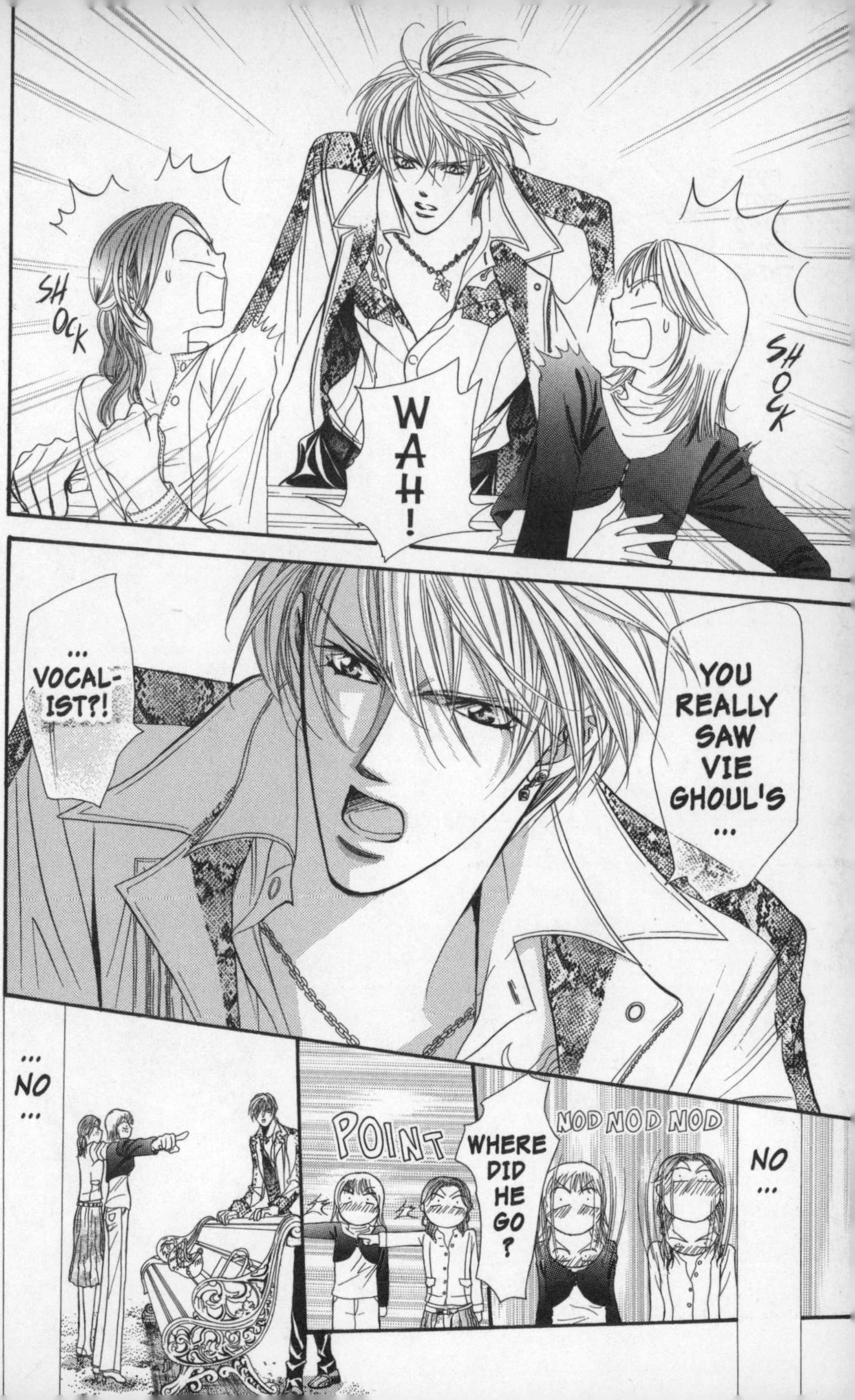
SHOCK
SHOCK
WAH!
YOU REALLY SAW VIE GHOUL'S ...
... VOCAL-IST?!
NO ...
NOD NOD NOD
WHERE DID HE GO?
POINT
... NO ...

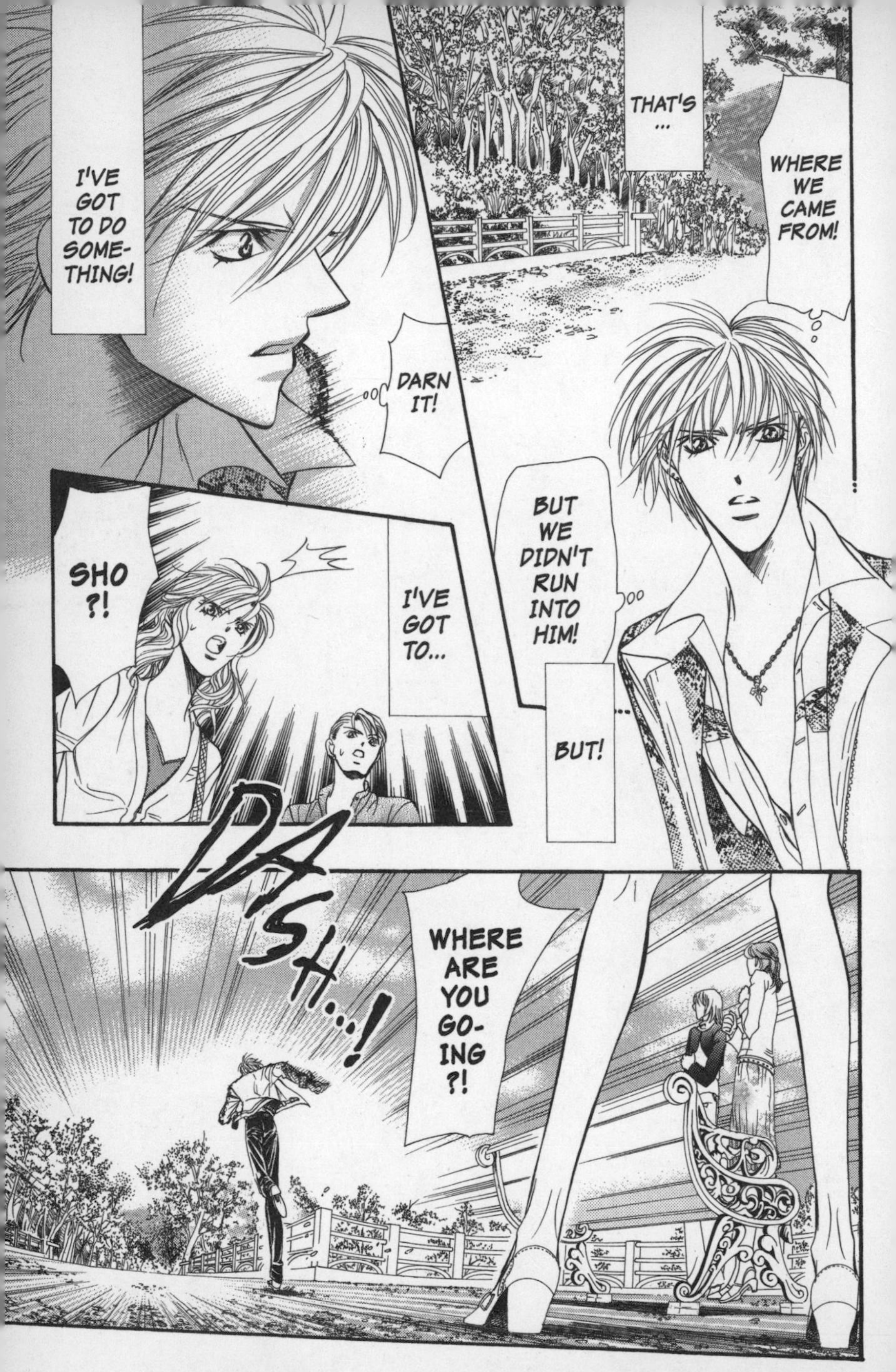
THAT'S ...
WHERE WE CAME FROM!
BUT WE DIDN'T RUN INTO HIM!
BUT!
DARN IT!
I'VE GOT TO DO SOME-THING!
I'VE GOT TO...
SHO ?!
WHERE ARE YOU GO-ING ?!
DASH...!

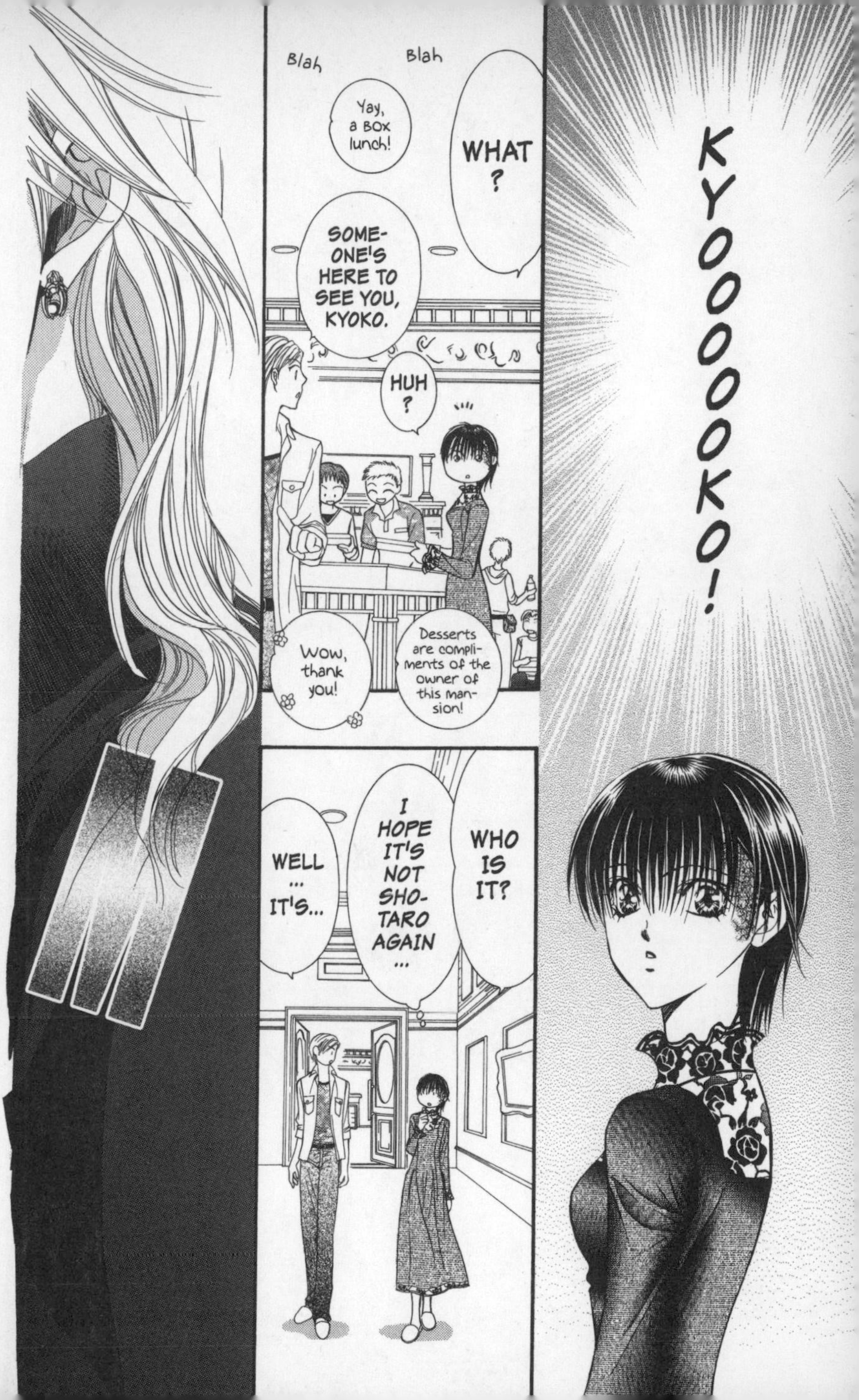
KYOOOOOKO!
WHAT?
Blah
Blah
Yay, a BOX lunch!
SOME-ONE'S HERE TO SEE YOU, KYOKO.
HUH?
Desserts are compli-ments of the owner of this man-sion!
Wow, thank you!
WHO IS IT?
I HOPE IT'S NOT SHO-TARO AGAIN...
WELL... IT'S...

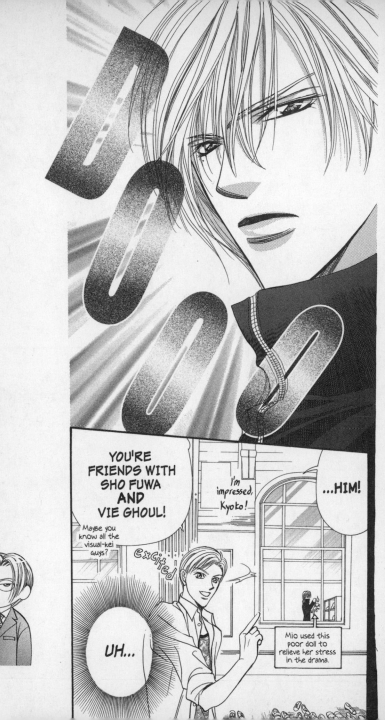

DOOO
...HIM!
I'm impressed, Kyoko!
YOU'RE FRIENDS WITH SHO FUWA AND VIE GHOUL!
Maybe you know all the visual-kei guys?
excited
Mio used this poor doll to relieve her stress in the drama.
UH...

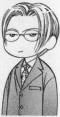

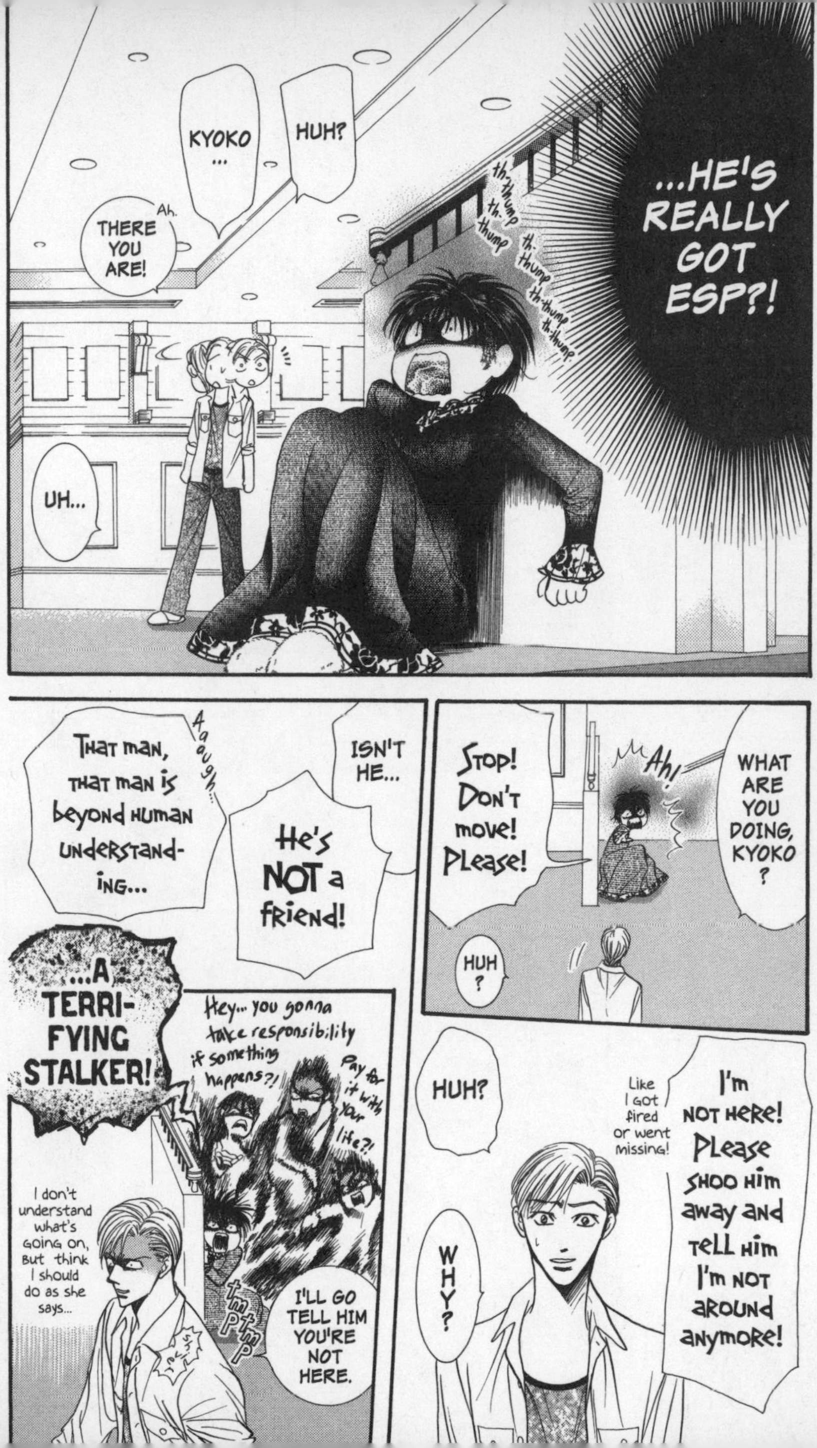
...HE'S REALLY GOT ESP?!
th-thump th-thump th-thump th-thump th-thump
HUH?
KYOKO...
Ah.
THERE YOU ARE!
UH...
Ah!
WHAT ARE YOU DOING, KYOKO?
Stop! Don't move! Please!
HUH?
ISN'T HE...
He's NOT a friend!
That man, that man is beyond human understand-ing...
Aaaugh...
Like I got fired or went missing!
I'm NOT HERE! Please shoo him away and tell him I'm NOT around anymore!
HUH?
WHY?
...A TERRI-FYING STALKER!
Hey... you gonna take responsibility if something happens?!
Pay for it with your life?!
I don't understand what's going on, but think I should do as she says...
I'LL GO TELL HIM YOU'RE NOT HERE.
tmp tmp

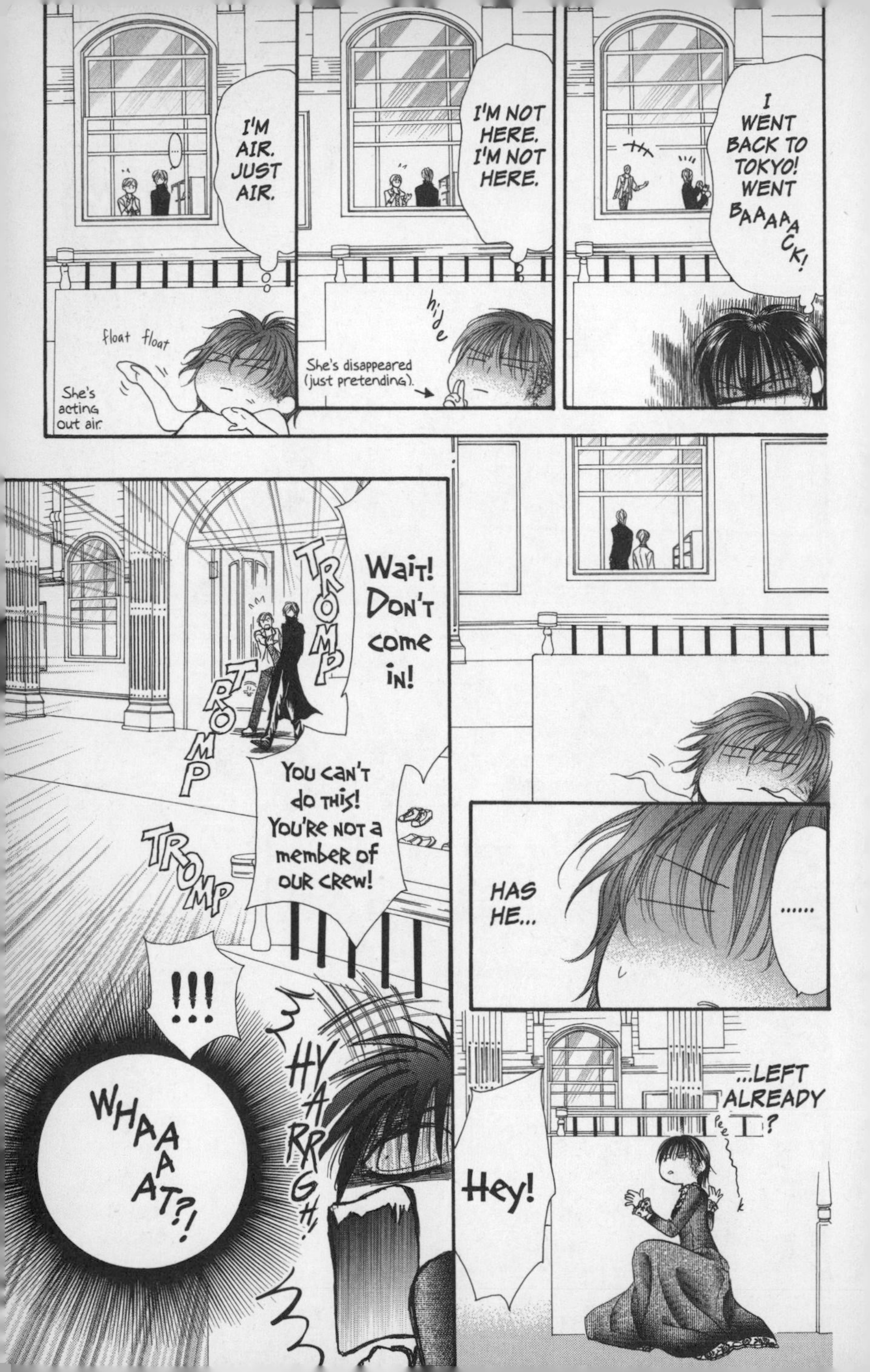
I WENT BACK TO TOKYO! WENT BAAAAACK!
I'M NOT HERE. I'M NOT HERE.
hide
She's disappeared (just pretending).
I'M AIR. JUST AIR.
...
float float
She's acting out air.
HAS HE...
......
...LEFT ALREADY?
Peek
Hey!
Wait! Don't come in!
TROMP
TROMP
You can't do this! You're not a member of our crew!
TROMP
!!!
HYAARRGH!
WHAAAAT?!

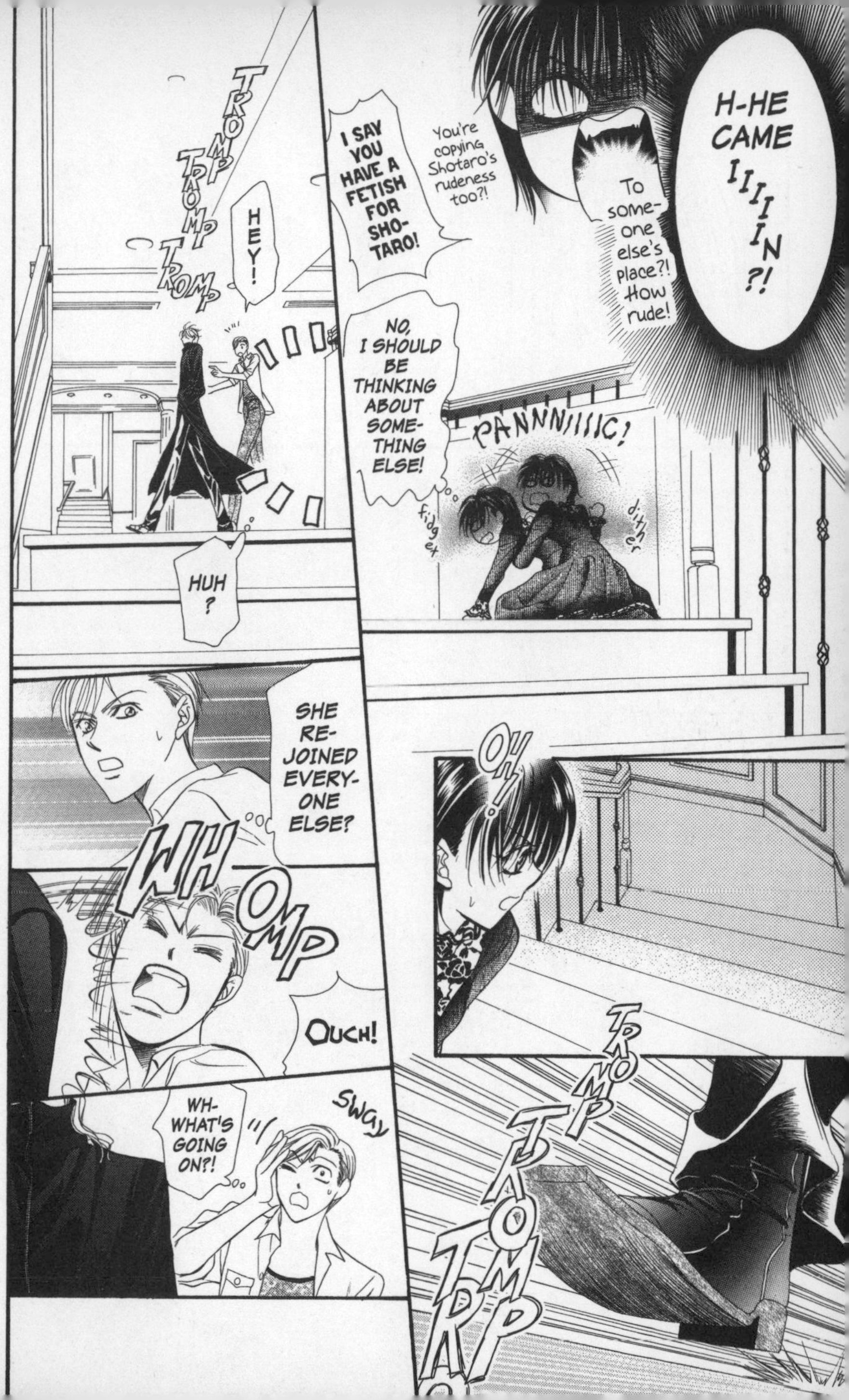
H-HE CAME IIIIIN?!
To someone else's place?! How rude!
You're copying Shotaro's rudeness too?!
I SAY YOU HAVE A FETISH FOR SHOTARO!
NO, I SHOULD BE THINKING ABOUT SOMETHING ELSE!
PANNNIIIIC!
fidget
dither
TROMP TROMP TROMP TROMP
HEY!
HUH?
OH!
TROMP TROMP TROMP
SHE REJOINED EVERYONE ELSE?
WHOMP
OUCH!
SWAY
WH-WHAT'S GOING ON?!

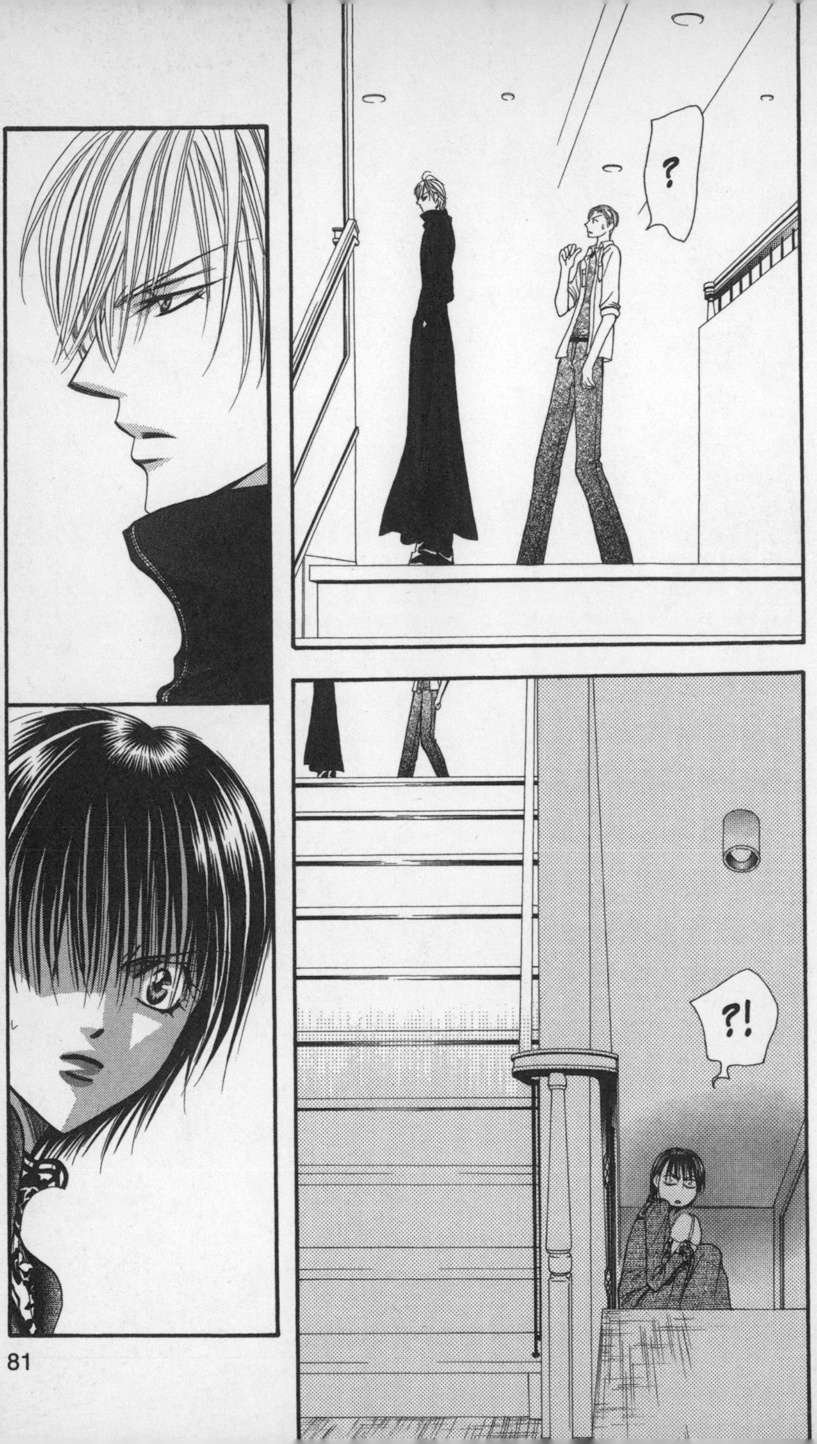
?
?!

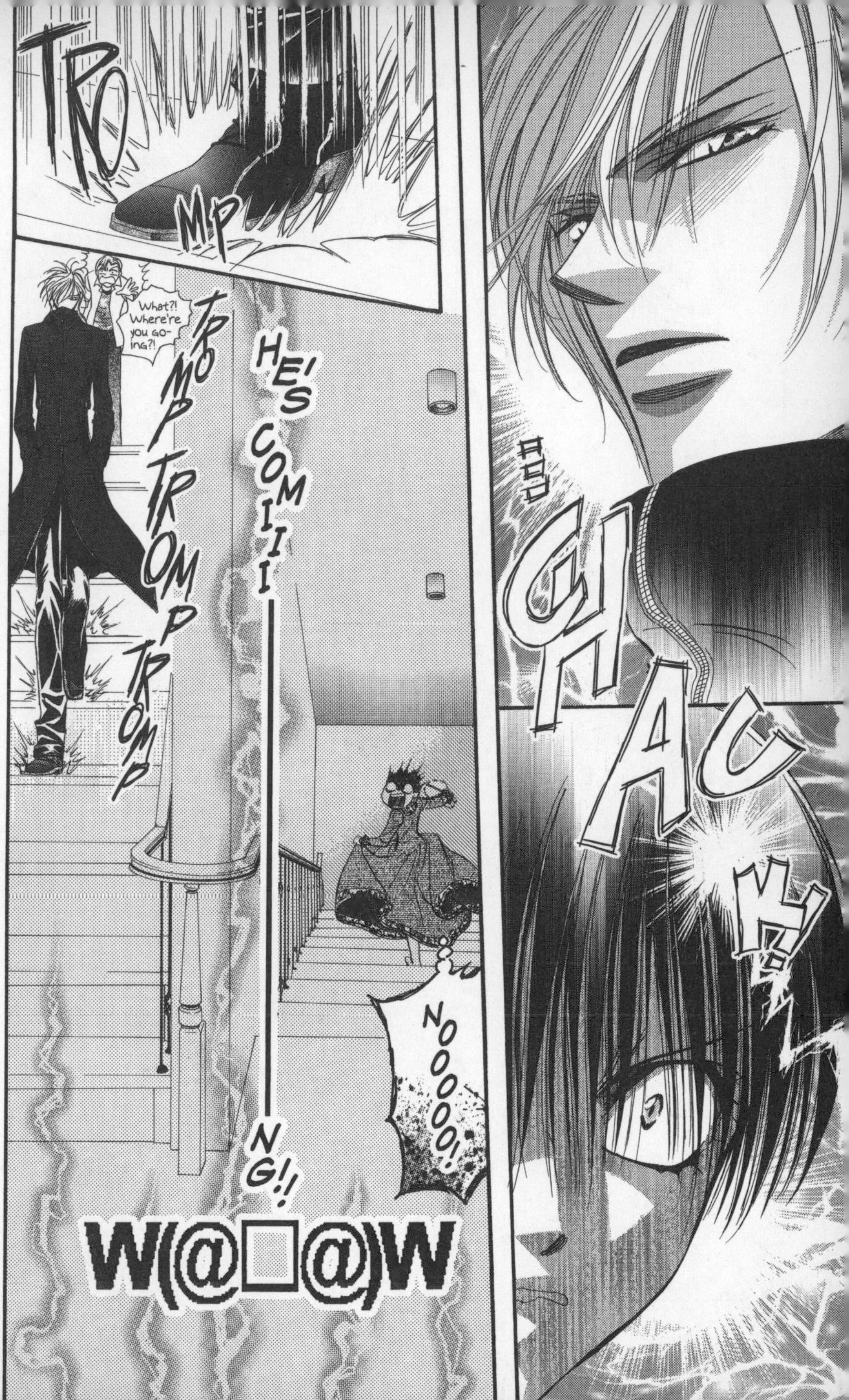
CHACK!
TROMP
What?! Where're you GO-ING?!
TROMP TROMP TROMP TROMP
HE'S COMIIII——NG!!
NOOOOOOO!
W(@□@)W

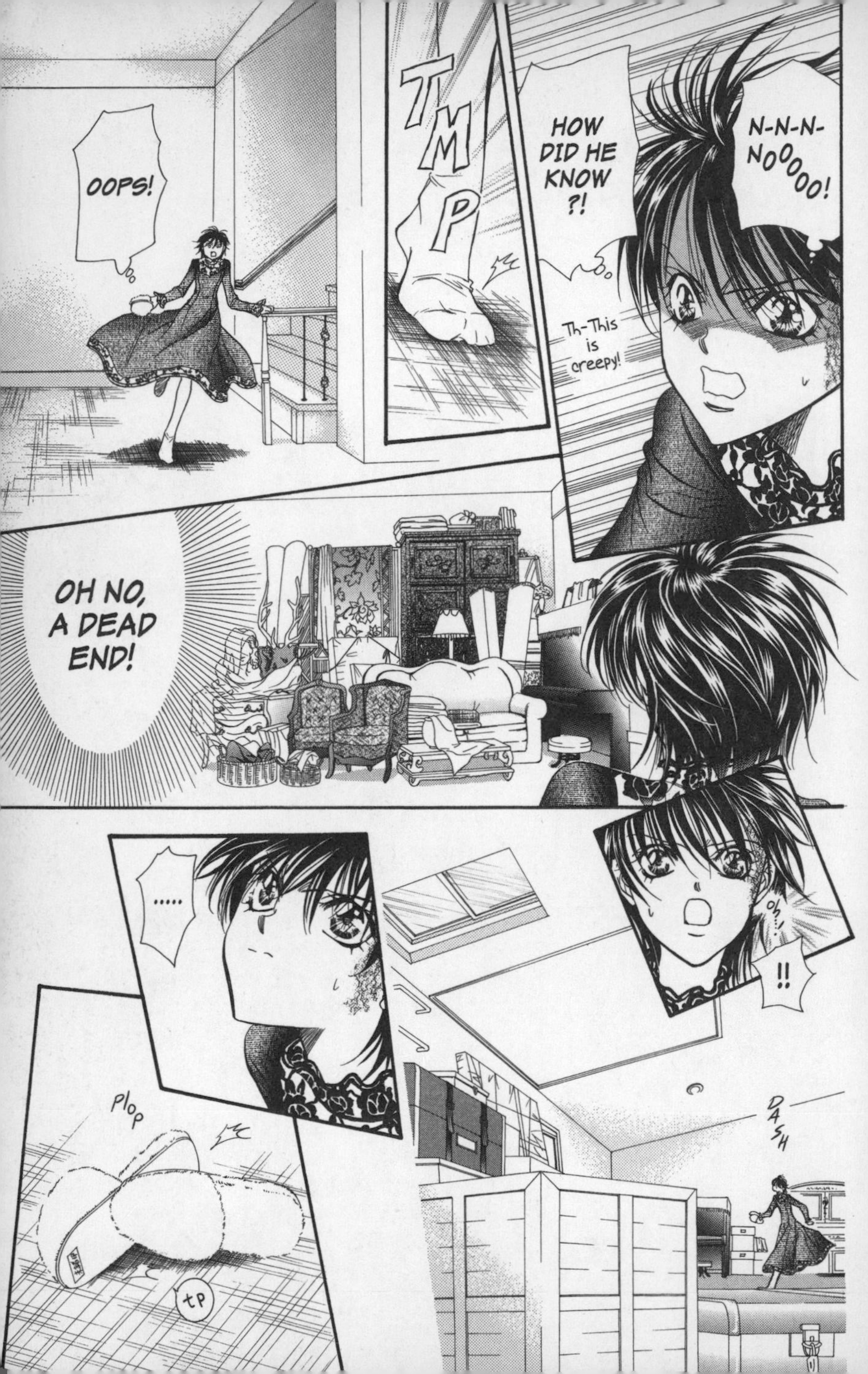
N-N-N-NOOOOOO!
HOW DID HE KNOW ?!
Th-This is creepy!
TMP
OOPS!
OH NO, A DEAD END!
oh...!
!!
.....
DASH
Plop
tp

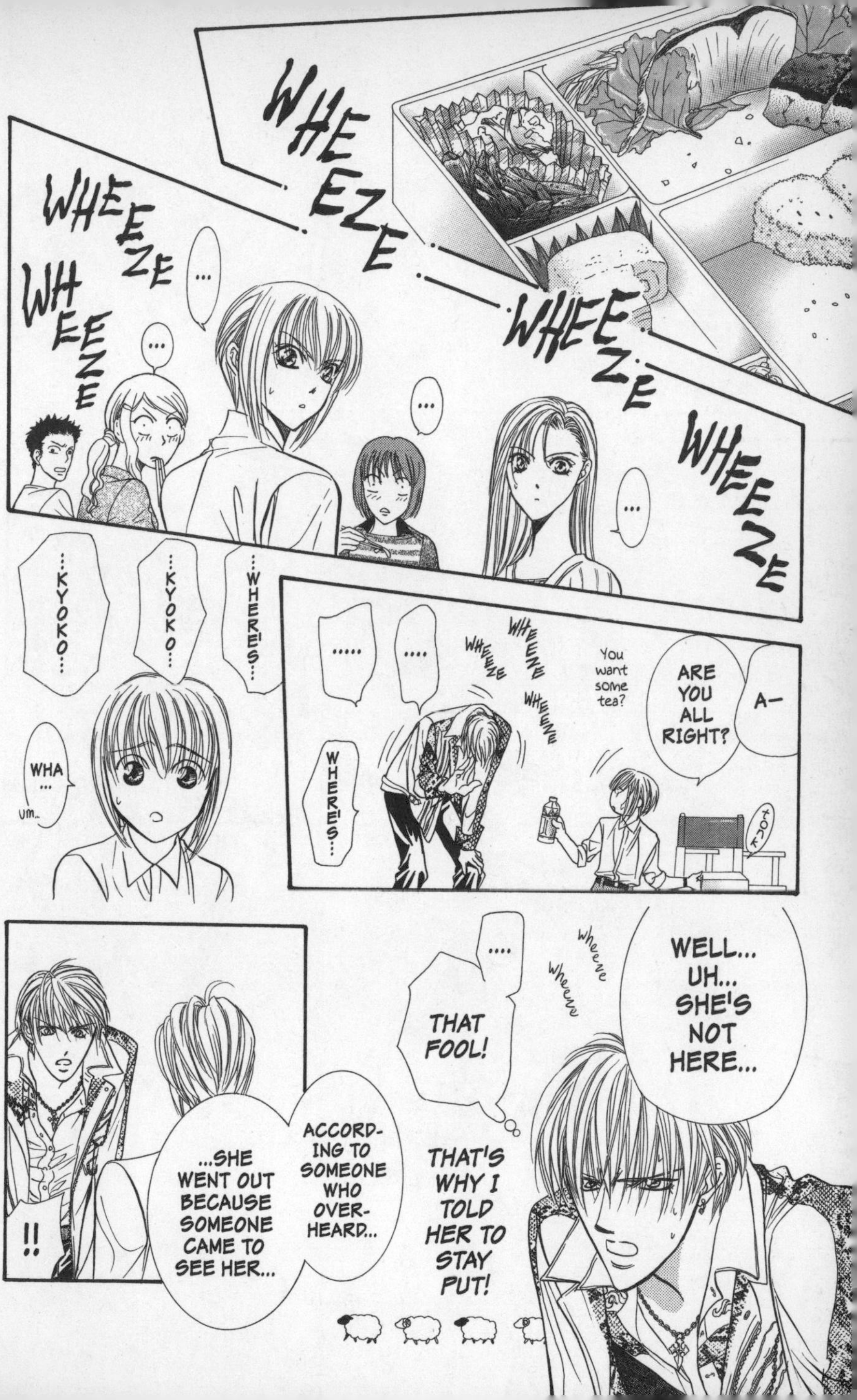
WHEEZE
WHEEZE
WHEEZE
WHEEZE
WHEEZE
...
....
....
...
....
A–
ARE YOU ALL RIGHT?
You want some tea?
WHEEZE
WHEEZE
WHEEZE
....
......
WHERE'S...
...WHERE'S...
...KYOKO...
...KYOKO...
WHA ...
um..
WELL... UH... SHE'S NOT HERE...
wheeze
wheeze
....
THAT FOOL!
THAT'S WHY I TOLD HER TO STAY PUT!
ACCORDING TO SOMEONE WHO OVERHEARD...
...SHE WENT OUT BECAUSE SOMEONE CAME TO SEE HER...
!!

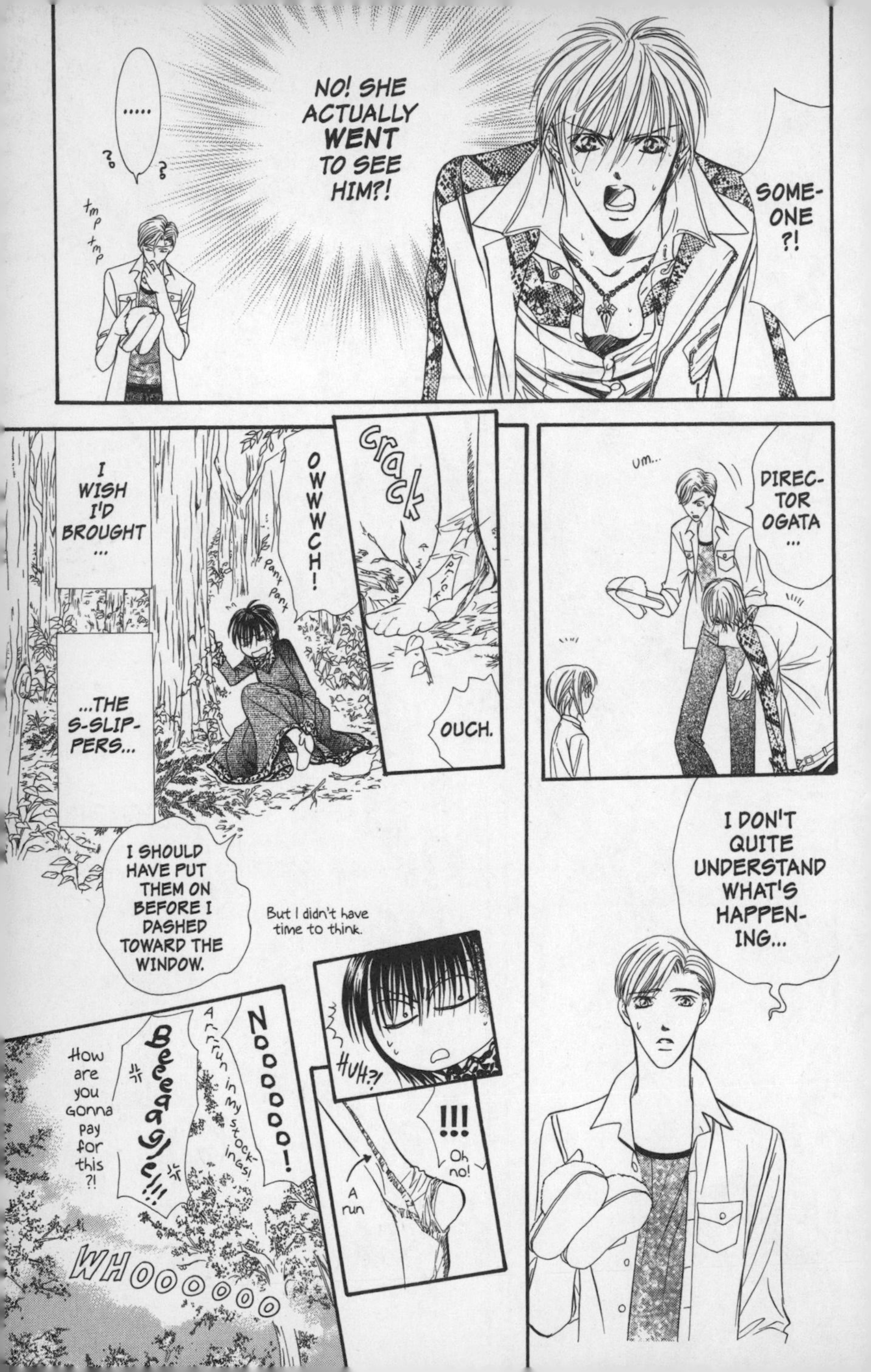
SOME-ONE ?!
NO! SHE ACTUALLY WENT TO SEE HIM?!
......
? ?
tmp tmp
DIREC-TOR OGATA ...
um...
I DON'T QUITE UNDERSTAND WHAT'S HAPPEN-ING...
Crack
prick
OWWWCH!
OUCH.
I WISH I'D BROUGHT ...
...THE S-SLIPPERS...
Pant Pant
I SHOULD HAVE PUT THEM ON BEFORE I DASHED TOWARD THE WINDOW.
But I didn't have time to think.
HUH?!
!!!
Oh no!
A run
Noooooo!
A r-run in my stock-ings!
Beeaagle!!!
How are you gonna pay for this ?!
WHOOOOOO

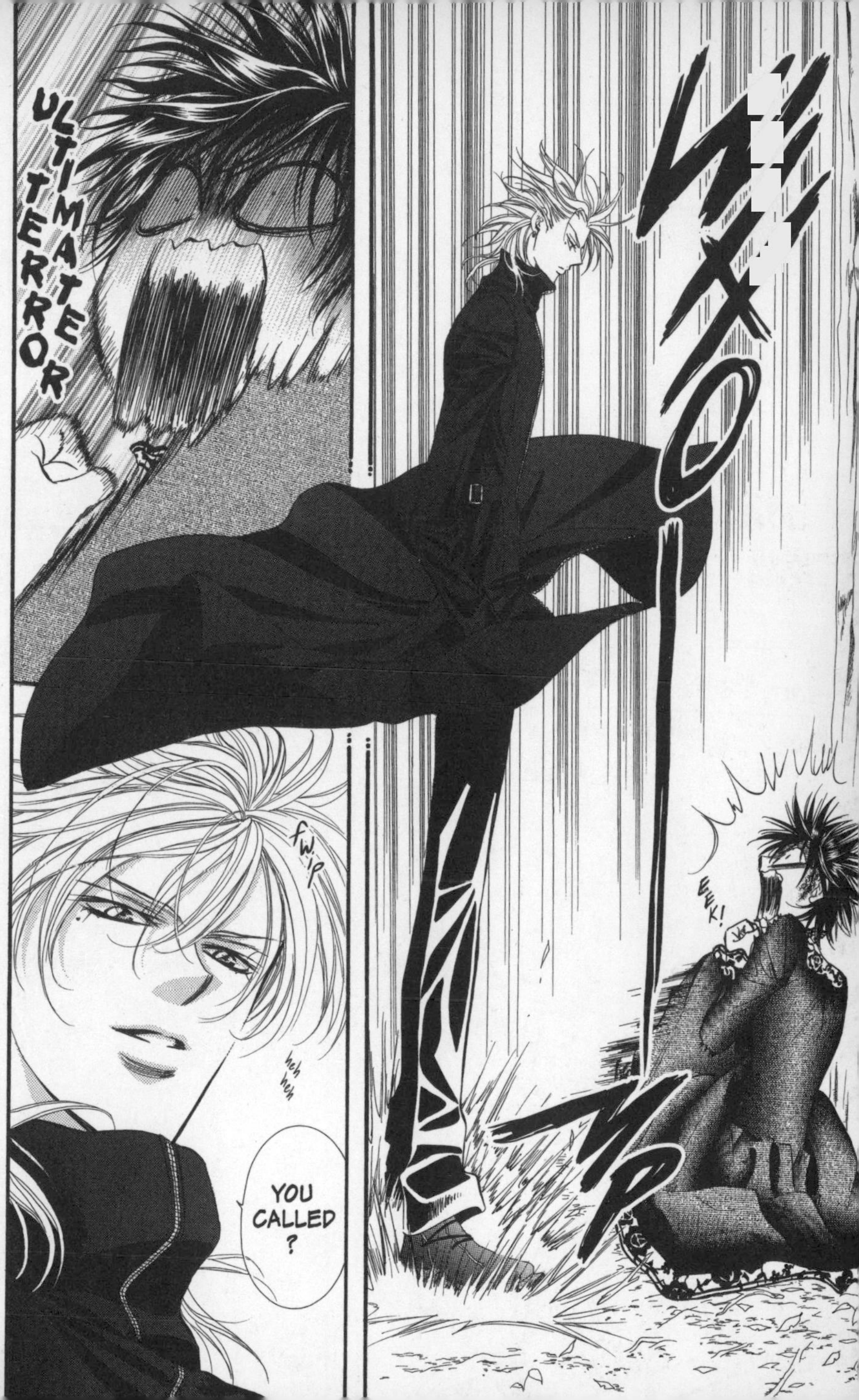
EEK!
ULTIMATE TERROR
FWIP
heh heh
YOU CALLED ?

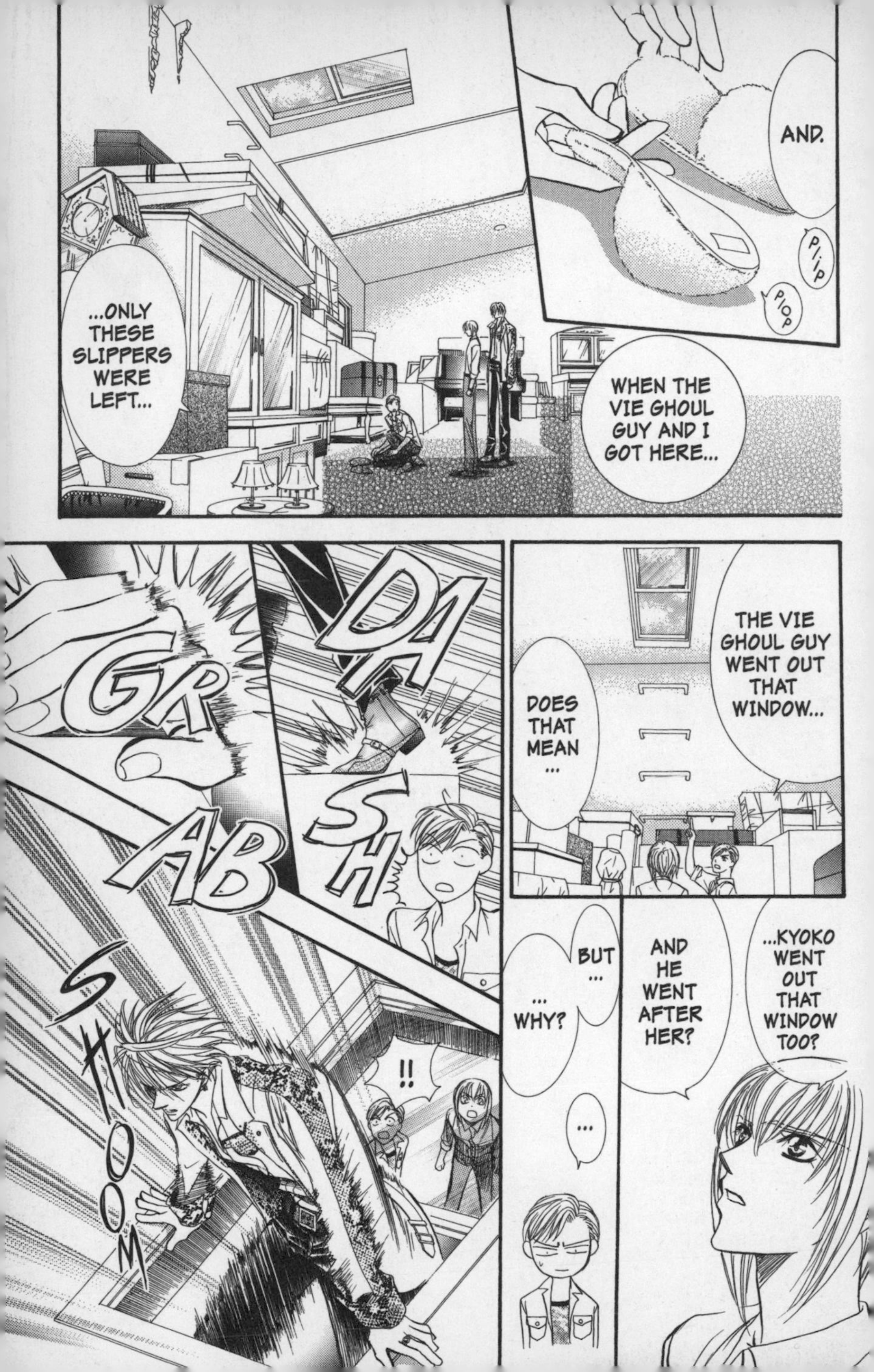
WHEN THE VIE GHOUL GUY AND I GOT HERE...
...ONLY THESE SLIPPERS WERE LEFT...
AND.
PLIP
PLOP
THE VIE GHOUL GUY WENT OUT THAT WINDOW...
DOES THAT MEAN ...
...KYOKO WENT OUT THAT WINDOW TOO?
AND HE WENT AFTER HER?
BUT ...
... WHY?
...
GRAB
DASH
!!
SHOOM

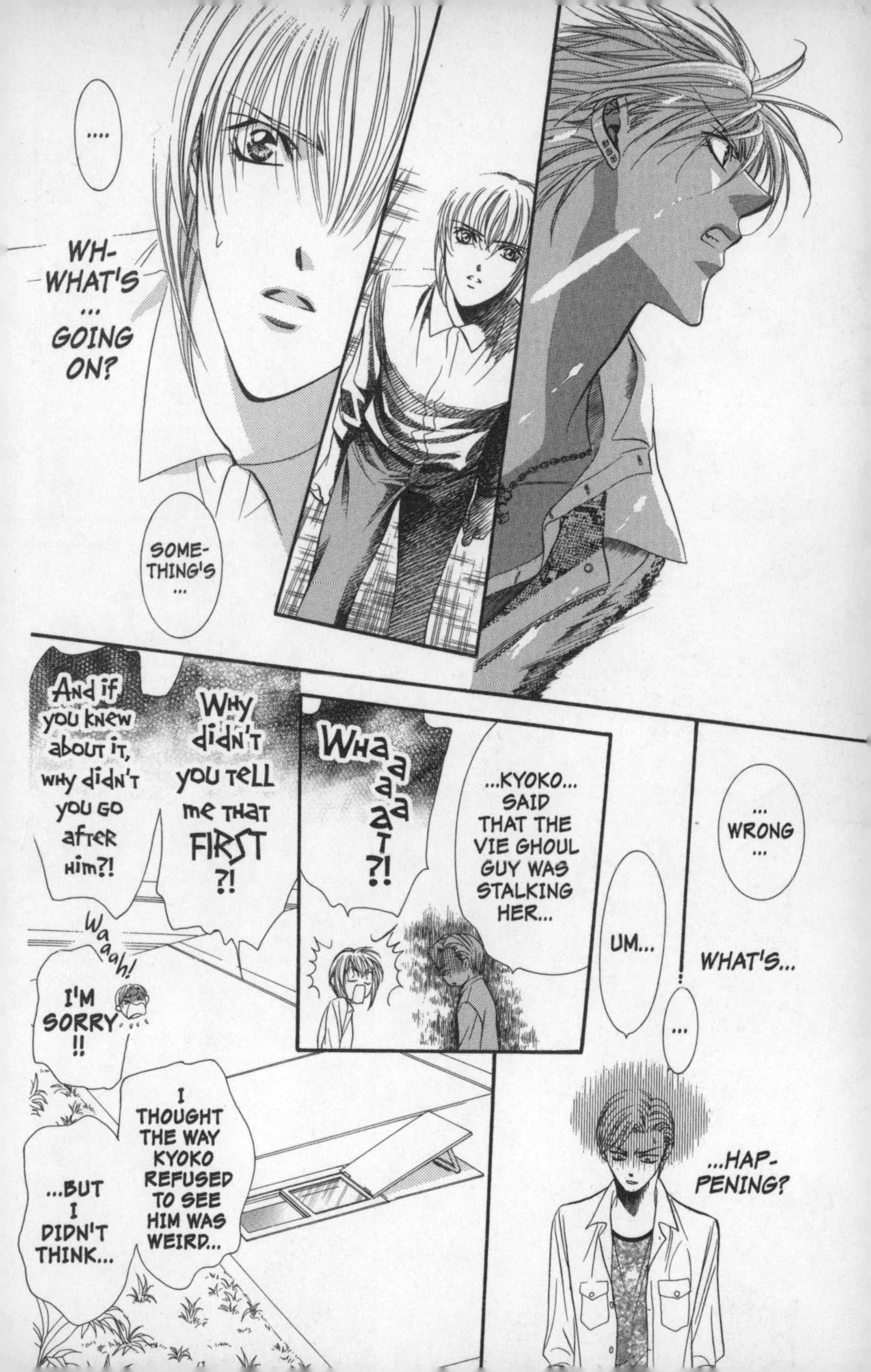
....
WH-WHAT'S ... GOING ON?
SOMETHING'S ...
... WRONG ...
WHAT'S...
UM...
...
...HAPPENING?
...KYOKO... SAID THAT THE VIE GHOUL GUY WAS STALKING HER...
Whaaaaat?!
Why didn't you tell me that FIRST?!
And if you knew about it, why didn't you go after him?!
Waaah!
I'M SORRY!!
I THOUGHT THE WAY KYOKO REFUSED TO SEE HIM WAS WEIRD...
...BUT I DIDN'T THINK...

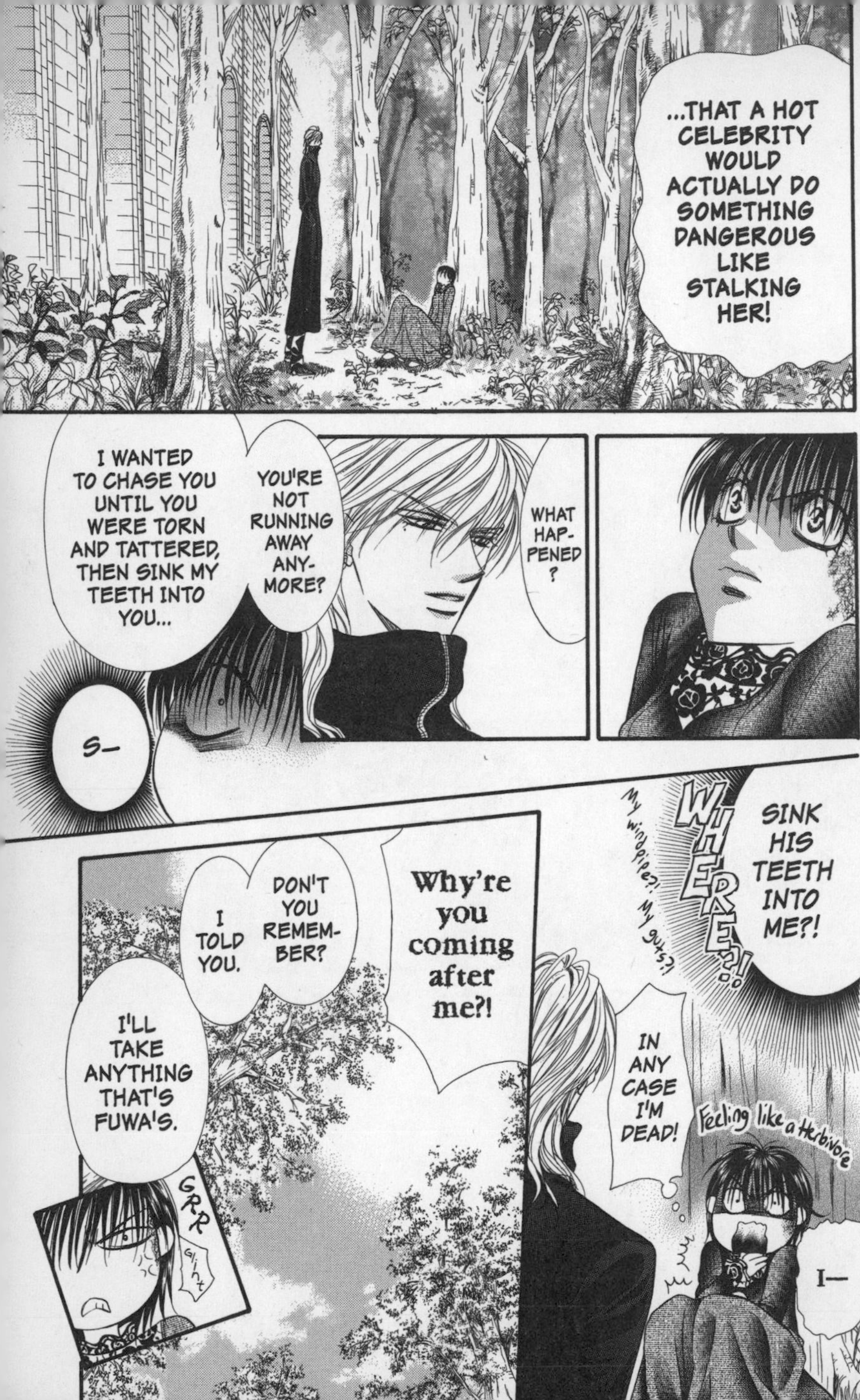
...THAT A HOT CELEBRITY WOULD ACTUALLY DO SOMETHING DANGEROUS LIKE STALKING HER!
WHAT HAP-PENED?
YOU'RE NOT RUNNING AWAY ANY-MORE?
I WANTED TO CHASE YOU UNTIL YOU WERE TORN AND TATTERED, THEN SINK MY TEETH INTO YOU...
S—
SINK HIS TEETH INTO ME?!
WHERE?!
My windpipe?! My guts?!
IN ANY CASE I'M DEAD!
Feeling like a Herbivore
I—
Why're you coming after me?!
DON'T YOU REMEMBER?
I TOLD YOU.
I'LL TAKE ANYTHING THAT'S FUWA'S.
GRR
Glint

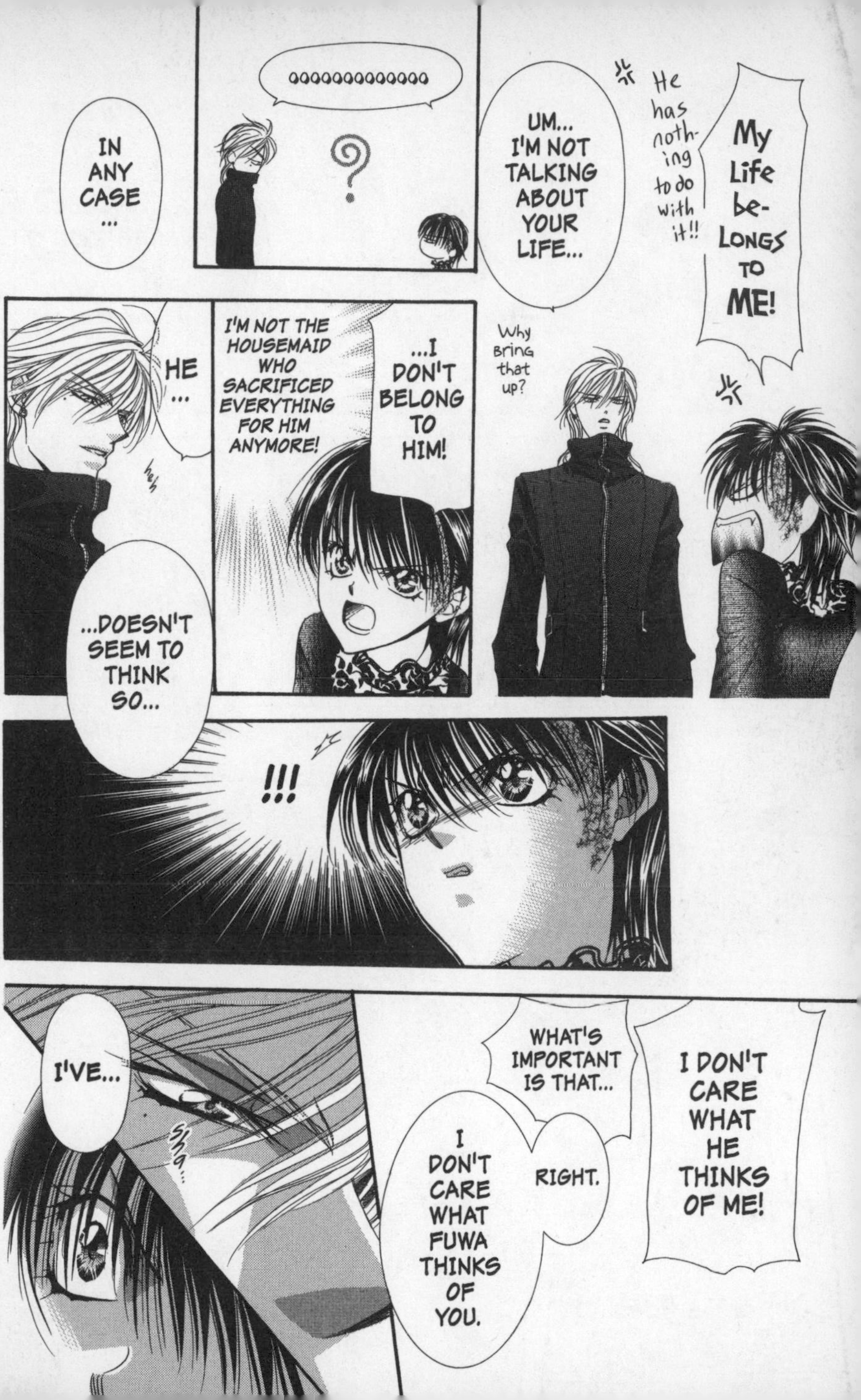
My Life belongs to ME!
He has nothing to do with it!!
UM... I'M NOT TALKING ABOUT YOUR LIFE...
oooooooooooooo
IN ANY CASE...
Why bring that up?
...I DON'T BELONG TO HIM!
I'M NOT THE HOUSEMAID WHO SACRIFICED EVERYTHING FOR HIM ANYMORE!
HE...
heh
...DOESN'T SEEM TO THINK SO...
!!!
I DON'T CARE WHAT HE THINKS OF ME!
WHAT'S IMPORTANT IS THAT...
RIGHT.
I DON'T CARE WHAT FUWA THINKS OF YOU.
I'VE...

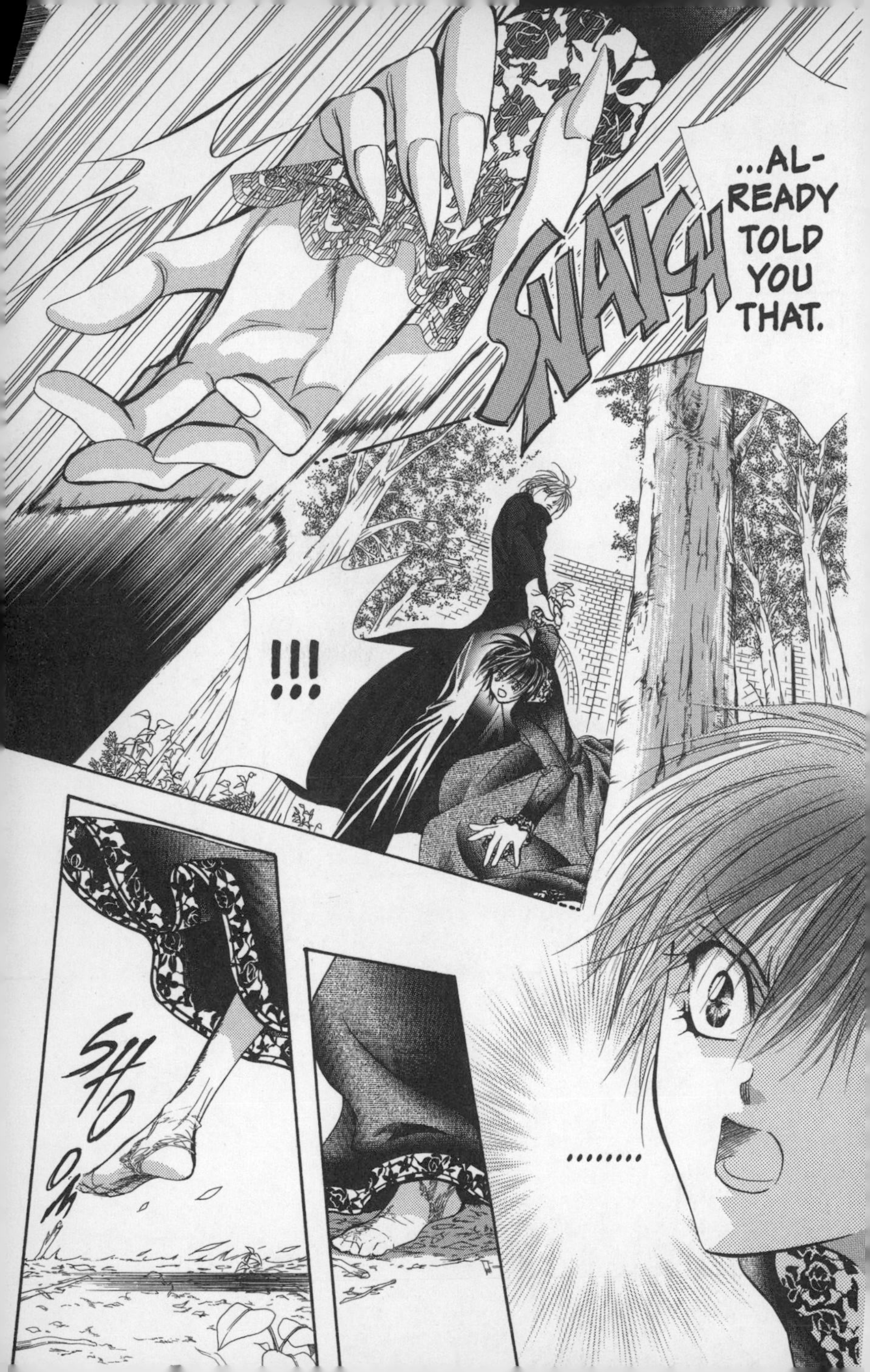

...AL-READY TOLD YOU THAT.
SNATCH
!!!
....
SHOOM

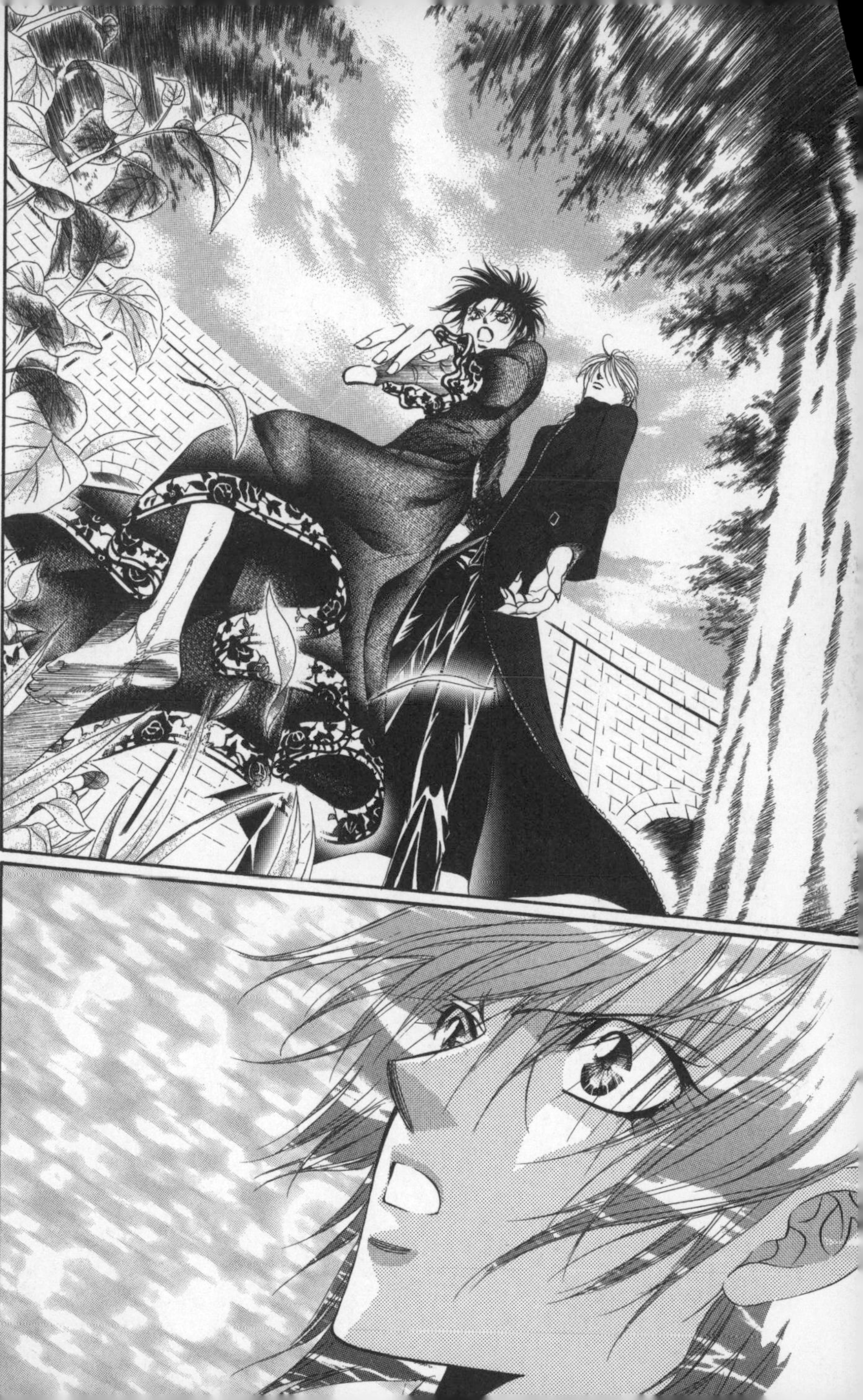

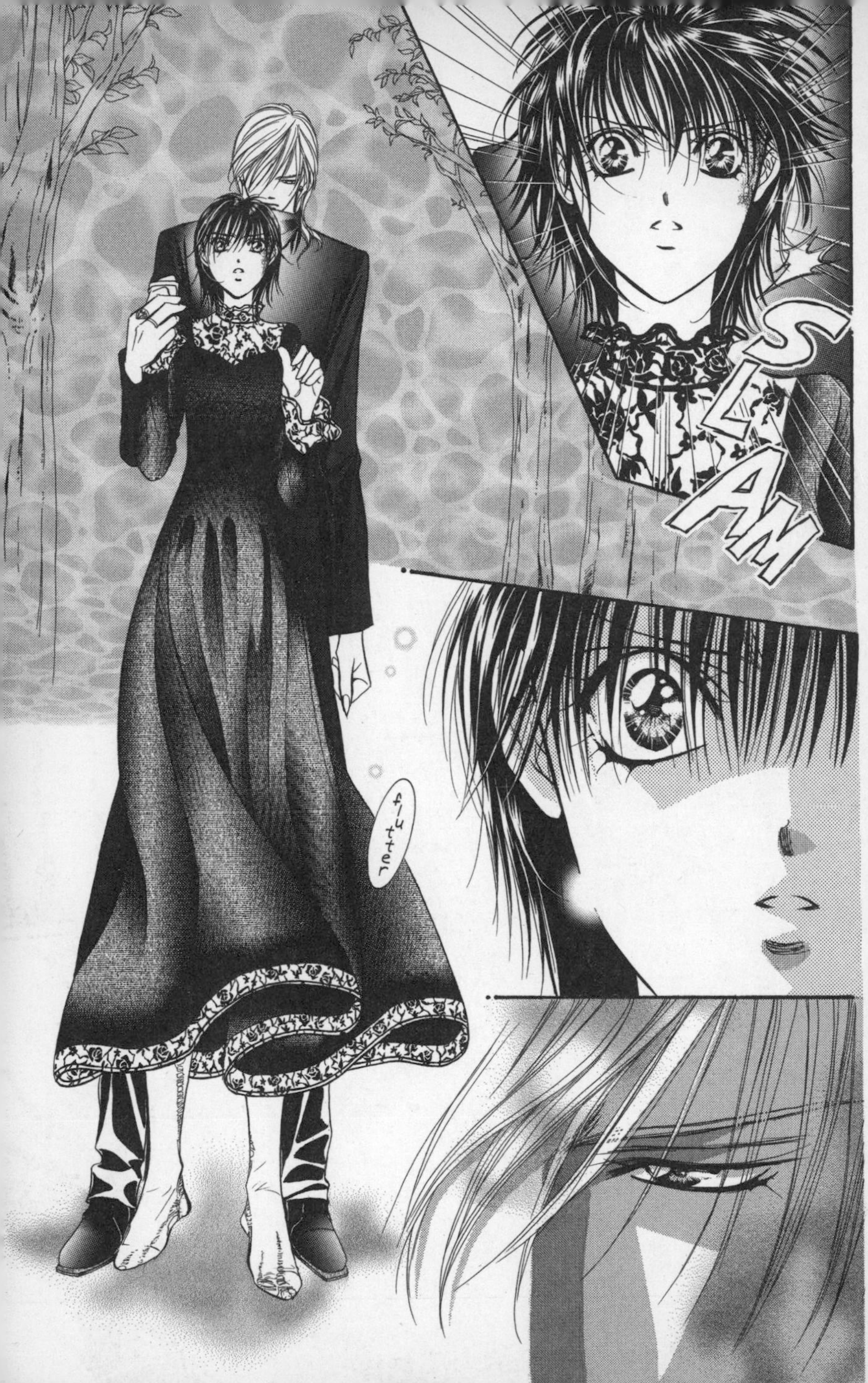
SLAM
flutter

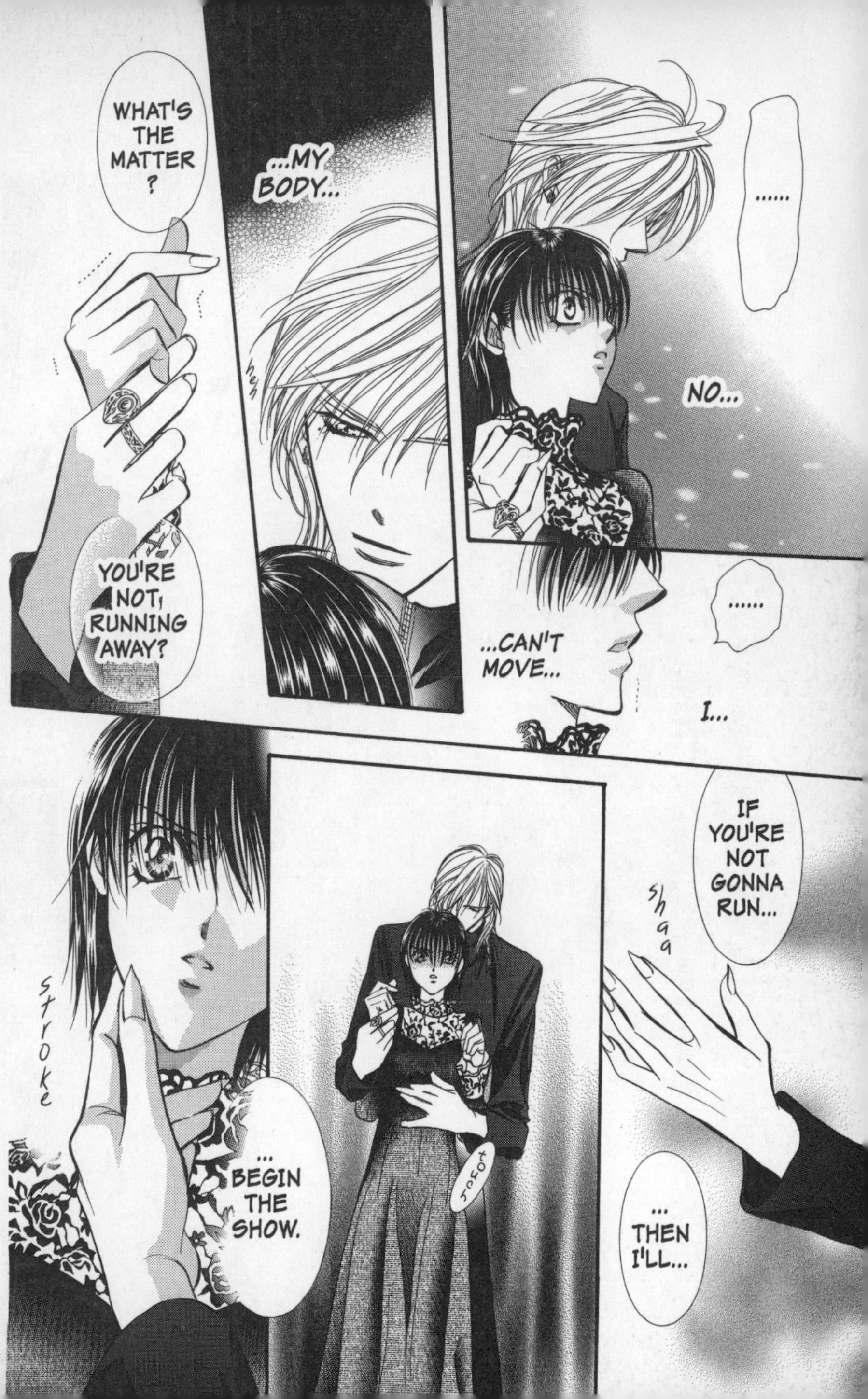
......
NO...
......
...CAN'T MOVE...
I...
...MY BODY...
heh
WHAT'S THE MATTER?
YOU'RE NOT RUNNING AWAY?
IF YOU'RE NOT GONNA RUN...
shaa
...THEN I'LL...
touch
stroke
...BEGIN THE SHOW.

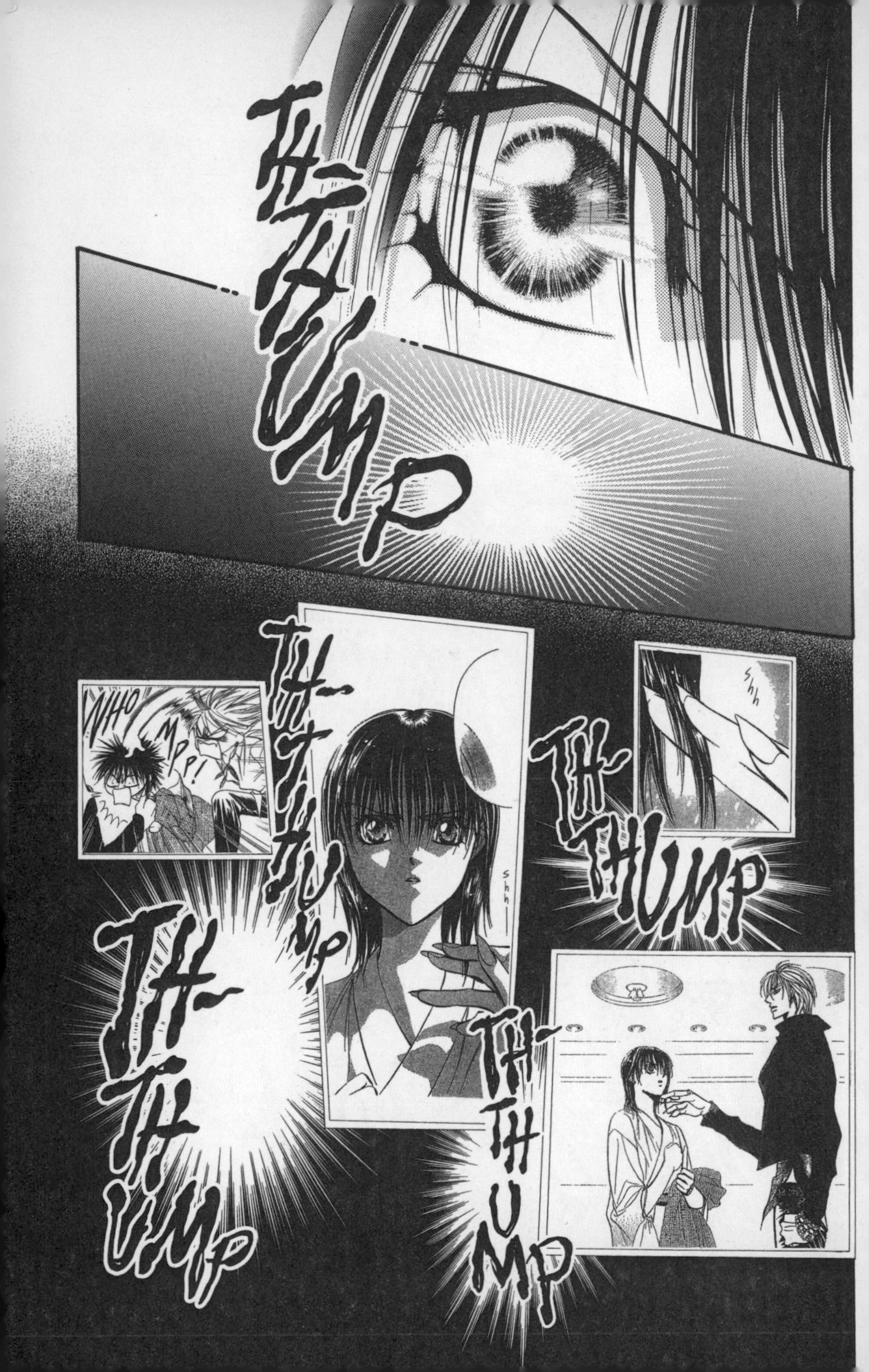
TH-THUMP
shh
TH-THUMP
TH-TH-THUMP
shh
WHOMP!
TH-TH-THUMP
TH-TH-THUMP

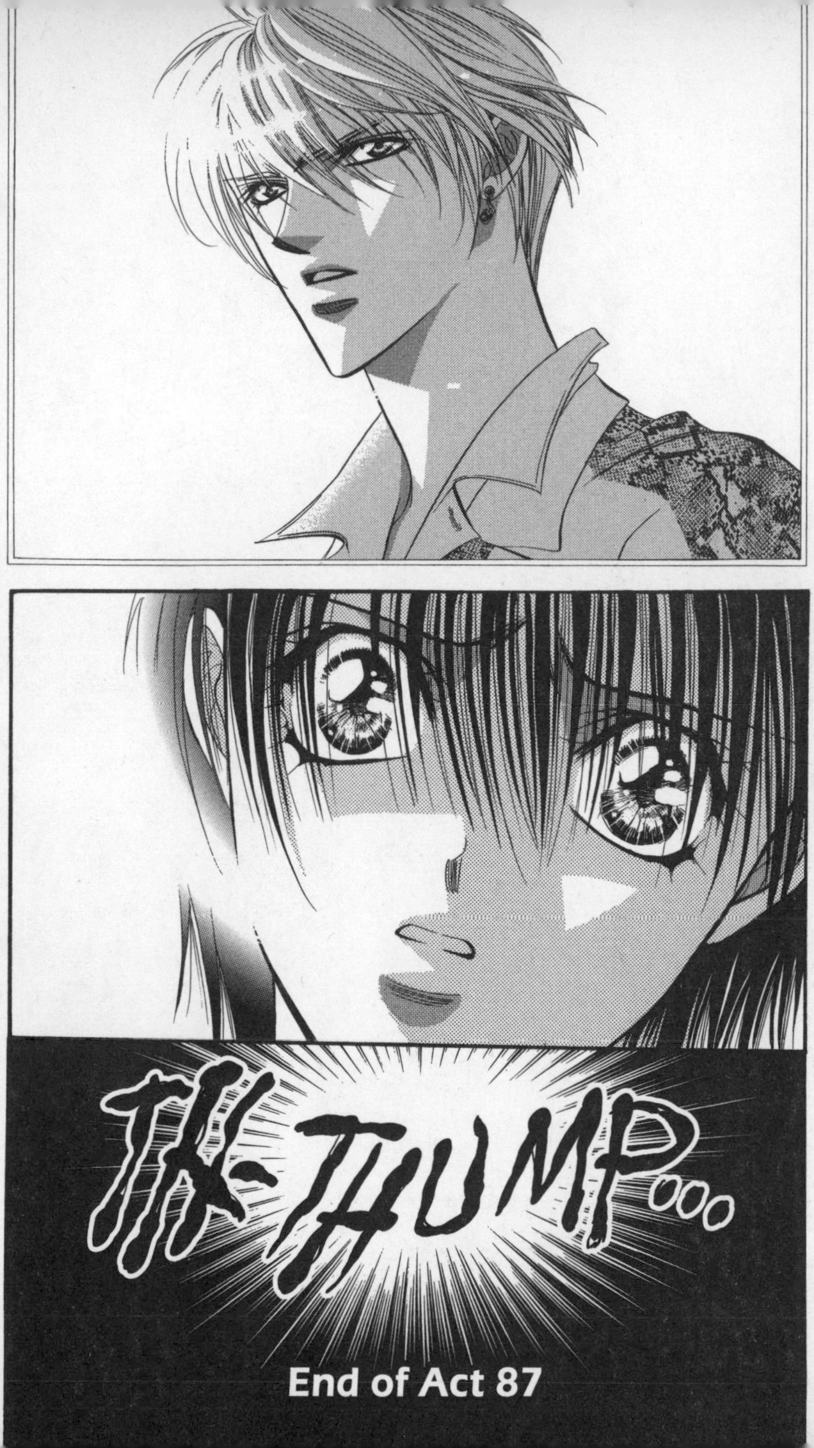
TH-THUMP...
End of Act 87

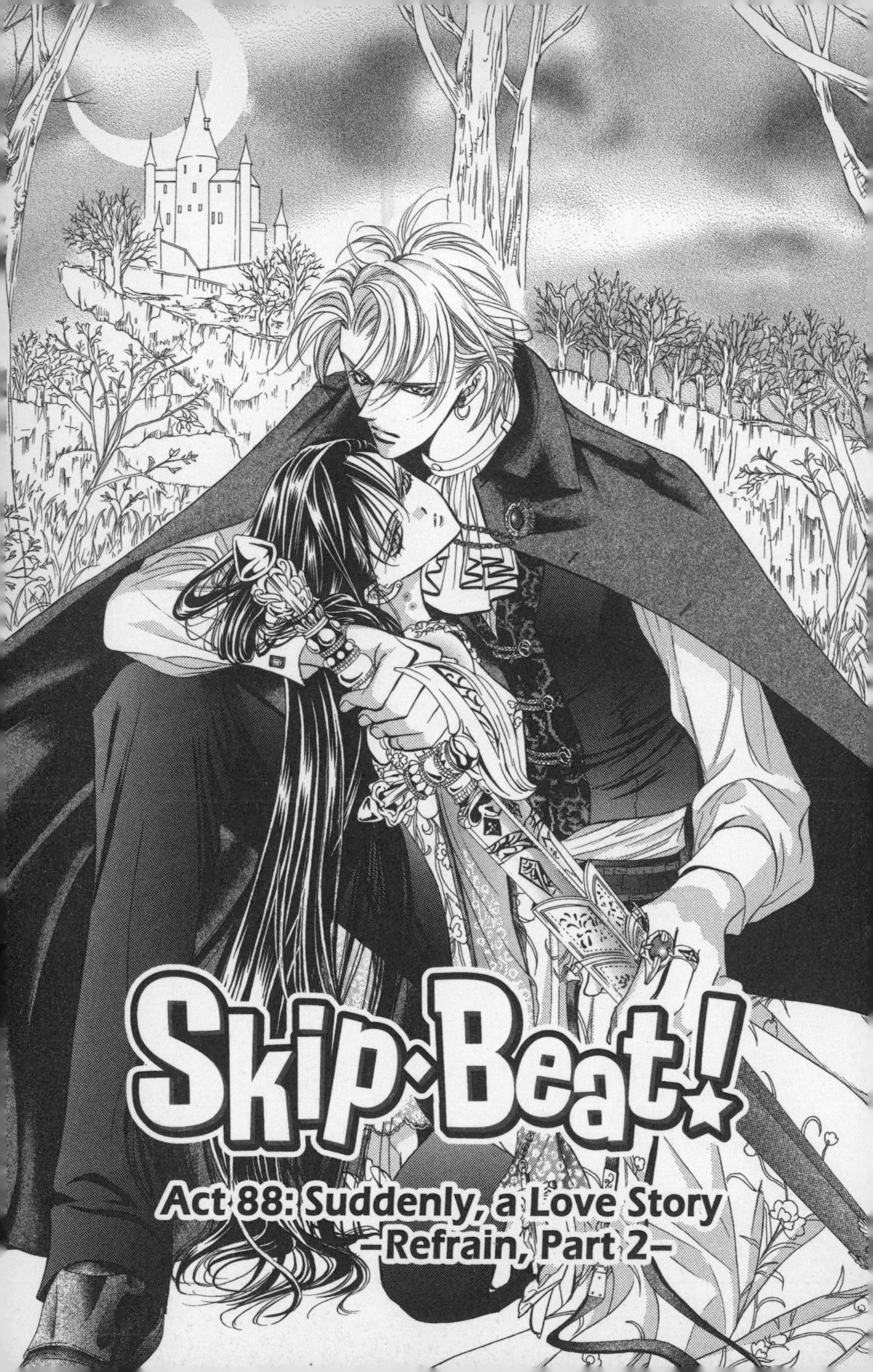
Skip·Beat!
Act 88: Suddenly, a Love Story
-Refrain, Part 2-

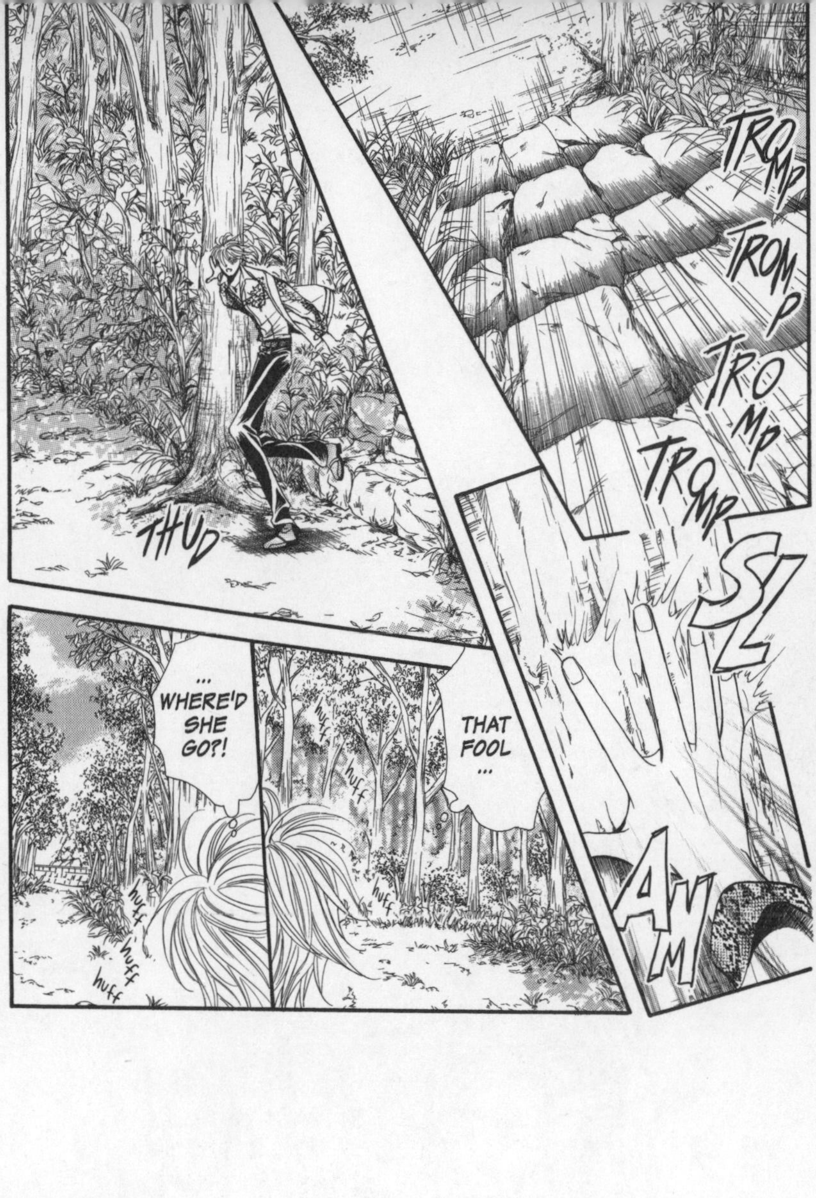
TROMP
TROMP
TROMP
TROMP
SLAM
THUD
huff
THAT FOOL ...
huff
huff
... WHERE'D SHE GO?!
huff
huff
huff

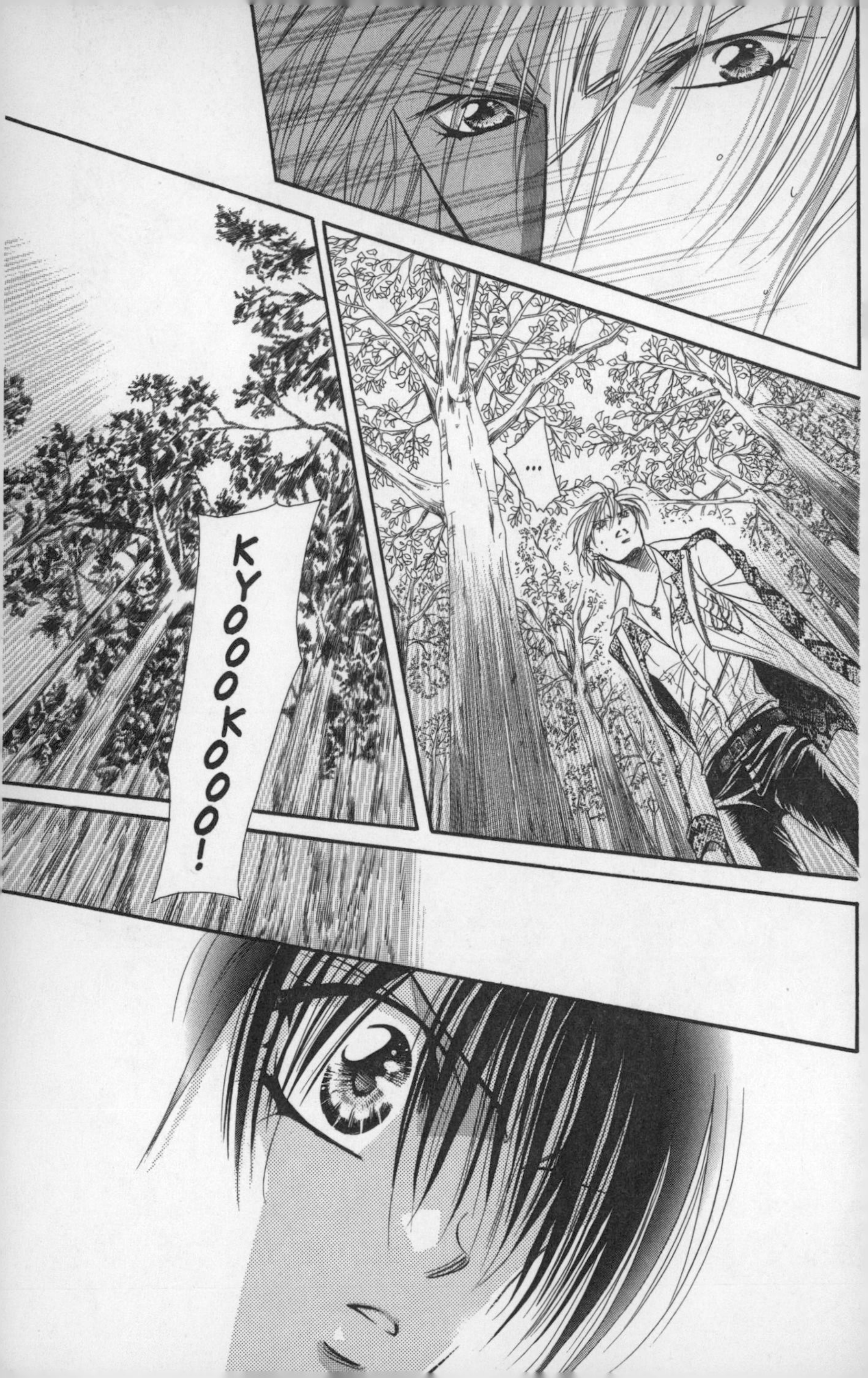
...
KYOOOKOOOO!

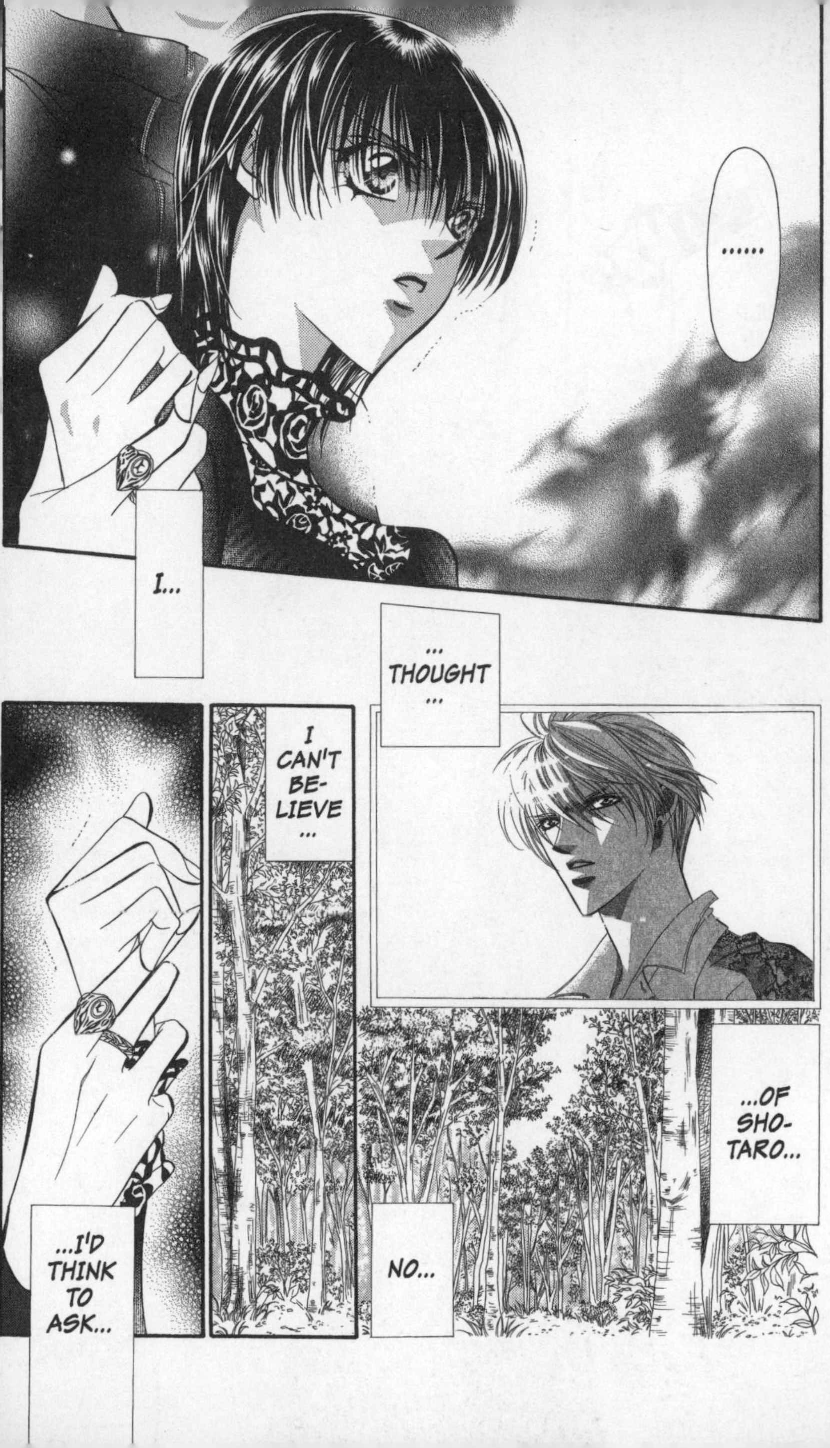
......
I...
...THOUGHT...
...OF SHO-TARO...
NO...
I CAN'T BE-LIEVE...
...I'D THINK TO ASK...

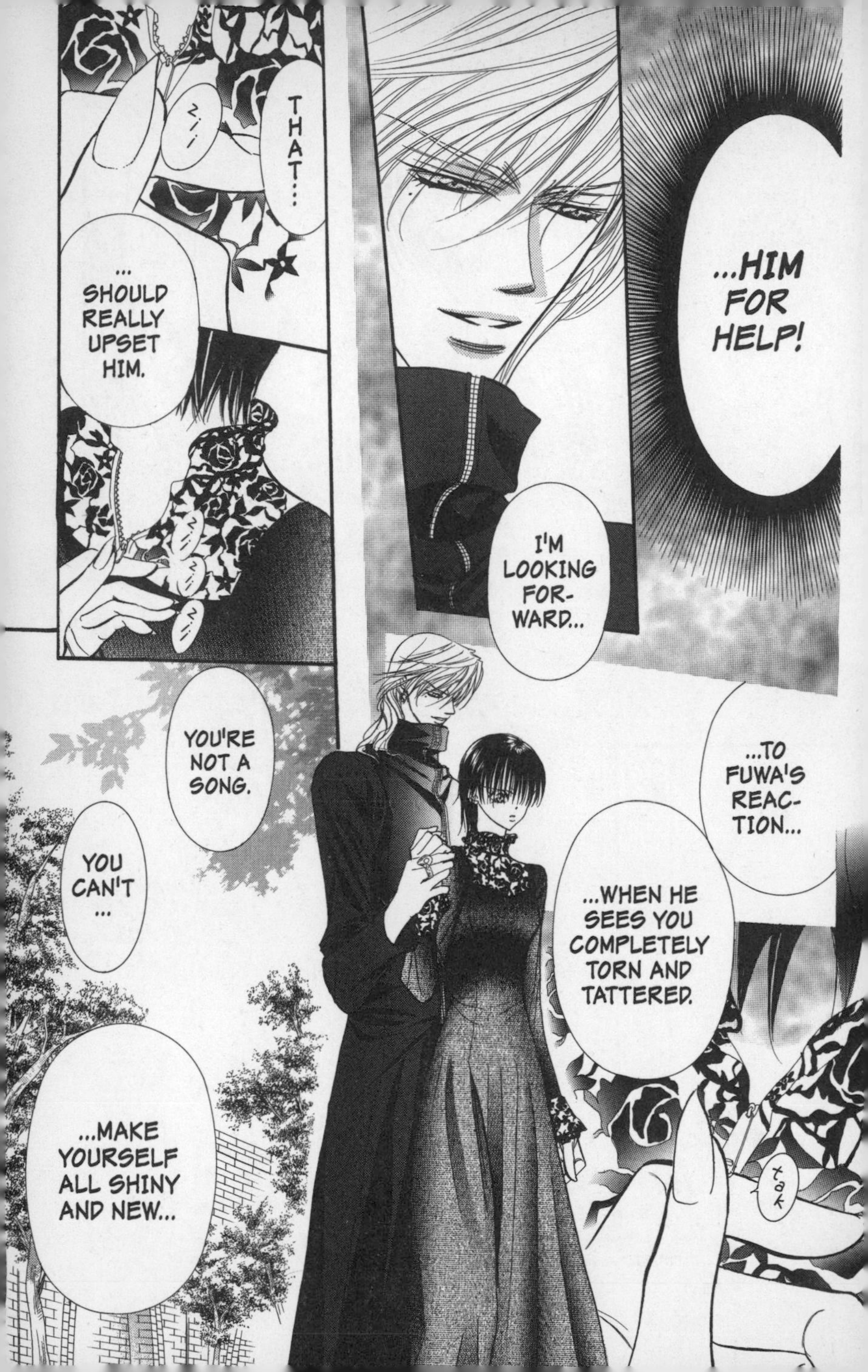
...HIM FOR HELP!
I'M LOOKING FOR-WARD...
THAT...
zii
...SHOULD REALLY UPSET HIM.
zii
zii
zii
...TO FUWA'S REAC-TION...
...WHEN HE SEES YOU COMPLETELY TORN AND TATTERED.
tak
YOU'RE NOT A SONG.
YOU CAN'T ...
...MAKE YOURSELF ALL SHINY AND NEW...

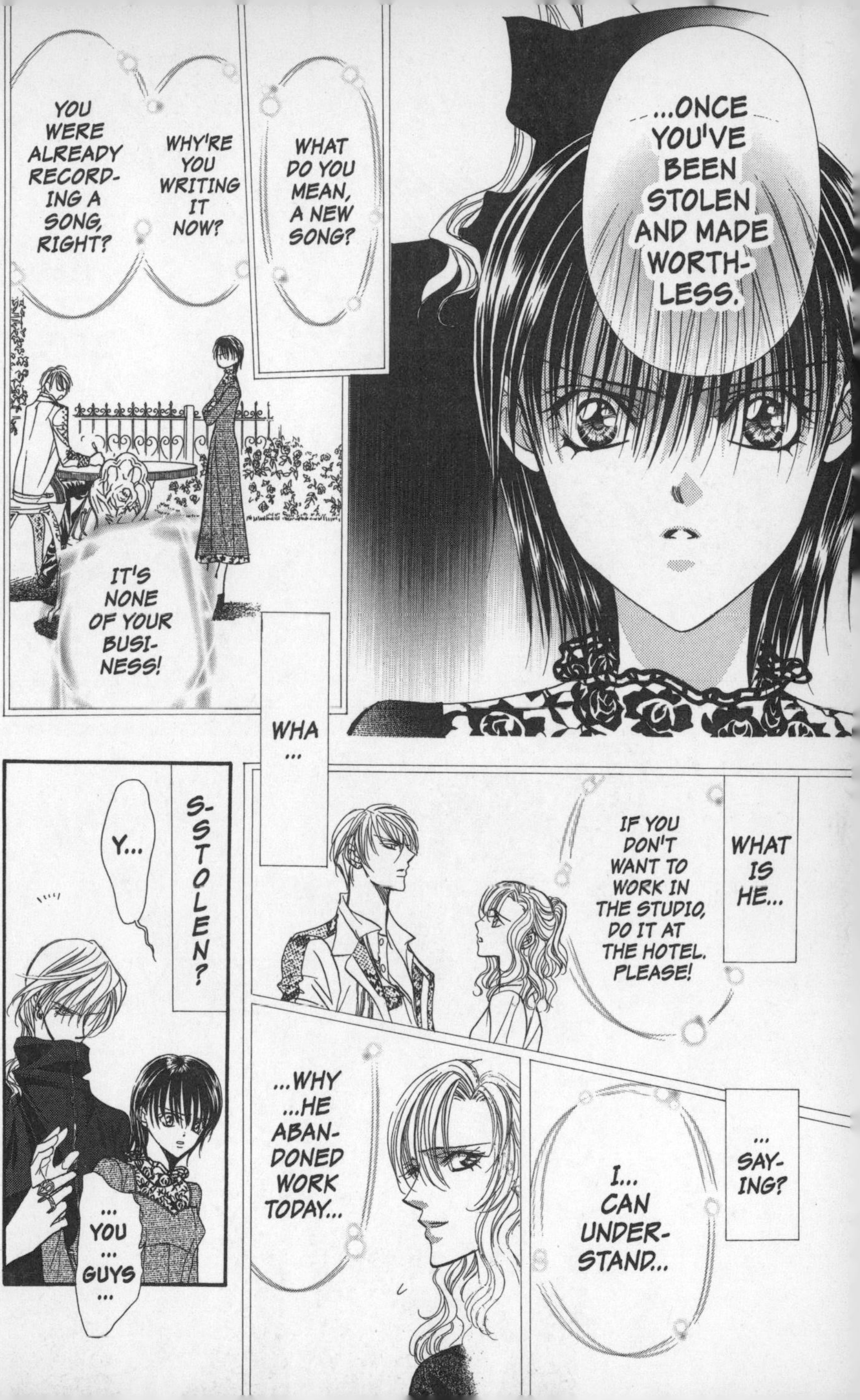
...ONCE YOU'VE BEEN STOLEN AND MADE WORTH-LESS.
WHAT DO YOU MEAN, A NEW SONG?
WHY'RE YOU WRITING IT NOW?
YOU WERE ALREADY RECORD-ING A SONG, RIGHT?
IT'S NONE OF YOUR BUSI-NESS!
WHA ...
WHAT IS HE...
IF YOU DON'T WANT TO WORK IN THE STUDIO, DO IT AT THE HOTEL. PLEASE!
... SAY-ING?
I... CAN UNDER-STAND...
...WHY ...HE ABAN-DONED WORK TODAY...
S-STOLEN?
Y...
... YOU ... GUYS ...

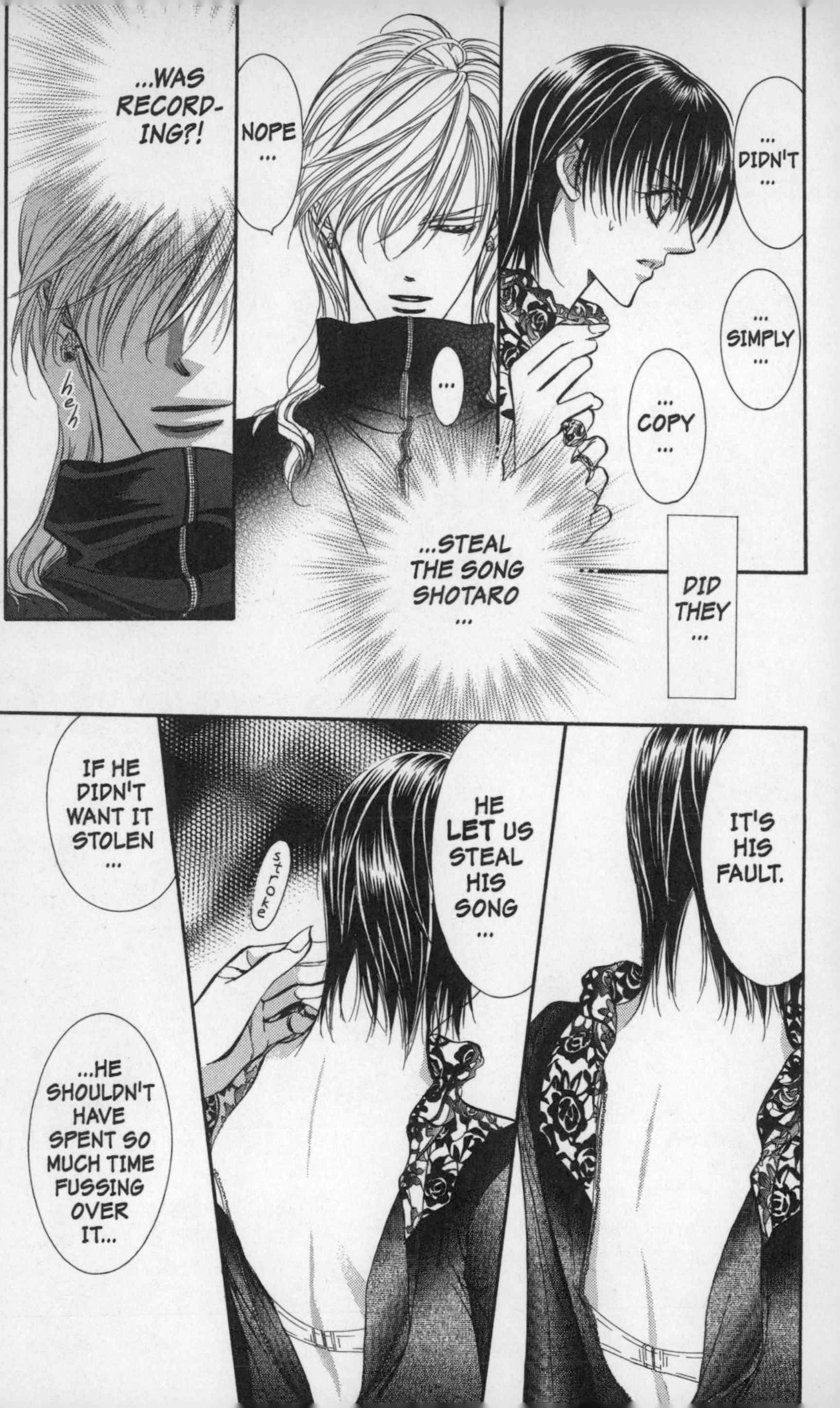
...DIDN'T...
...SIMPLY...
...COPY...
DID THEY...
...STEAL THE SONG SHOTARO...
NOPE...
...
...WAS RECORD-ING?!
heh
IT'S HIS FAULT.
HE LET US STEAL HIS SONG...
stroke
IF HE DIDN'T WANT IT STOLEN...
...HE SHOULDN'T HAVE SPENT SO MUCH TIME FUSSING OVER IT...

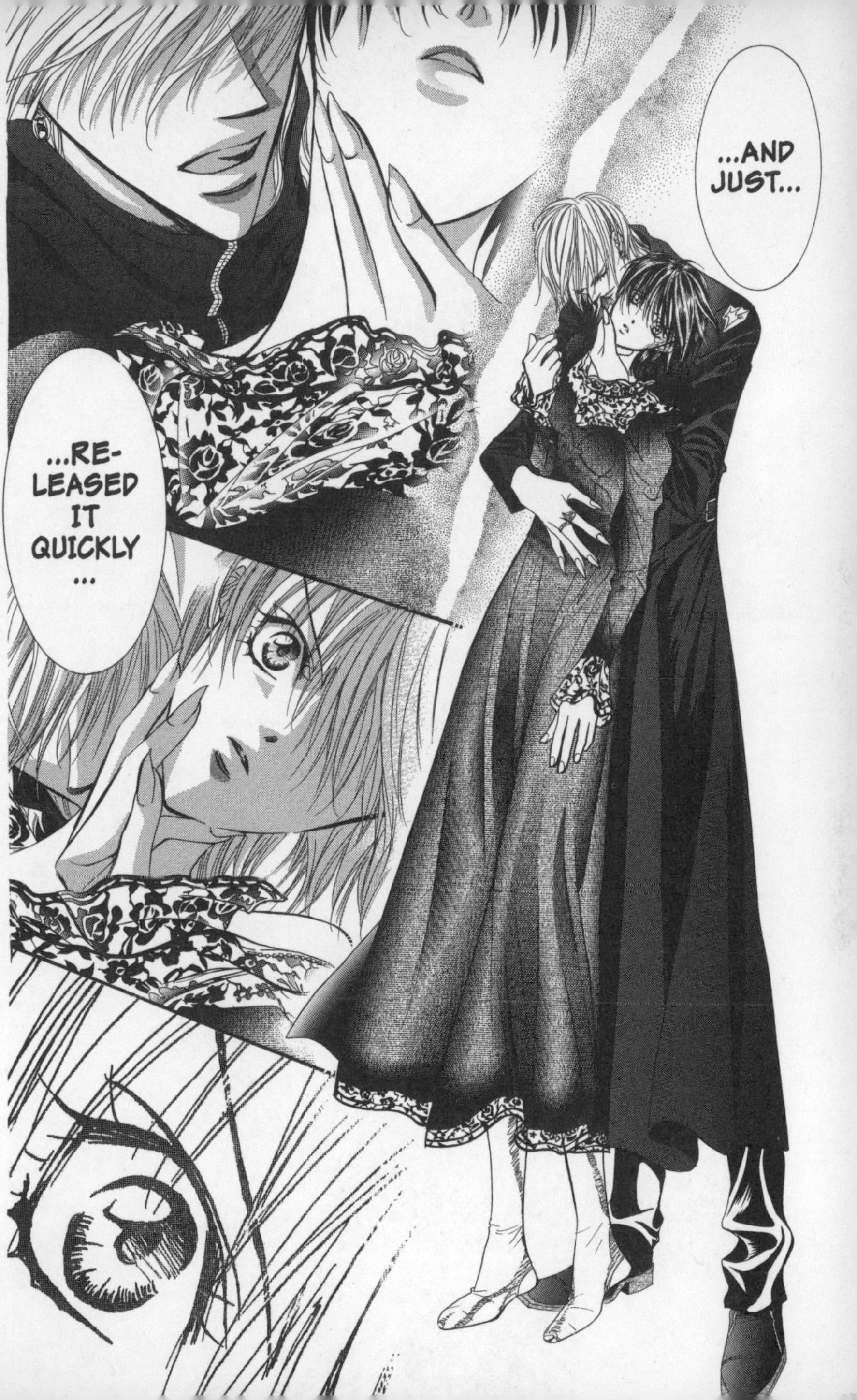
...AND JUST...
...RE-LEASED IT QUICKLY ...

GRAB
?!

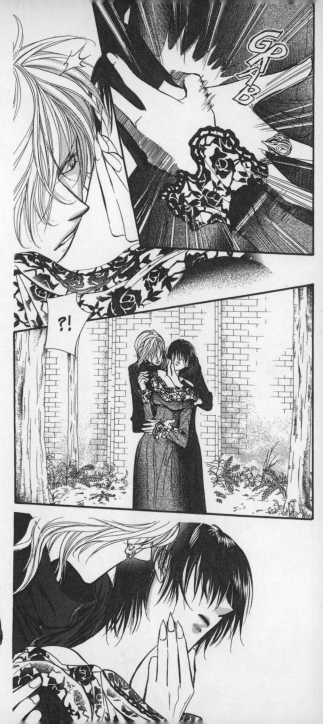

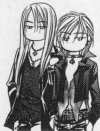

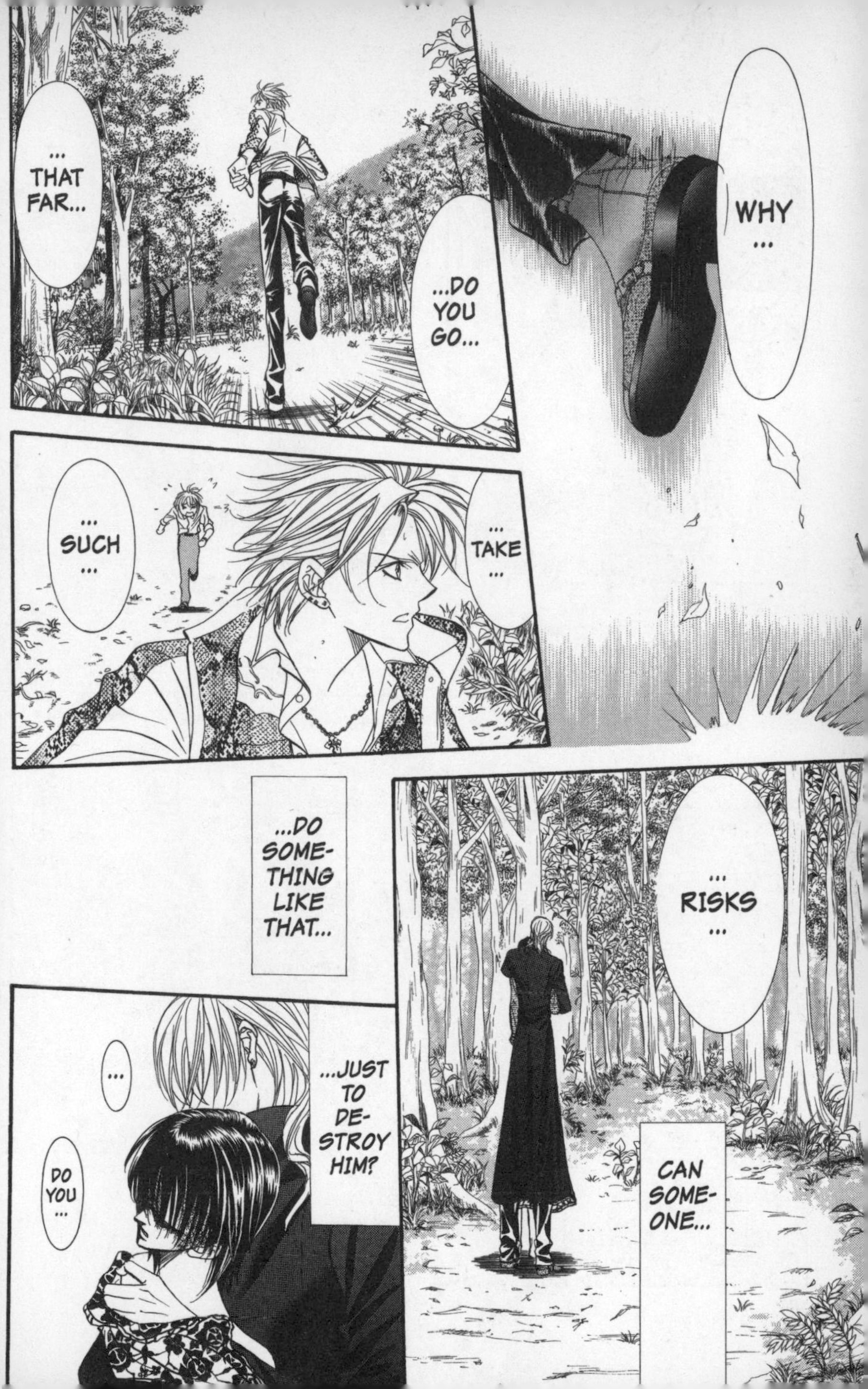
WHY ...
...DO YOU GO...
... THAT FAR...
... TAKE ...
... SUCH ...
... RISKS ...
CAN SOME-ONE...
...DO SOME-THING LIKE THAT...
...JUST TO DE-STROY HIM?
...
DO YOU ...

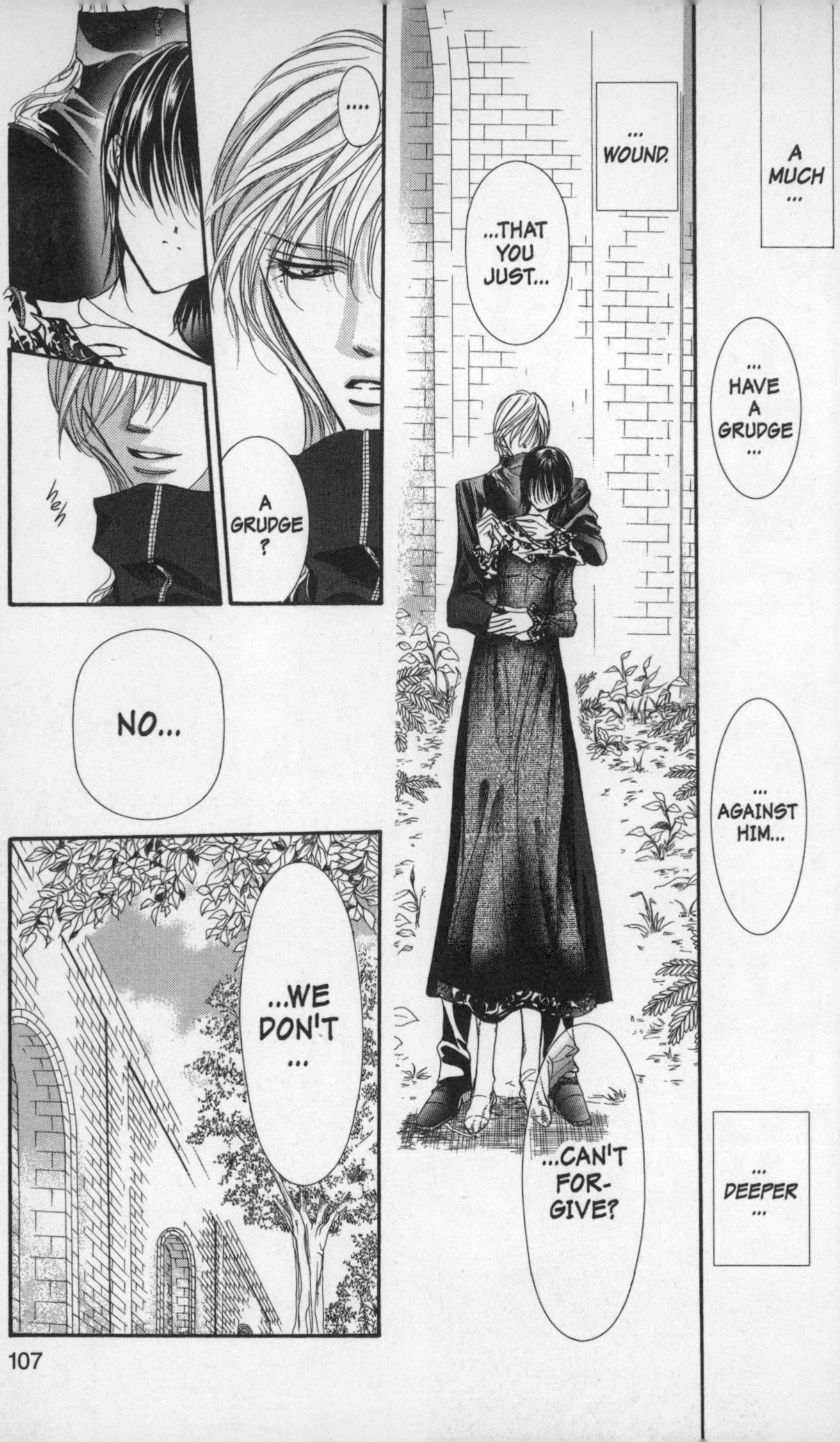
A MUCH ...
... HAVE A GRUDGE ...
... AGAINST HIM...
... DEEPER ...
... WOUND.
...THAT YOU JUST...
...CAN'T FOR- GIVE?
....
A GRUDGE ?
heh
NO...
...WE DON'T ...

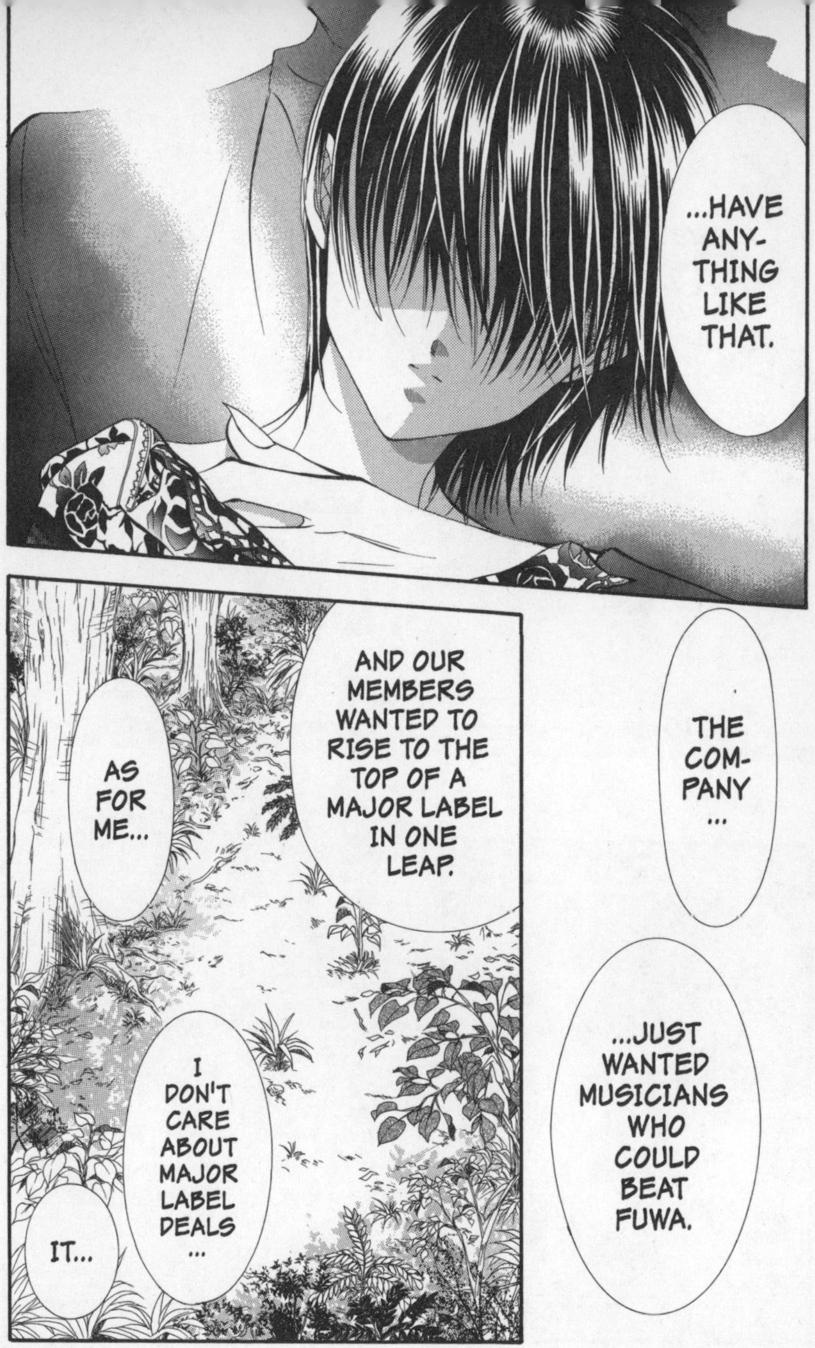
...HAVE ANY-THING LIKE THAT.
THE COM-PANY ...
...JUST WANTED MUSICIANS WHO COULD BEAT FUWA.
AND OUR MEMBERS WANTED TO RISE TO THE TOP OF A MAJOR LABEL IN ONE LEAP.
AS FOR ME...
I DON'T CARE ABOUT MAJOR LABEL DEALS ...
IT...

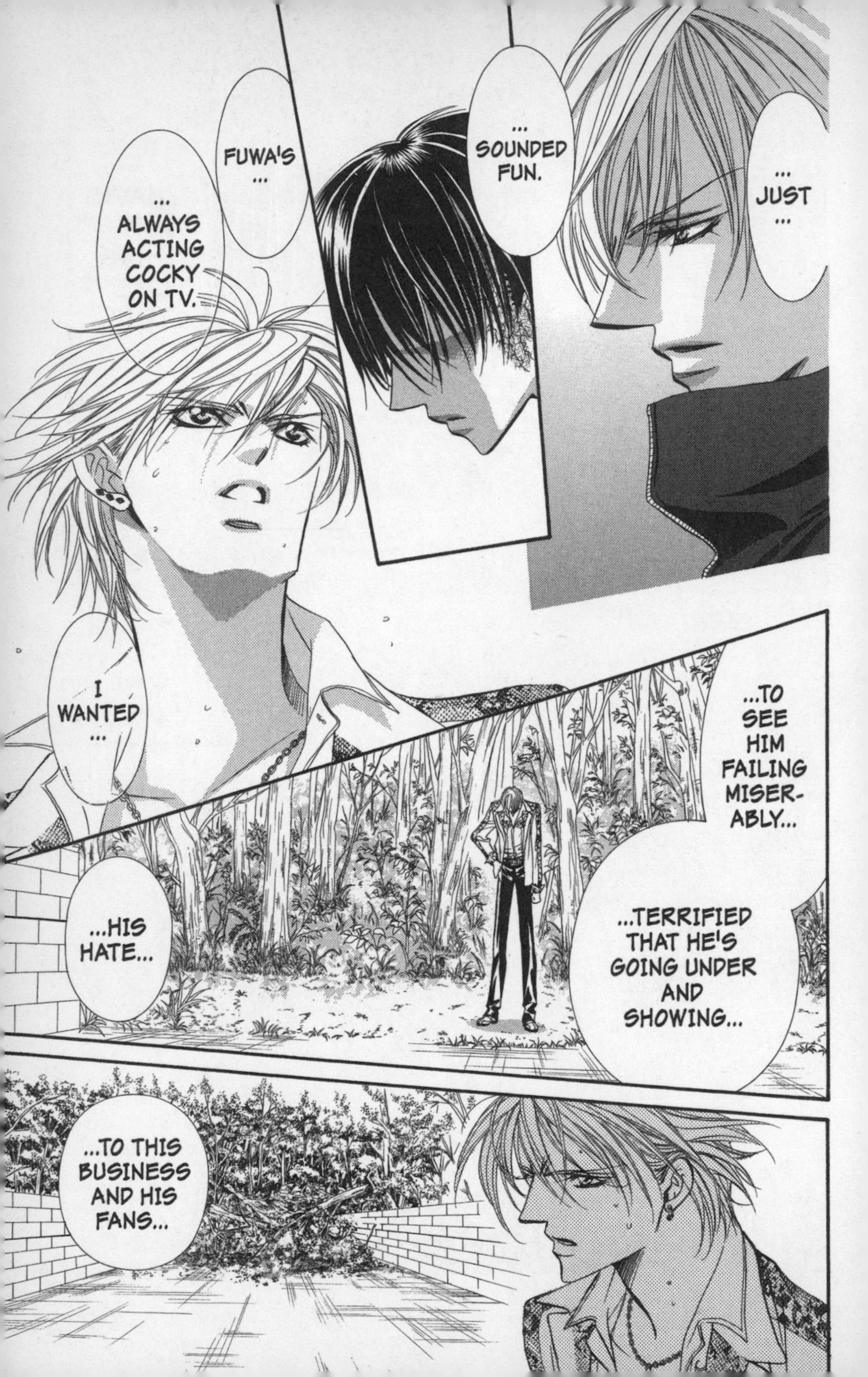

... JUST ...
... SOUNDED FUN.
FUWA'S ...
... ALWAYS ACTING COCKY ON TV.
I WANTED ...
...TO SEE HIM FAILING MISER-ABLY...
...TERRIFIED THAT HE'S GOING UNDER AND SHOWING...
...HIS HATE...
...TO THIS BUSINESS AND HIS FANS...

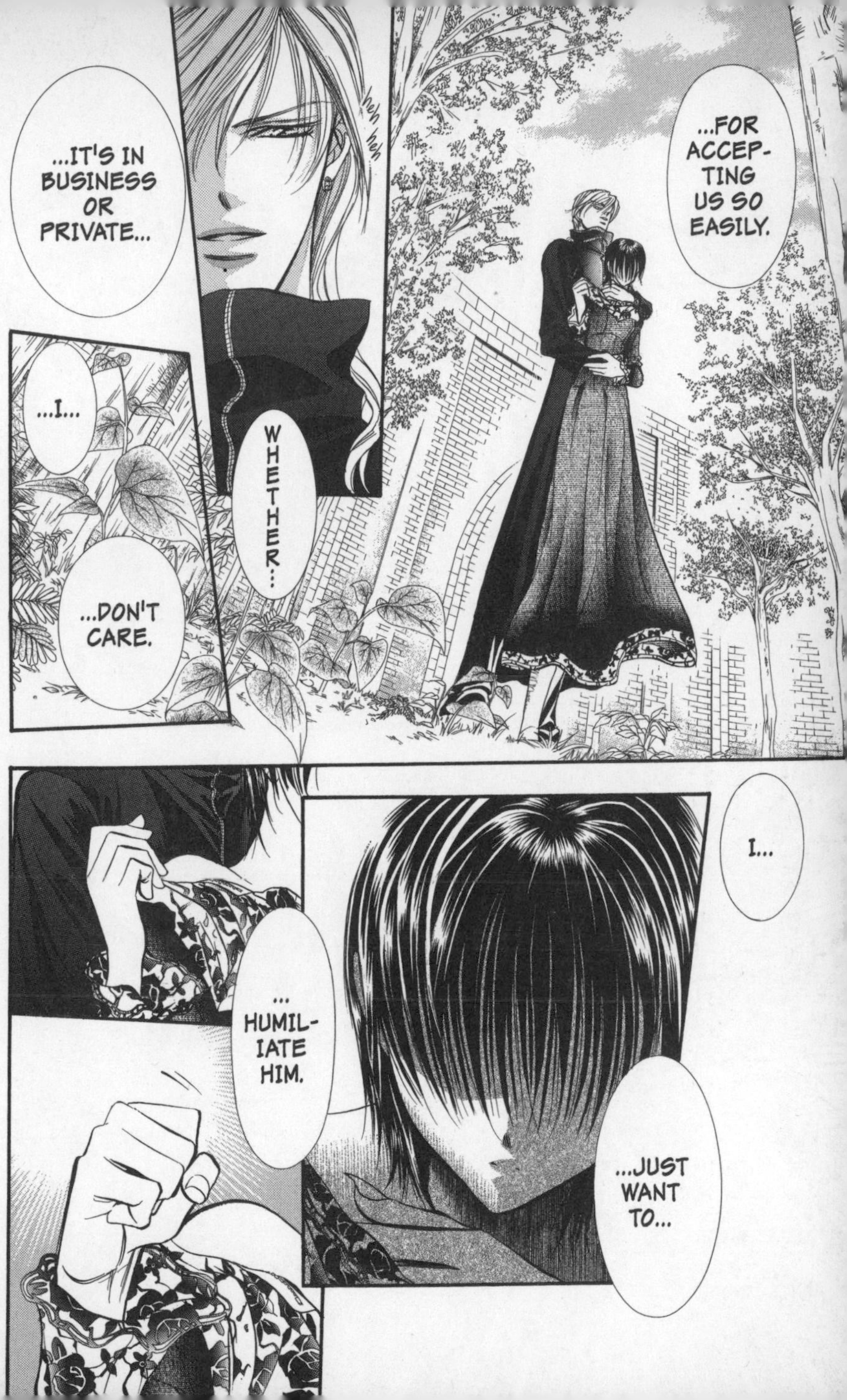

...FOR ACCEPTING US SO EASILY.
heh heh
WHETHER...
...IT'S IN BUSINESS OR PRIVATE...
...I...
...DON'T CARE.
I...
...JUST WANT TO...
... HUMILIATE HIM.

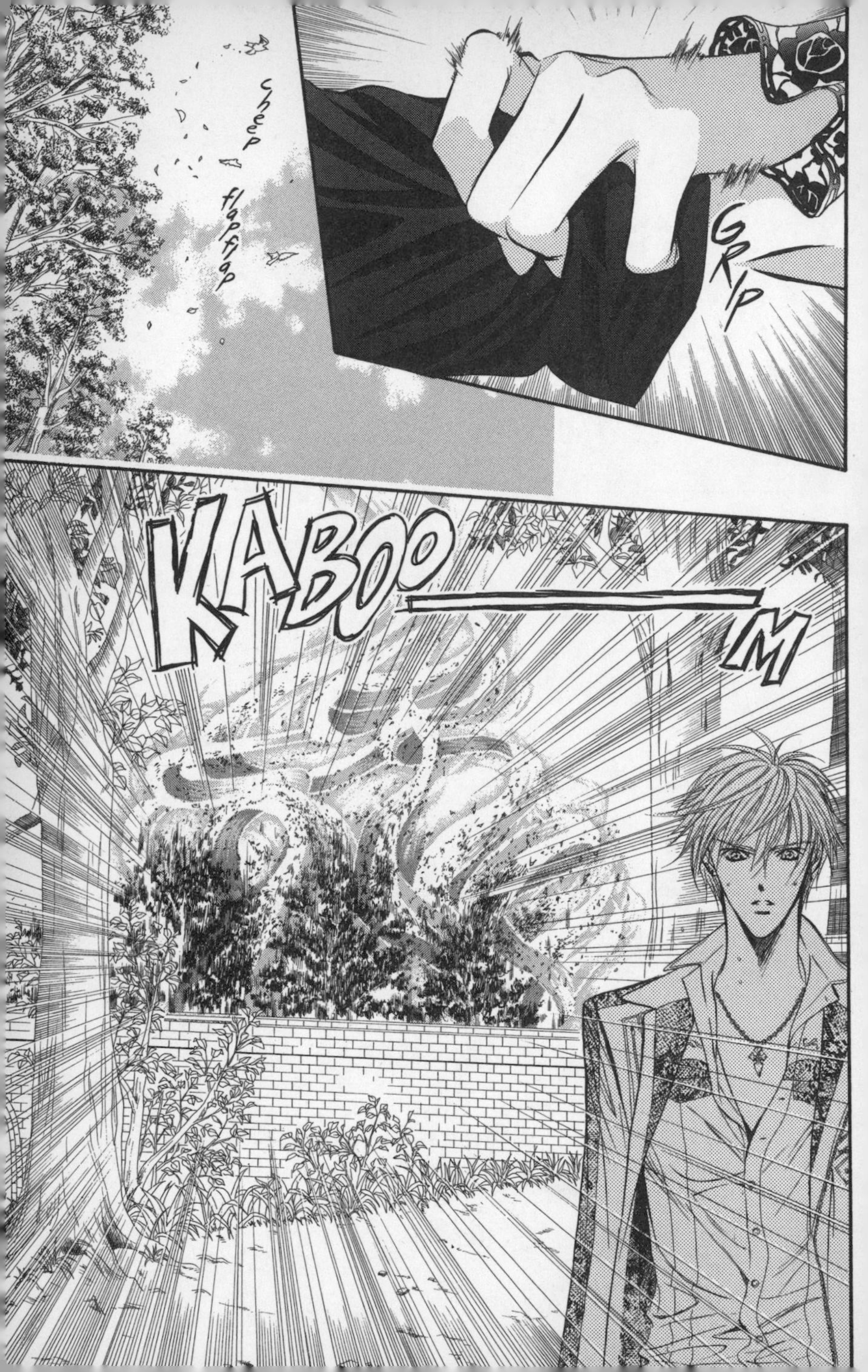
GRIP
Cheep
flapflap
KABOO—M

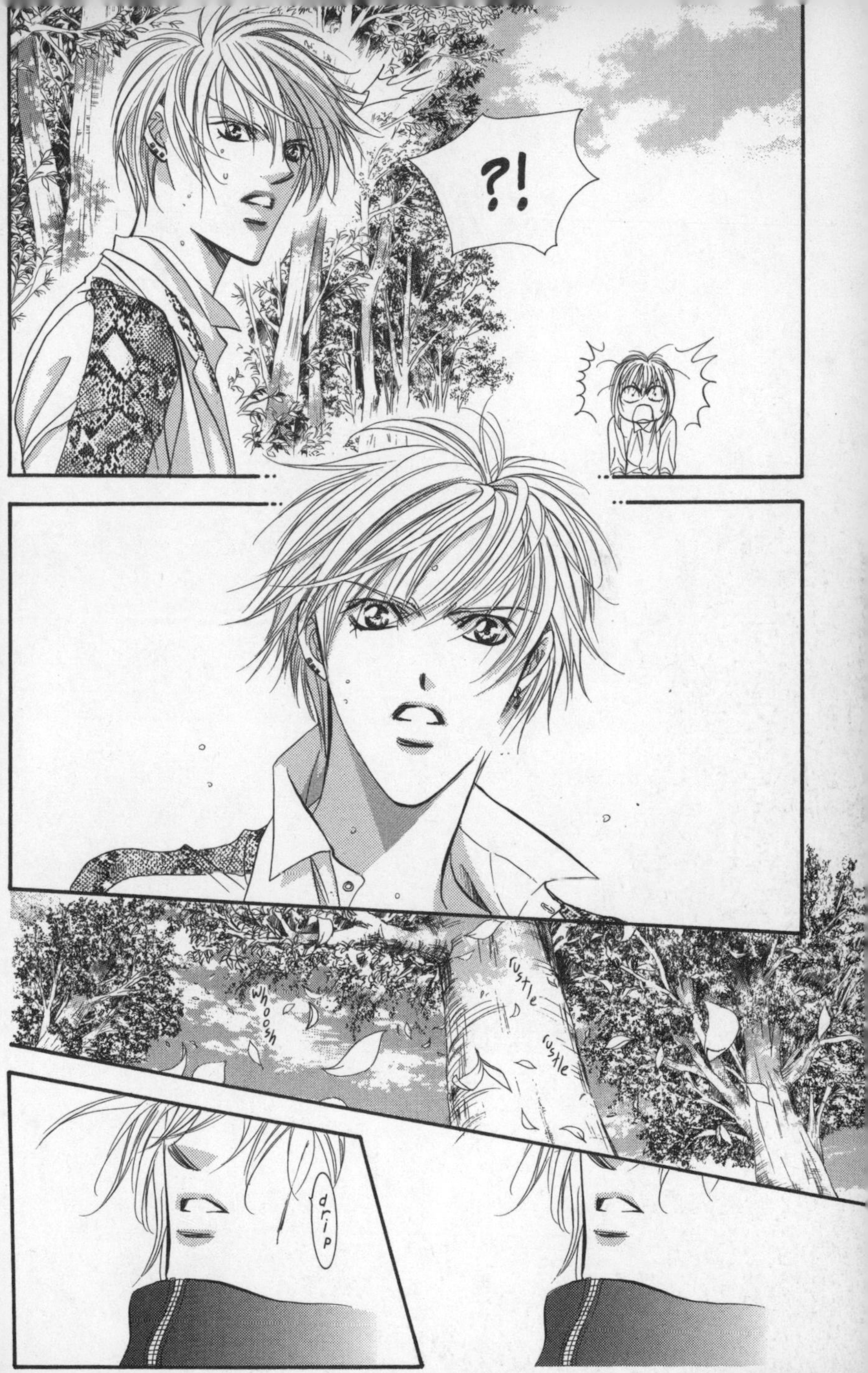
?!
whoosh
rustle
rustle
drip

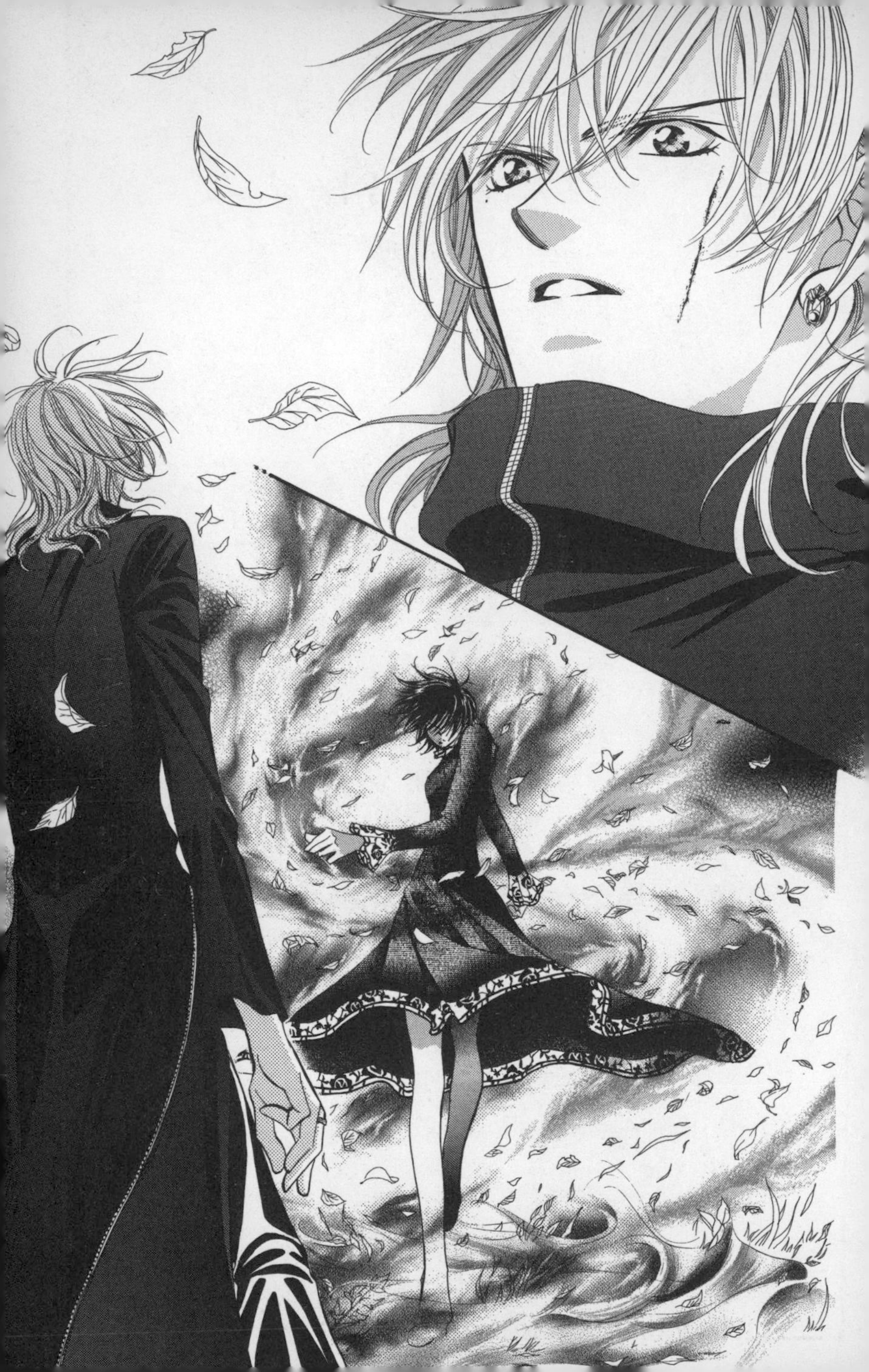

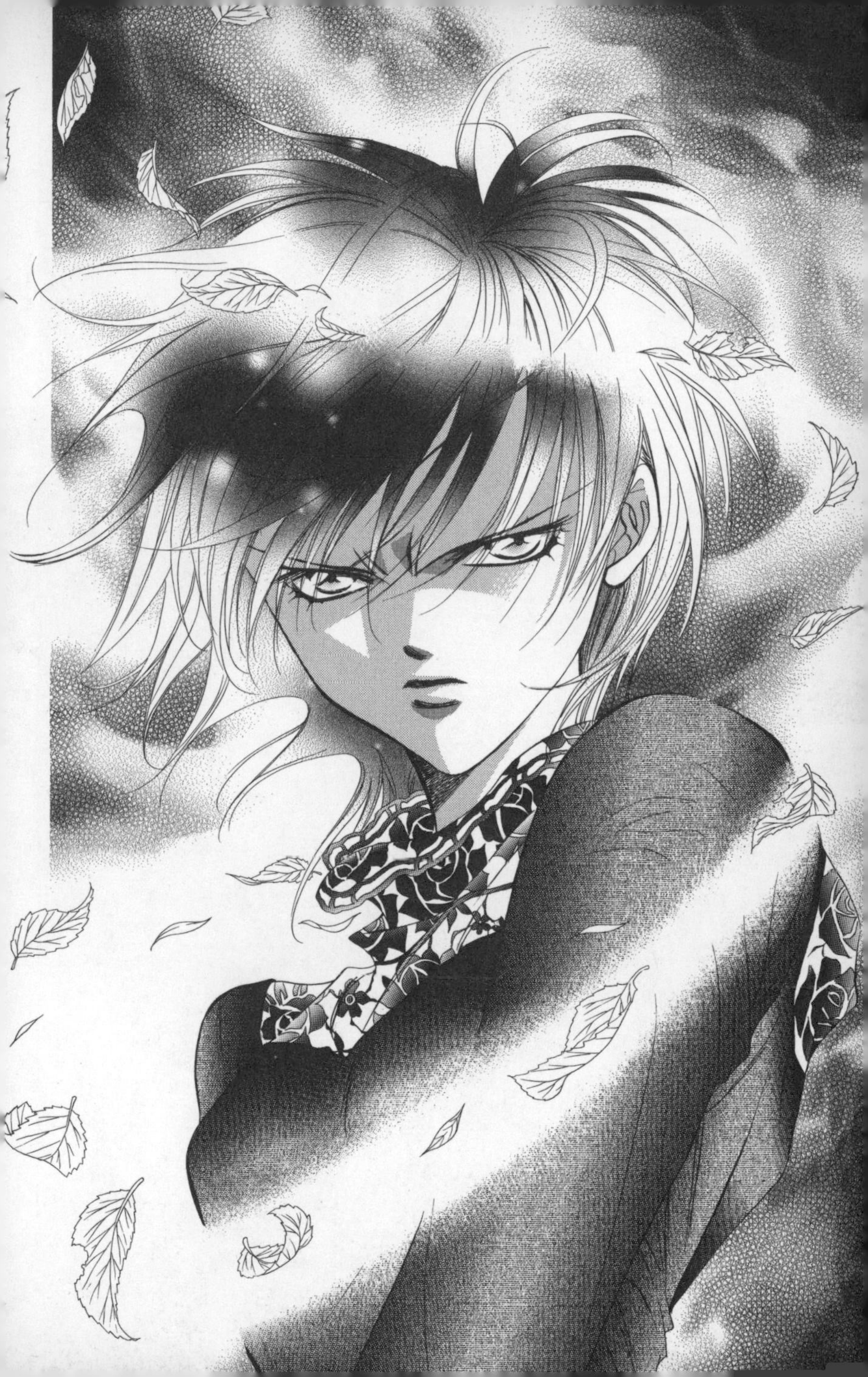

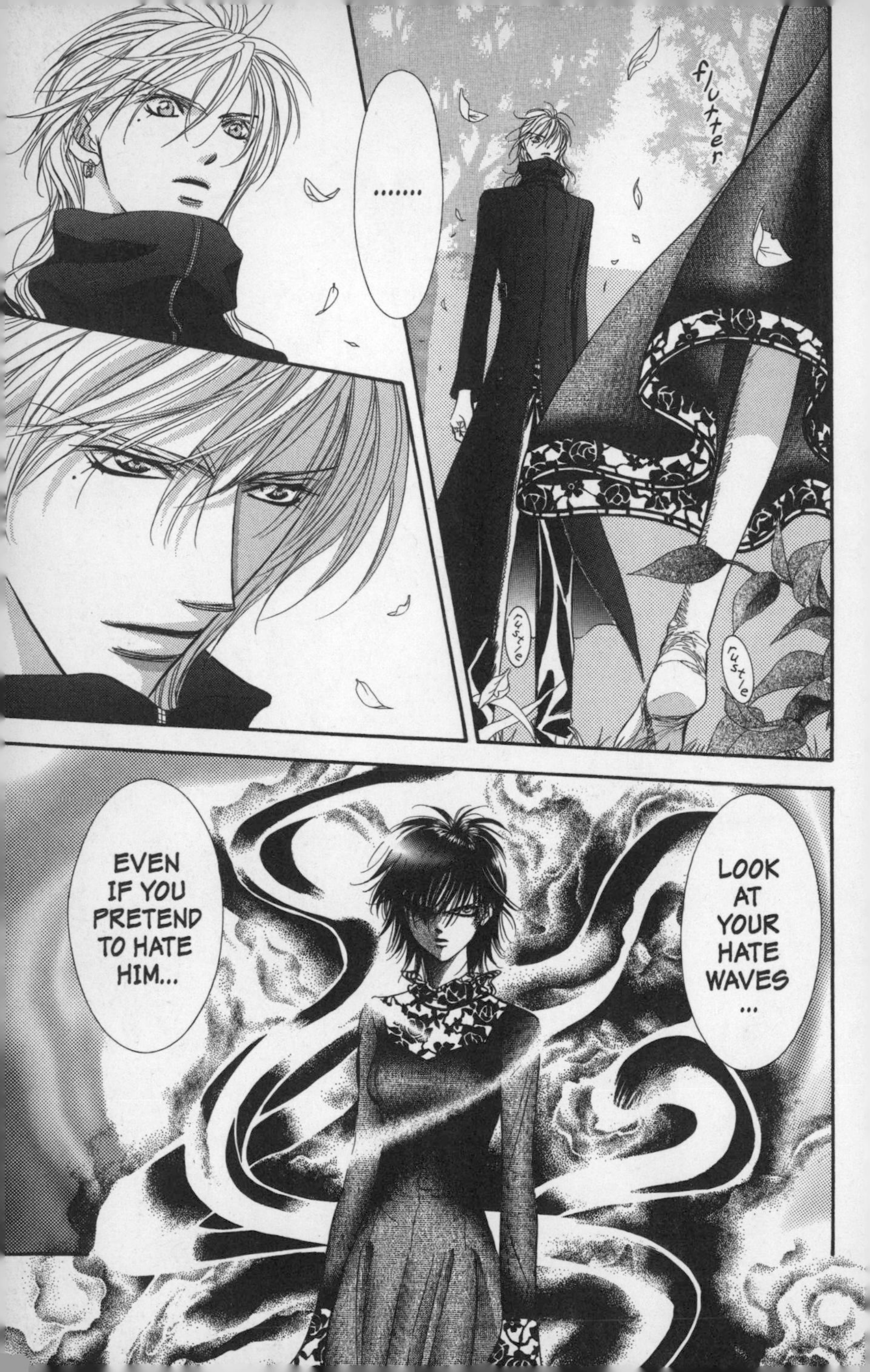
flutter
....
rustle
rustle
LOOK AT YOUR HATE WAVES ...
EVEN IF YOU PRETEND TO HATE HIM...

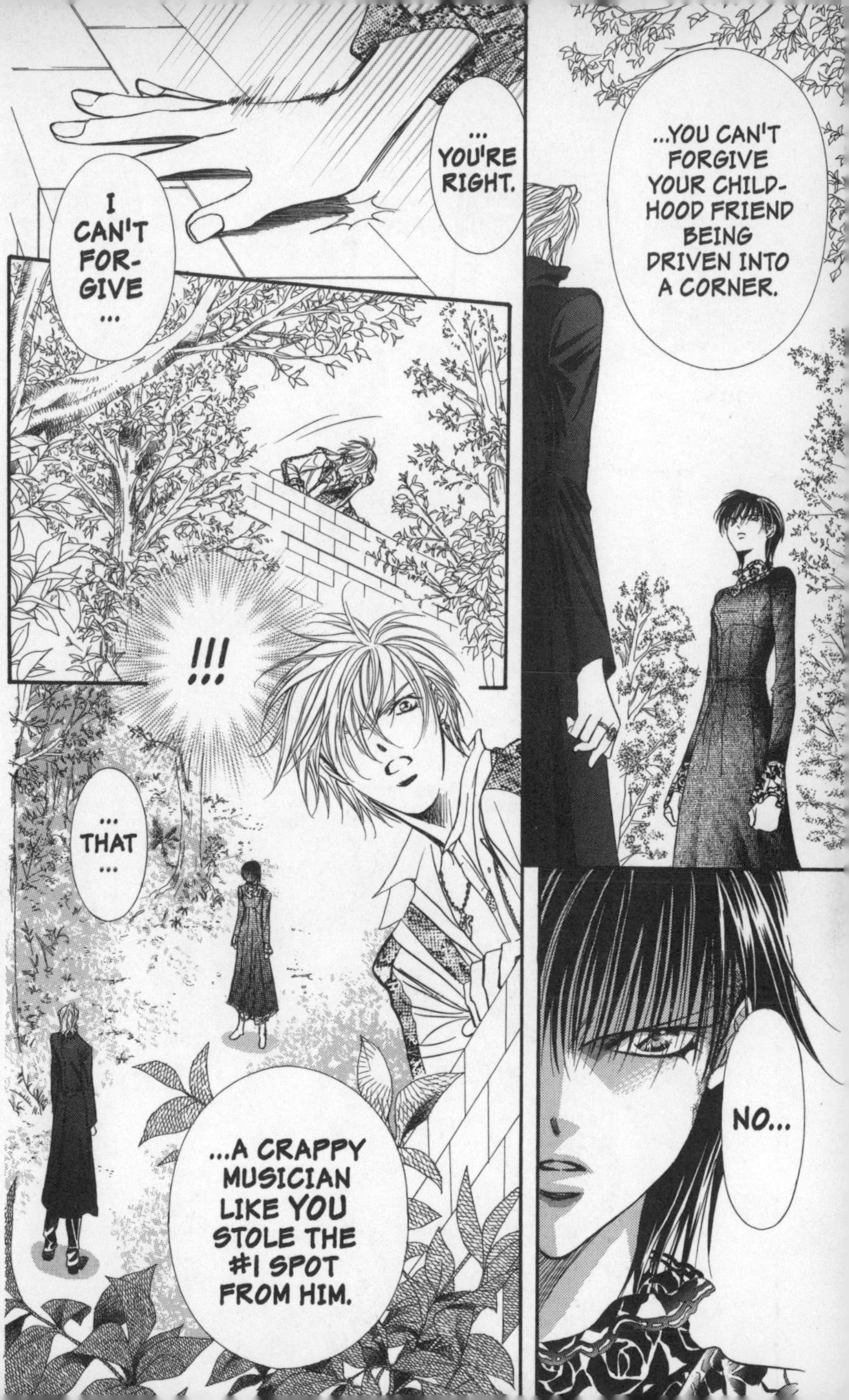
...YOU CAN'T FORGIVE YOUR CHILDHOOD FRIEND BEING DRIVEN INTO A CORNER.
NO...
... YOU'RE RIGHT.
I CAN'T FORGIVE ...
!!!
... THAT ...
...A CRAPPY MUSICIAN LIKE YOU STOLE THE #1 SPOT FROM HIM.

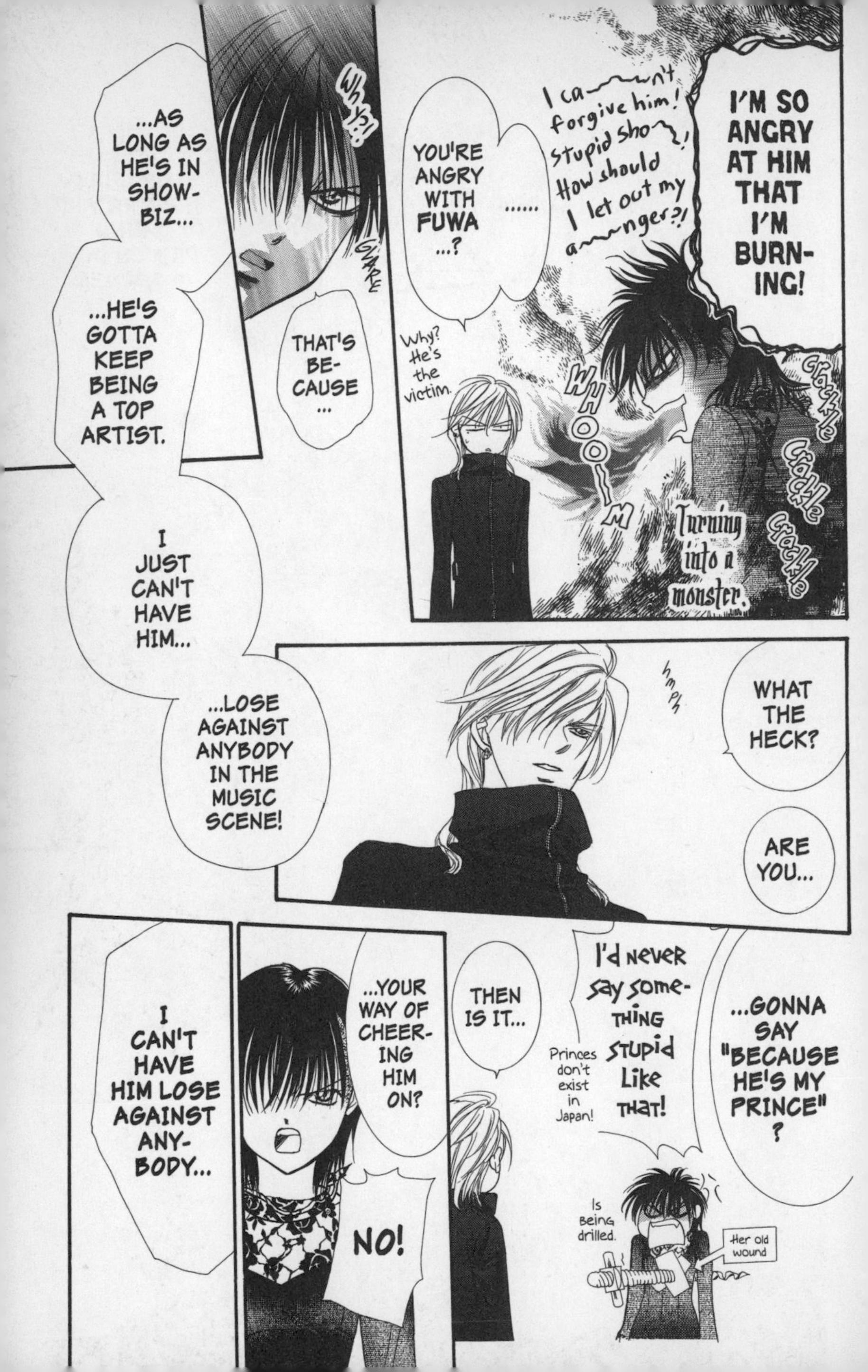
I'M SO ANGRY AT HIM THAT I'M BURNING!
I ca~~n't forgive him! Stupid Sho~! How should I let out my a~~nger?!
WHOO~M
Crackle
Crackle
Crackle
Turning into a monster.
Why? He's the victim.
......
YOU'RE ANGRY WITH FUWA ...?
THAT'S BE-CAUSE ...
Why?!
GLARE
...AS LONG AS HE'S IN SHOW-BIZ...
...HE'S GOTTA KEEP BEING A TOP ARTIST.
I JUST CAN'T HAVE HIM...
...LOSE AGAINST ANYBODY IN THE MUSIC SCENE!
WHAT THE HECK?
hmph
ARE YOU...
...GONNA SAY "BECAUSE HE'S MY PRINCE"?
I'd never say some-thing stupid like that!
Princes don't exist in Japan!
Is being drilled.
Her old wound
THEN IS IT...
...YOUR WAY OF CHEER-ING HIM ON?
NO!
I CAN'T HAVE HIM LOSE AGAINST ANY-BODY...

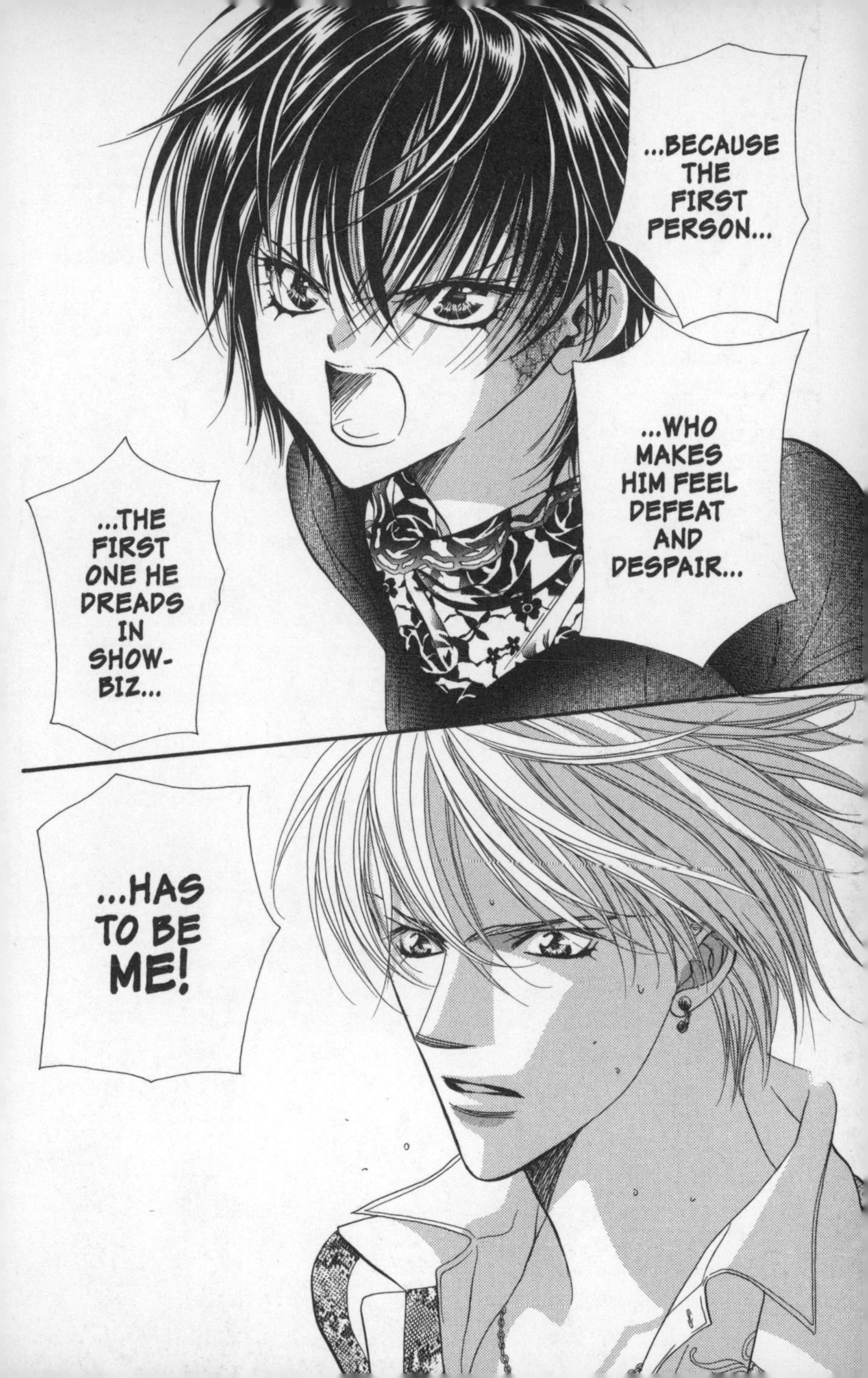
...BECAUSE THE FIRST PERSON...
...WHO MAKES HIM FEEL DEFEAT AND DESPAIR...
...THE FIRST ONE HE DREADS IN SHOW-BIZ...
...HAS TO BE ME!

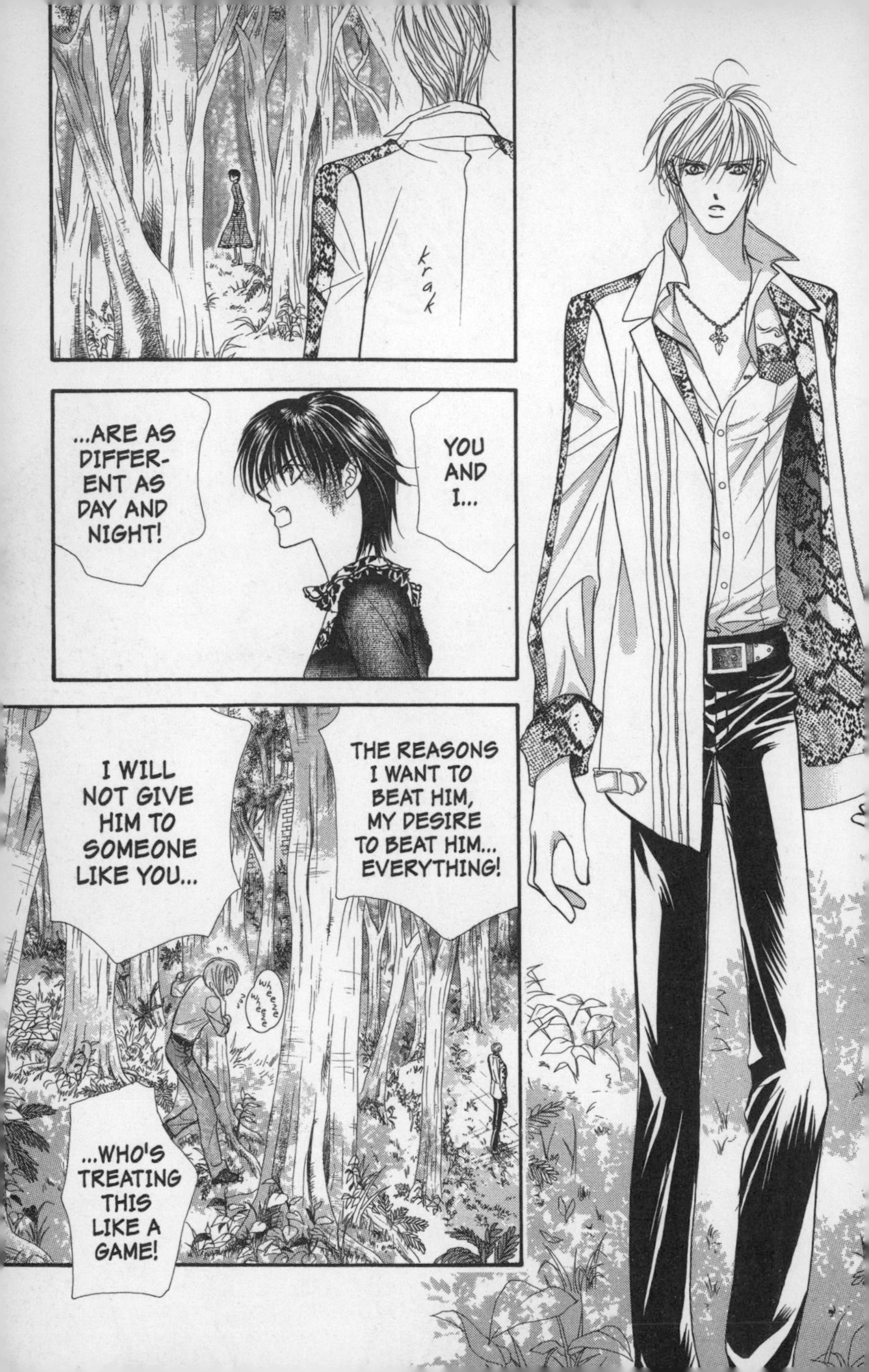
krak
YOU AND I...
...ARE AS DIFFERENT AS DAY AND NIGHT!
THE REASONS I WANT TO BEAT HIM, MY DESIRE TO BEAT HIM... EVERYTHING!
I WILL NOT GIVE HIM TO SOMEONE LIKE YOU...
wheeze wheeze
...WHO'S TREATING THIS LIKE A GAME!

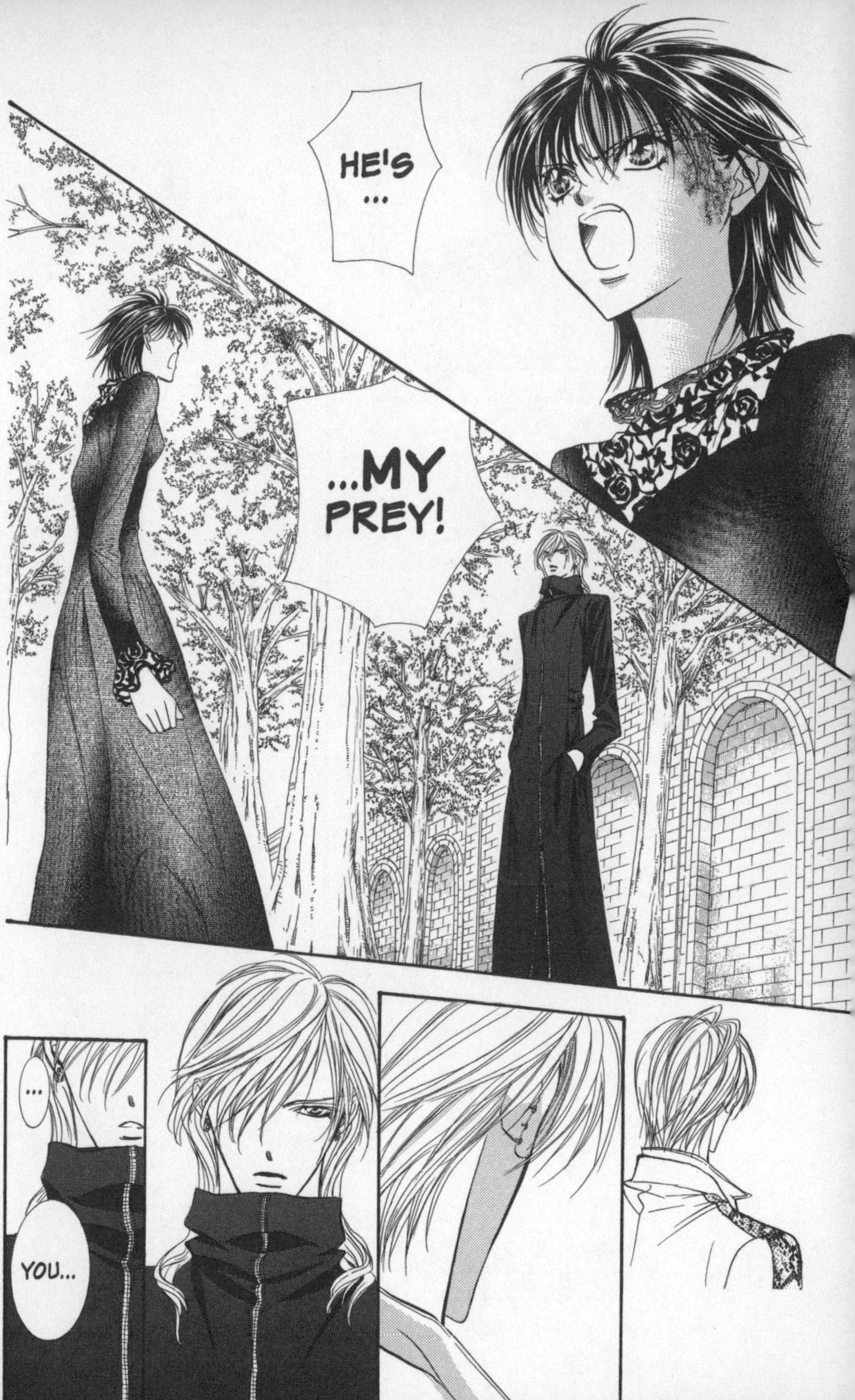
HE'S ...
...MY PREY!
...
YOU...

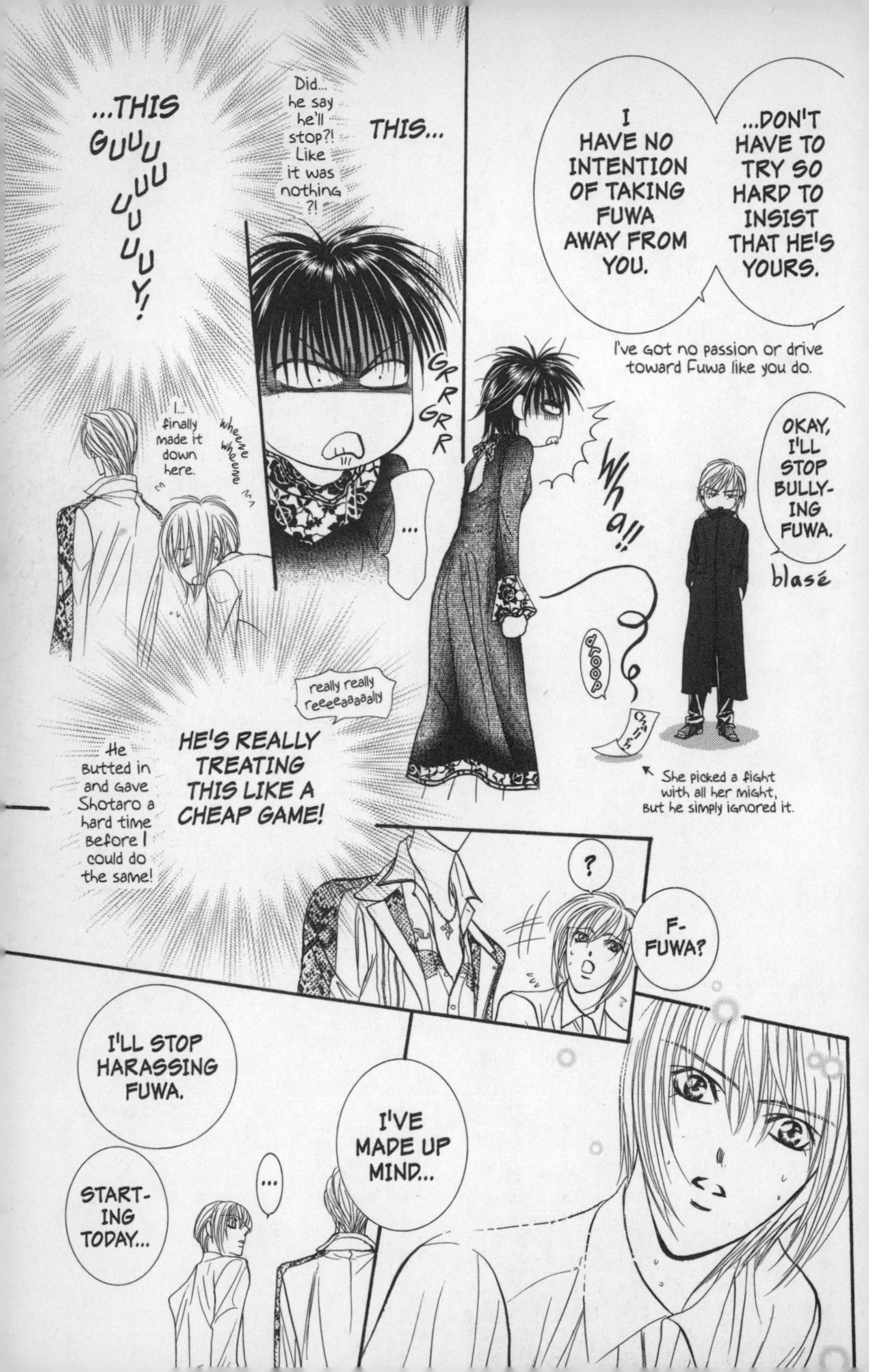
I HAVE NO INTENTION OF TAKING FUWA AWAY FROM YOU.
...DON'T HAVE TO TRY SO HARD TO INSIST THAT HE'S YOURS.
I've got no passion or drive toward Fuwa like you do.
OKAY, I'LL STOP BULLY-ING FUWA.
blasé
Wha!!
droop
She picked a fight with all her might, but he simply ignored it.
Did... he say he'll stop?! Like it was nothing?!
THIS...
GRR GRR
...
...THIS GUUUUUUUUUY!
I... finally made it down here.
wheeze wheeze
really really reeeeaaaally
HE'S REALLY TREATING THIS LIKE A CHEAP GAME!
He butted in and gave Shotaro a hard time before I could do the same!
?
F-FUWA?
I'VE MADE UP MIND...
I'LL STOP HARASSING FUWA.
START-ING TODAY...
...

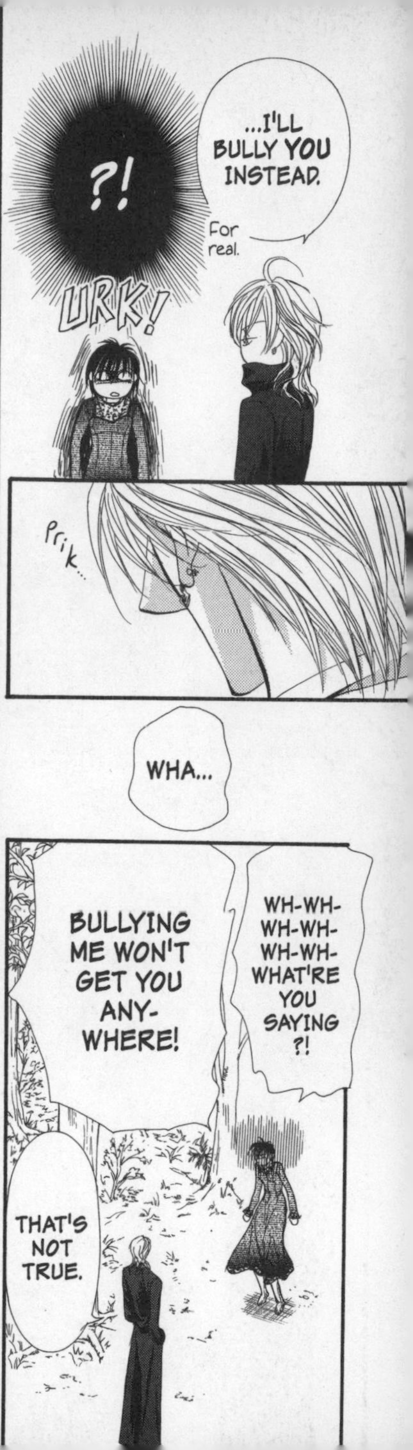
...I'LL BULLY YOU INSTEAD.
For real.
?!
URK!
Prik...
WHA...
WH-WH-WH-WH-WH-WH-WHAT'RE YOU SAYING?!
BULLYING ME WON'T GET YOU ANYWHERE!
THAT'S NOT TRUE.
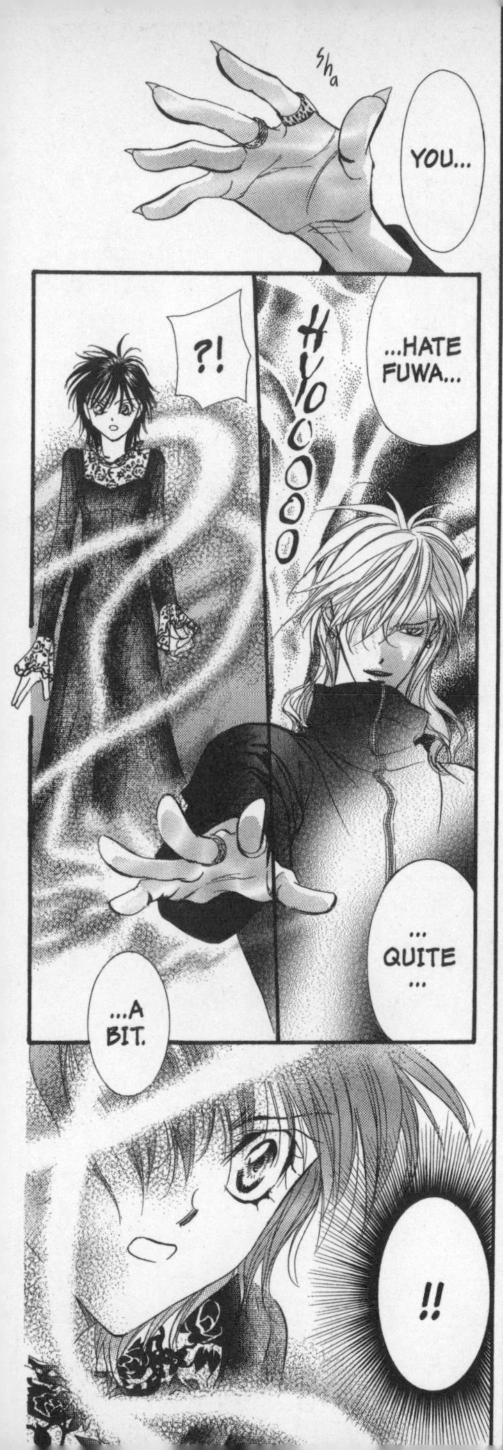
YOU...
Sha
HYOOOOOO
...HATE FUWA...
... QUITE ...
?!
...A BIT.
!!

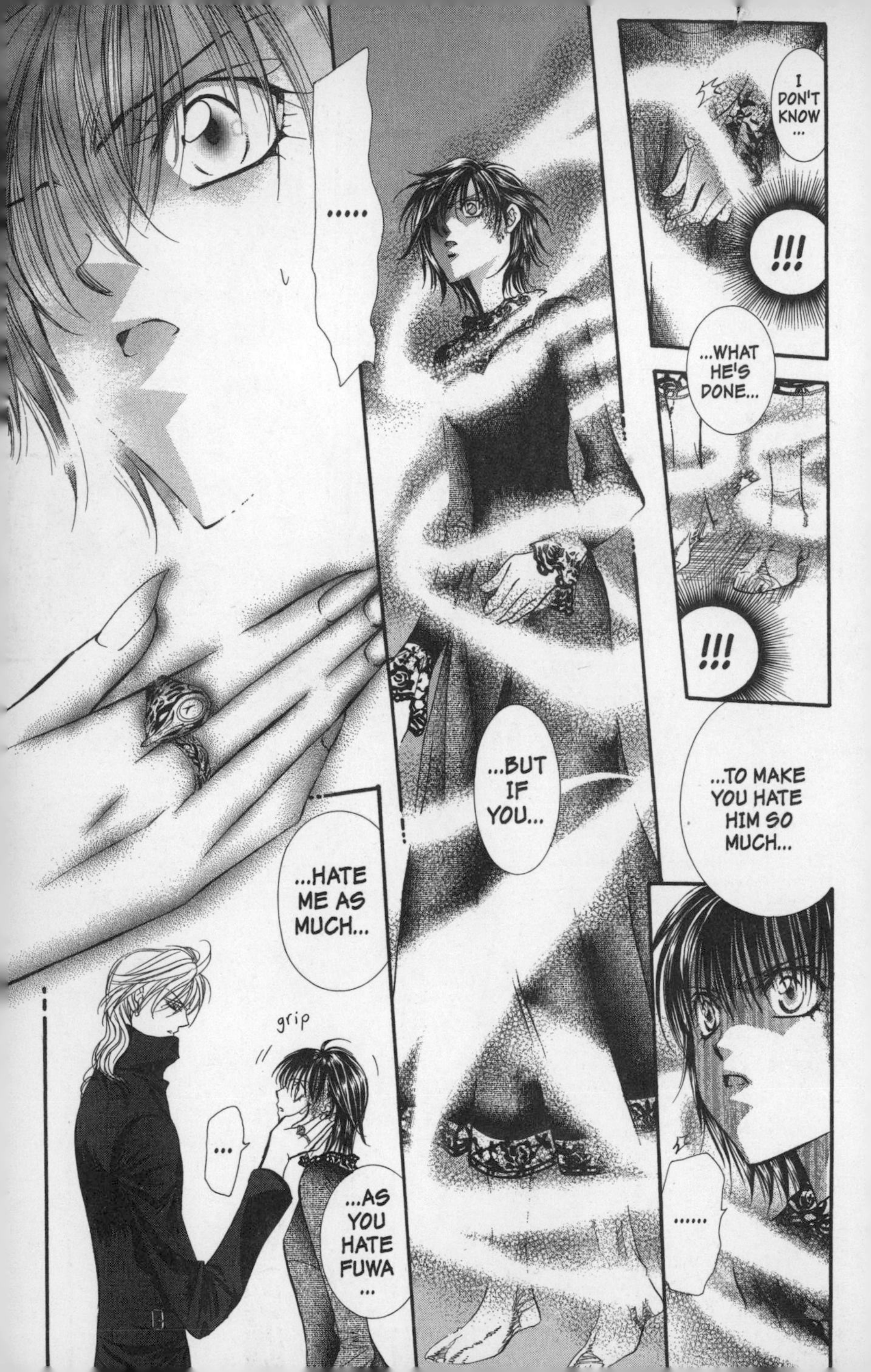
I DON'T KNOW ...
!!!
...WHAT HE'S DONE...
!!!
...TO MAKE YOU HATE HIM SO MUCH...
......
...BUT IF YOU...
......
...HATE ME AS MUCH...
grip
...
...AS YOU HATE FUWA ...

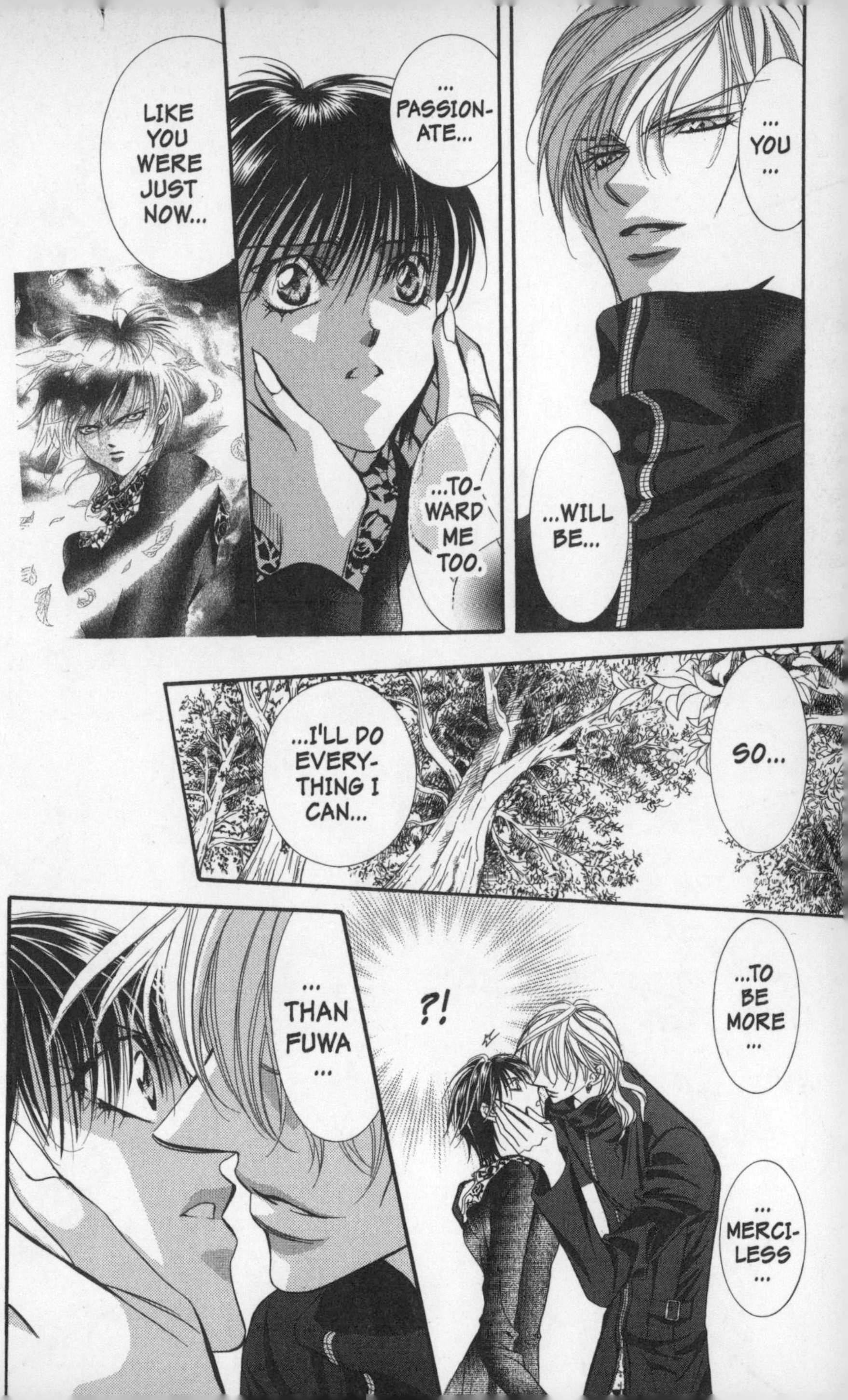
... YOU ...
...WILL BE...
... PASSION-ATE...
...TO-WARD ME TOO.
LIKE YOU WERE JUST NOW...
SO...
...I'LL DO EVERY-THING I CAN...
...TO BE MORE ...
... MERCI-LESS ...
?!
... THAN FUWA ...

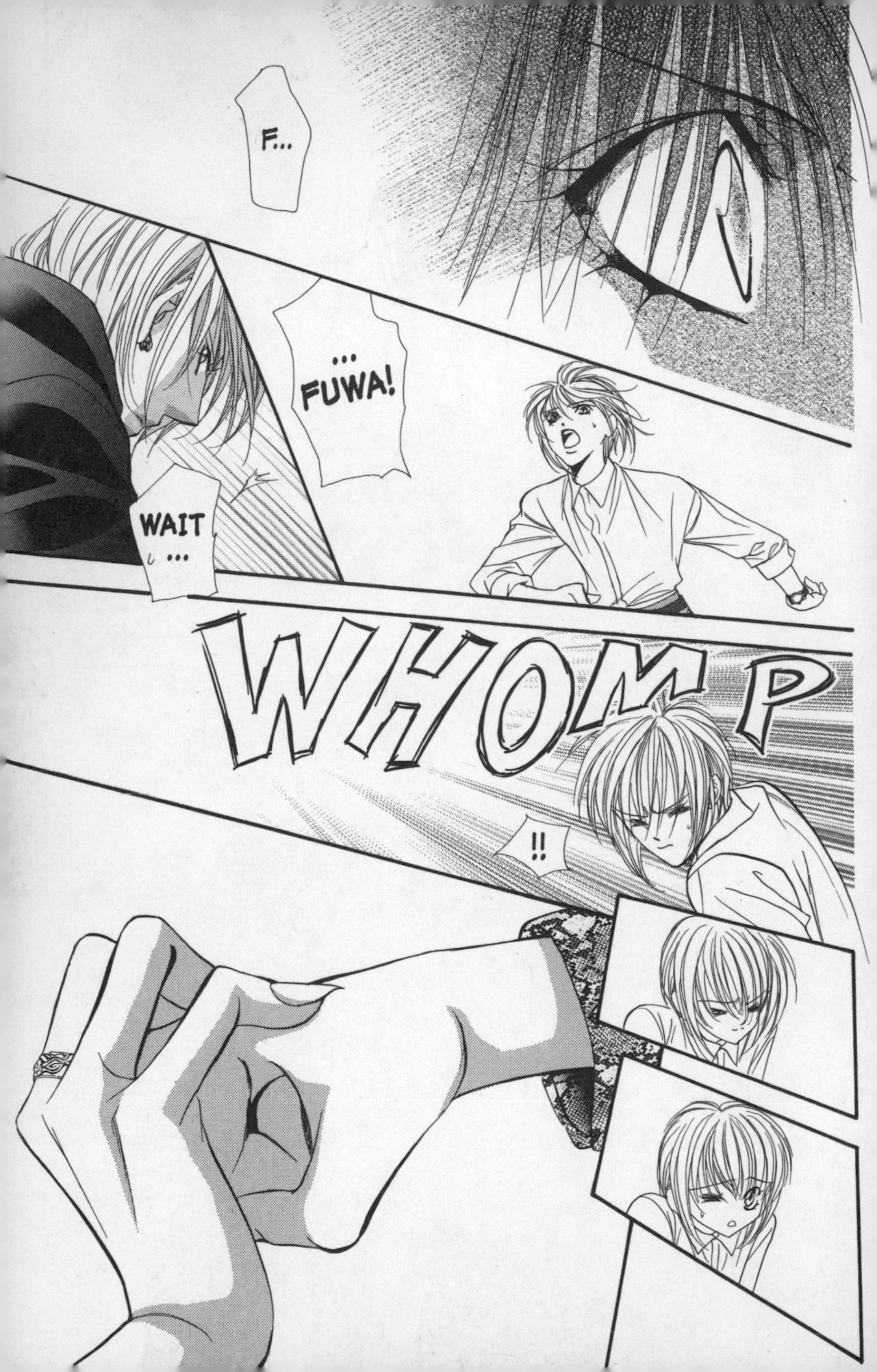
F...
...FUWA!
WAIT ...
WHOMP
!!

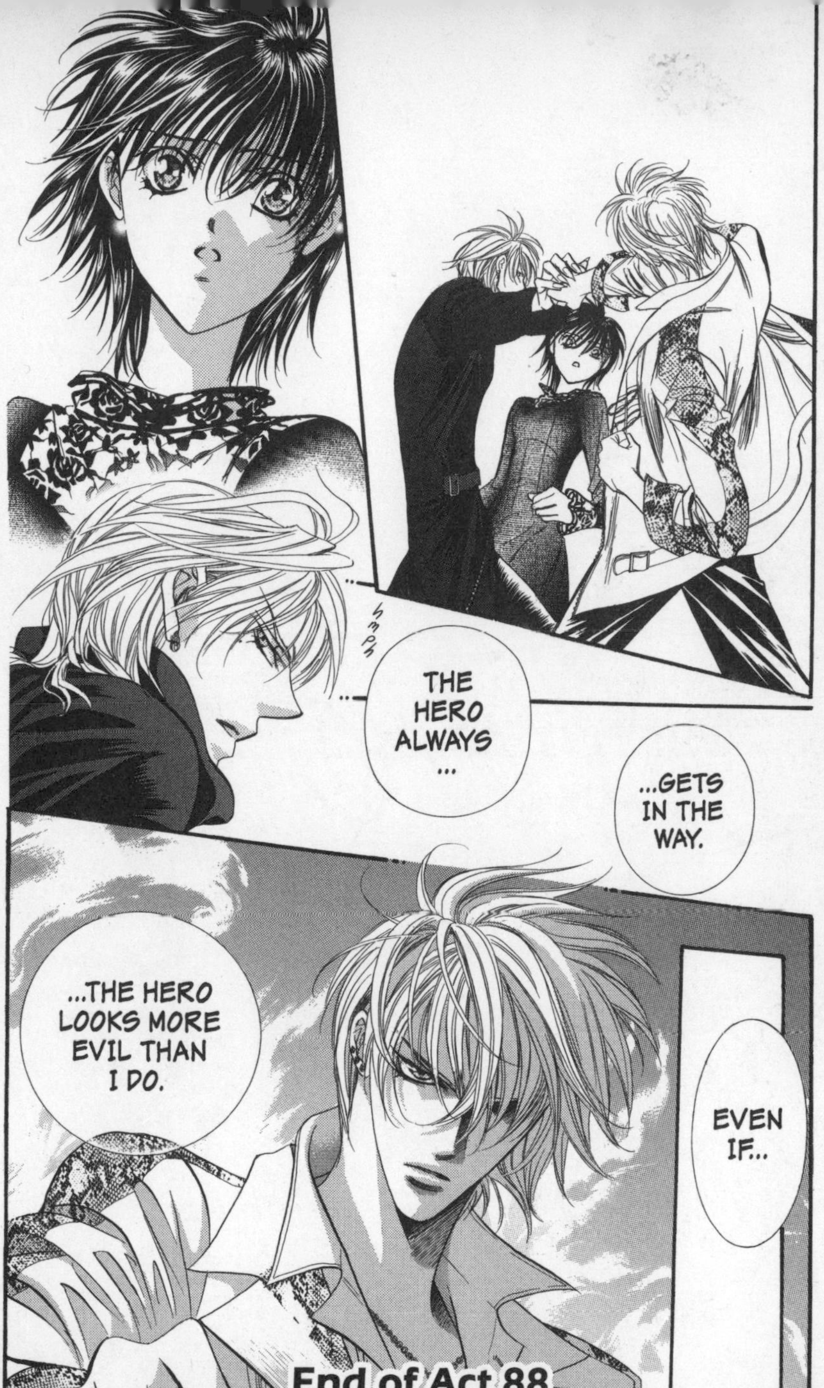
smph
THE HERO ALWAYS ...
...GETS IN THE WAY.
EVEN IF...
...THE HERO LOOKS MORE EVIL THAN I DO.
End of Act 88

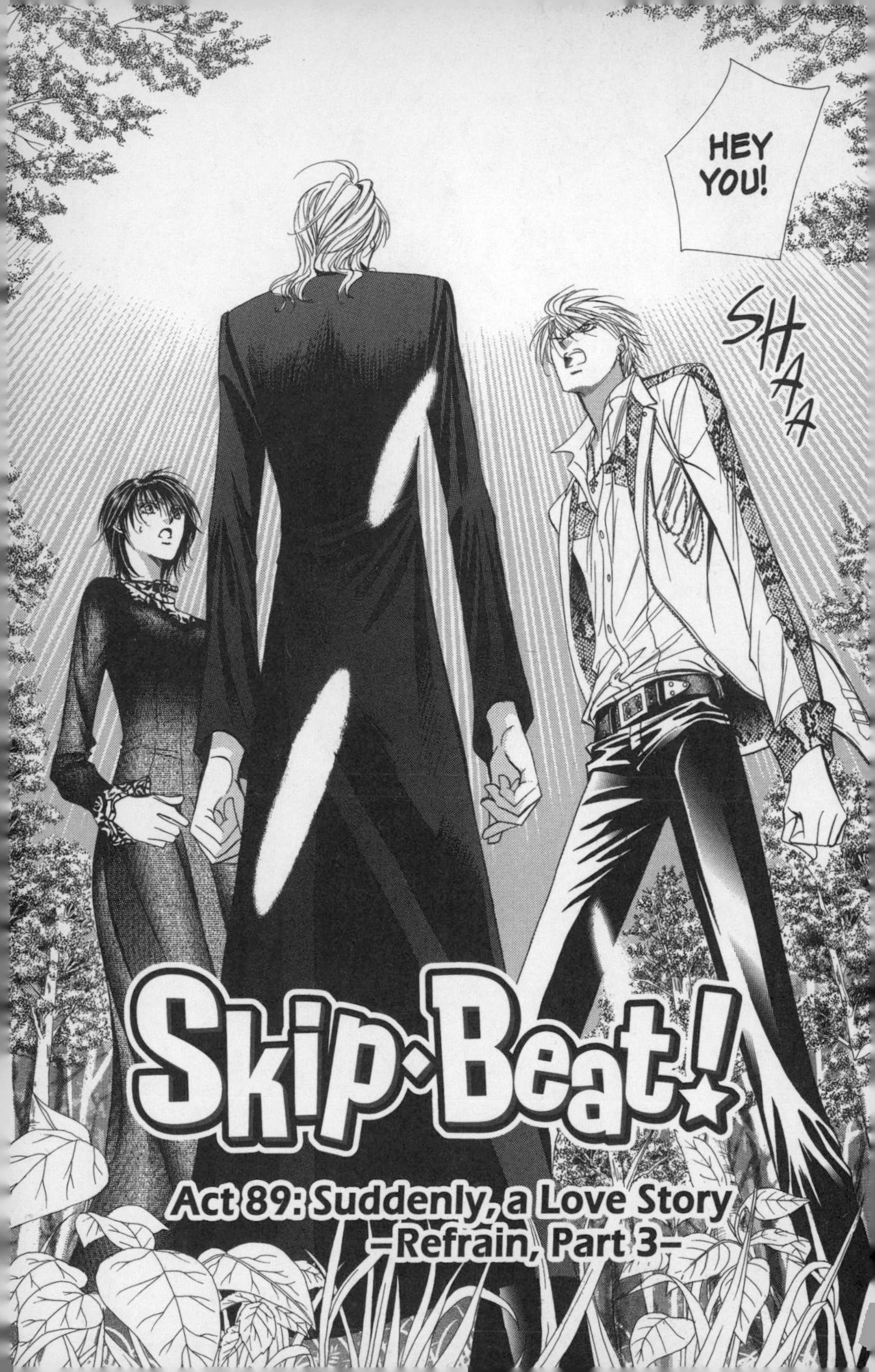
HEY YOU!
SHAA
Skip·Beat!
Act 89: Suddenly, a Love Story
-Refrain, Part 3-

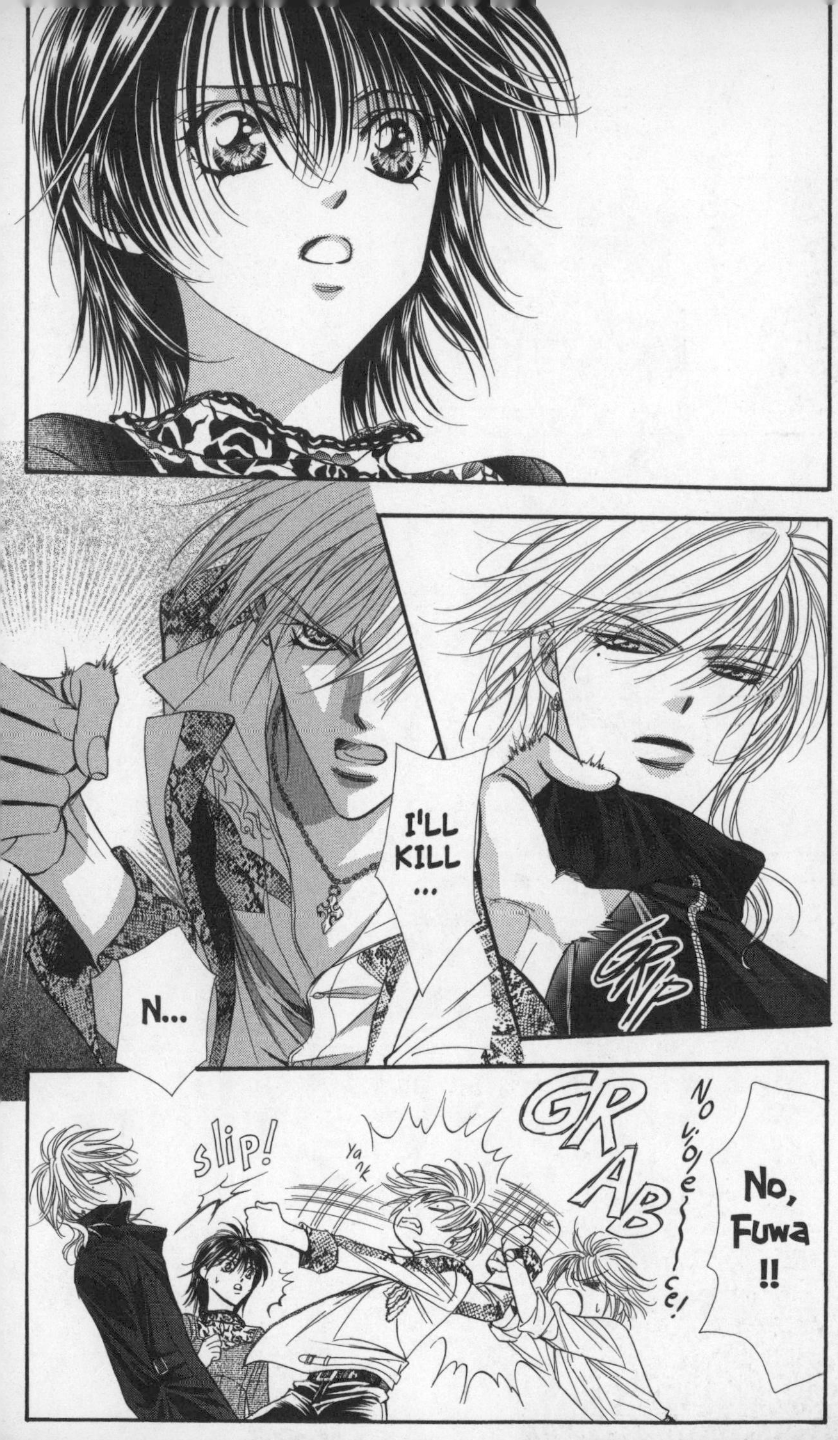
GRIP
I'LL KILL ...
N...
No, Fuwa !!
No violence!
GRAB
yank
slip!

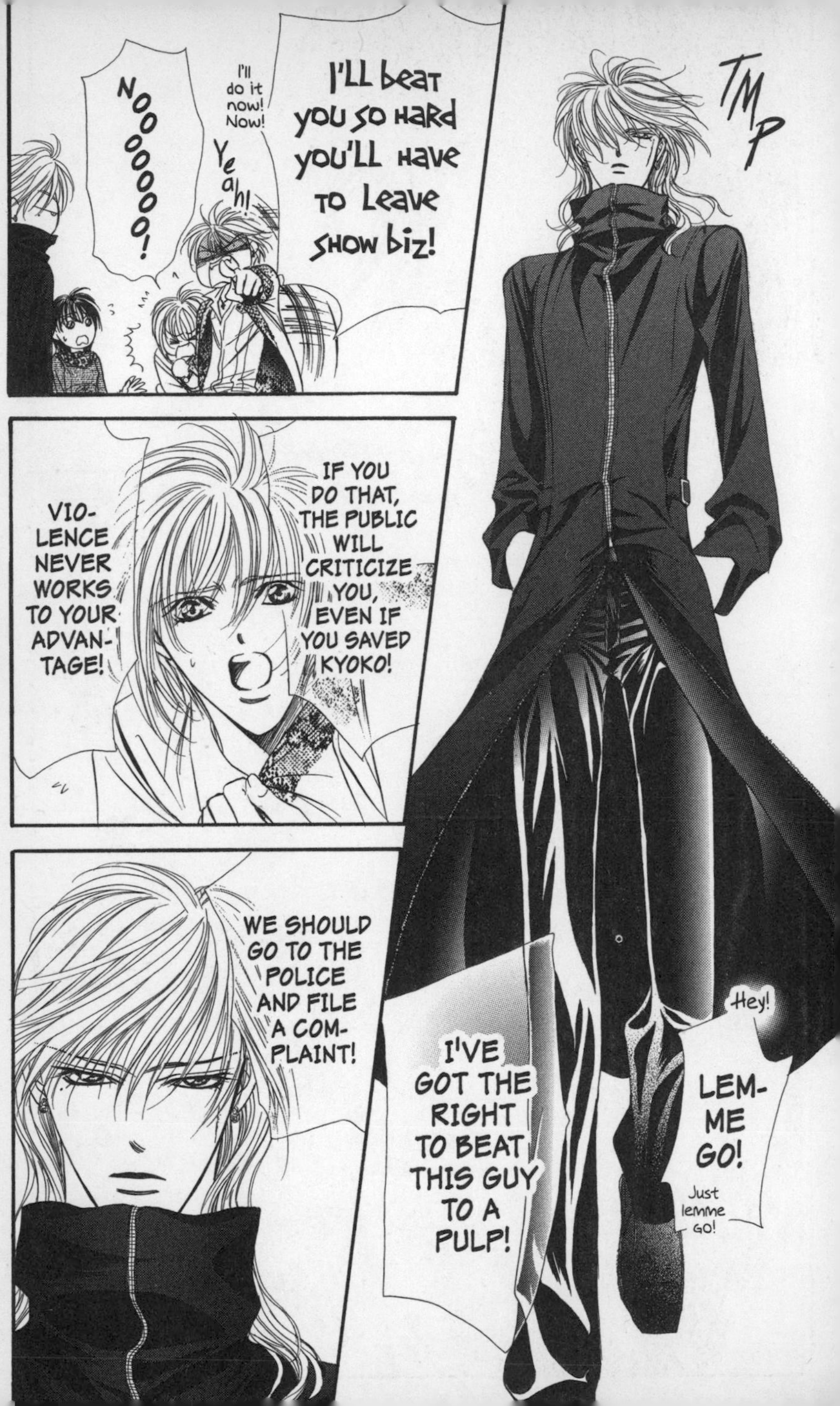
TMP
Hey!
LEM-ME GO!
Just lemme GO!
I'VE GOT THE RIGHT TO BEAT THIS GUY TO A PULP!
I'LL beat you so hard you'LL have to Leave show biz!
I'll do it now! Now!
Yeah!
NOOOOOOOO!
IF YOU DO THAT, THE PUBLIC WILL CRITICIZE YOU, EVEN IF YOU SAVED KYOKO!
VIO-LENCE NEVER WORKS TO YOUR ADVAN-TAGE!
WE SHOULD GO TO THE POLICE AND FILE A COM-PLAINT!

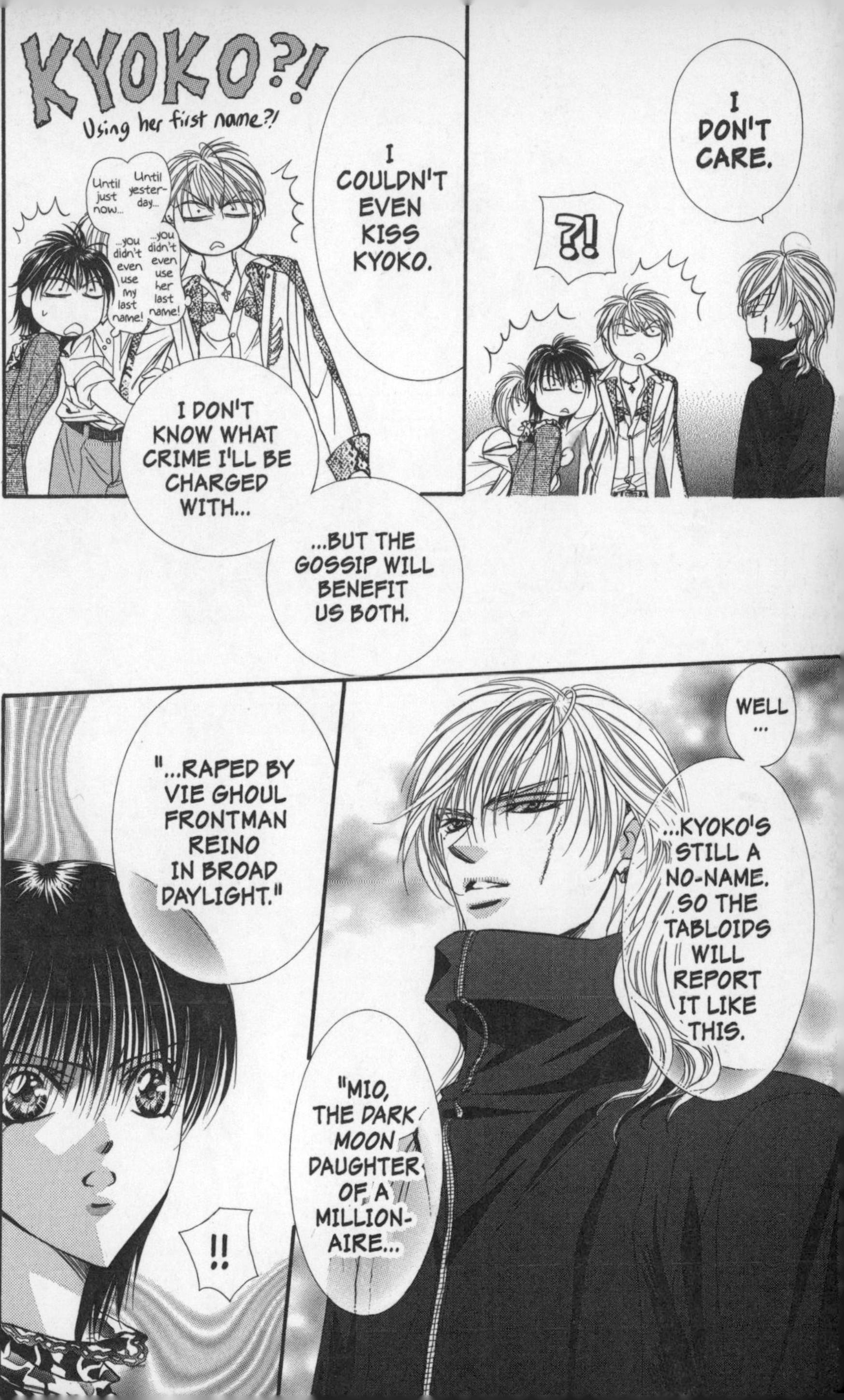
I DON'T CARE.
?!
I COULDN'T EVEN KISS KYOKO.
KYOKO?!
Using her first name?!
Until yesterday... ...you didn't even use her last name!
Until just now... ...you didn't even use my last name!
I DON'T KNOW WHAT CRIME I'LL BE CHARGED WITH...
...BUT THE GOSSIP WILL BENEFIT US BOTH.
WELL...
...KYOKO'S STILL A NO-NAME. SO THE TABLOIDS WILL REPORT IT LIKE THIS.
"MIO, THE DARK MOON DAUGHTER OF A MILLIONAIRE...
"...RAPED BY VIE GHOUL FRONTMAN REINO IN BROAD DAYLIGHT."
!!

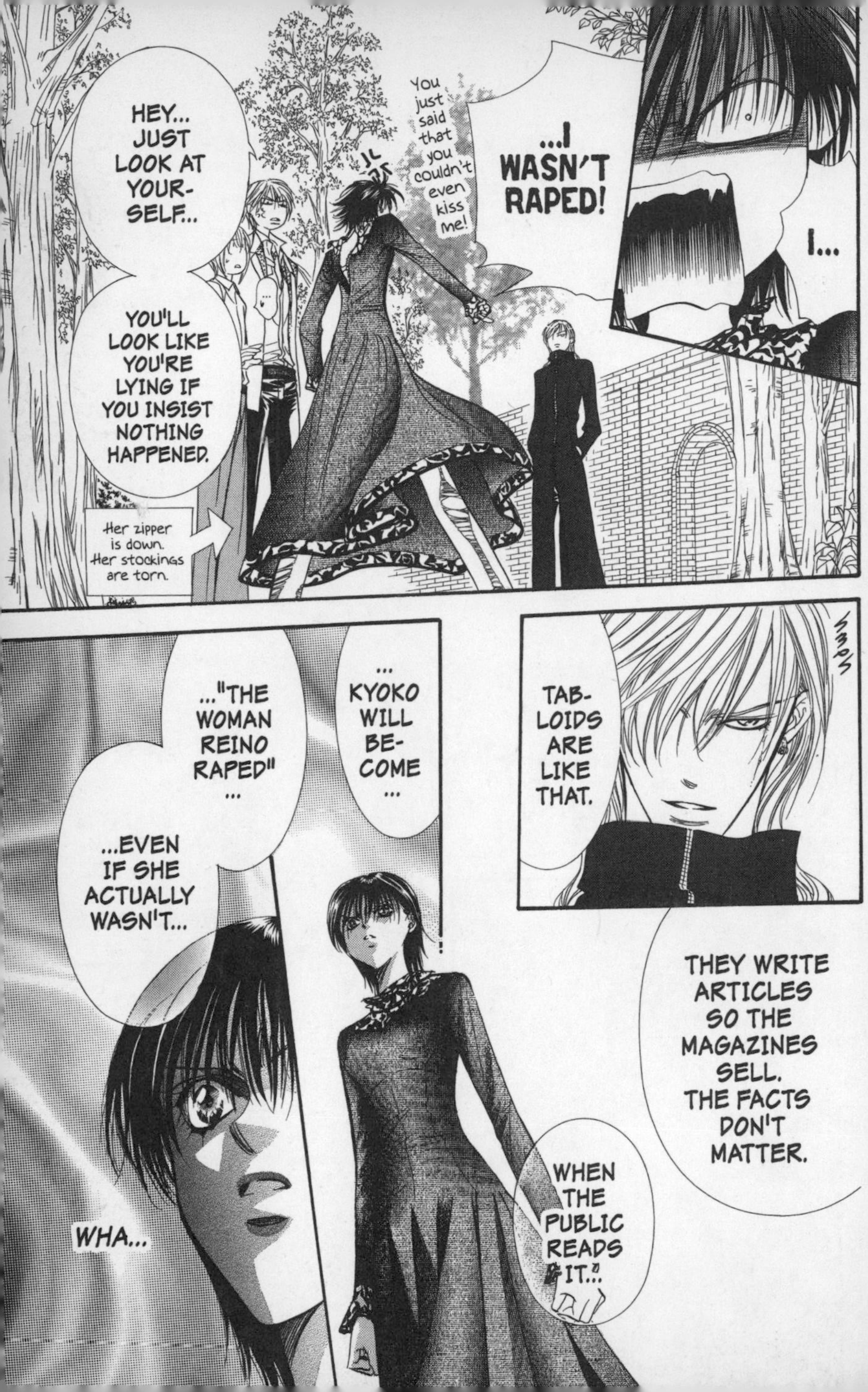
I...
...I WASN'T RAPED!
You just said that you couldn't even kiss me!
HEY... JUST LOOK AT YOURSELF...
YOU'LL LOOK LIKE YOU'RE LYING IF YOU INSIST NOTHING HAPPENED.
...
Her zipper is down. Her stockings are torn.
TABLOIDS ARE LIKE THAT.
THEY WRITE ARTICLES SO THE MAGAZINES SELL. THE FACTS DON'T MATTER.
WHEN THE PUBLIC READS IT...
...KYOKO WILL BECOME...
..."THE WOMAN REINO RAPED"...
...EVEN IF SHE ACTUALLY WASN'T...
WHA...

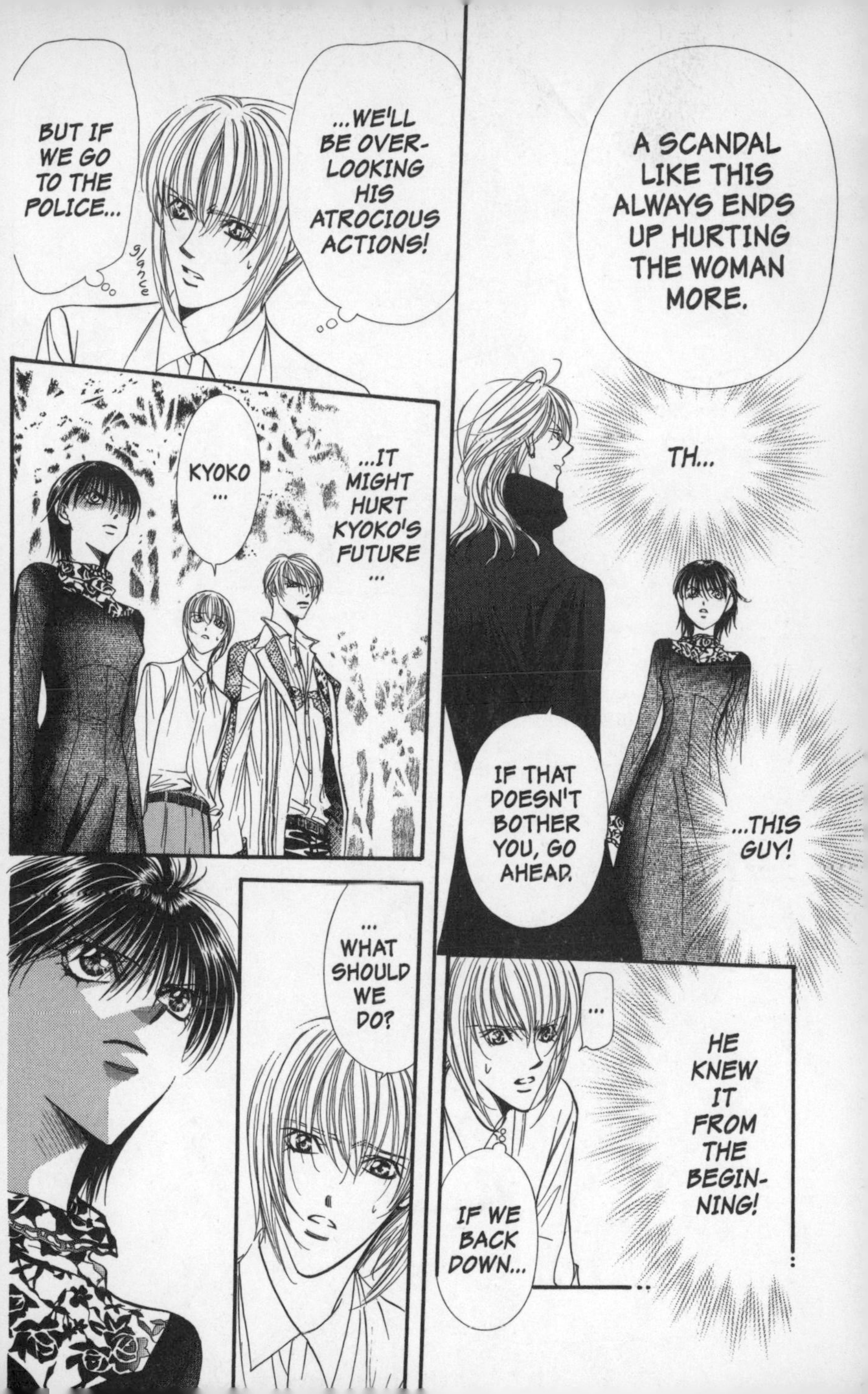
A SCANDAL LIKE THIS ALWAYS ENDS UP HURTING THE WOMAN MORE.
TH...
IF THAT DOESN'T BOTHER YOU, GO AHEAD.
...THIS GUY!
...
HE KNEW IT FROM THE BEGIN-NING!
IF WE BACK DOWN...
...WE'LL BE OVER-LOOKING HIS ATROCIOUS ACTIONS!
glance
BUT IF WE GO TO THE POLICE...
...IT MIGHT HURT KYOKO'S FUTURE...
KYOKO...
...WHAT SHOULD WE DO?

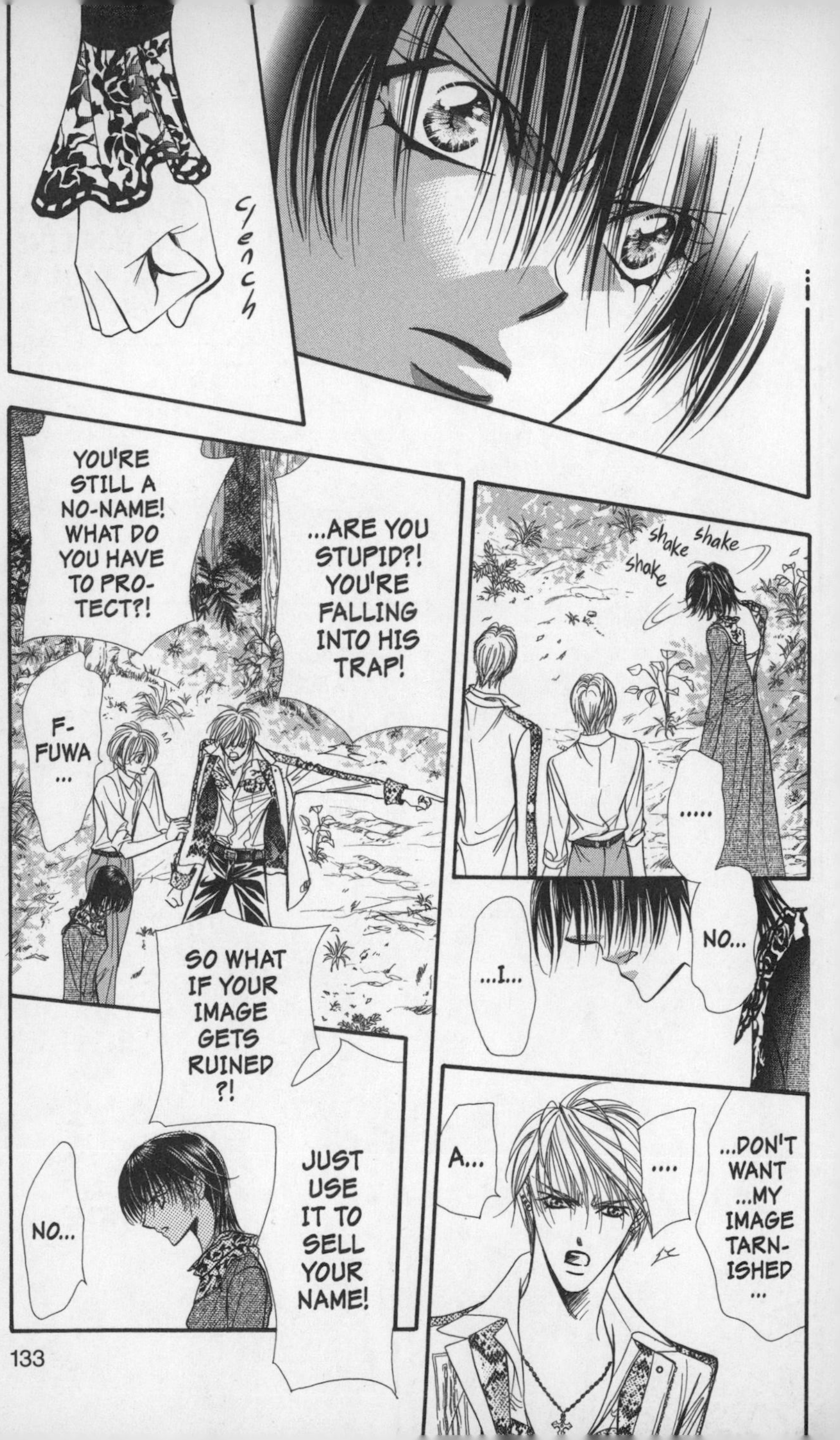
Clench
shake shake shake
.....
NO...
...I...
...ARE YOU STUPID?! YOU'RE FALLING INTO HIS TRAP!
YOU'RE STILL A NO-NAME! WHAT DO YOU HAVE TO PRO-TECT?!
F-FUWA...
SO WHAT IF YOUR IMAGE GETS RUINED?!
...DON'T WANT ...MY IMAGE TARN-ISHED...
....
A...
JUST USE IT TO SELL YOUR NAME!
NO...

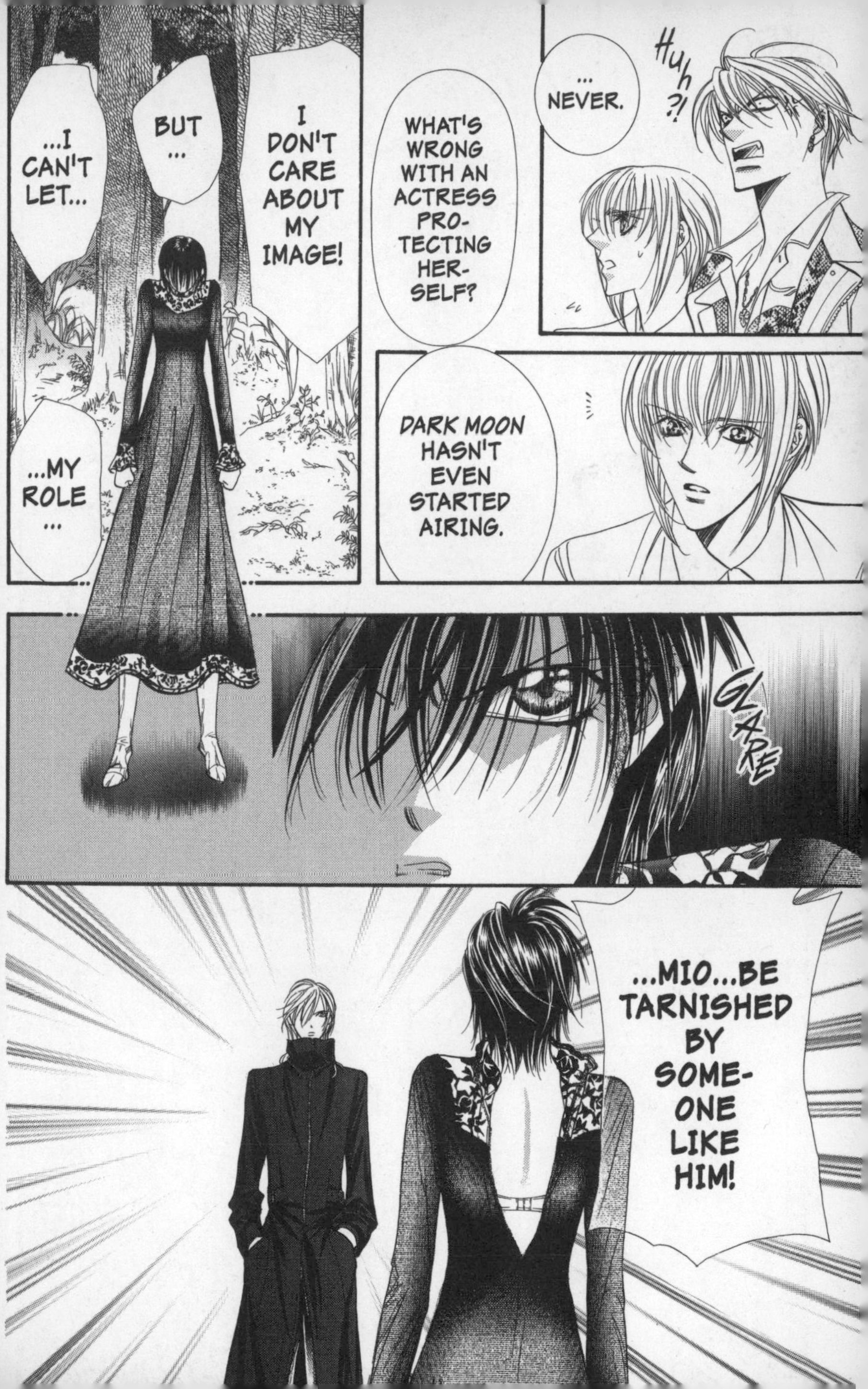
Huh ?!
... NEVER.
WHAT'S WRONG WITH AN ACTRESS PRO-TECTING HER-SELF?
DARK MOON HASN'T EVEN STARTED AIRING.
I DON'T CARE ABOUT MY IMAGE!
BUT ...
...I CAN'T LET...
...MY ROLE ...
GLARE
...MIO...BE TARNISHED BY SOME-ONE LIKE HIM!

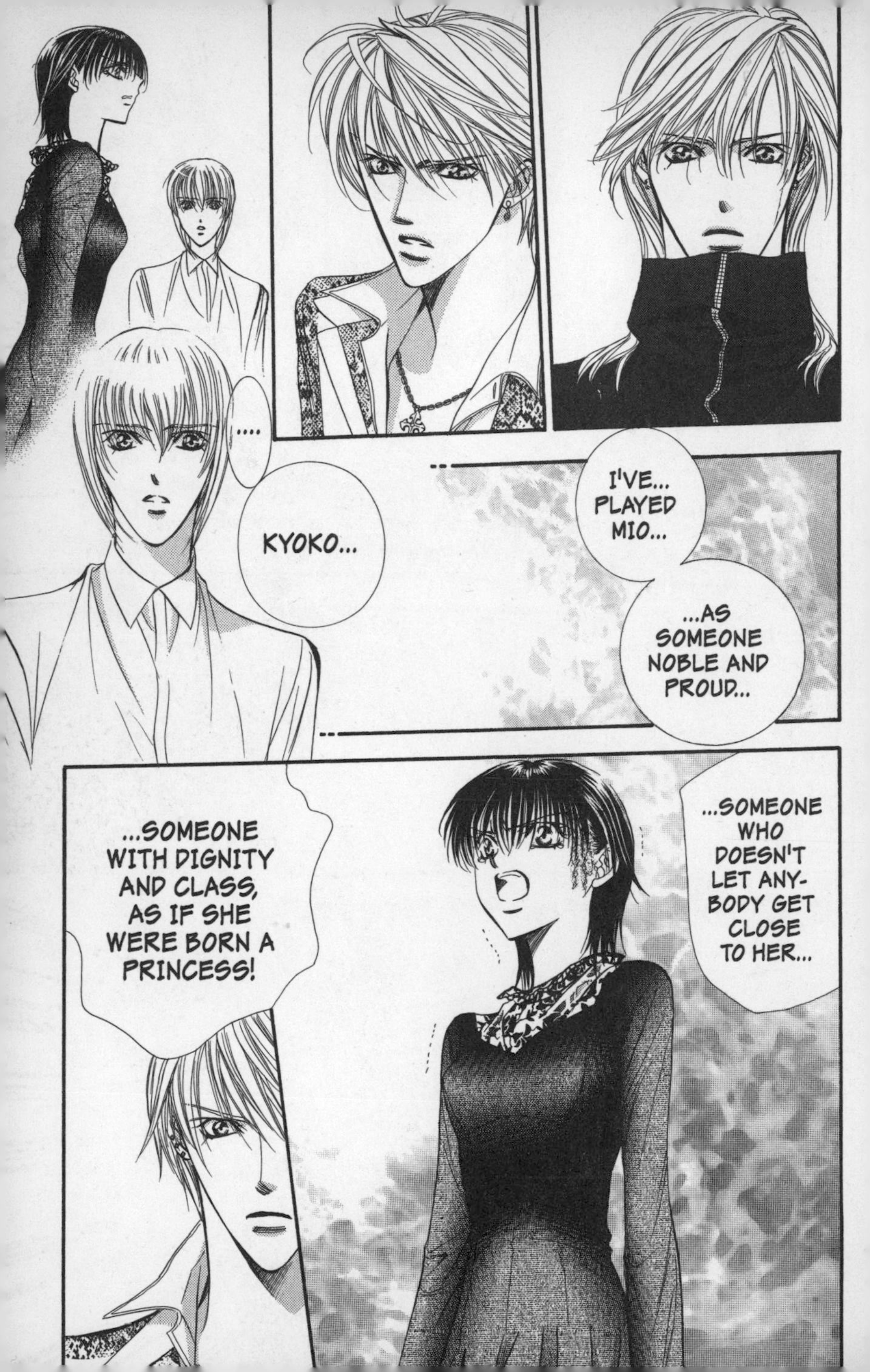
I'VE... PLAYED MIO...
...AS SOMEONE NOBLE AND PROUD...
....
KYOKO...
...SOMEONE WHO DOESN'T LET ANY-BODY GET CLOSE TO HER...
...SOMEONE WITH DIGNITY AND CLASS, AS IF SHE WERE BORN A PRINCESS!

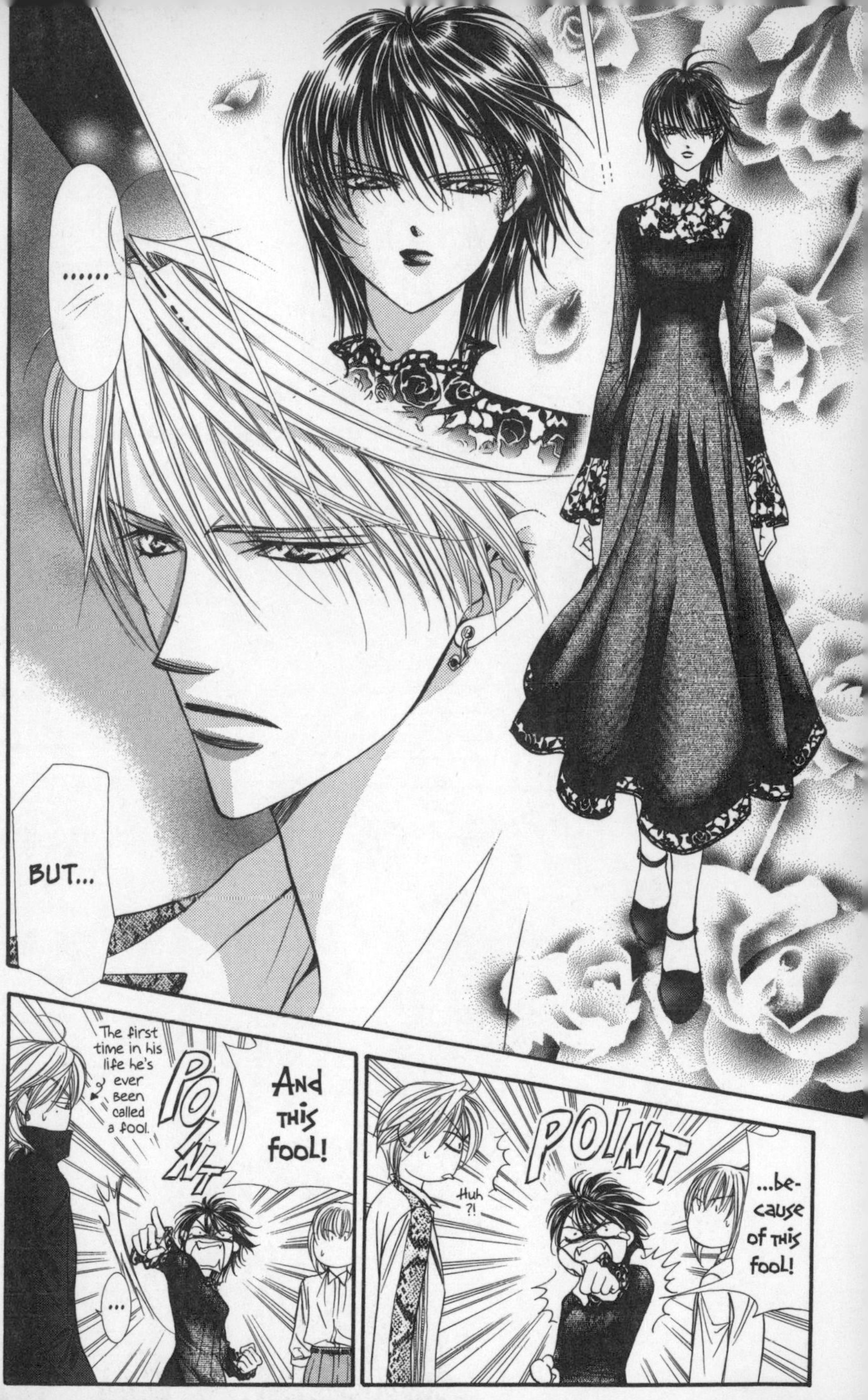

......
BUT...
...because of this fool!
POINT
Huh ?!
And this fool!
POINT
The first time in his life he's ever been called a fool.
...

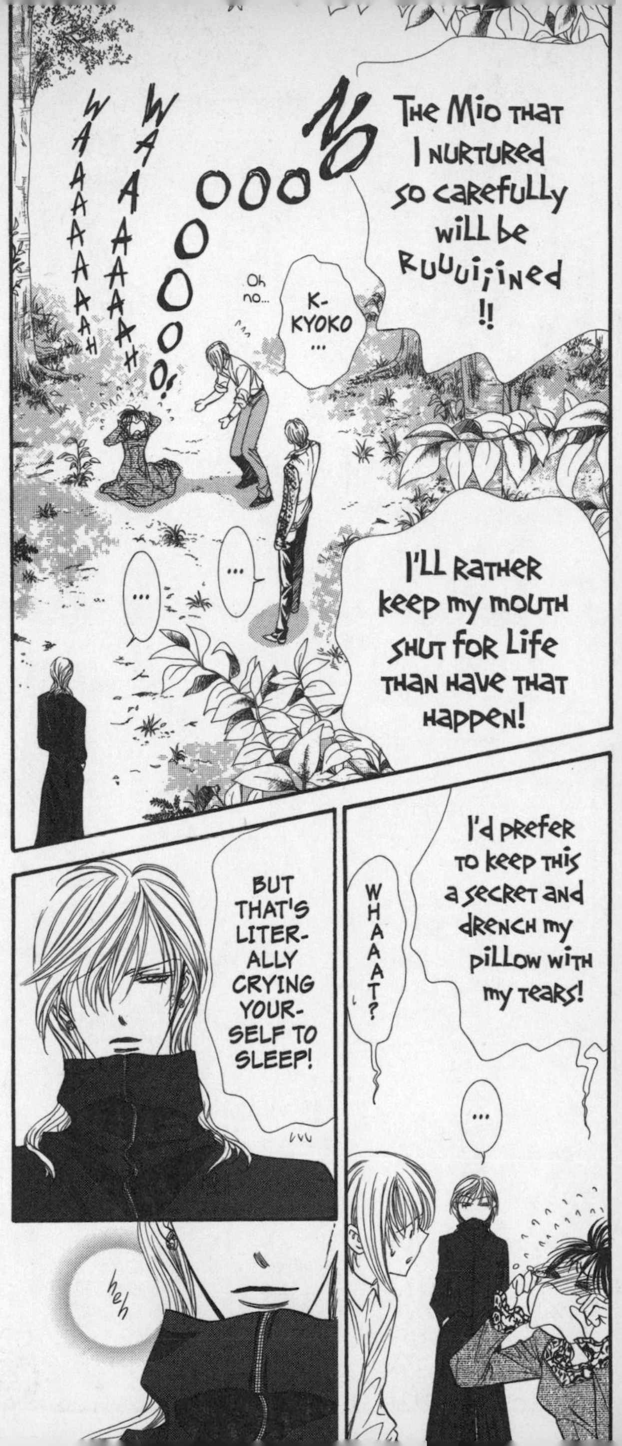
The Mio that I nurtured so carefully will be ruuuiiined!!
NOOOOOOOO
K-KYOKO...
Oh no...
WAAAAAAAH
WAAAAAAAAH
...
...
I'll rather keep my mouth shut for life than have that happen!
I'd prefer to keep this a secret and drench my pillow with my tears!
WHAAAT?
BUT THAT'S LITERALLY CRYING YOURSELF TO SLEEP!
...
heh

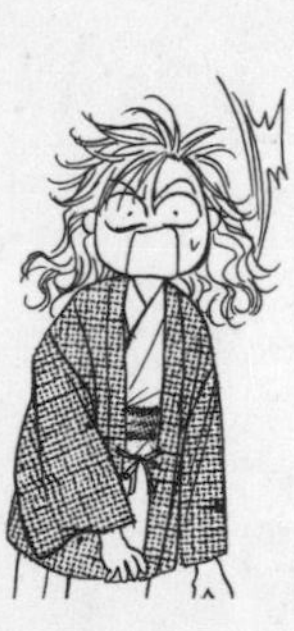

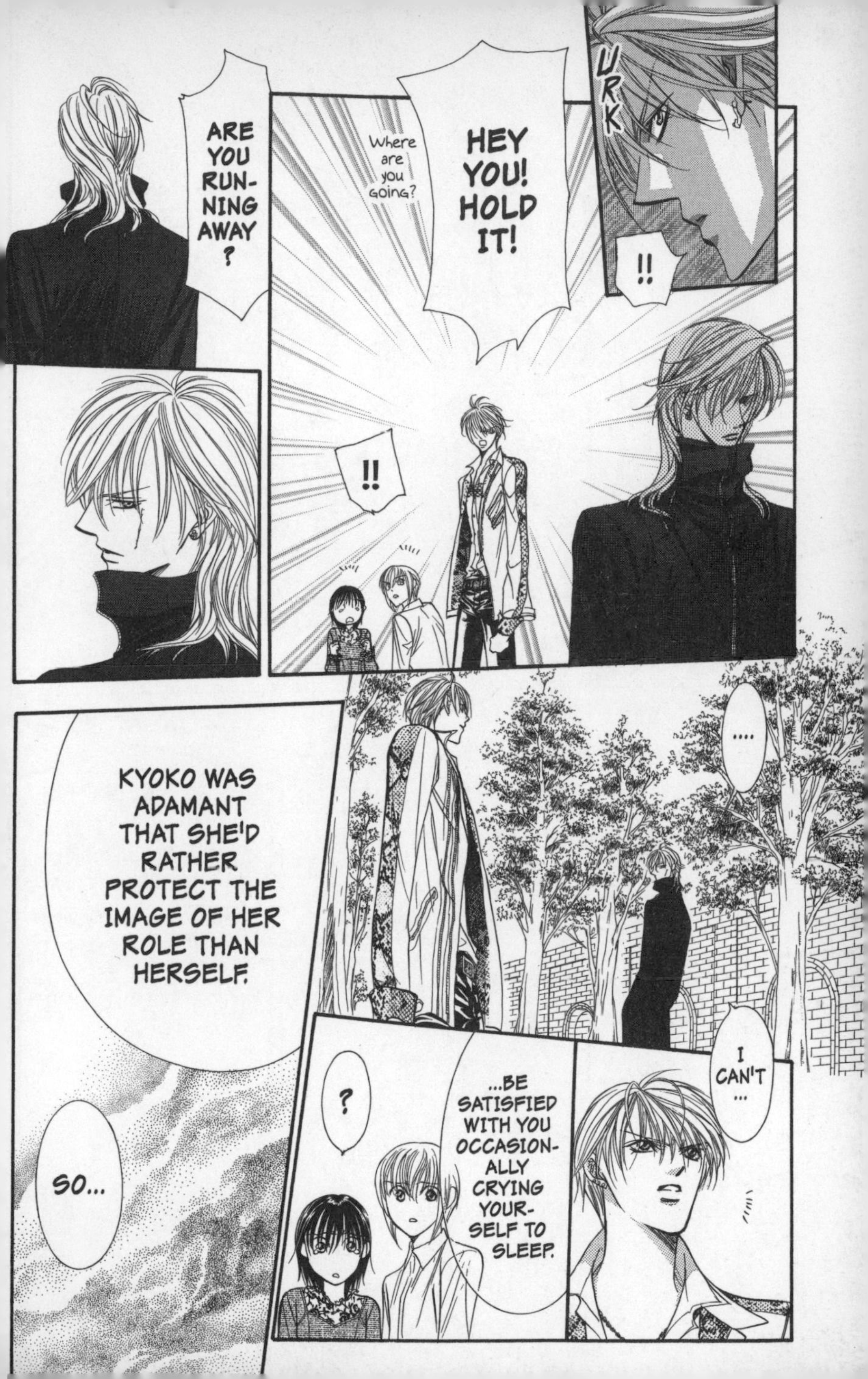
URK
!!
HEY YOU! HOLD IT!
Where are you going?
!!
ARE YOU RUN-NING AWAY?
....
I CAN'T...
...BE SATISFIED WITH YOU OCCASION-ALLY CRYING YOUR-SELF TO SLEEP.
?
KYOKO WAS ADAMANT THAT SHE'D RATHER PROTECT THE IMAGE OF HER ROLE THAN HERSELF.
SO...

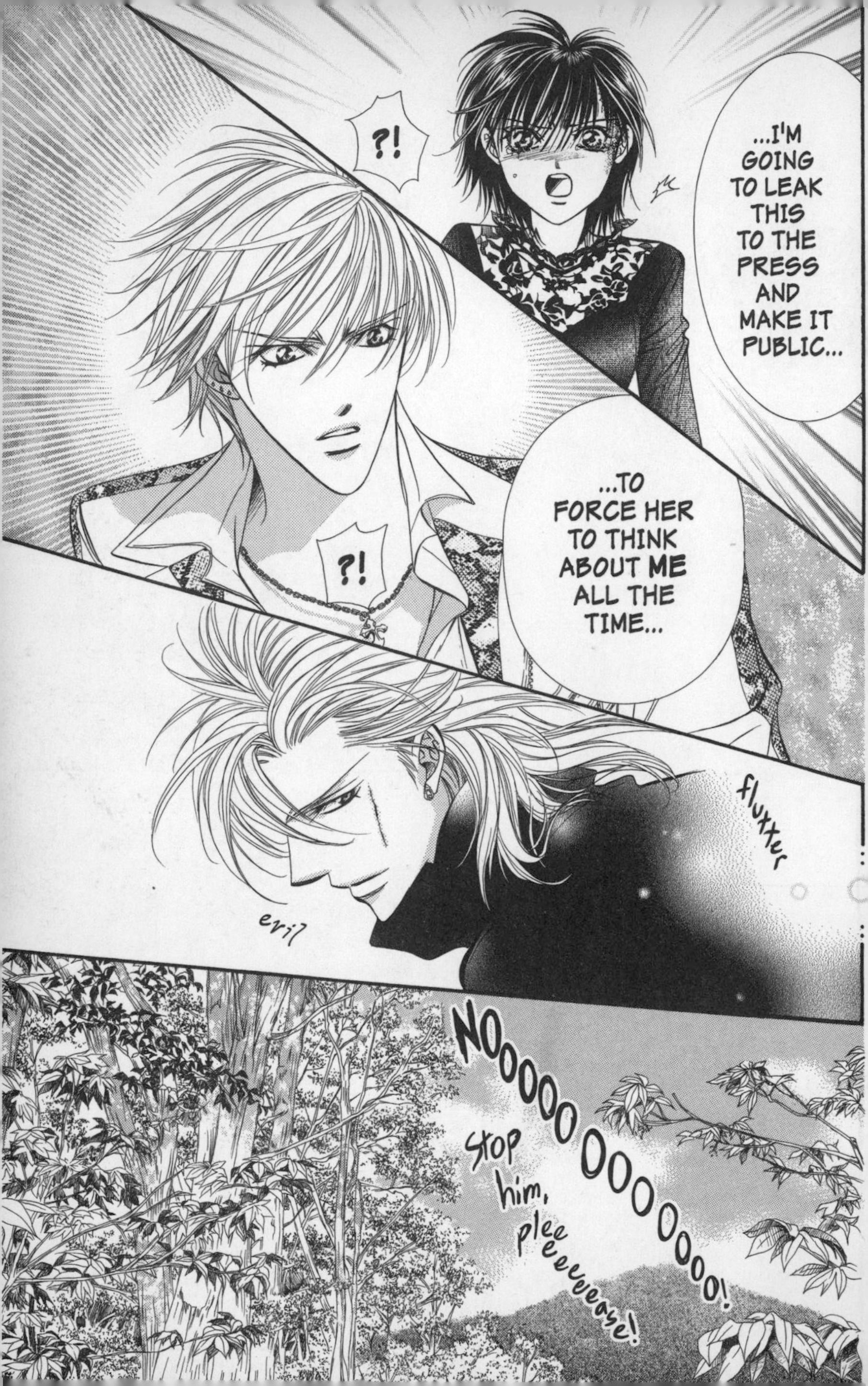
...I'M GOING TO LEAK THIS TO THE PRESS AND MAKE IT PUBLIC...
?!
...TO FORCE HER TO THINK ABOUT ME ALL THE TIME...
?!
flutter
evil
NOOOOOOOOOOOO!
Stop him, pleeeeeeease!

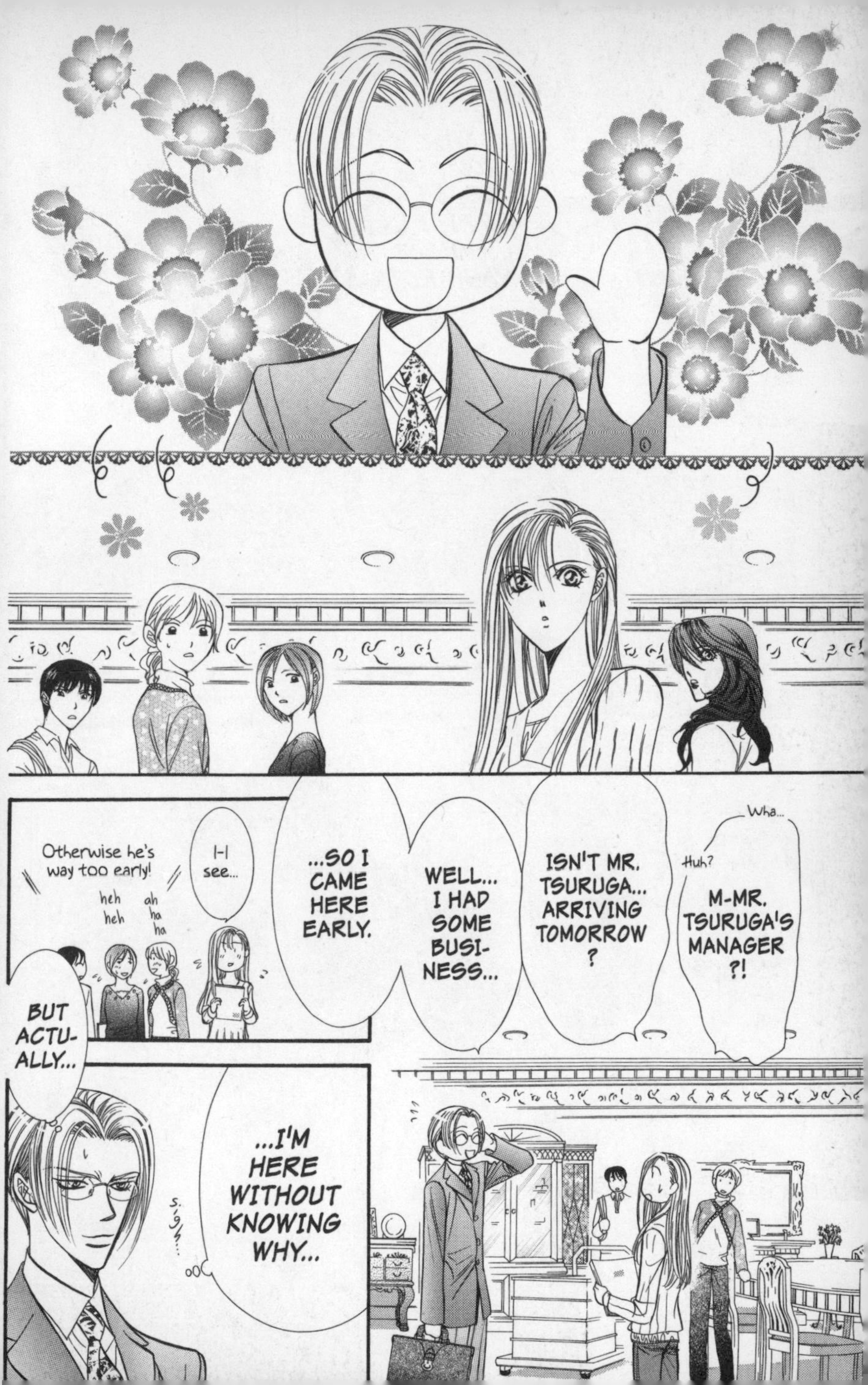
Wha...
Huh?
M-MR. TSURUGA'S MANAGER?!
ISN'T MR. TSURUGA... ARRIVING TOMORROW?
WELL... I HAD SOME BUSINESS...
...SO I CAME HERE EARLY.
I-I see...
Otherwise he's way too early!
heh heh
ah ha ha
BUT ACTUALLY...
...I'M HERE WITHOUT KNOWING WHY...
sigh...

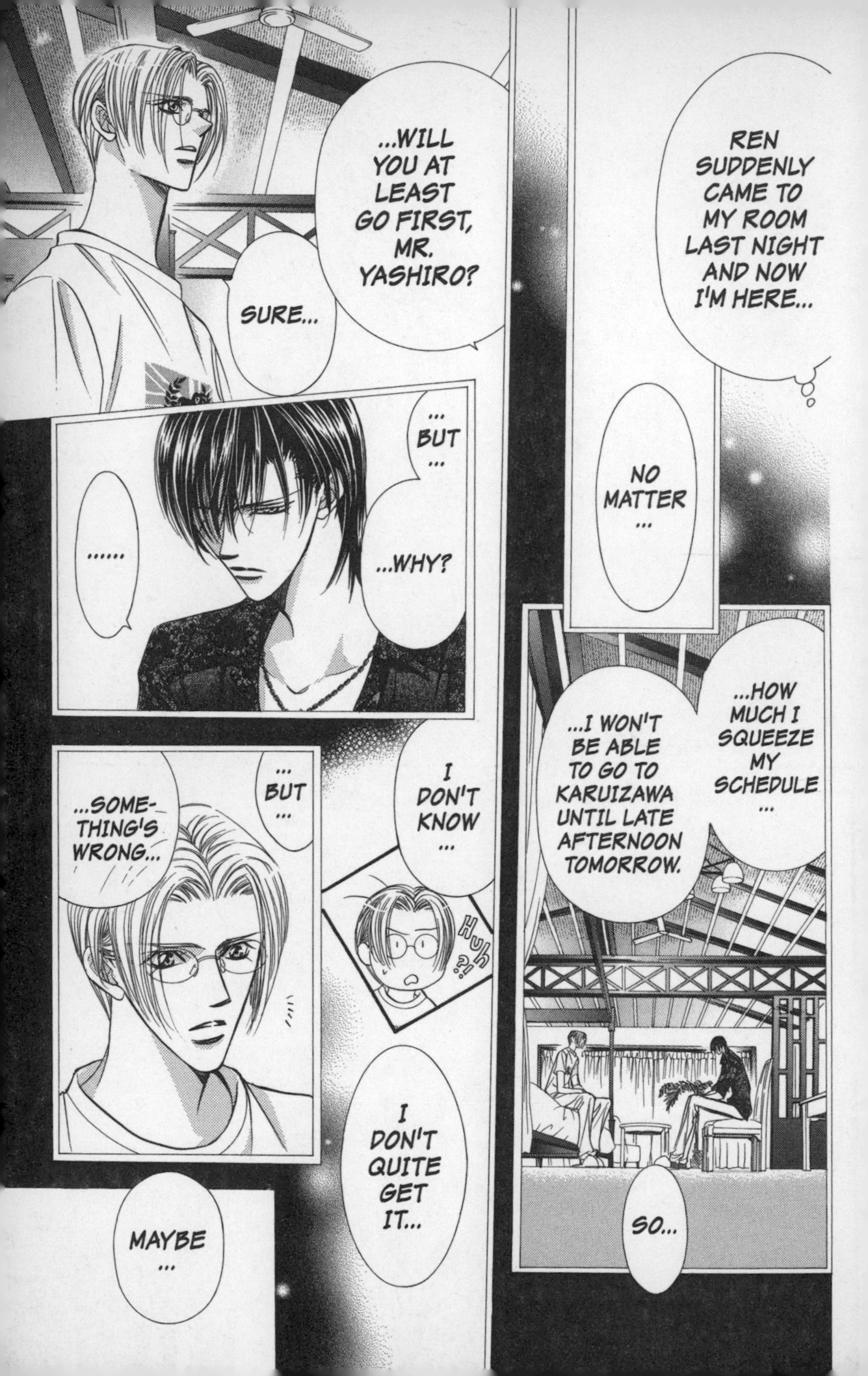
REN SUDDENLY CAME TO MY ROOM LAST NIGHT AND NOW I'M HERE...
NO MATTER ...
...HOW MUCH I SQUEEZE MY SCHEDULE ...
...I WON'T BE ABLE TO GO TO KARUIZAWA UNTIL LATE AFTERNOON TOMORROW.
SO...
...WILL YOU AT LEAST GO FIRST, MR. YASHIRO?
SURE...
... BUT ...
...WHY?
......
I DON'T KNOW ...
... BUT ...
...SOME-THING'S WRONG...
Huh ?!
I DON'T QUITE GET IT...
MAYBE ...

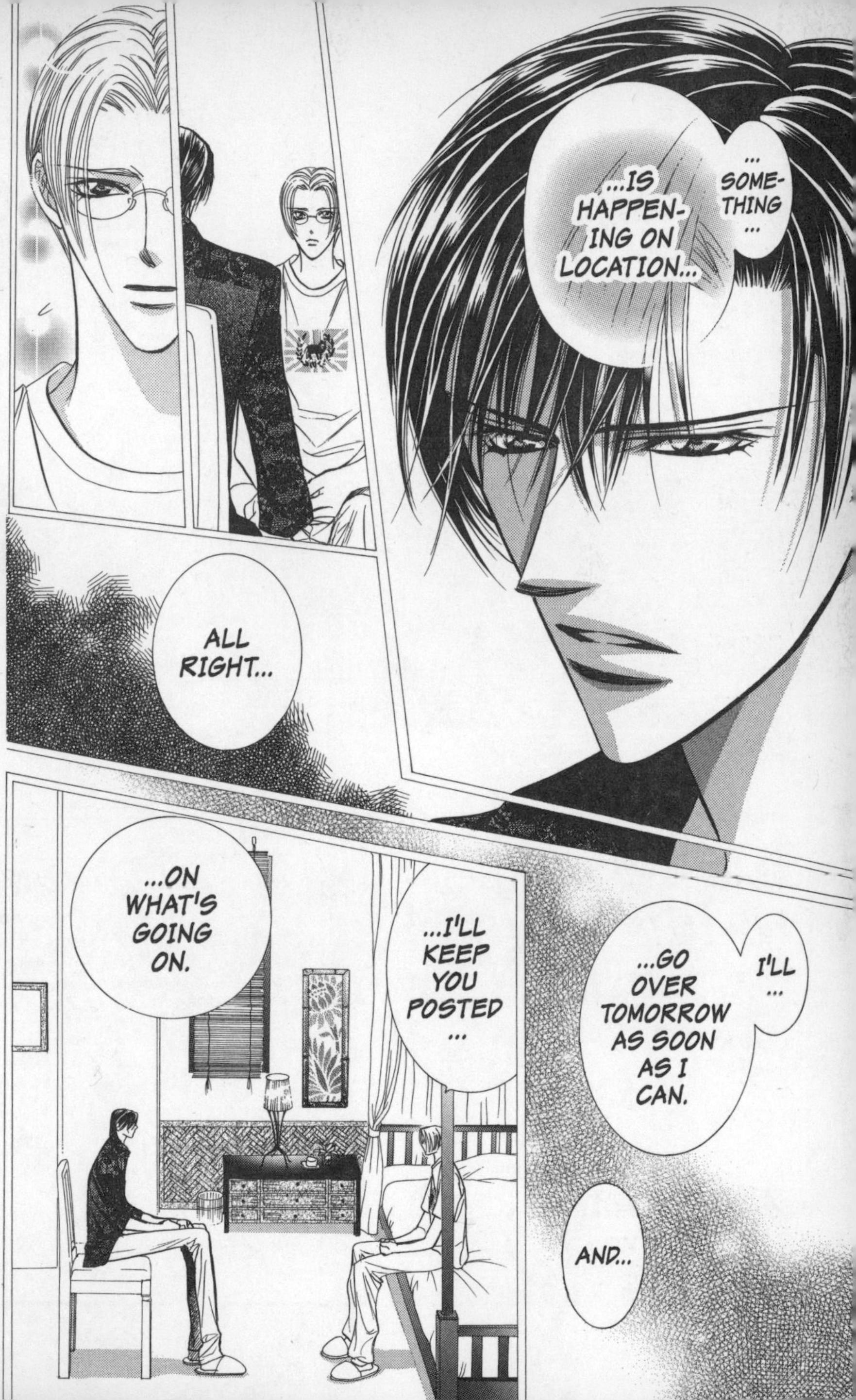
...SOMETHING...
...IS HAPPENING ON LOCATION...
ALL RIGHT...
I'LL...
...GO OVER TOMORROW AS SOON AS I CAN.
AND...
...I'LL KEEP YOU POSTED...
...ON WHAT'S GOING ON.

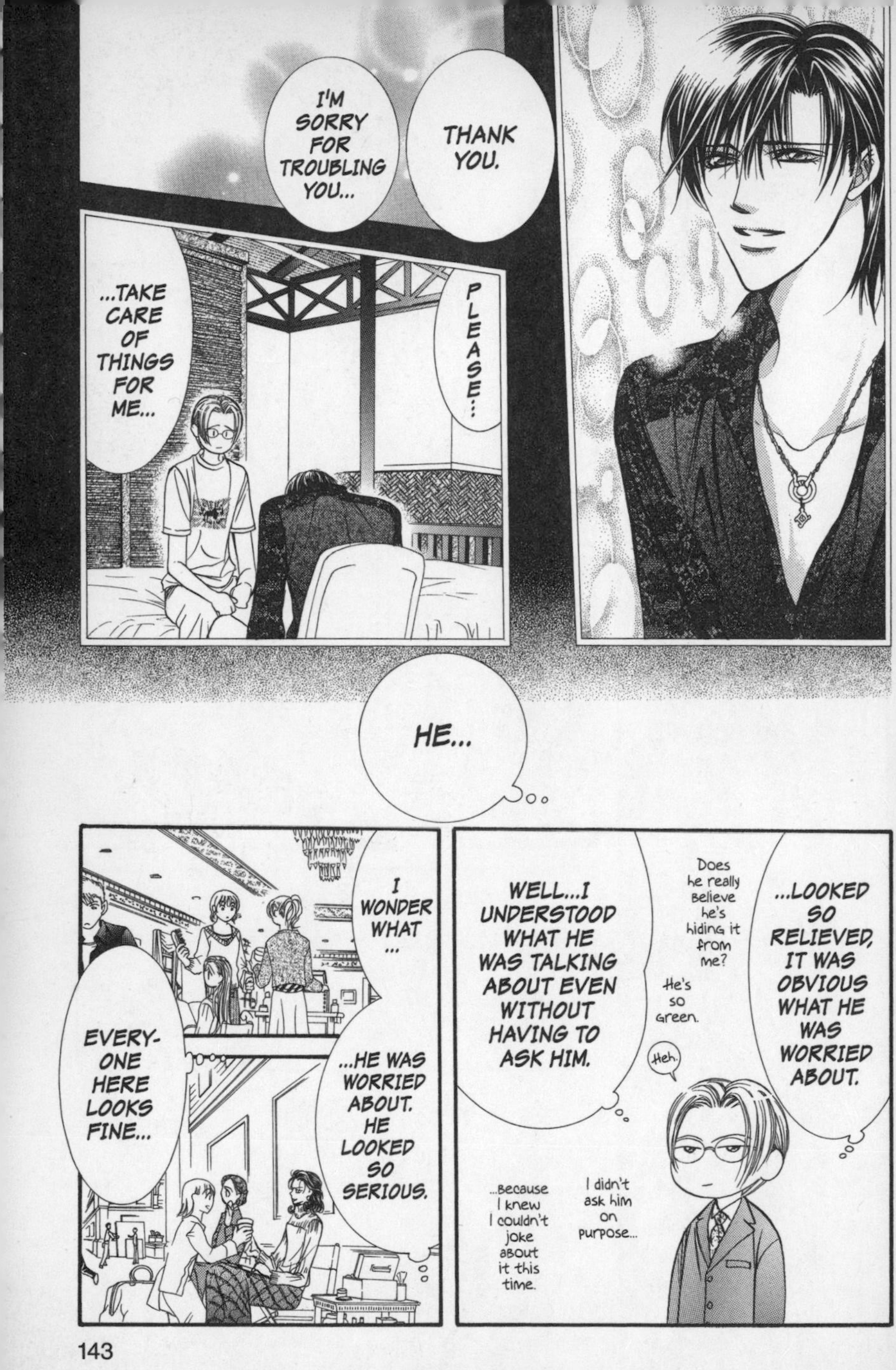
THANK YOU.
I'M SORRY FOR TROUBLING YOU...
PLEASE...
...TAKE CARE OF THINGS FOR ME...
HE...
...LOOKED SO RELIEVED, IT WAS OBVIOUS WHAT HE WAS WORRIED ABOUT.
Does he really believe he's hiding it from me?
WELL...I UNDERSTOOD WHAT HE WAS TALKING ABOUT EVEN WITHOUT HAVING TO ASK HIM.
He's so Green.
Heh.
I didn't ask him on purpose...
...Because I knew I couldn't joke about it this time.
I WONDER WHAT ...
...HE WAS WORRIED ABOUT. HE LOOKED SO SERIOUS.
EVERY-ONE HERE LOOKS FINE...

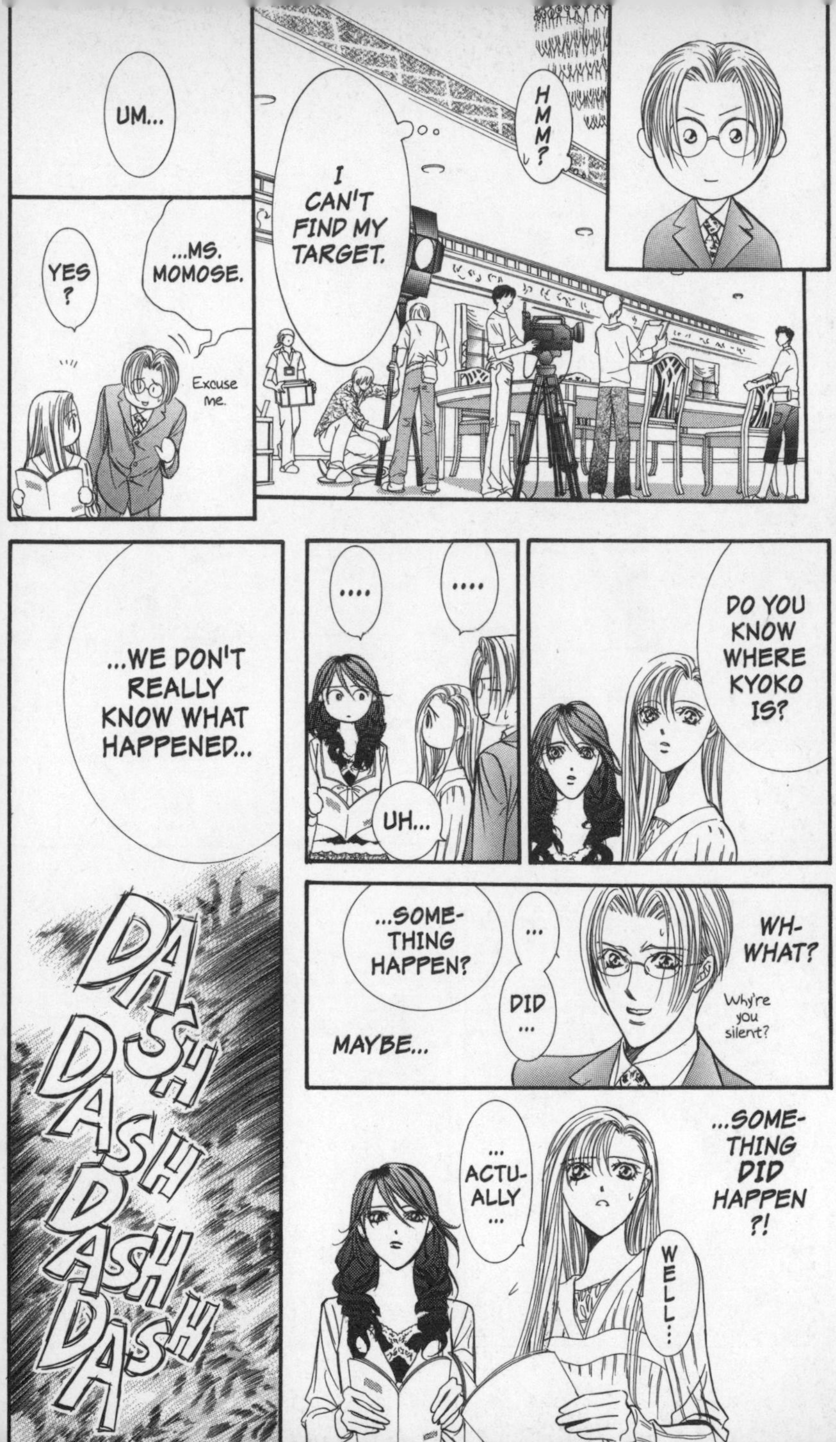
HMM?
I CAN'T FIND MY TARGET.
UM...
...MS. MOMOSE.
Excuse me.
YES?
DO YOU KNOW WHERE KYOKO IS?
....
....
UH...
WH-WHAT?
Why're you silent?
... DID ...
...SOMETHING HAPPEN?
MAYBE...
...SOMETHING DID HAPPEN?!
WELL...
...ACTUALLY...
...WE DON'T REALLY KNOW WHAT HAPPENED...
DASH DASH DASH DASH

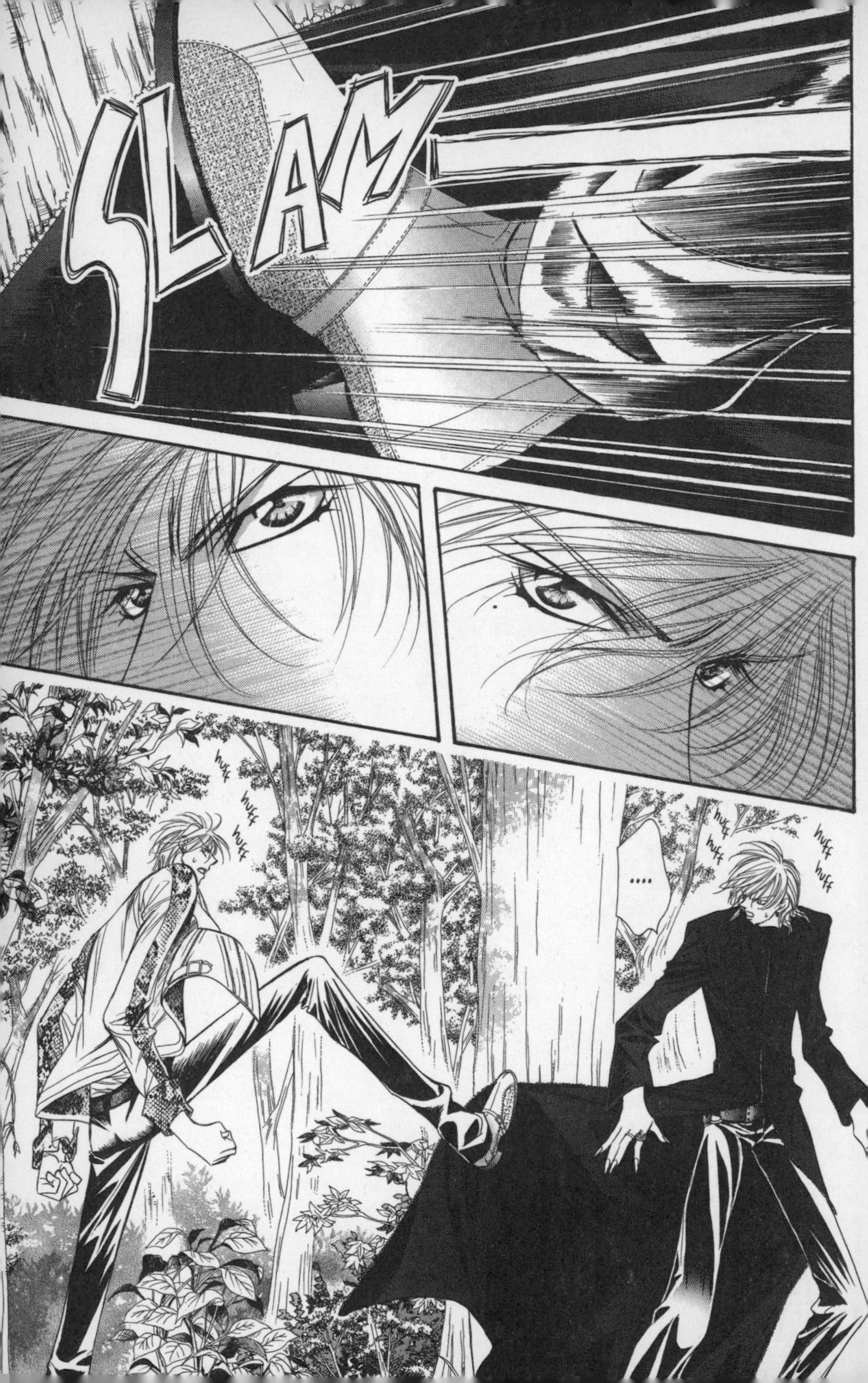
SLAM
huff
huff
huff
huff
....
huff
huff
huff

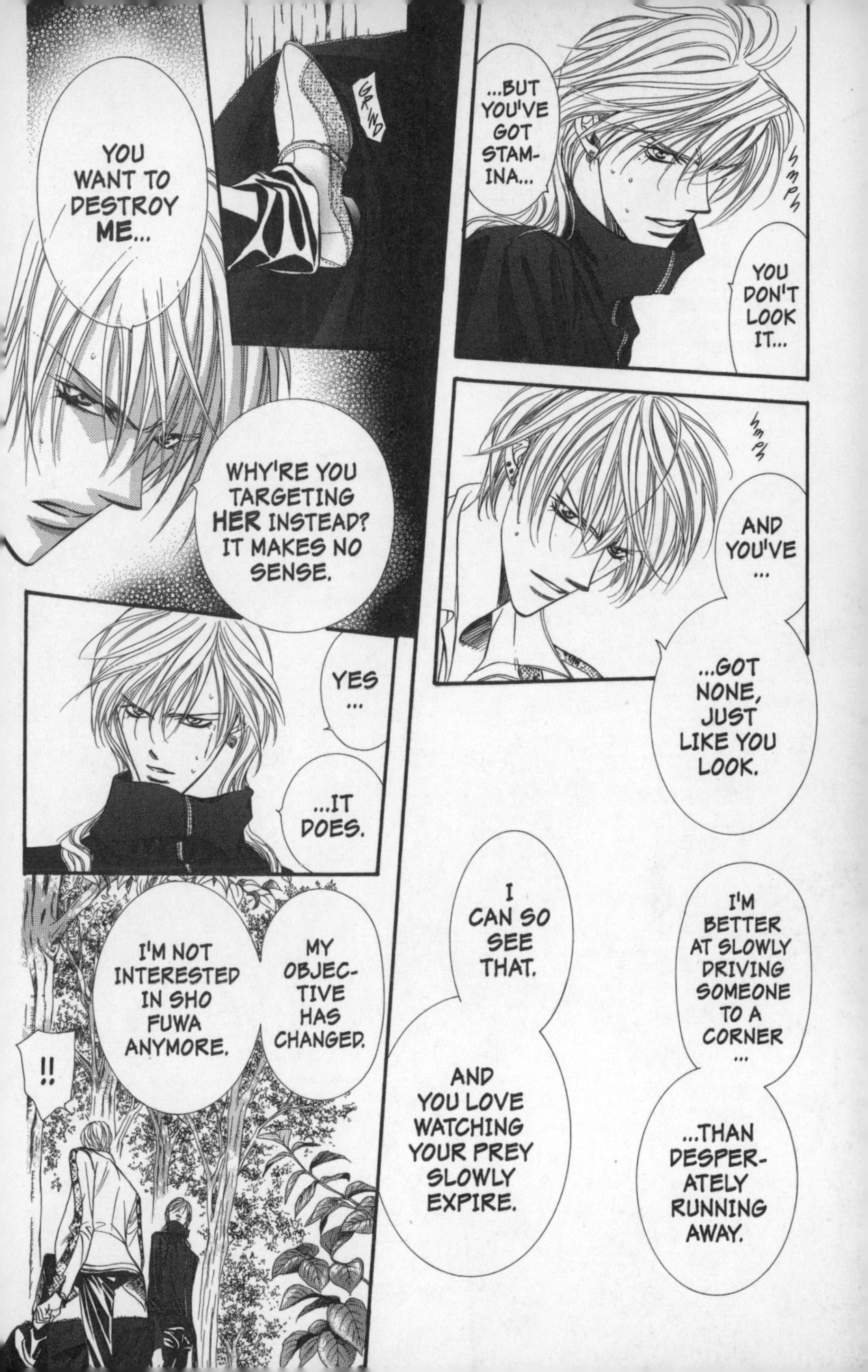

...BUT YOU'VE GOT STAM-INA...
HMPH
YOU DON'T LOOK IT...
HMPH
AND YOU'VE ...
...GOT NONE, JUST LIKE YOU LOOK.
I'M BETTER AT SLOWLY DRIVING SOMEONE TO A CORNER ...
...THAN DESPER-ATELY RUNNING AWAY.
I CAN SO SEE THAT.
AND YOU LOVE WATCHING YOUR PREY SLOWLY EXPIRE.
GRIND
YOU WANT TO DESTROY ME...
WHY'RE YOU TARGETING HER INSTEAD? IT MAKES NO SENSE.
YES ...
...IT DOES.
MY OBJECT-TIVE HAS CHANGED.
I'M NOT INTERESTED IN SHO FUWA ANYMORE.
!!

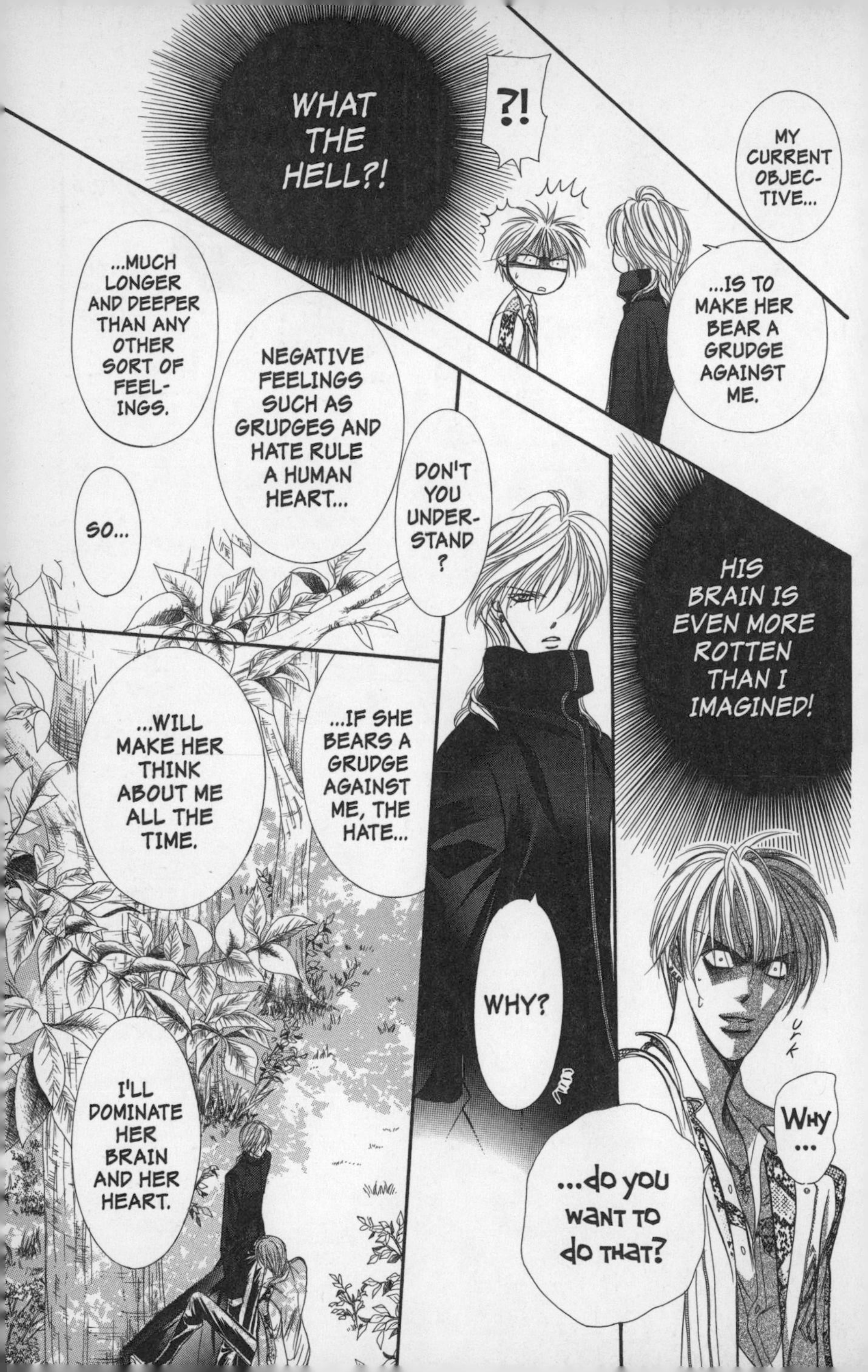

MY CURRENT OBJECTIVE...
...IS TO MAKE HER BEAR A GRUDGE AGAINST ME.
?!
WHAT THE HELL?!
HIS BRAIN IS EVEN MORE ROTTEN THAN I IMAGINED!
URK
Why...
...do you want to do that?
WHY?
DON'T YOU UNDERSTAND?
NEGATIVE FEELINGS SUCH AS GRUDGES AND HATE RULE A HUMAN HEART...
...MUCH LONGER AND DEEPER THAN ANY OTHER SORT OF FEELINGS.
SO...
...IF SHE BEARS A GRUDGE AGAINST ME, THE HATE...
...WILL MAKE HER THINK ABOUT ME ALL THE TIME.
I'LL DOMINATE HER BRAIN AND HER HEART.

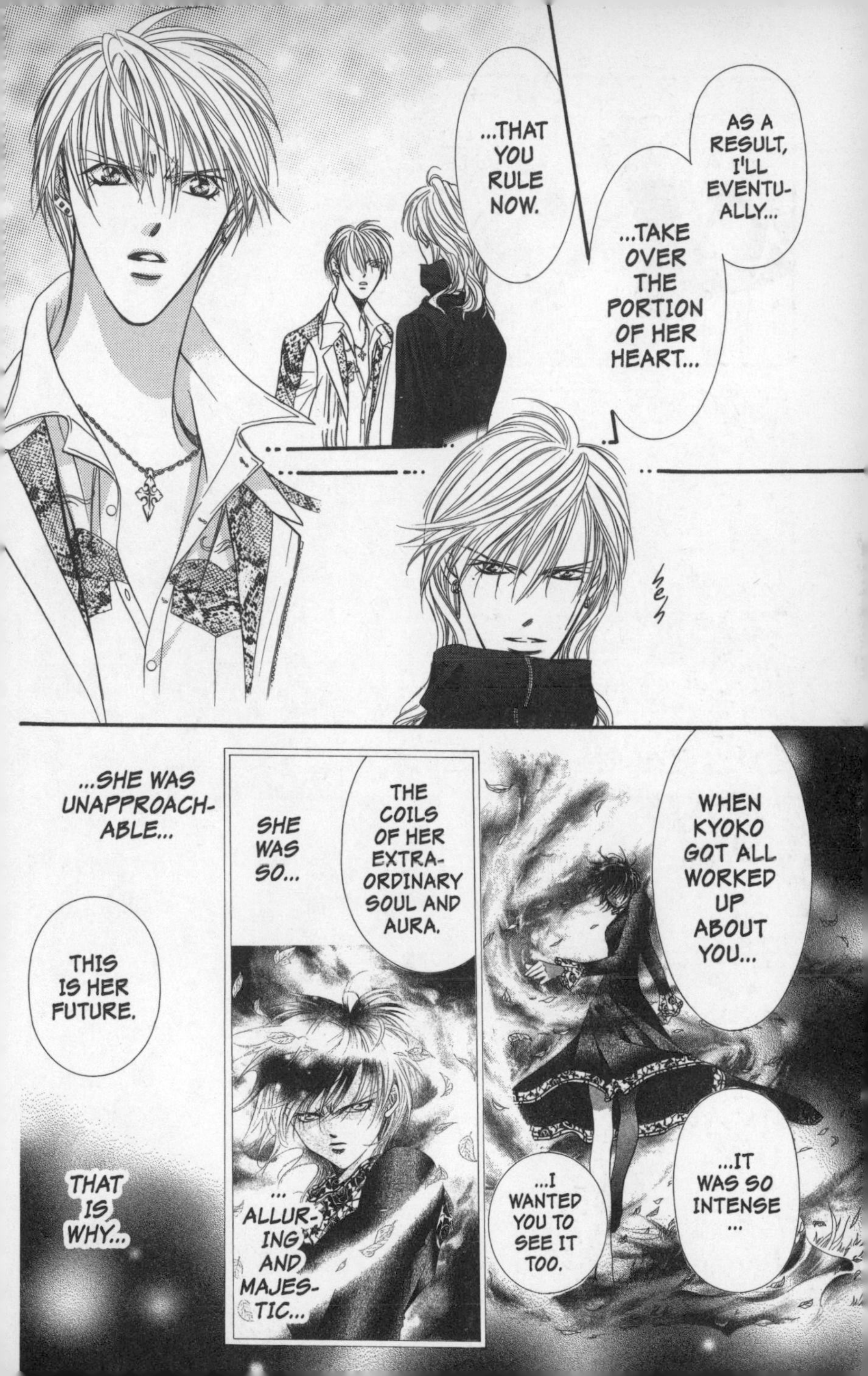
AS A RESULT, I'LL EVENTU-ALLY...
...TAKE OVER THE PORTION OF HER HEART...
...THAT YOU RULE NOW.
WHEN KYOKO GOT ALL WORKED UP ABOUT YOU...
...IT WAS SO INTENSE...
...I WANTED YOU TO SEE IT TOO.
THE COILS OF HER EXTRA-ORDINARY SOUL AND AURA.
SHE WAS SO...
...ALLUR-ING AND MAJES-TIC...
...SHE WAS UNAPPROACH-ABLE...
THIS IS HER FUTURE.
THAT IS WHY...

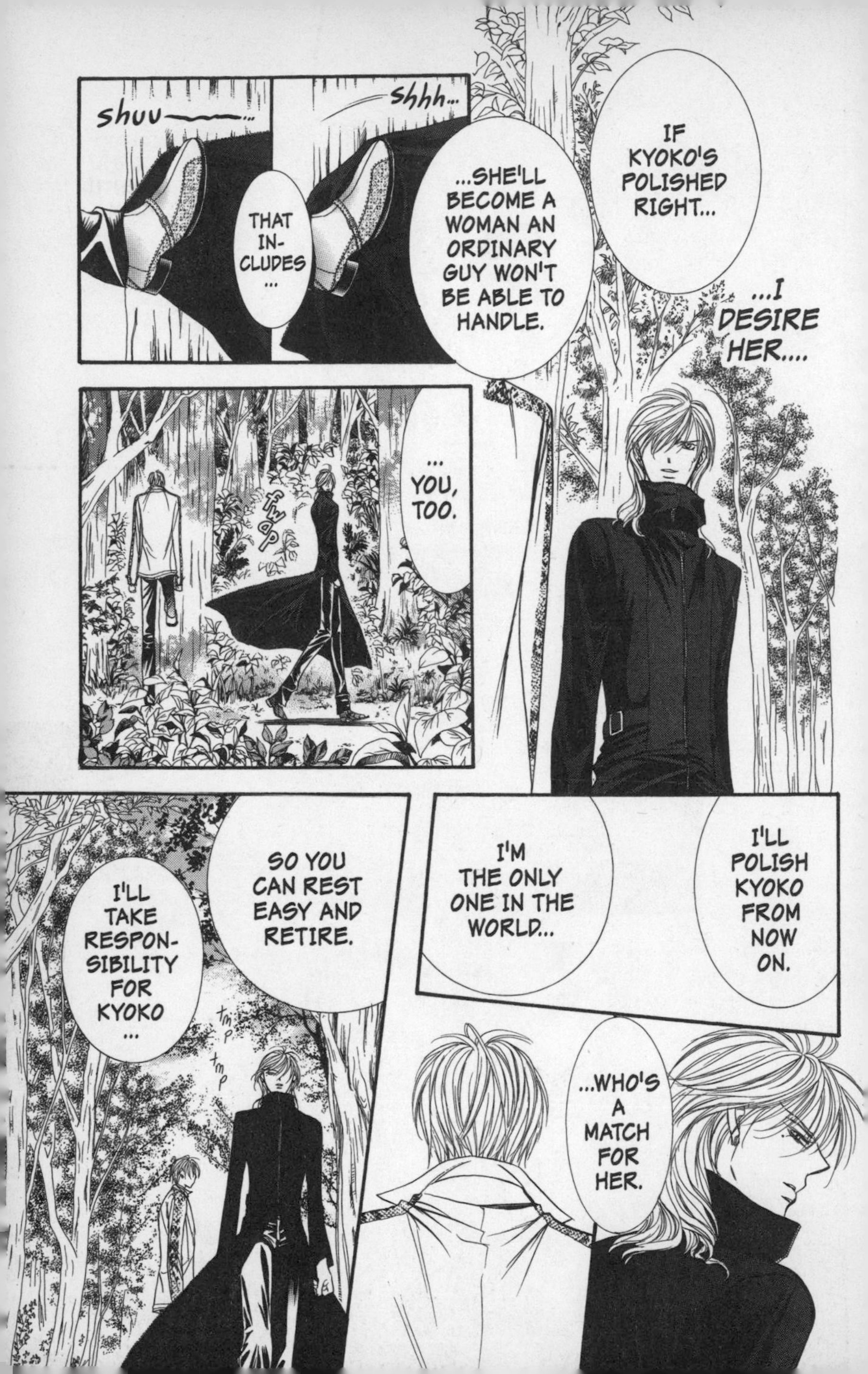
IF KYOKO'S POLISHED RIGHT...
...SHE'LL BECOME A WOMAN AN ORDINARY GUY WON'T BE ABLE TO HANDLE.
...I DESIRE HER....
shhh...
THAT IN-CLUDES ...
shuu——...
... YOU, TOO.
fwap
I'LL POLISH KYOKO FROM NOW ON.
I'M THE ONLY ONE IN THE WORLD...
...WHO'S A MATCH FOR HER.
SO YOU CAN REST EASY AND RETIRE.
I'LL TAKE RESPON-SIBILITY FOR KYOKO ...
tmp tmp

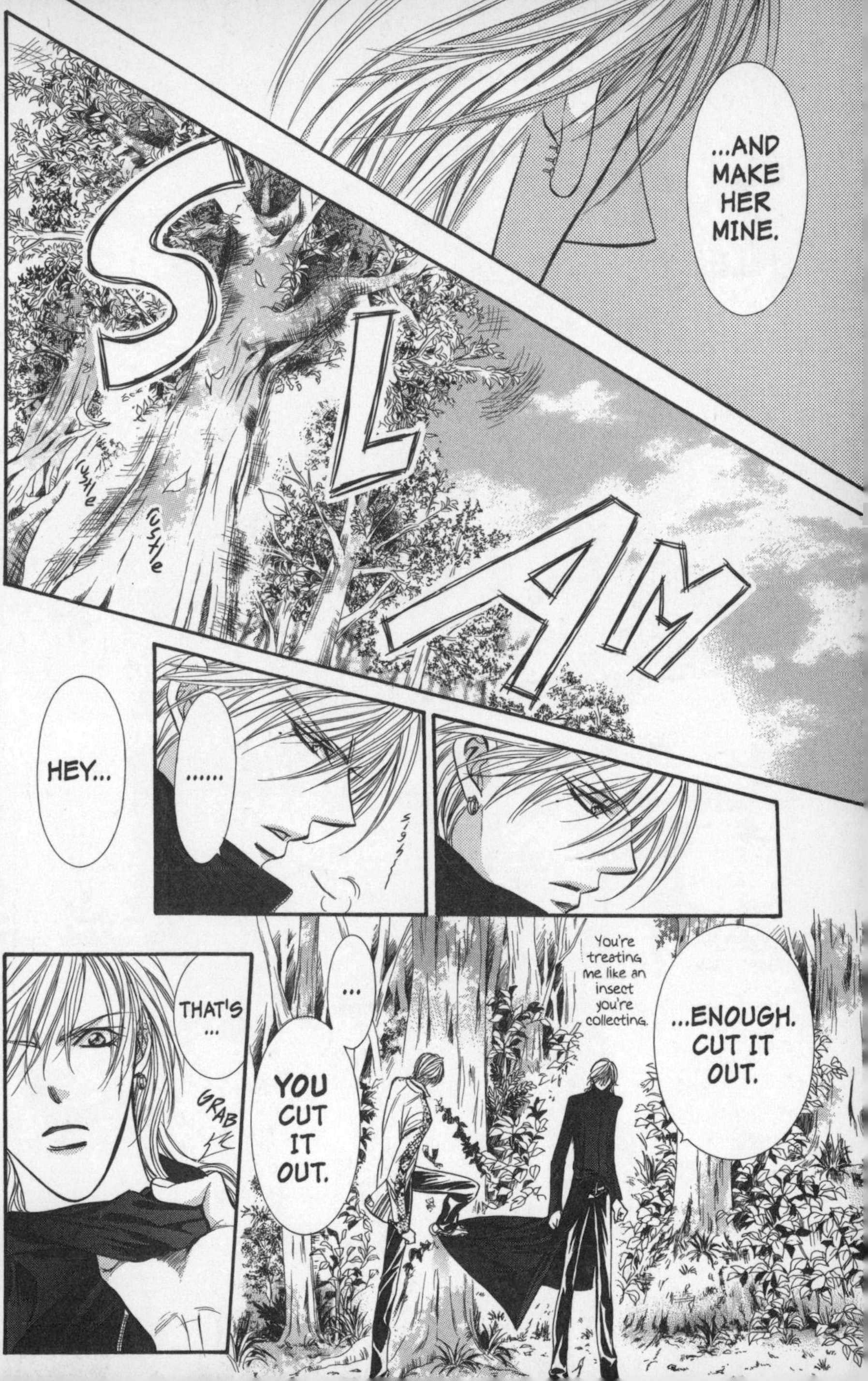
...AND MAKE HER MINE.
SLAM
rustle
rustle
......
sigh
HEY...
...ENOUGH. CUT IT OUT.
You're treating me like an insect you're collecting.
...
YOU CUT IT OUT.
THAT'S ...
GRAB

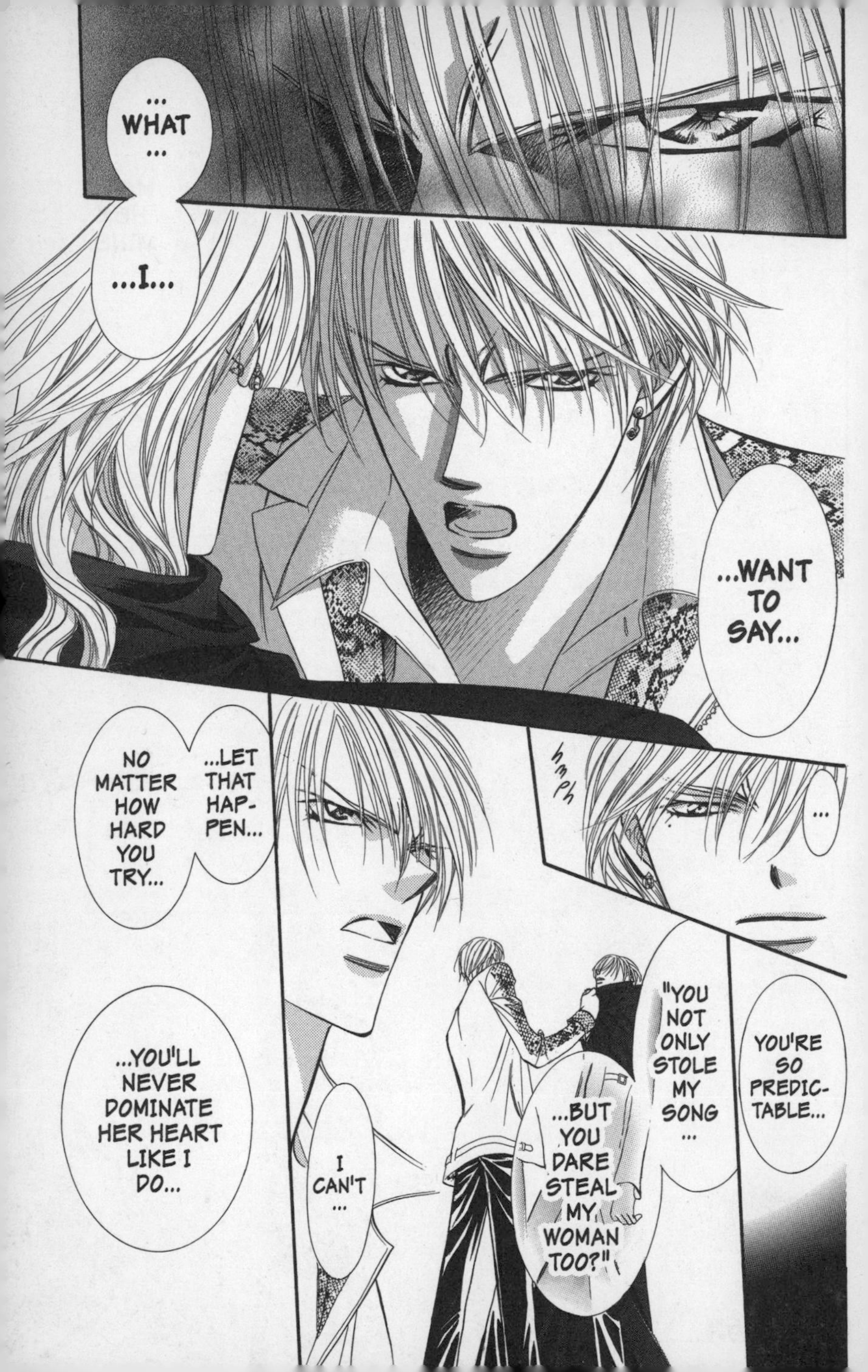

... WHAT ...
...I...
...WANT TO SAY...
hmph
...
YOU'RE SO PREDIC-TABLE...
"YOU NOT ONLY STOLE MY SONG ...
...BUT YOU DARE STEAL MY WOMAN TOO?"
I CAN'T ...
...LET THAT HAP-PEN...
NO MATTER HOW HARD YOU TRY...
...YOU'LL NEVER DOMINATE HER HEART LIKE I DO...

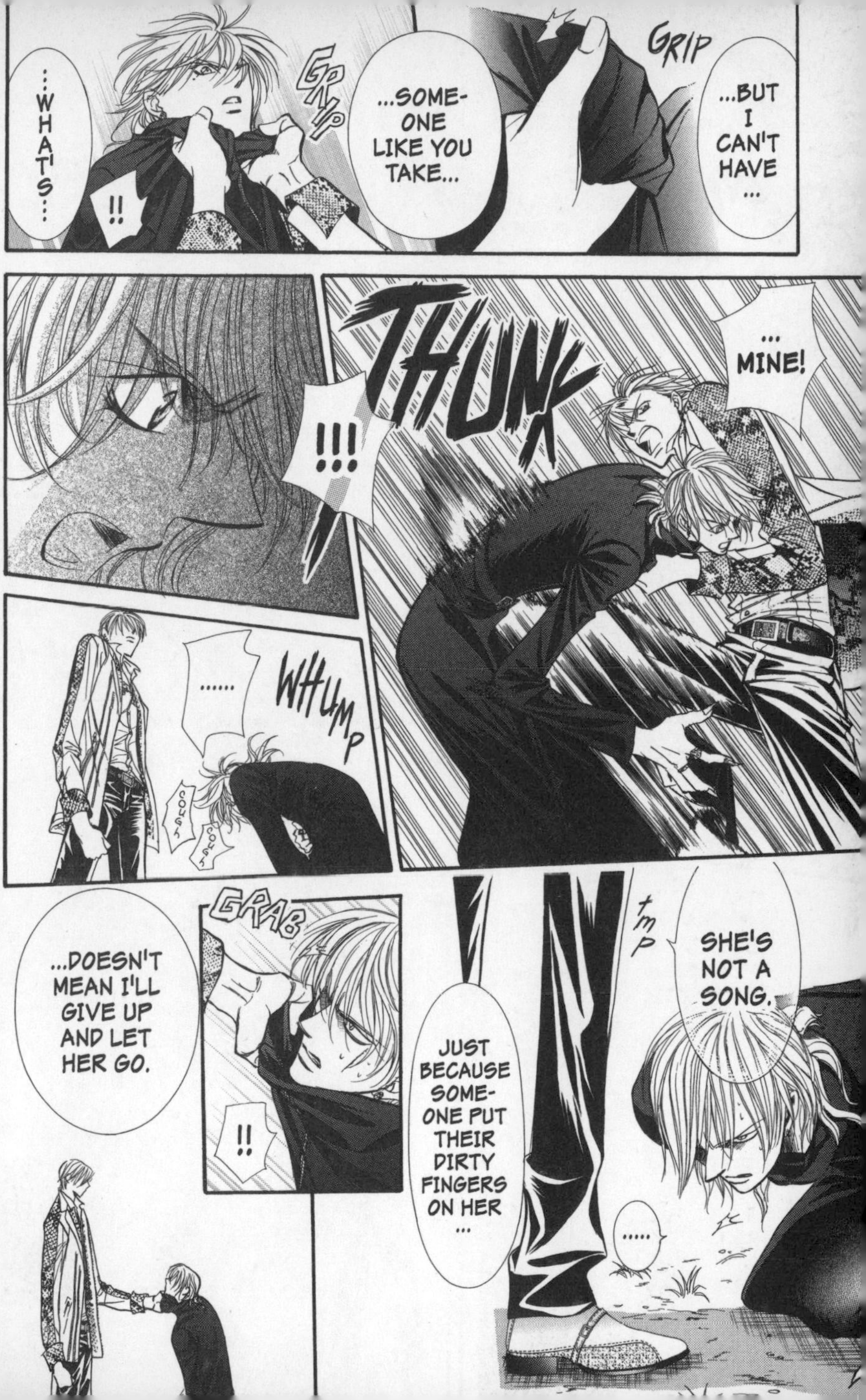
GRIP
...BUT I CAN'T HAVE ...
...SOME-ONE LIKE YOU TAKE...
GRIP
...WHAT'S...
!!
... MINE!
THUNK
!!!
WHUMP
......
COUGH
COUGH
tmp
SHE'S NOT A SONG.
JUST BECAUSE SOME-ONE PUT THEIR DIRTY FINGERS ON HER ...
......
GRAB
!!
...DOESN'T MEAN I'LL GIVE UP AND LET HER GO.

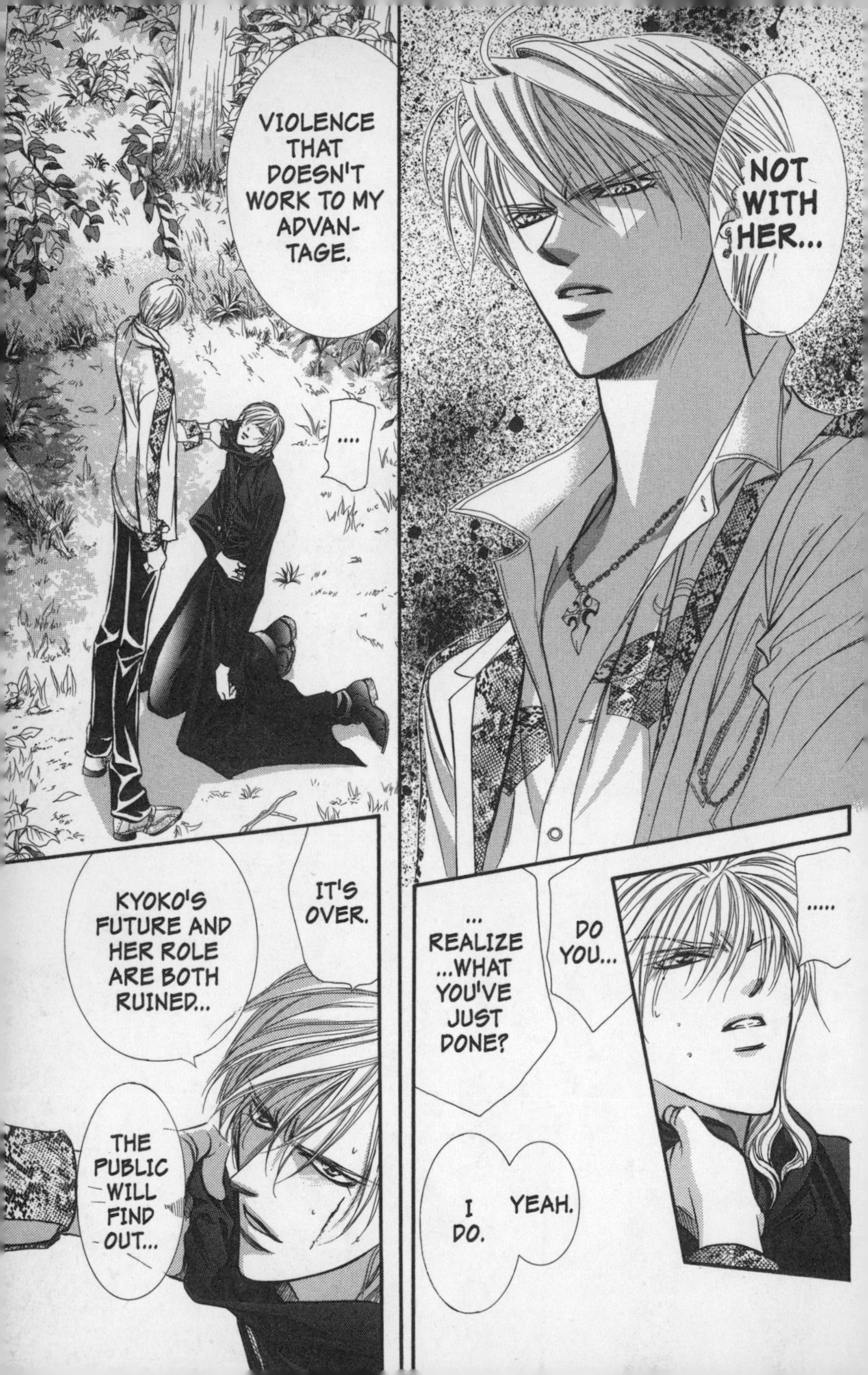
NOT WITH HER...
.....
DO YOU...
... REALIZE ...WHAT YOU'VE JUST DONE?
YEAH. I DO.
VIOLENCE THAT DOESN'T WORK TO MY ADVANTAGE.
....
IT'S OVER.
KYOKO'S FUTURE AND HER ROLE ARE BOTH RUINED...
THE PUBLIC WILL FIND OUT...

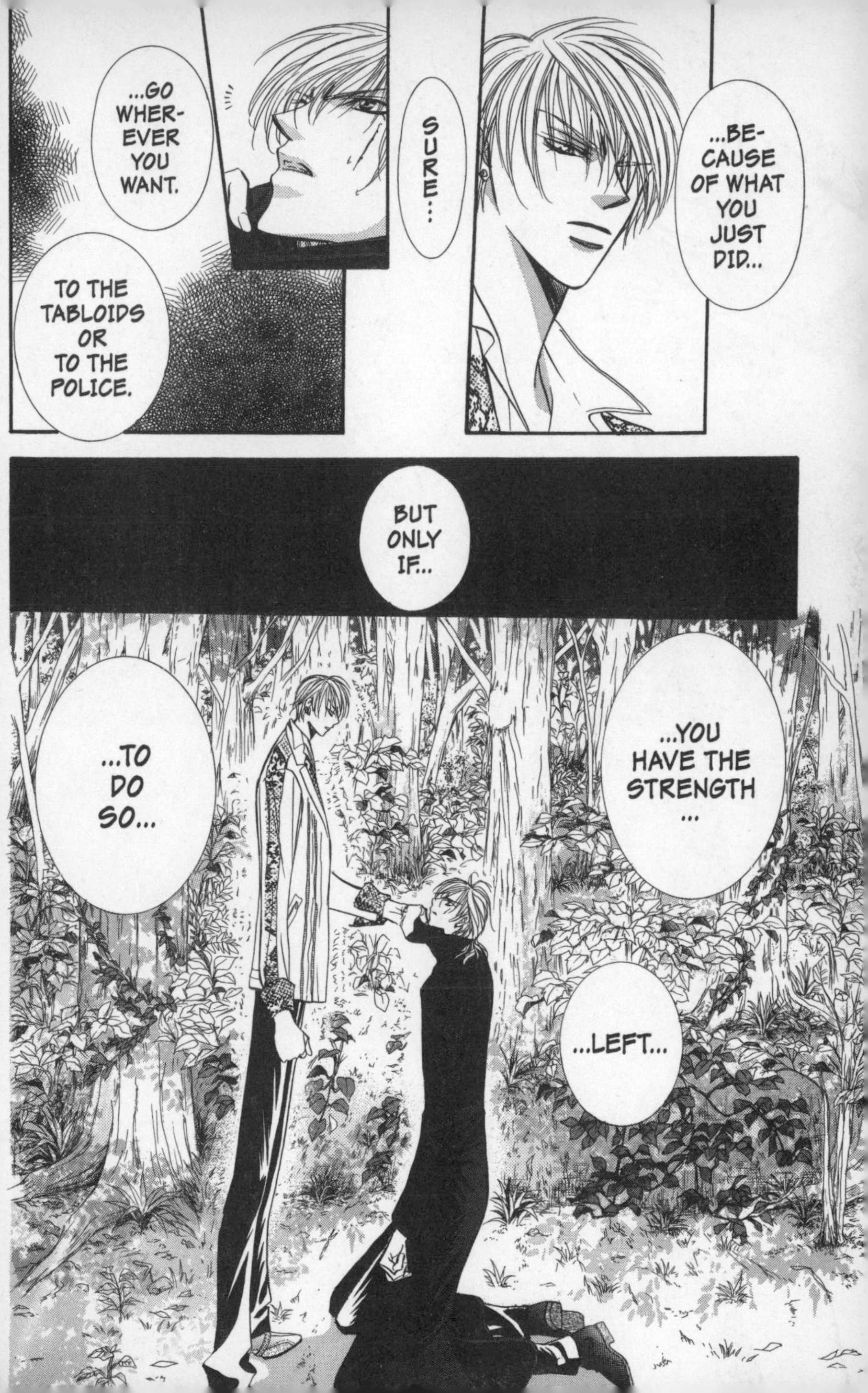
...BE-CAUSE OF WHAT YOU JUST DID...
SURE...
...GO WHER-EVER YOU WANT.
TO THE TABLOIDS OR TO THE POLICE.
BUT ONLY IF...
...YOU HAVE THE STRENGTH ...
...LEFT...
...TO DO SO...

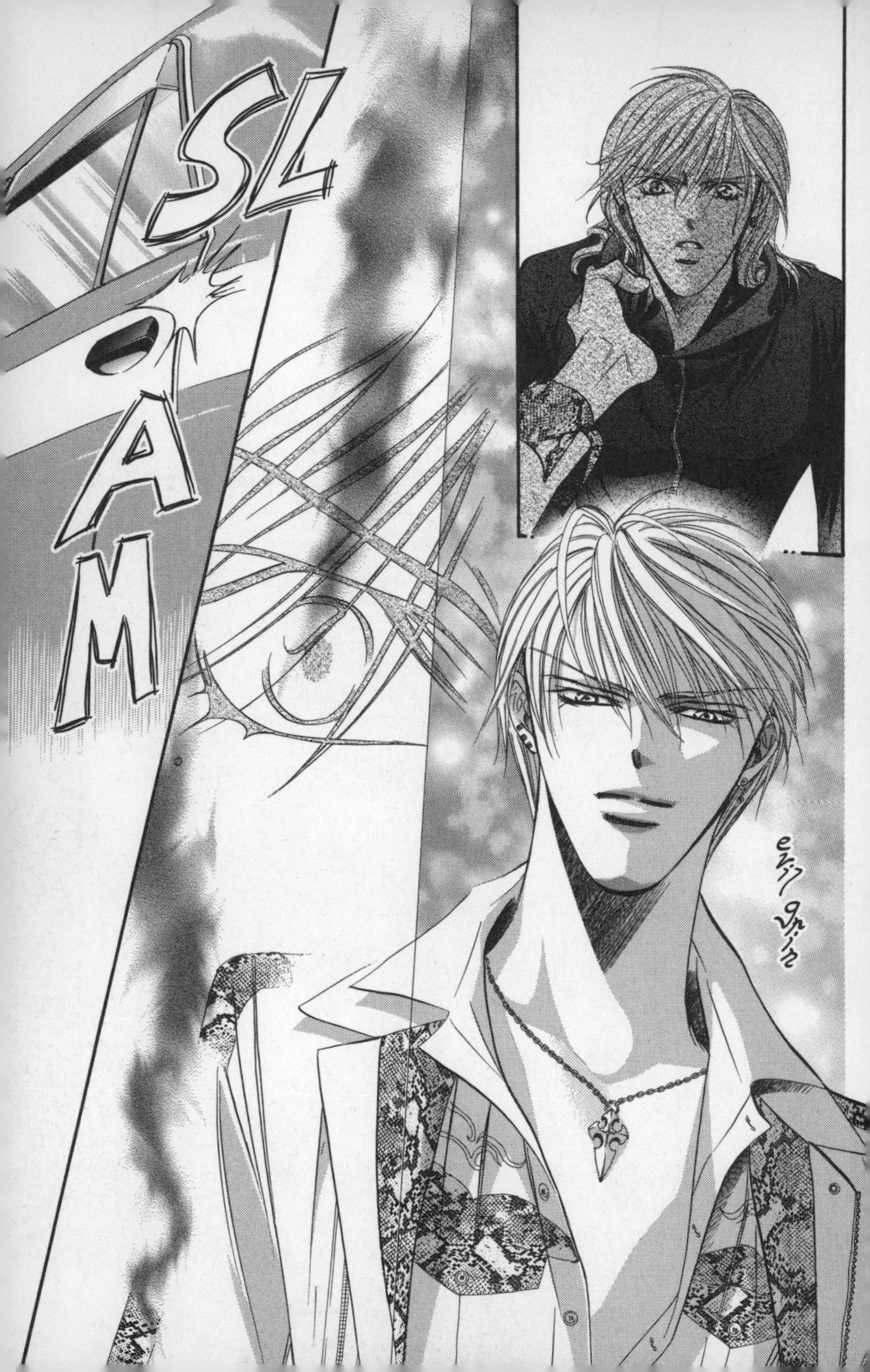
SLAM
grin grin

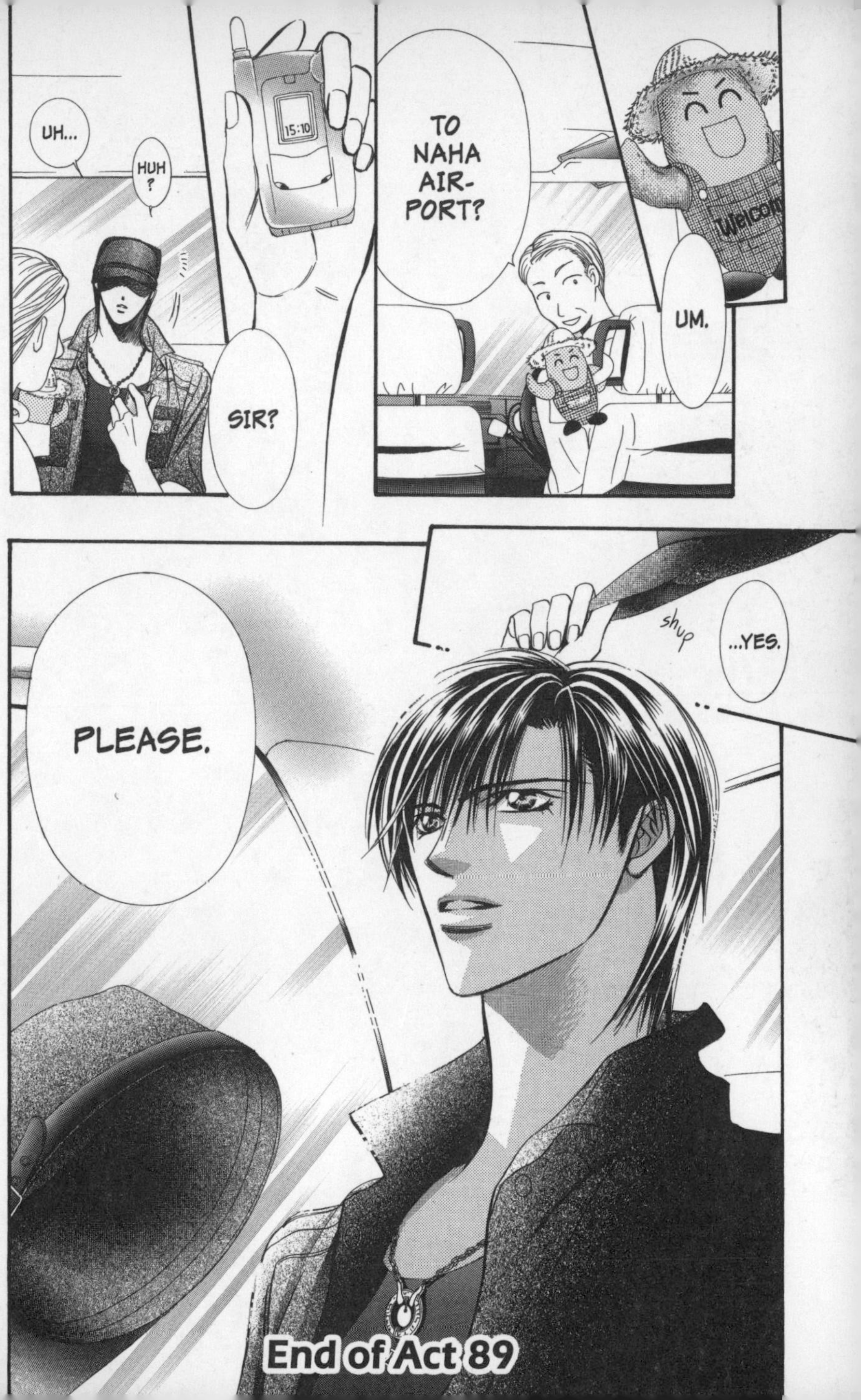
Welcom
UM.
TO NAHA AIR-PORT?
SIR?
HUH?
UH...
15:10
...YES.
shup
...
PLEASE.
End of Act 89

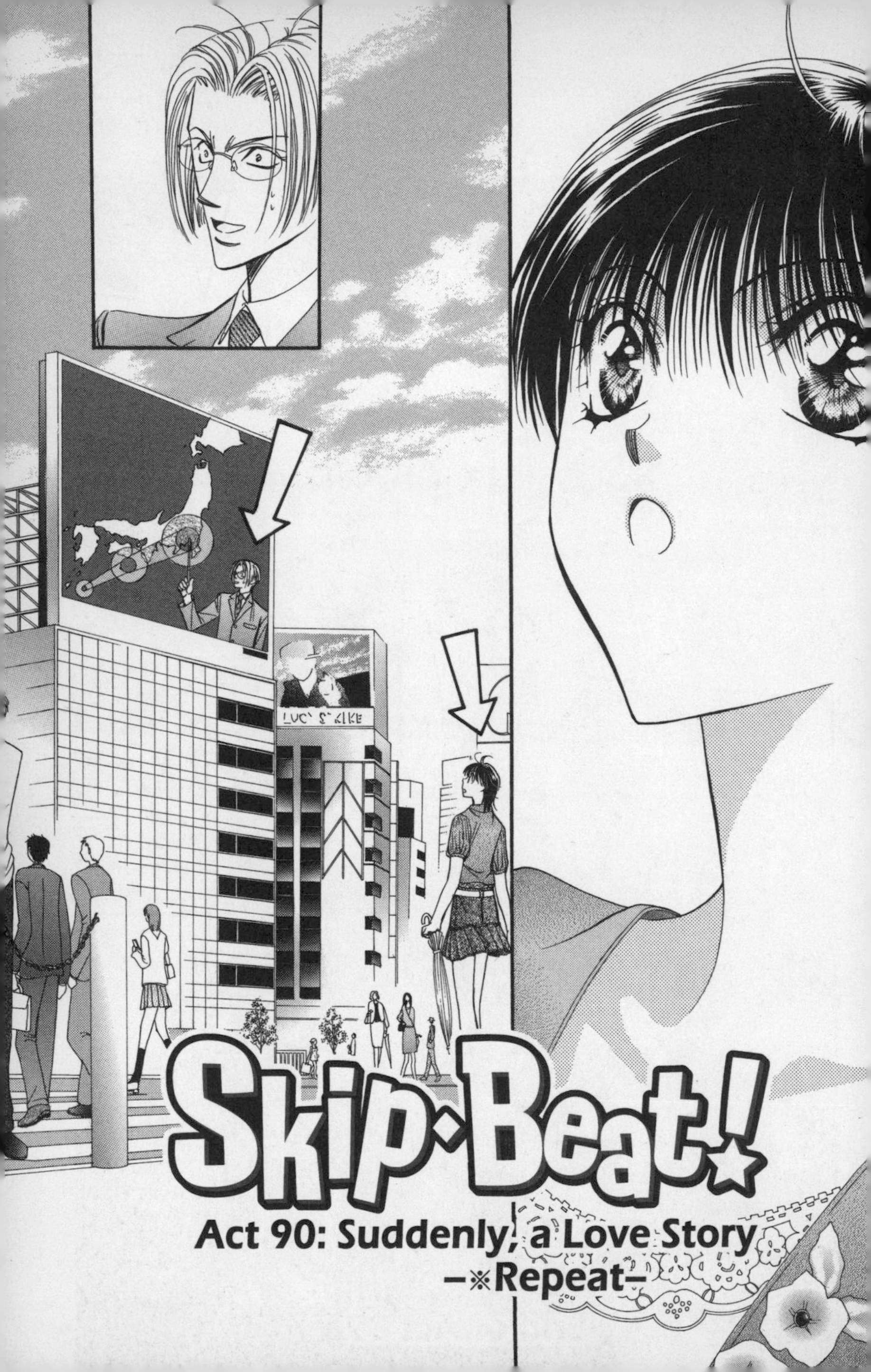
Skip·Beat!
Act 90: Suddenly, a Love Story
—※Repeat—

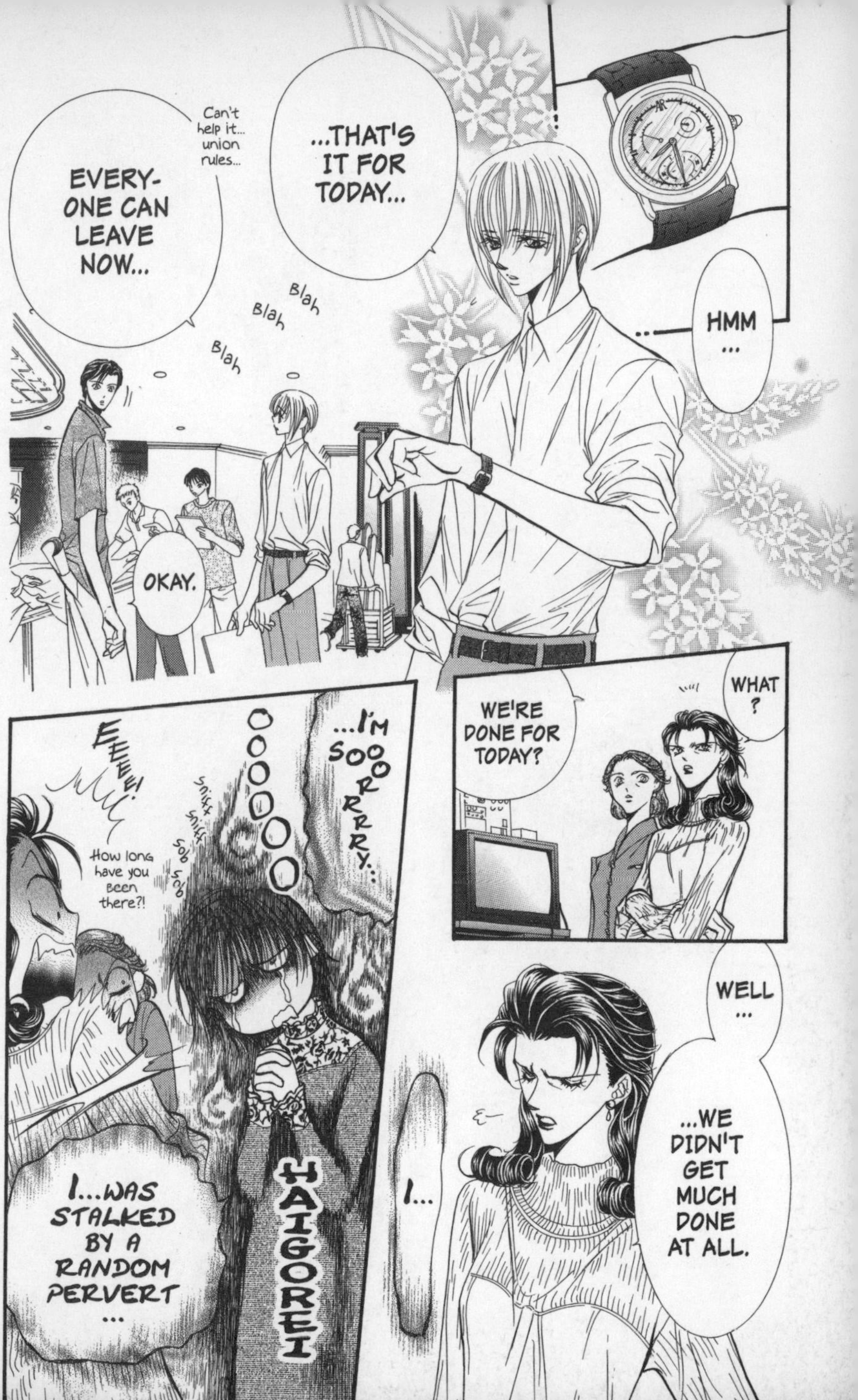
HMM ...
...THAT'S IT FOR TODAY...
Can't help it... union rules...
EVERY-ONE CAN LEAVE NOW...
Blah
Blah
Blah
OKAY.
WHAT ?
WE'RE DONE FOR TODAY?
WELL ...
...WE DIDN'T GET MUCH DONE AT ALL.
I...
...I'M SOOOORRRRY...
EEEE!
How long have you been there?!
Sniff sniff
sob sob
I...WAS STALKED BY A RANDOM PERVERT ...
HAIGOREI

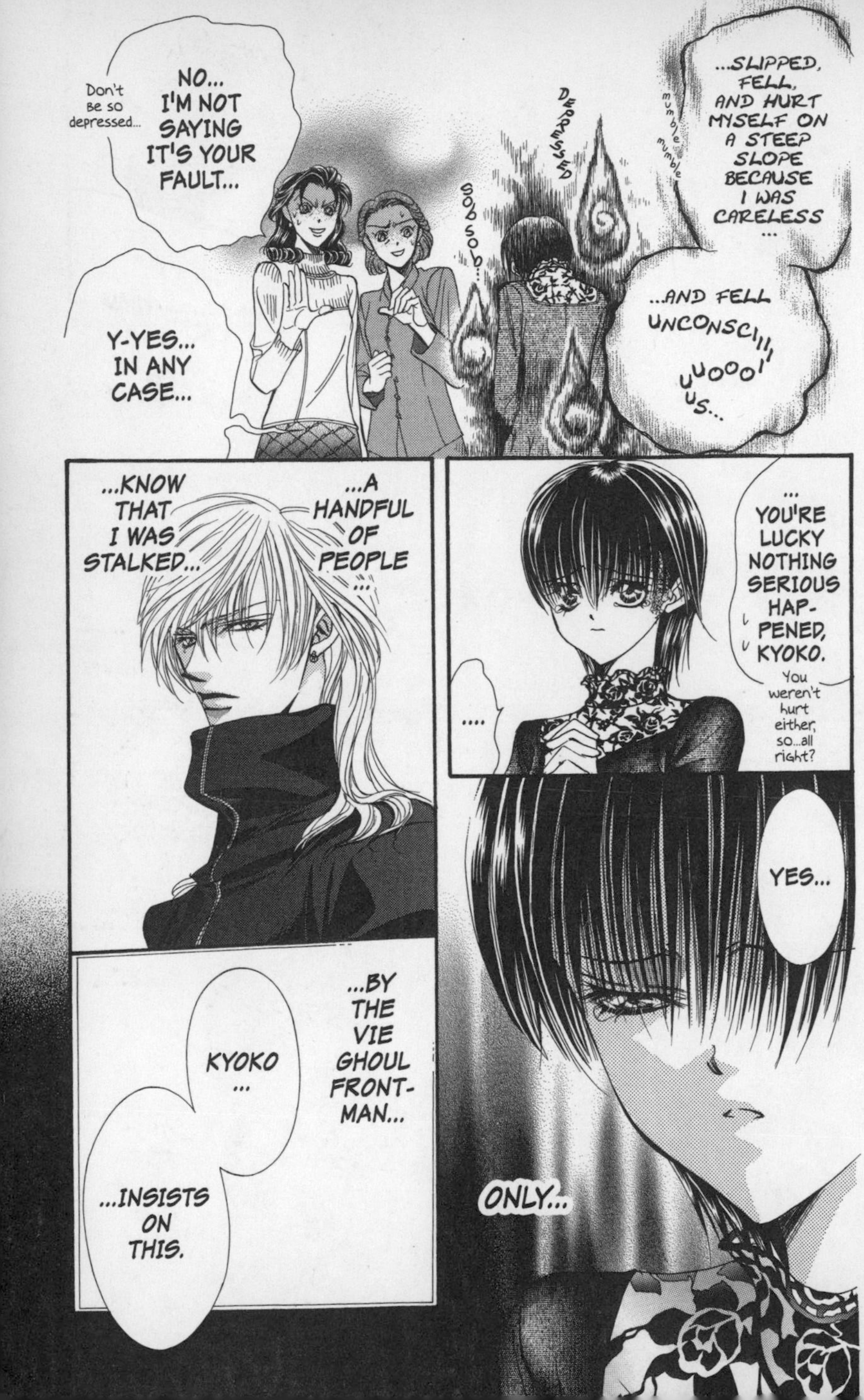
...SLIPPED, FELL, AND HURT MYSELF ON A STEEP SLOPE BECAUSE I WAS CARELESS...
mumble mumble
DEPRESSED
...AND FELL UNCONSCIIII UUOOO! US...
sob sob...
NO... I'M NOT SAYING IT'S YOUR FAULT...
Don't be so depressed...
Y-YES... IN ANY CASE...
... YOU'RE LUCKY NOTHING SERIOUS HAP-PENED, KYOKO.
You weren't hurt either, so...all right?
....
YES...
ONLY...
...A HANDFUL OF PEOPLE...
...KNOW THAT I WAS STALKED...
...BY THE VIE GHOUL FRONT-MAN...
KYOKO...
...INSISTS ON THIS.

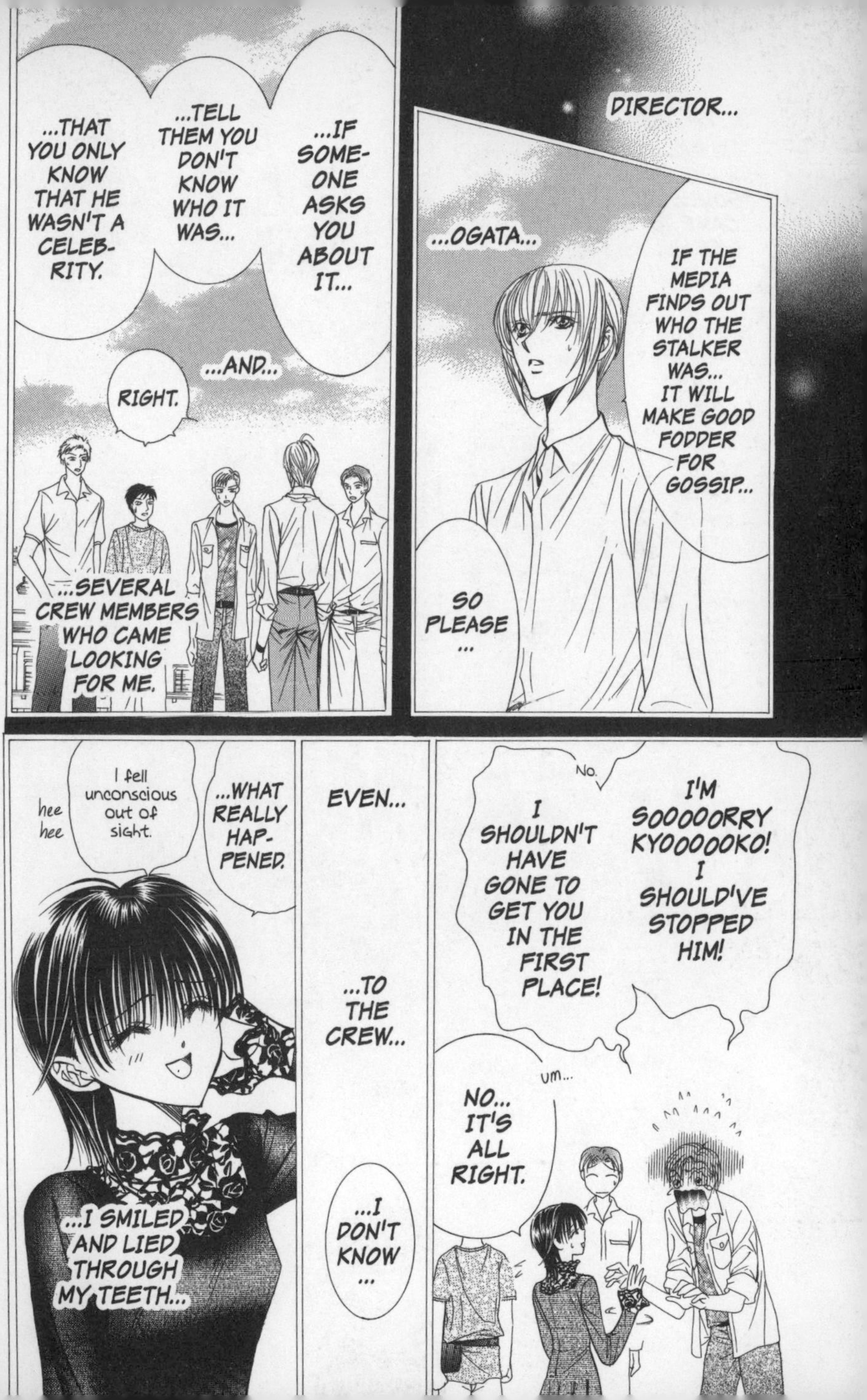
DIRECTOR...
...OGATA...
IF THE MEDIA FINDS OUT WHO THE STALKER WAS... IT WILL MAKE GOOD FODDER FOR GOSSIP...
SO PLEASE ...
...IF SOME-ONE ASKS YOU ABOUT IT...
...TELL THEM YOU DON'T KNOW WHO IT WAS...
...THAT YOU ONLY KNOW THAT HE WASN'T A CELEB-RITY.
...AND...
RIGHT.
...SEVERAL CREW MEMBERS WHO CAME LOOKING FOR ME.
I'M SOOOOORRY KYOOOOOKO! I SHOULD'VE STOPPED HIM!
No.
I SHOULDN'T HAVE GONE TO GET YOU IN THE FIRST PLACE!
um...
NO... IT'S ALL RIGHT.
EVEN...
...TO THE CREW...
...I DON'T KNOW ...
...WHAT REALLY HAP-PENED.
I fell unconscious out of sight.
hee hee
...I SMILED AND LIED THROUGH MY TEETH...

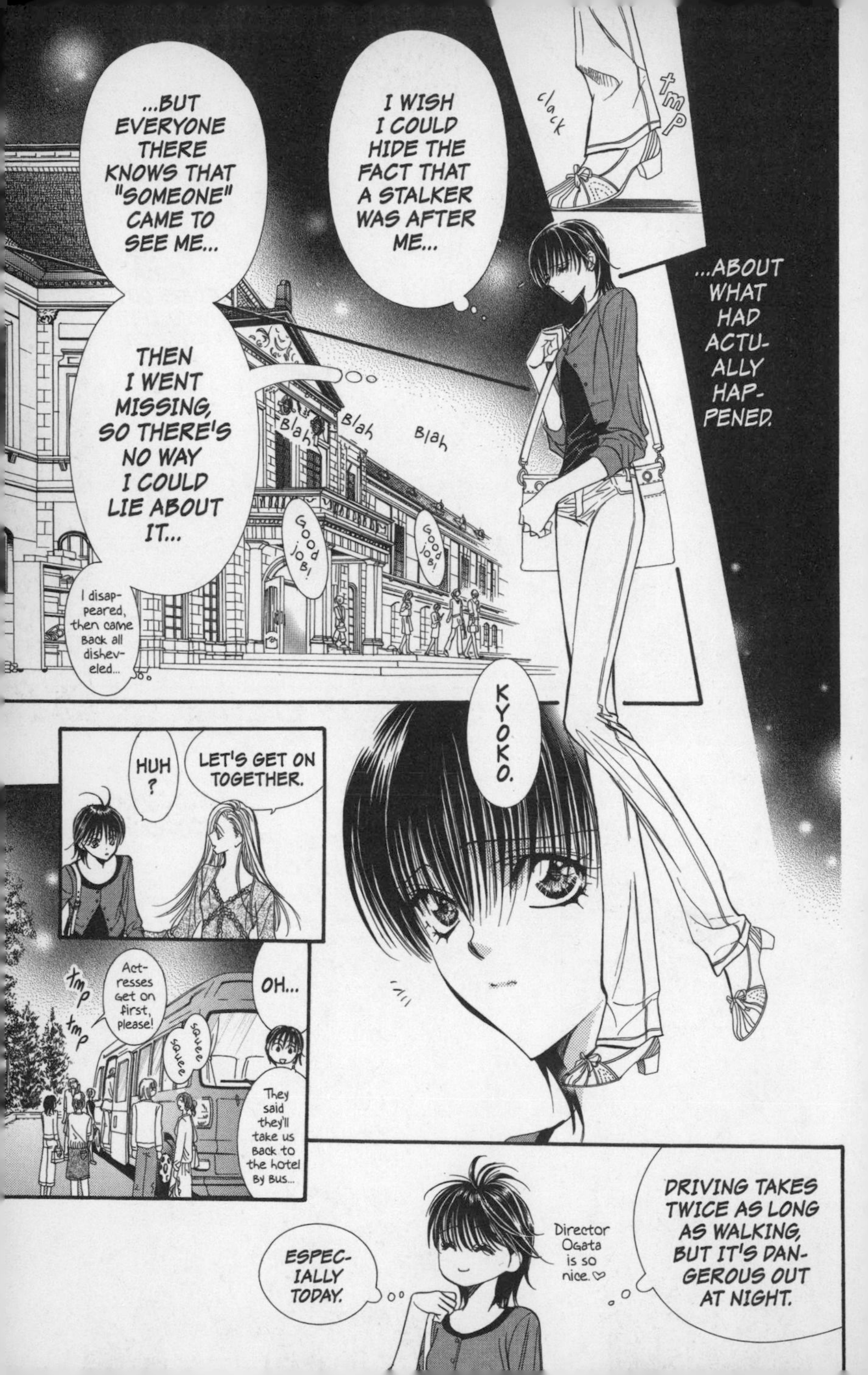

clack
tmp
...ABOUT WHAT HAD ACTUALLY HAPPENED.
I WISH I COULD HIDE THE FACT THAT A STALKER WAS AFTER ME...
...BUT EVERYONE THERE KNOWS THAT "SOMEONE" CAME TO SEE ME...
THEN I WENT MISSING, SO THERE'S NO WAY I COULD LIE ABOUT IT...
Blah
Blah
Blah
Good job!
Good job!
I disappeared, then came back all disheveled...
KYOKO.
LET'S GET ON TOGETHER.
HUH?
OH...
Actresses get on first, please!
xmp
xmp
squee
squee
They said they'll take us back to the hotel by bus...
DRIVING TAKES TWICE AS LONG AS WALKING, BUT IT'S DANGEROUS OUT AT NIGHT.
Director Ogata is so nice.♡
ESPECIALLY TODAY.

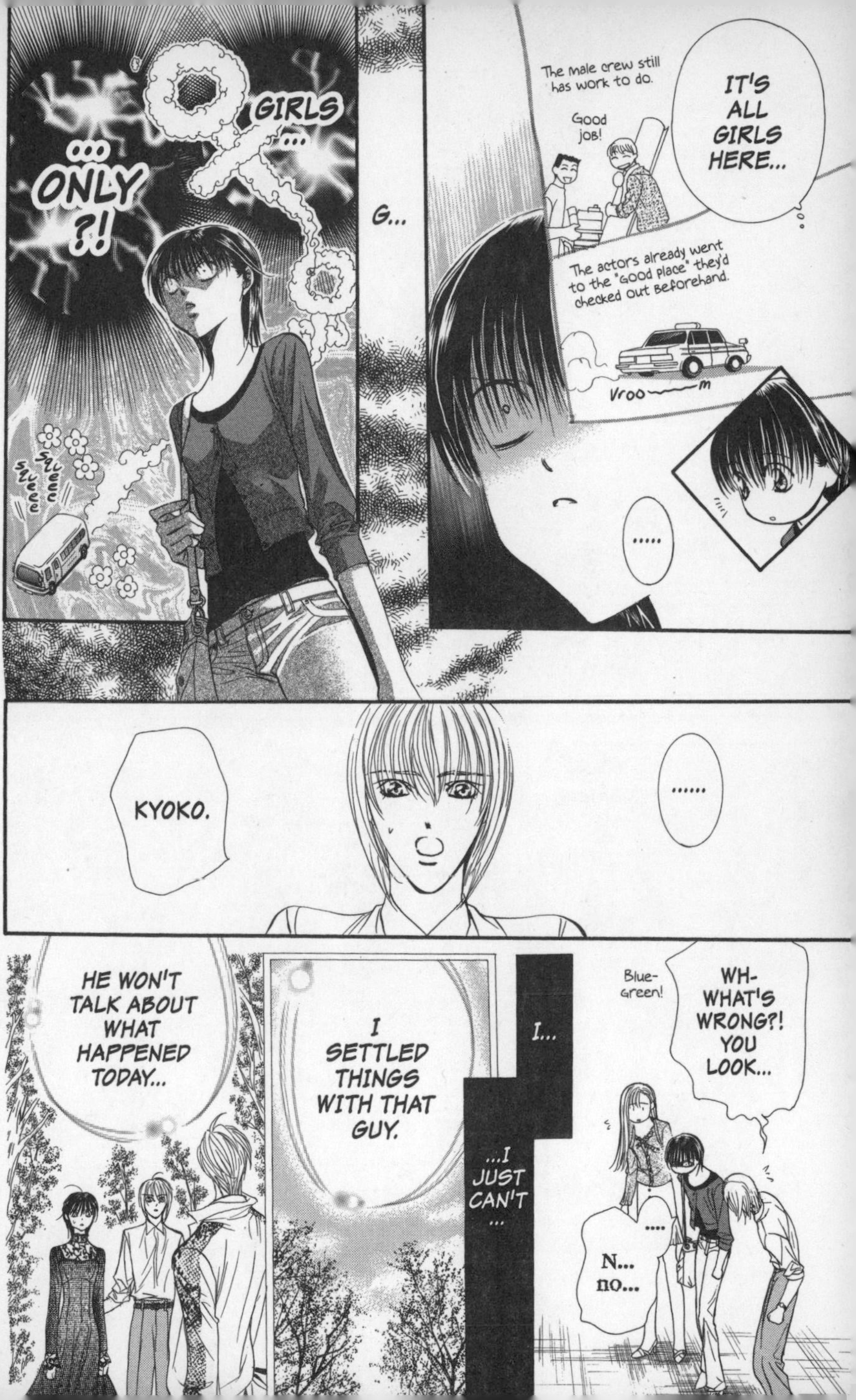
IT'S ALL GIRLS HERE...
The male crew still has work to do.
Good job!
The actors already went to the "Good place" they'd checked out beforehand.
Vroo——m
......
G...
GIRLS...
...ONLY?!
......
KYOKO.
WH-WHAT'S WRONG?! YOU LOOK...
Blue-Green!
....
N... no...
I...
...I JUST CAN'T ...
I SETTLED THINGS WITH THAT GUY.
HE WON'T TALK ABOUT WHAT HAPPENED TODAY...

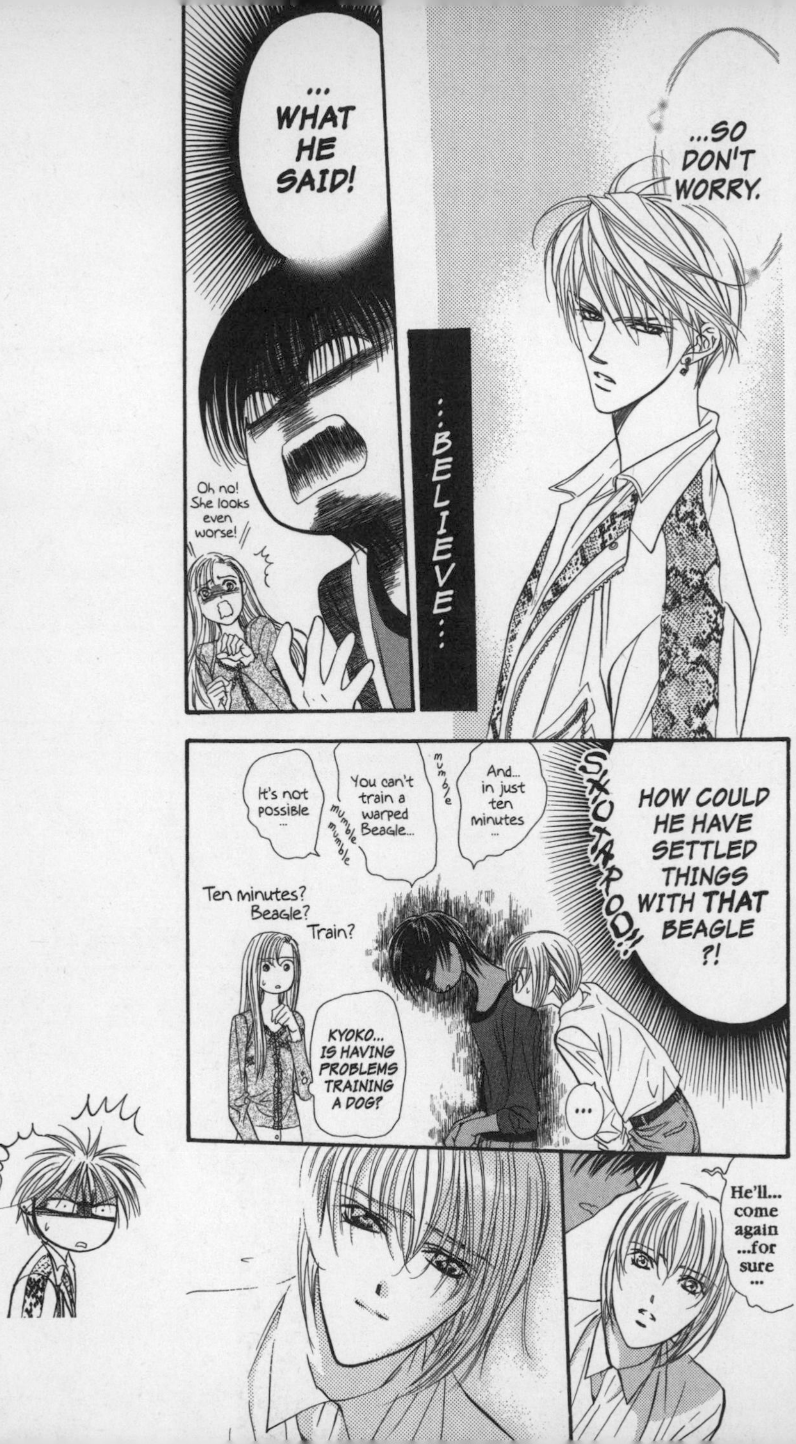
...SO DON'T WORRY.
...BELIEVE...
... WHAT HE SAID!
Oh no! She looks even worse!
HOW COULD HE HAVE SETTLED THINGS WITH THAT BEAGLE ?!
SHOTAROO!!
And... in just ten minutes ...
mumble
You can't train a warped Beagle...
mumble mumble
It's not possible ...
Ten minutes? Beagle? Train?
KYOKO... IS HAVING PROBLEMS TRAINING A DOG?
...
He'll... come again ...for sure ...

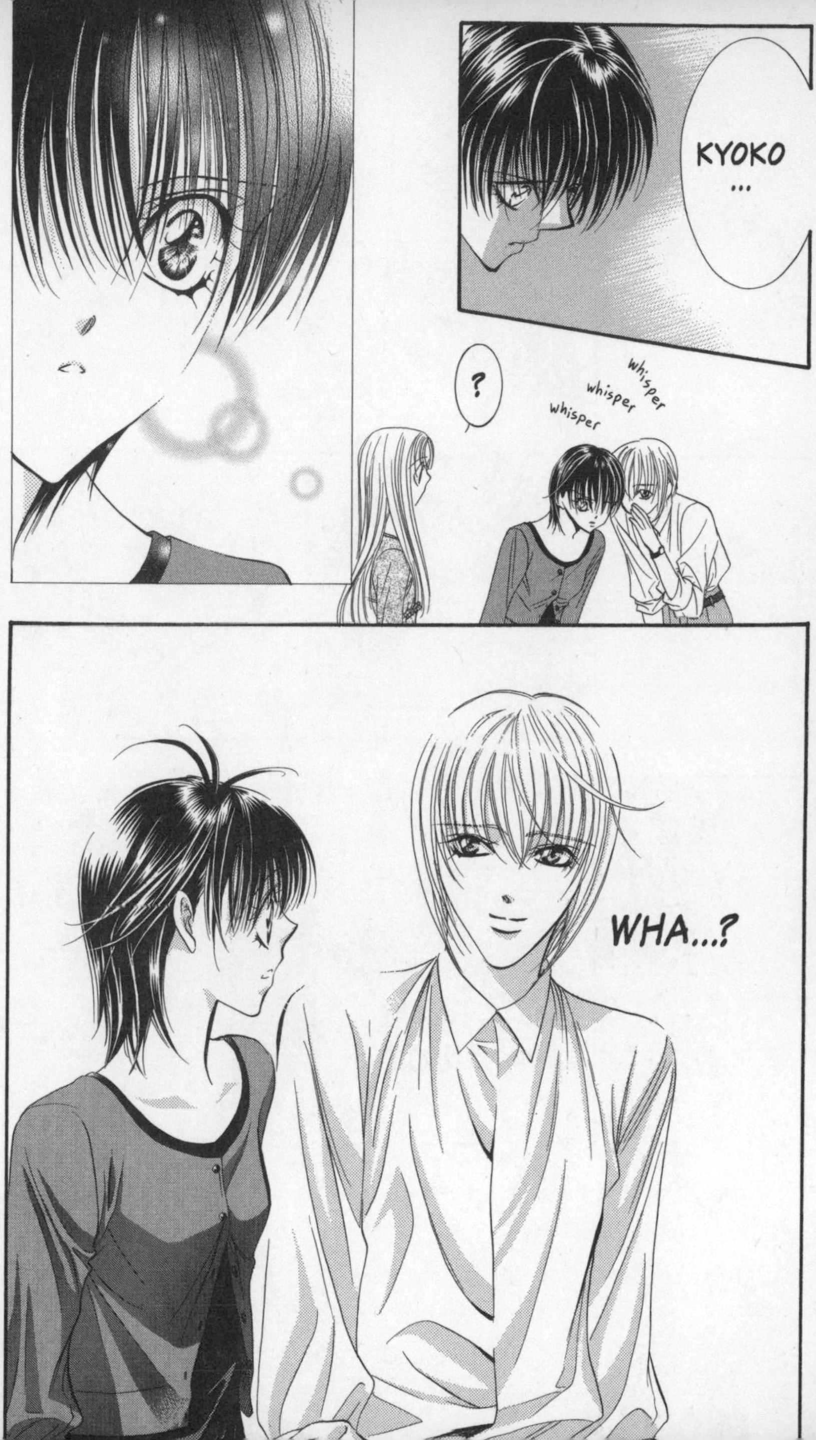
KYOKO ...
whisper
whisper
whisper
?
WHA...?

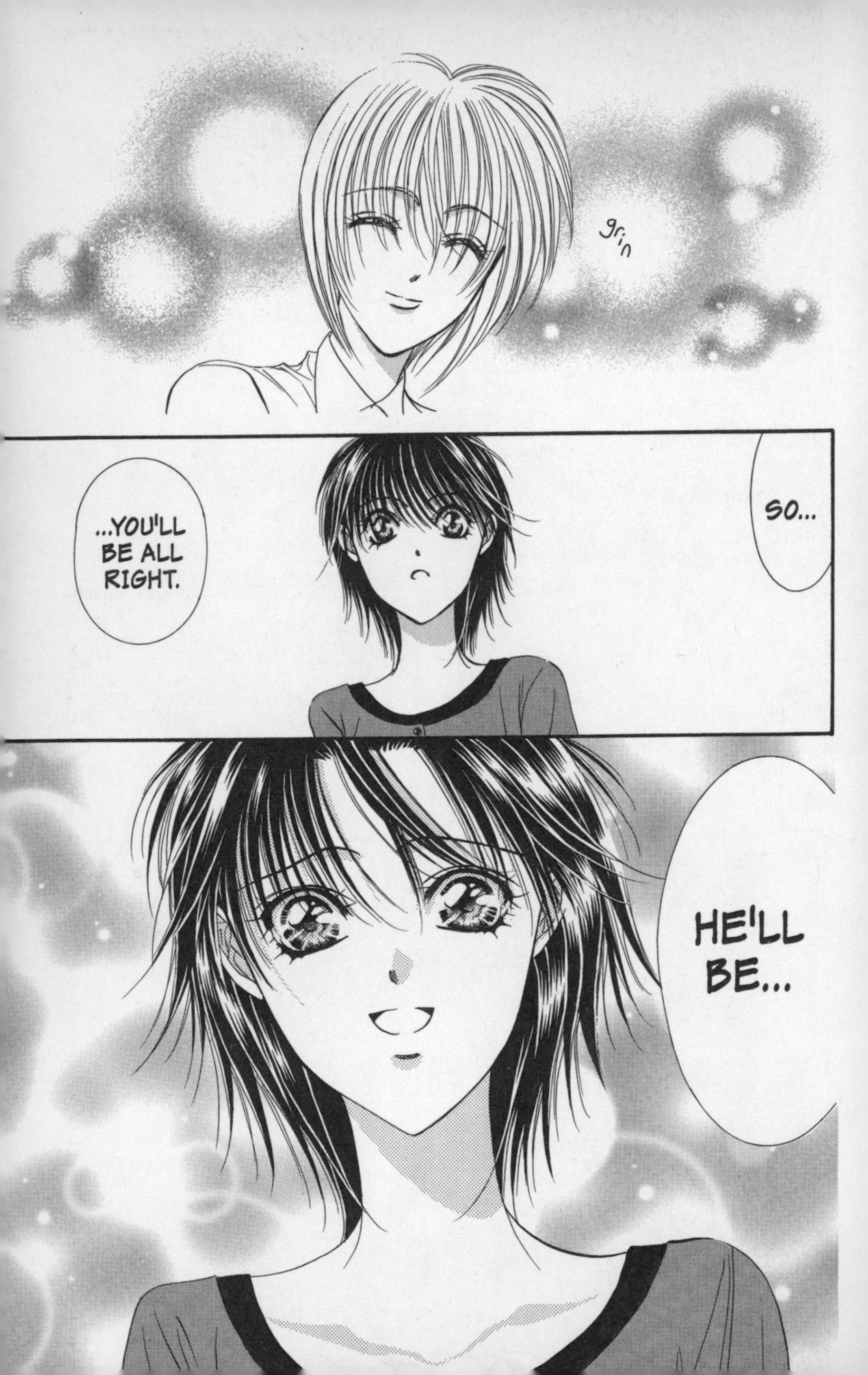
grin
SO...
...YOU'LL BE ALL RIGHT.
HE'LL BE...

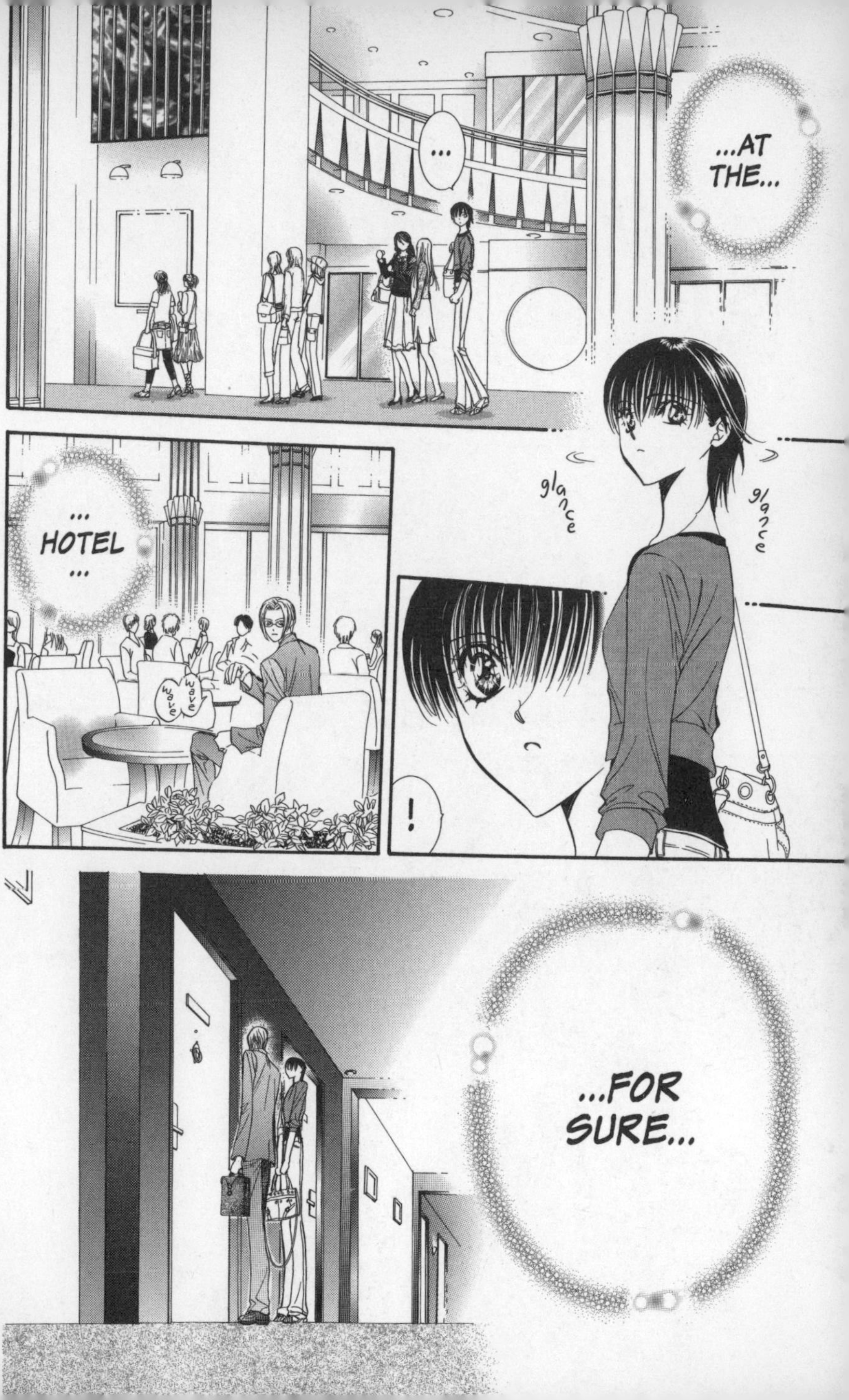
...AT THE...
...
glance glance
!
... HOTEL ...
wave wave
...FOR SURE...

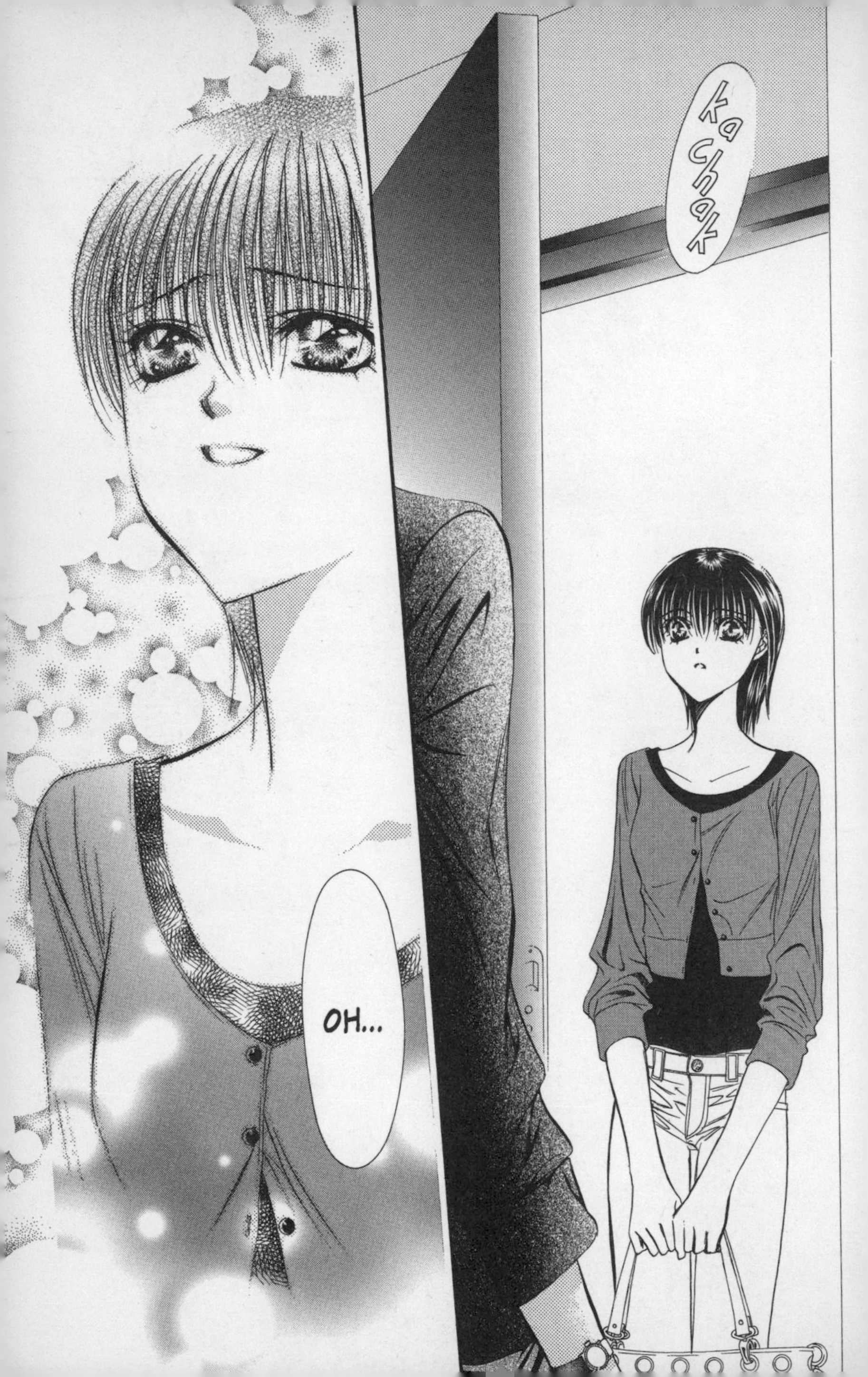
ka chak
OH...

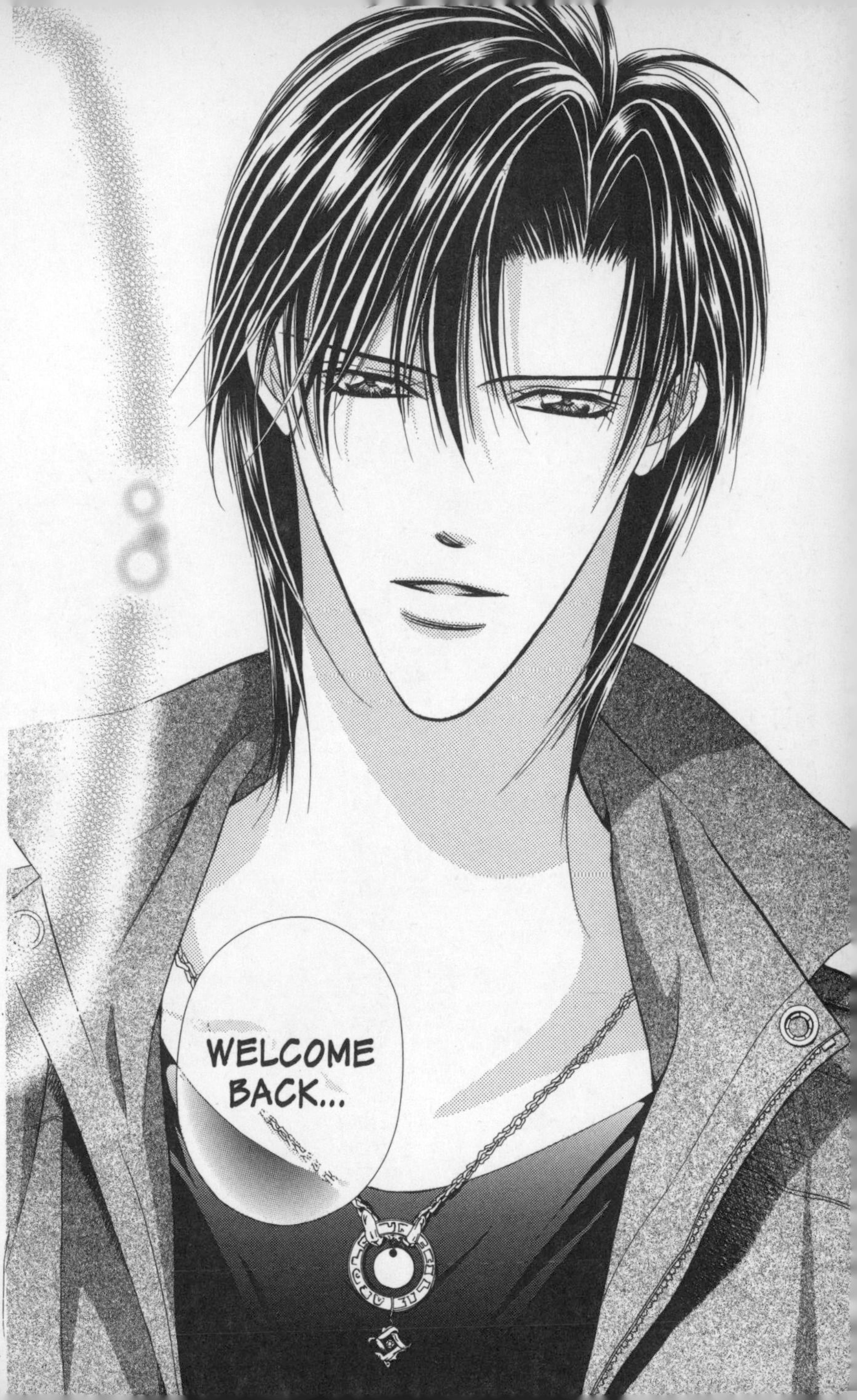
WELCOME BACK...

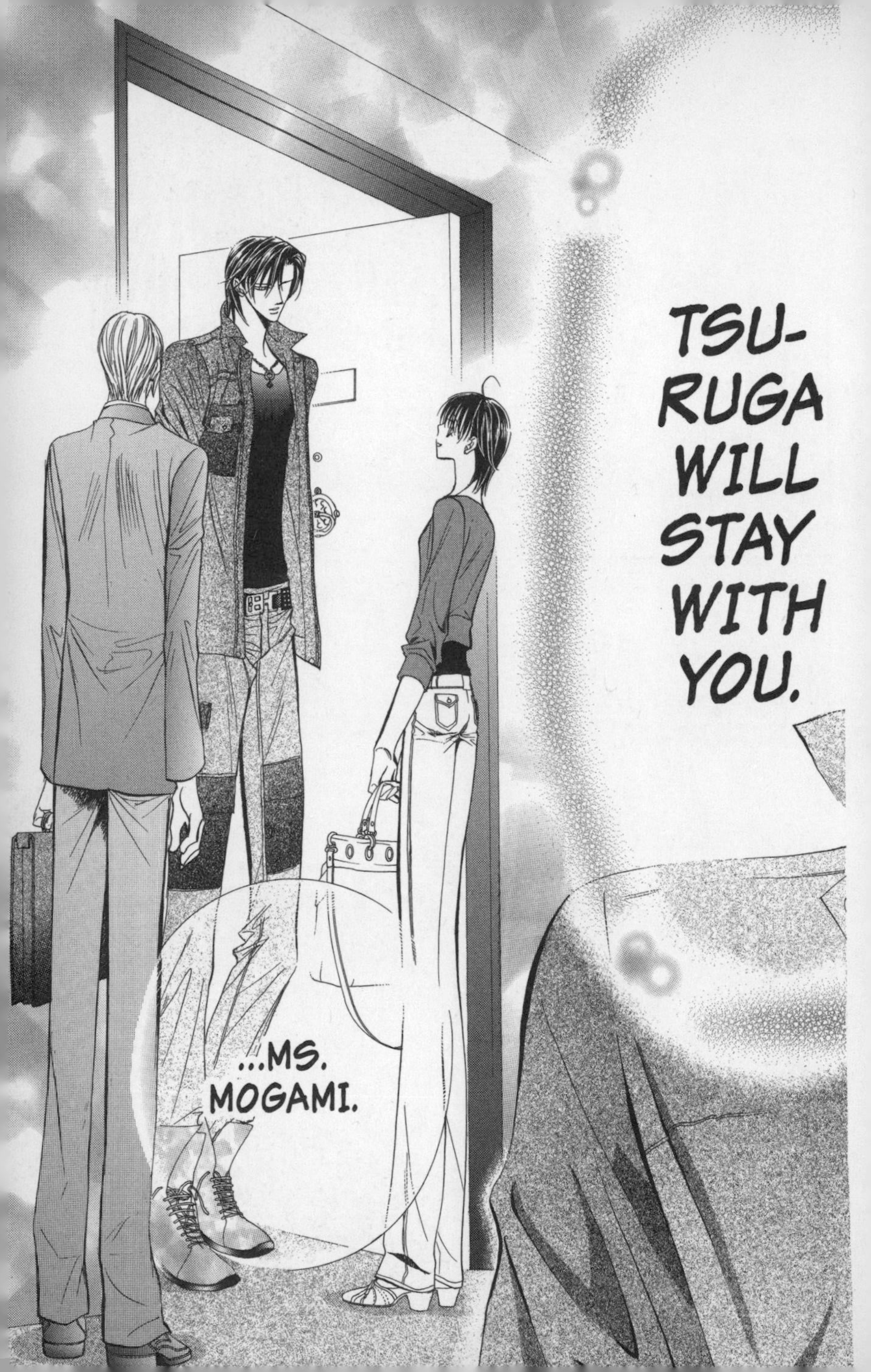
TSU-RUGA WILL STAY WITH YOU.
...MS. MOGAMI.

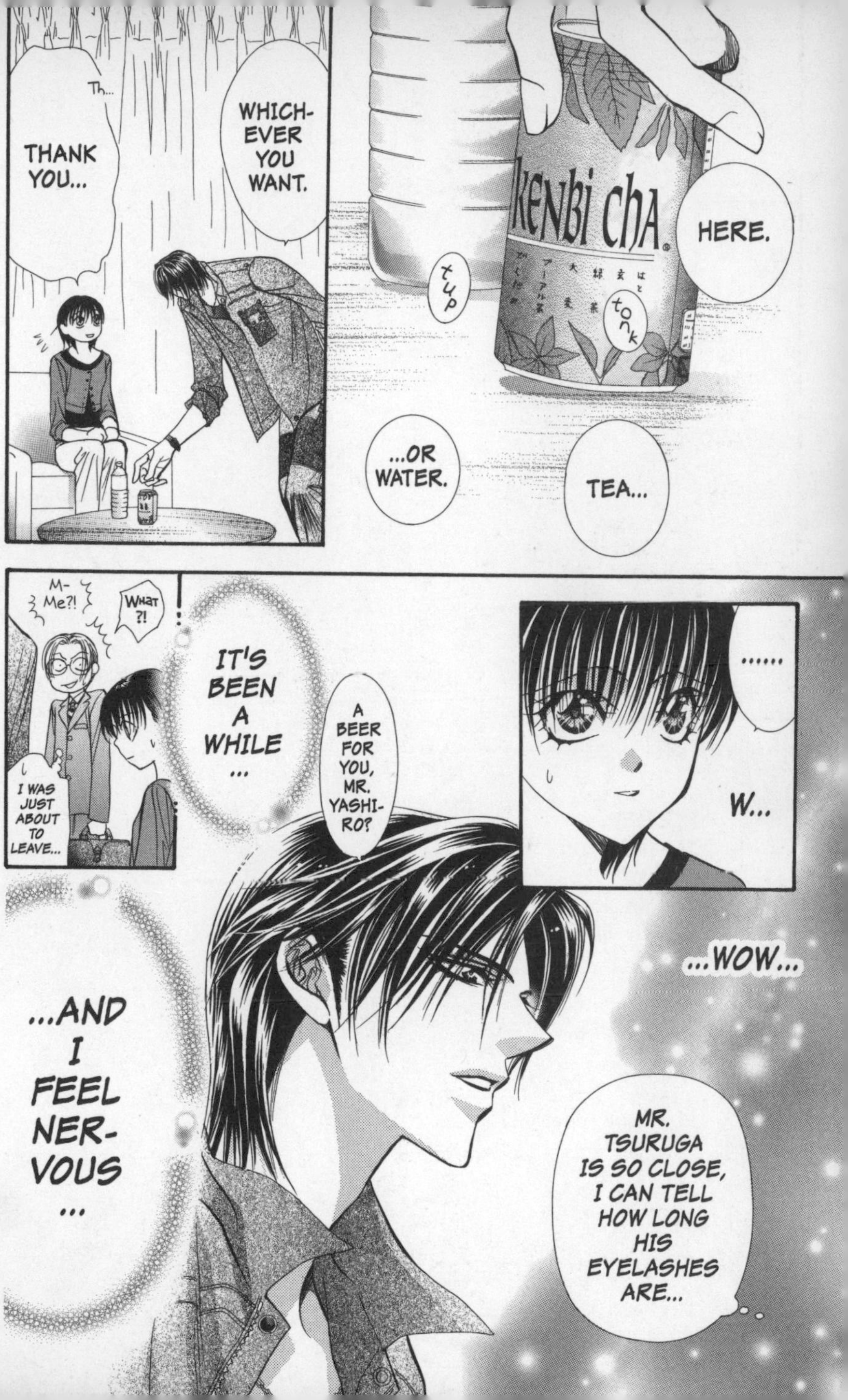
HERE.
tonk
tup
TEA...
...OR WATER.
WHICH-EVER YOU WANT.
Th...
THANK YOU...
KENBI CHA
......
W...
...WOW...
MR. TSURUGA IS SO CLOSE, I CAN TELL HOW LONG HIS EYELASHES ARE...
A BEER FOR YOU, MR. YASHIRO?
M- Me?!
What ?!
I WAS JUST ABOUT TO LEAVE...
IT'S BEEN A WHILE...
...AND I FEEL NER-VOUS...

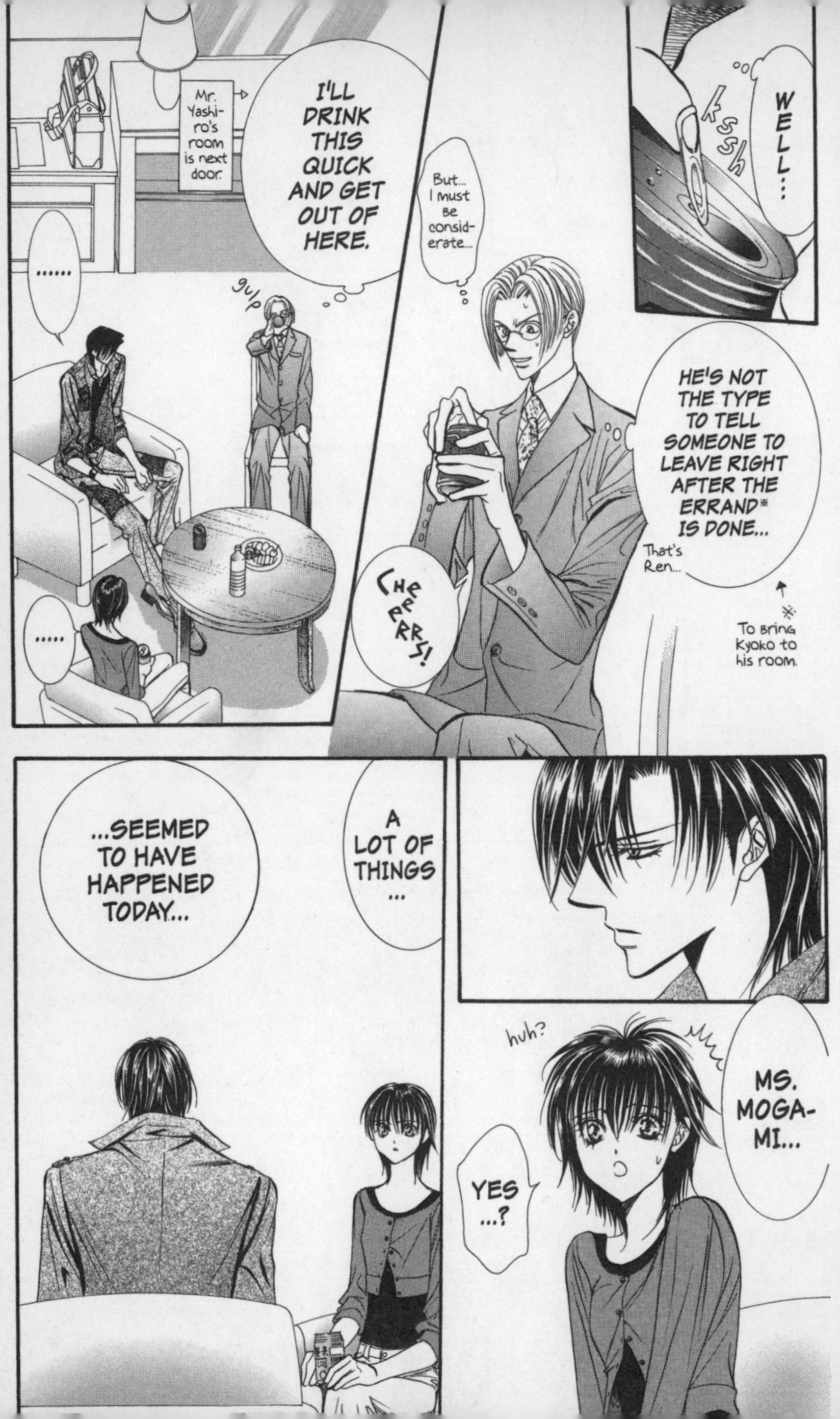
WELL...
kssh
But... I must be consid-erate...
HE'S NOT THE TYPE TO TELL SOMEONE TO LEAVE RIGHT AFTER THE ERRAND※ IS DONE...
That's Ren...
※ To bring Kyoko to his room.
CHEERRS!
I'LL DRINK THIS QUICK AND GET OUT OF HERE.
Mr. Yashi-ro's room is next door.
gulp
......
......
MS. MOGA-MI...
huh?
YES ...?
A LOT OF THINGS ...
...SEEMED TO HAVE HAPPENED TODAY...

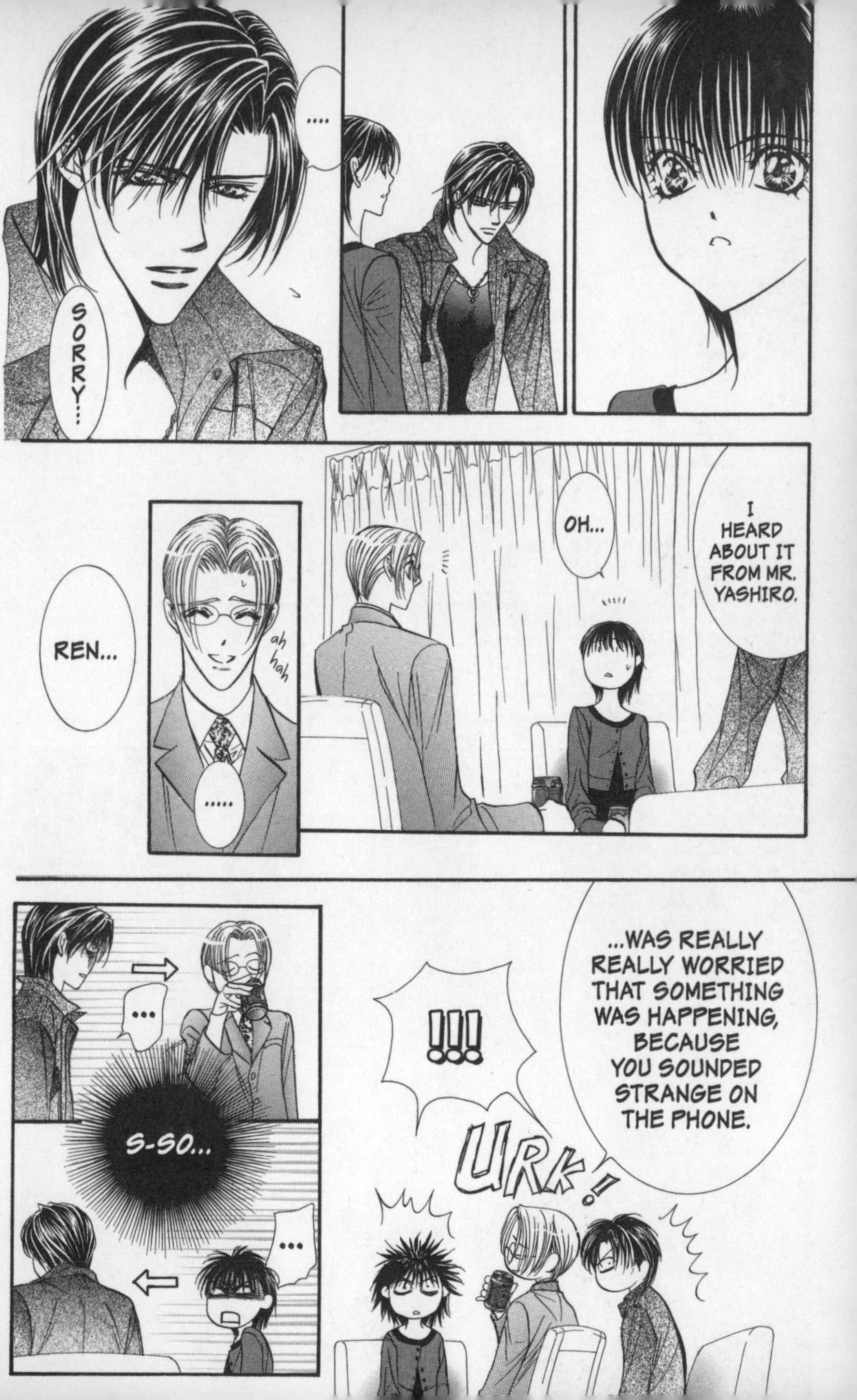
....
SORRY...
I HEARD ABOUT IT FROM MR. YASHIRO.
OH...
REN...
ah hah
......
...WAS REALLY REALLY WORRIED THAT SOMETHING WAS HAPPENING, BECAUSE YOU SOUNDED STRANGE ON THE PHONE.
!!!
URK!
...
S-SO...
...

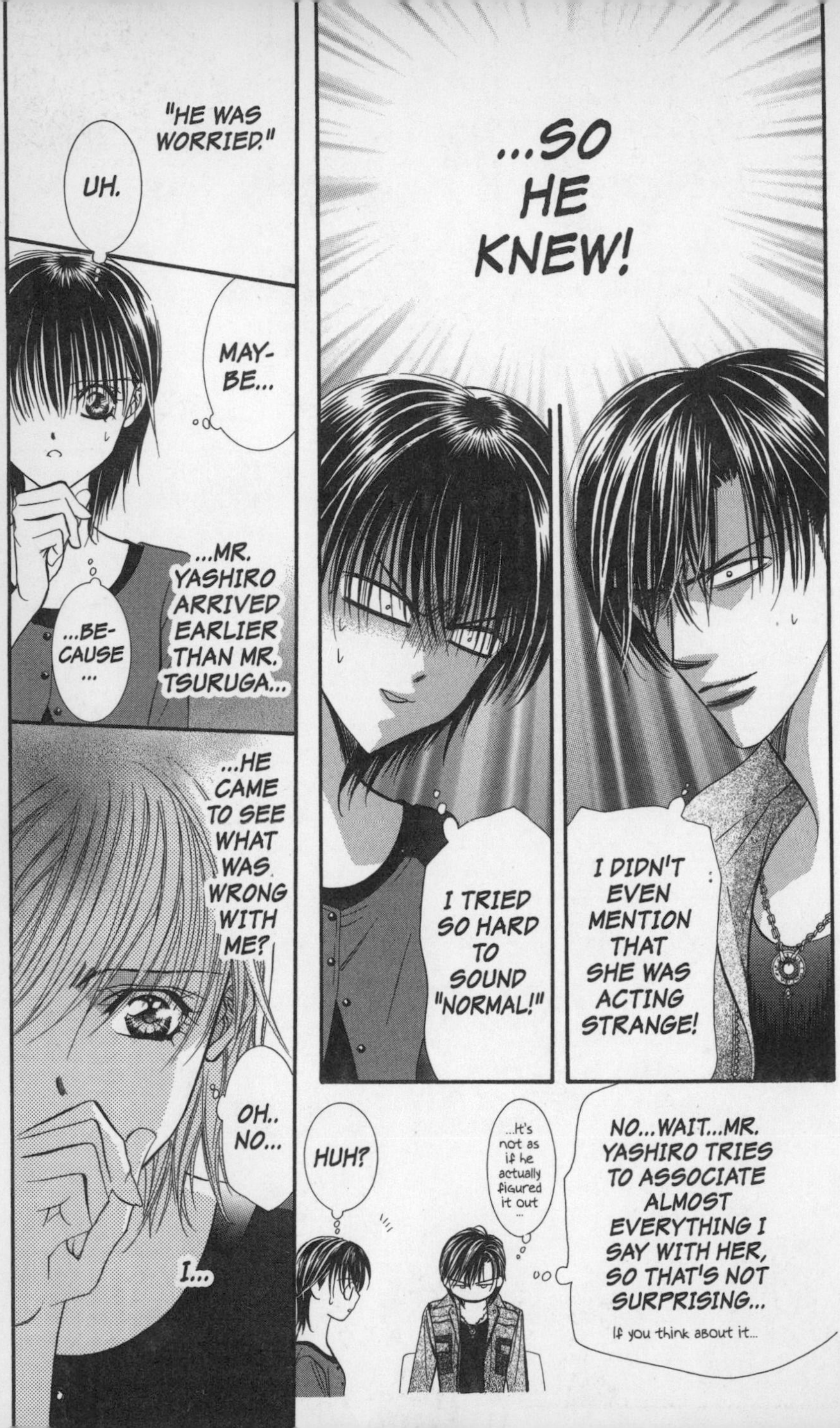
...SO HE KNEW!
I DIDN'T EVEN MENTION THAT SHE WAS ACTING STRANGE!
I TRIED SO HARD TO SOUND "NORMAL!"
NO...WAIT...MR. YASHIRO TRIES TO ASSOCIATE ALMOST EVERYTHING I SAY WITH HER, SO THAT'S NOT SURPRISING...
If you think about it...
...It's not as if he actually figured it out ...
HUH?
"HE WAS WORRIED."
UH.
MAY-BE...
...BE-CAUSE ...
...MR. YASHIRO ARRIVED EARLIER THAN MR. TSURUGA...
...HE CAME TO SEE WHAT WAS WRONG WITH ME?
OH.. NO...
I...

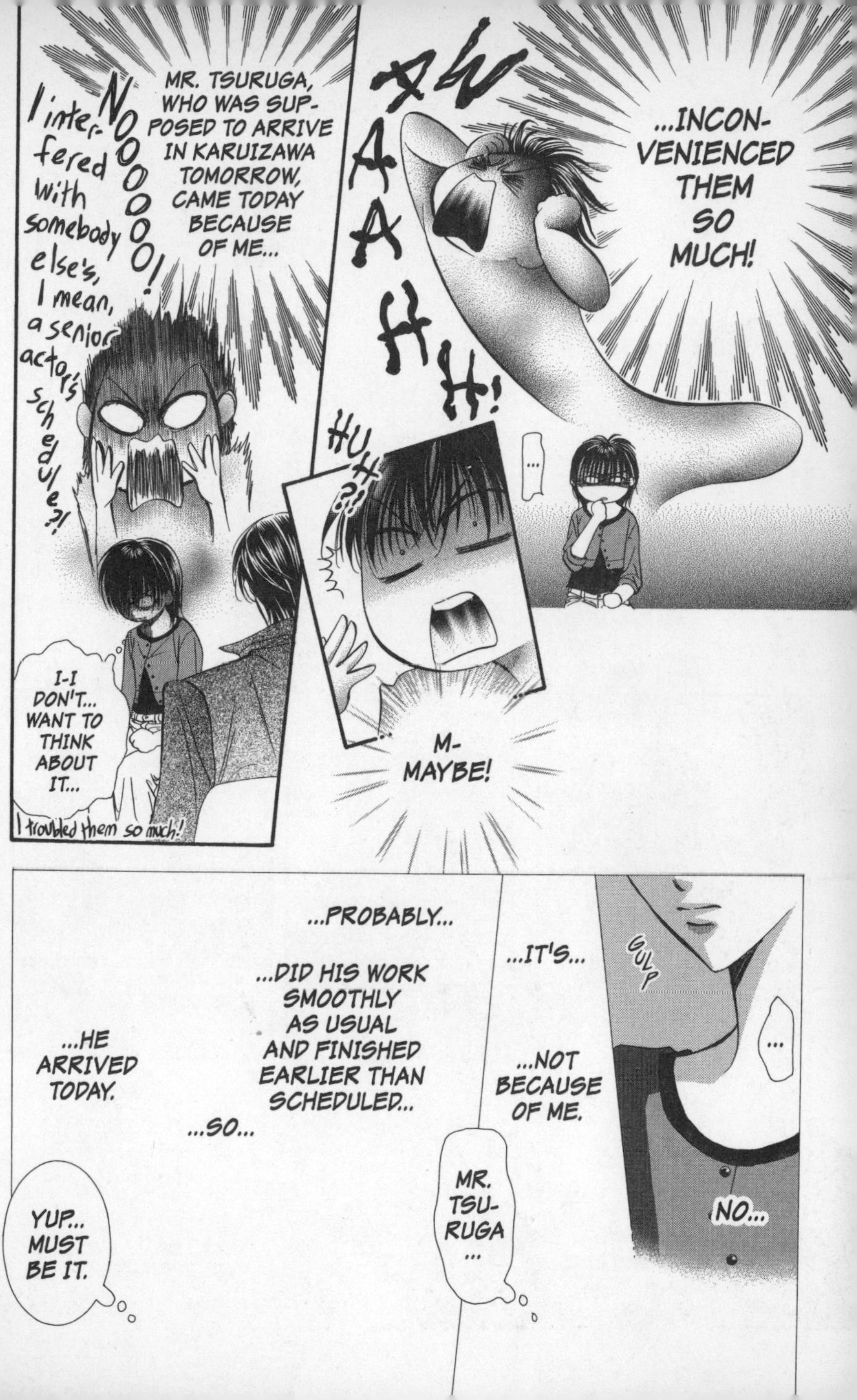
...INCONVENIENCED THEM SO MUCH!
AWAHHH!
...
HUH?!
M-MAYBE!
MR. TSURUGA, WHO WAS SUPPOSED TO ARRIVE IN KARUIZAWA TOMORROW, CAME TODAY BECAUSE OF ME...
NOOOOOOO!
I interfered with somebody else's, I mean, a senior actor's schedule?!
I-I DON'T... WANT TO THINK ABOUT IT...
I troubled them so much!
GULP
...
NO...
...IT'S...
...NOT BECAUSE OF ME.
MR. TSURUGA...
...PROBABLY...
...DID HIS WORK SMOOTHLY AS USUAL AND FINISHED EARLIER THAN SCHEDULED...
...SO...
...HE ARRIVED TODAY.
YUP... MUST BE IT.

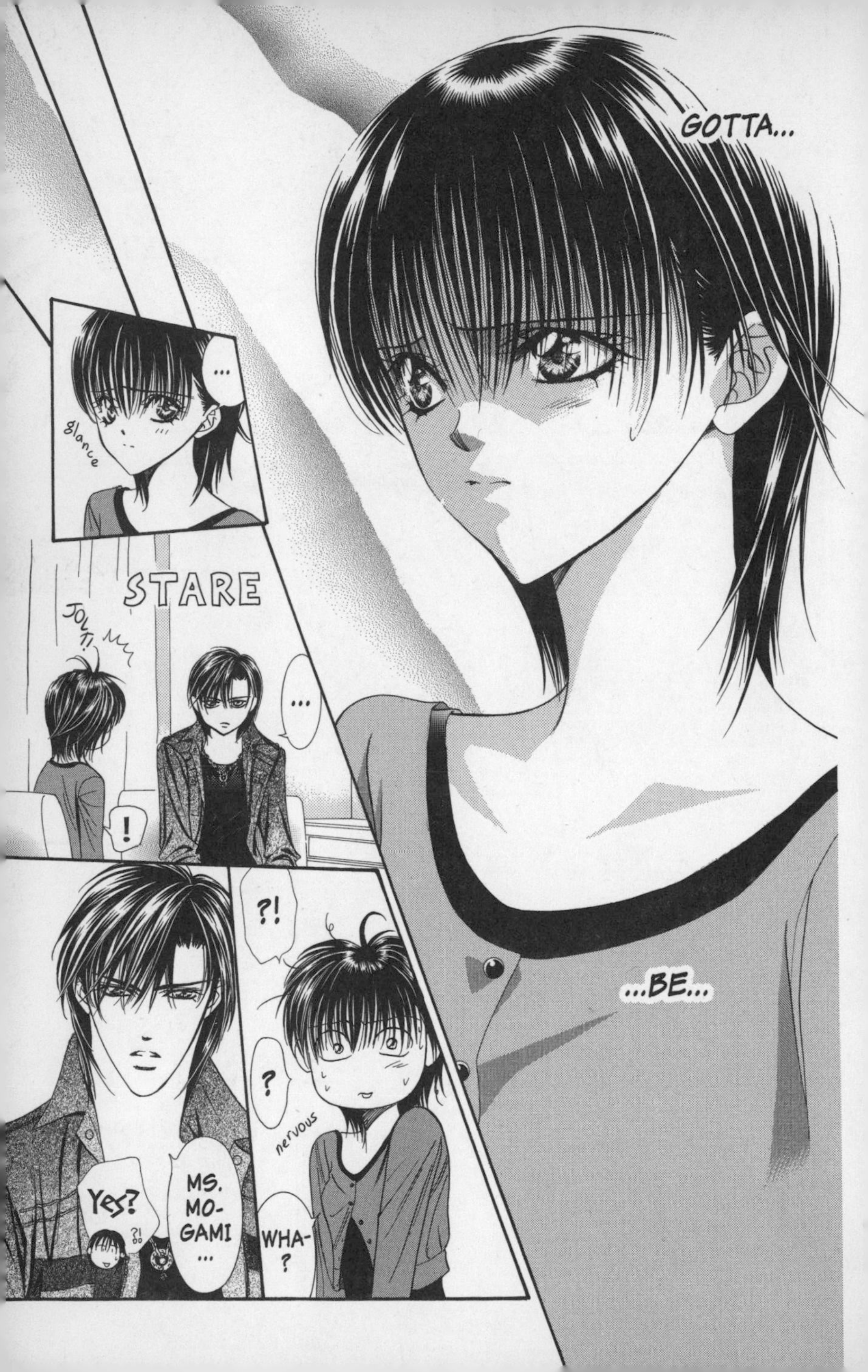
GOTTA...
...BE...
...
glance
STARE
JOLT!
...
!
?!
?
nervous
WHA-?
MS. MO-GAMI...
Yes?
?!

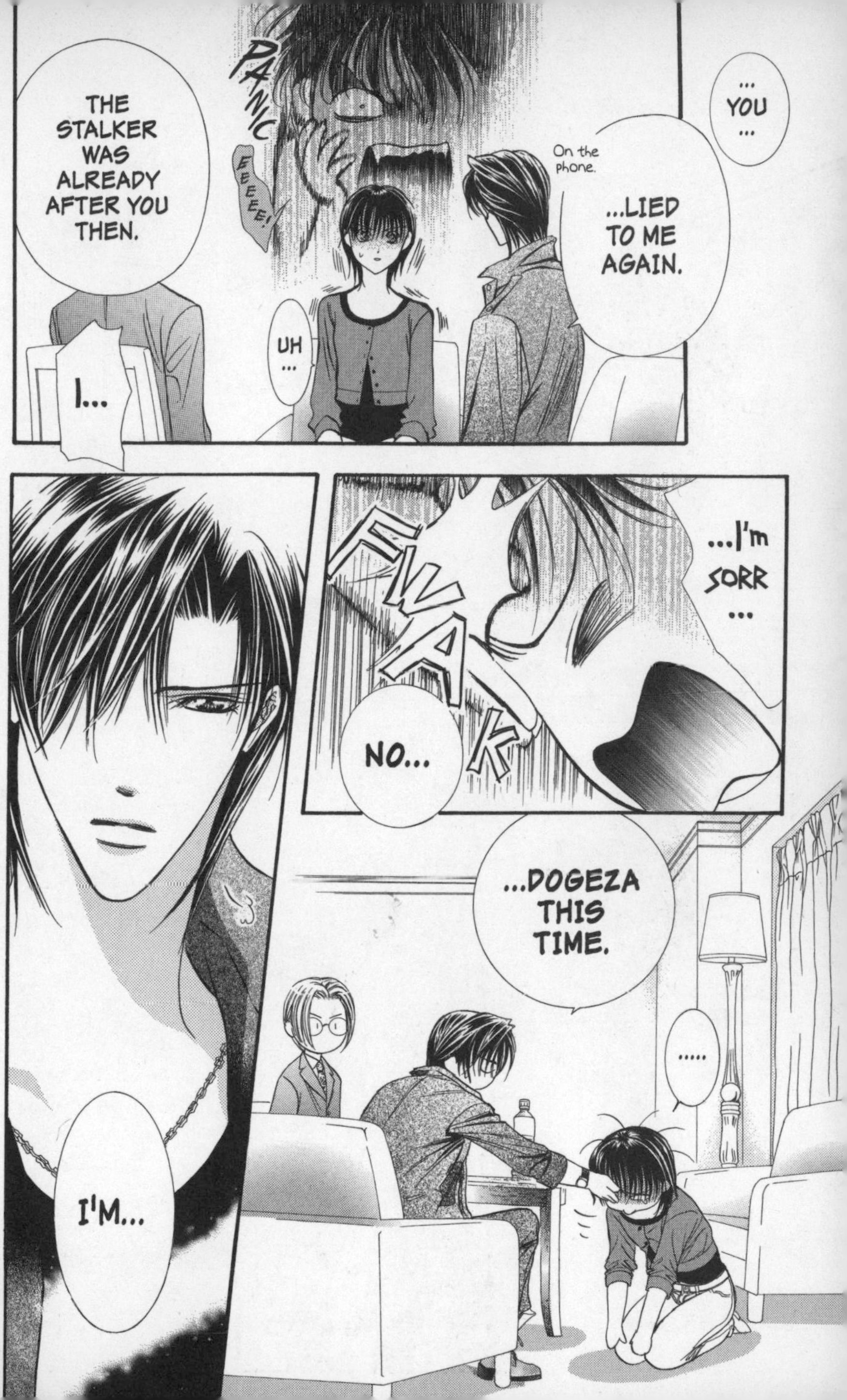

... YOU ...
On the phone.
...LIED TO ME AGAIN.
PANIC
EEEEE!
THE STALKER WAS ALREADY AFTER YOU THEN.
UH ...
I...
...I'm SORR ...
FWAK
NO...
...DOGEZA THIS TIME.
.....
I'M...

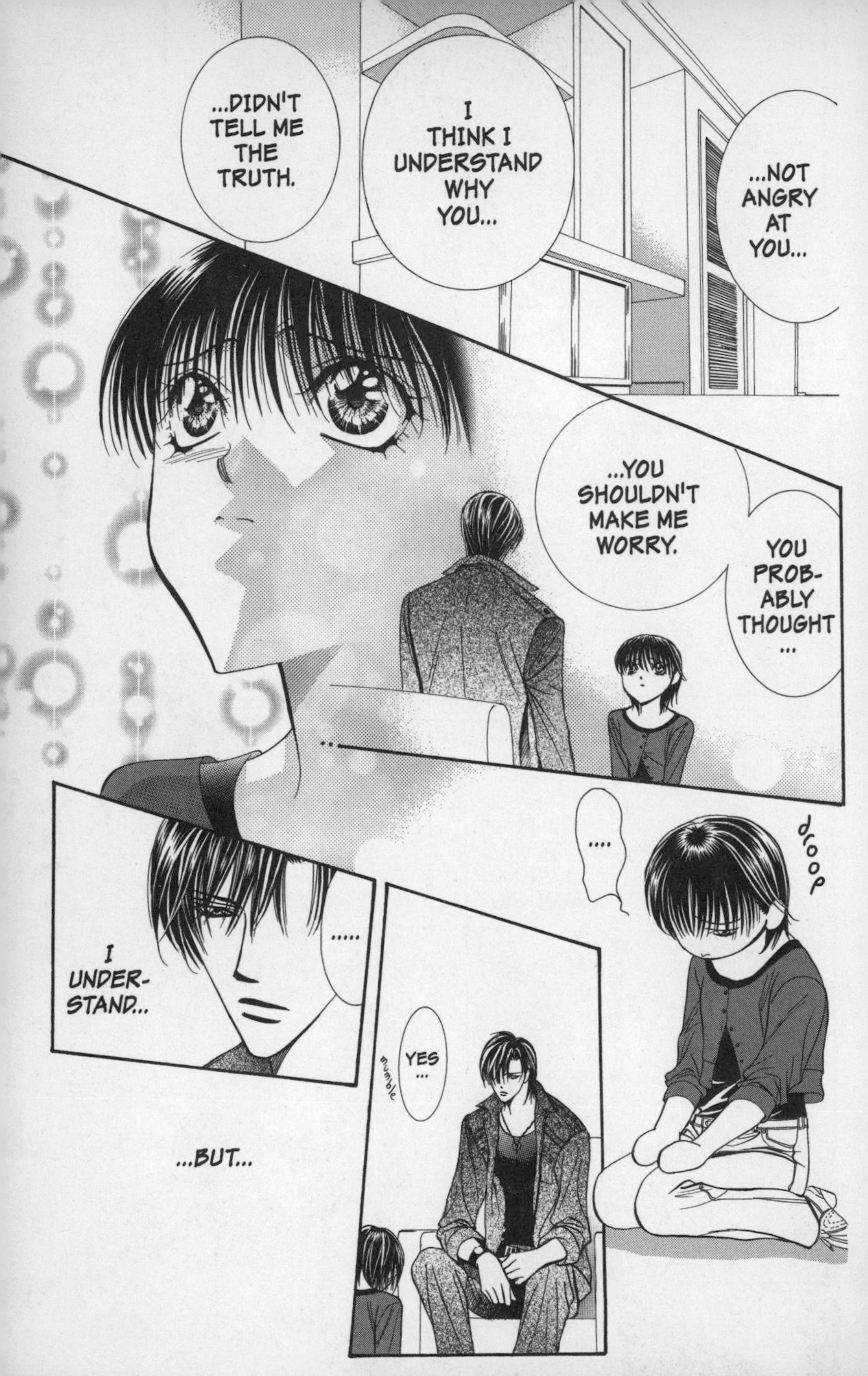
...NOT ANGRY AT YOU...
I THINK I UNDERSTAND WHY YOU...
...DIDN'T TELL ME THE TRUTH.
YOU PROBABLY THOUGHT...
...YOU SHOULDN'T MAKE ME WORRY.
...
....
droop
.....
YES ...
mumble
I UNDERSTAND...
...BUT...

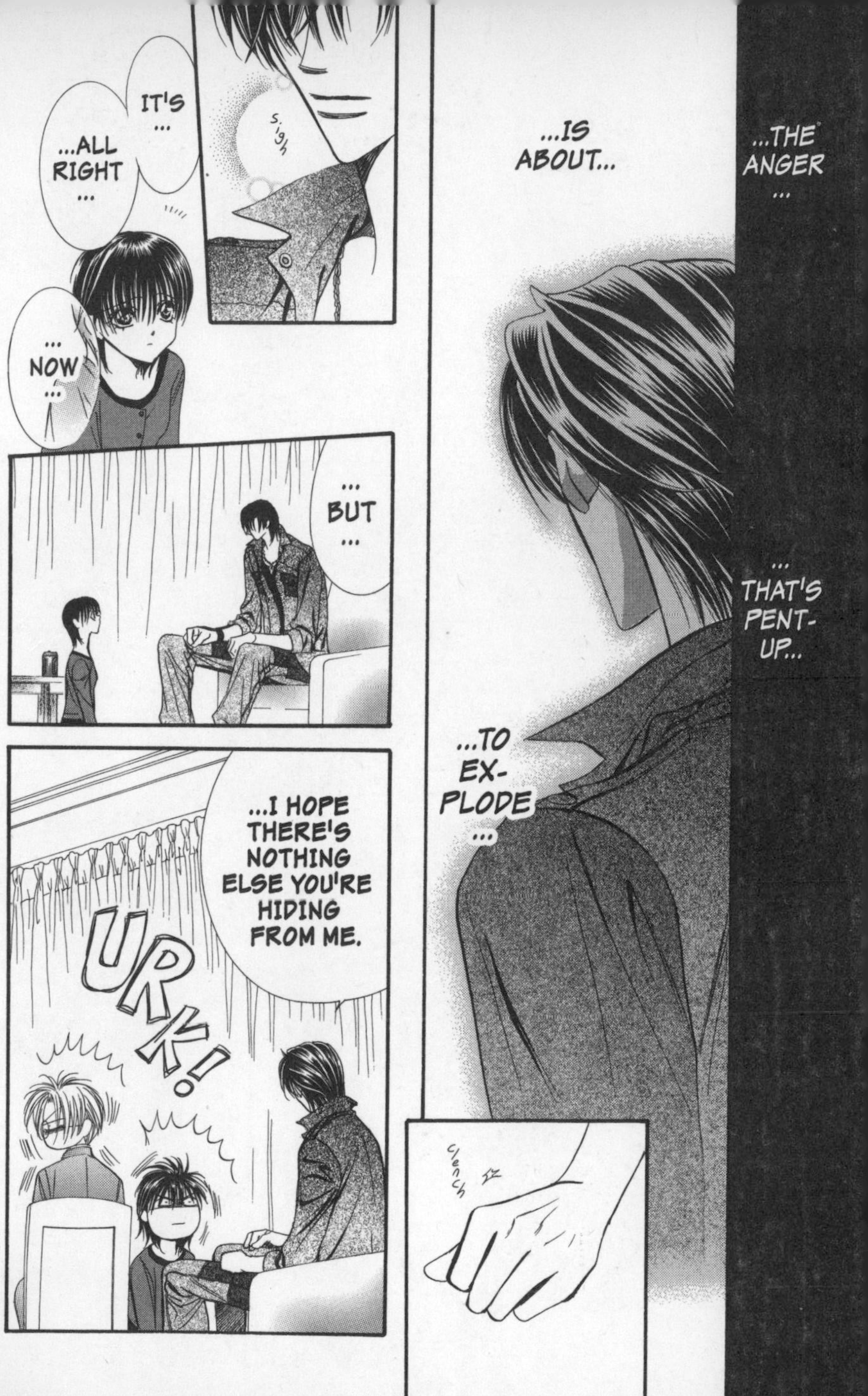
...THE ANGER ...
...IS ABOUT...
... THAT'S PENT-UP...
...TO EX-PLODE ...
clench
sigh
IT'S ...
...ALL RIGHT ...
... NOW ...
... BUT ...
...I HOPE THERE'S NOTHING ELSE YOU'RE HIDING FROM ME.
URK!

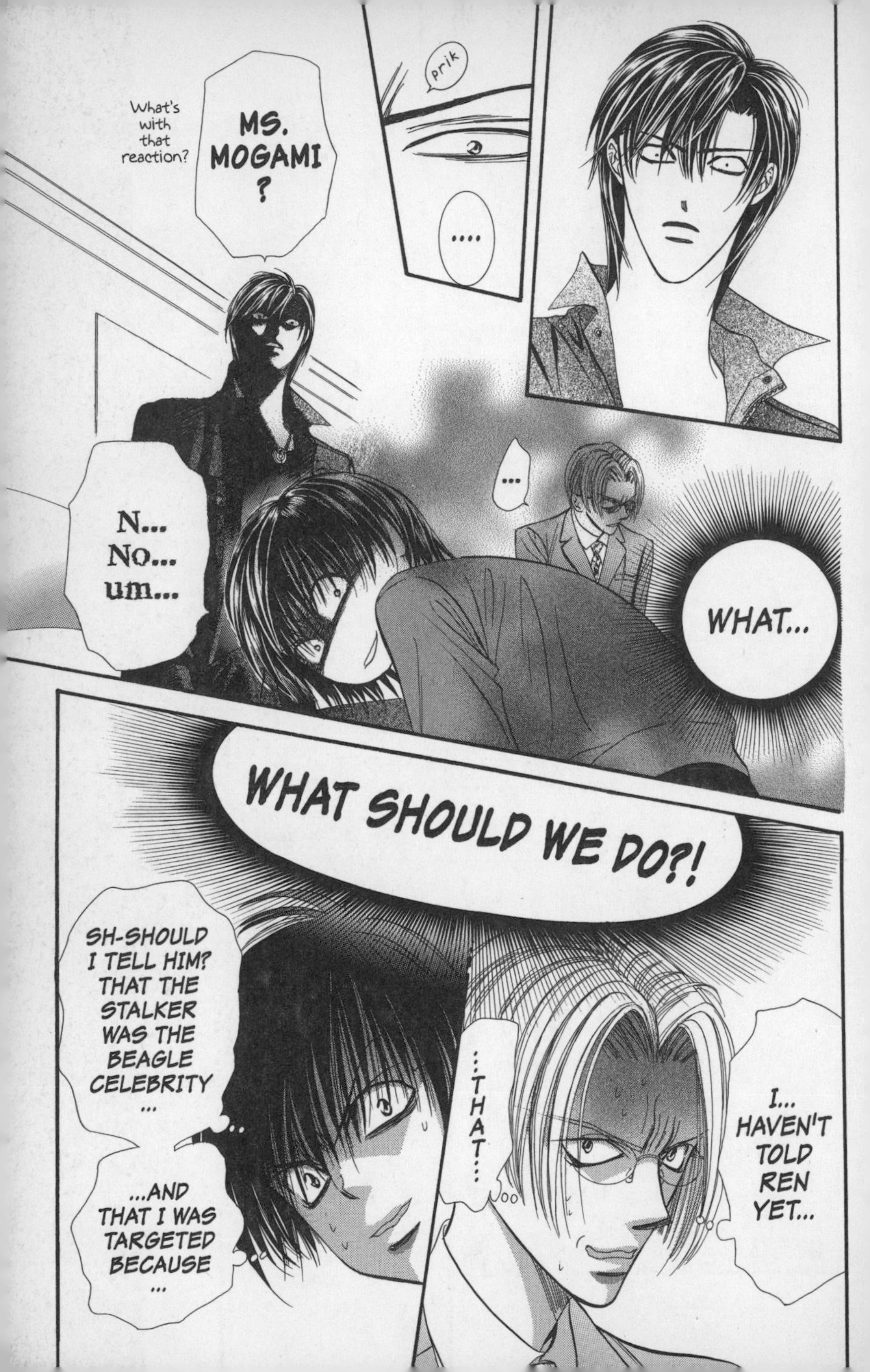
prik
....
MS. MOGAMI?
What's with that reaction?
N... No... um...
...
WHAT...
WHAT SHOULD WE DO?!
I... HAVEN'T TOLD REN YET...
...THAT...
SH-SHOULD I TELL HIM? THAT THE STALKER WAS THE BEAGLE CELEBRITY...
...AND THAT I WAS TARGETED BECAUSE...

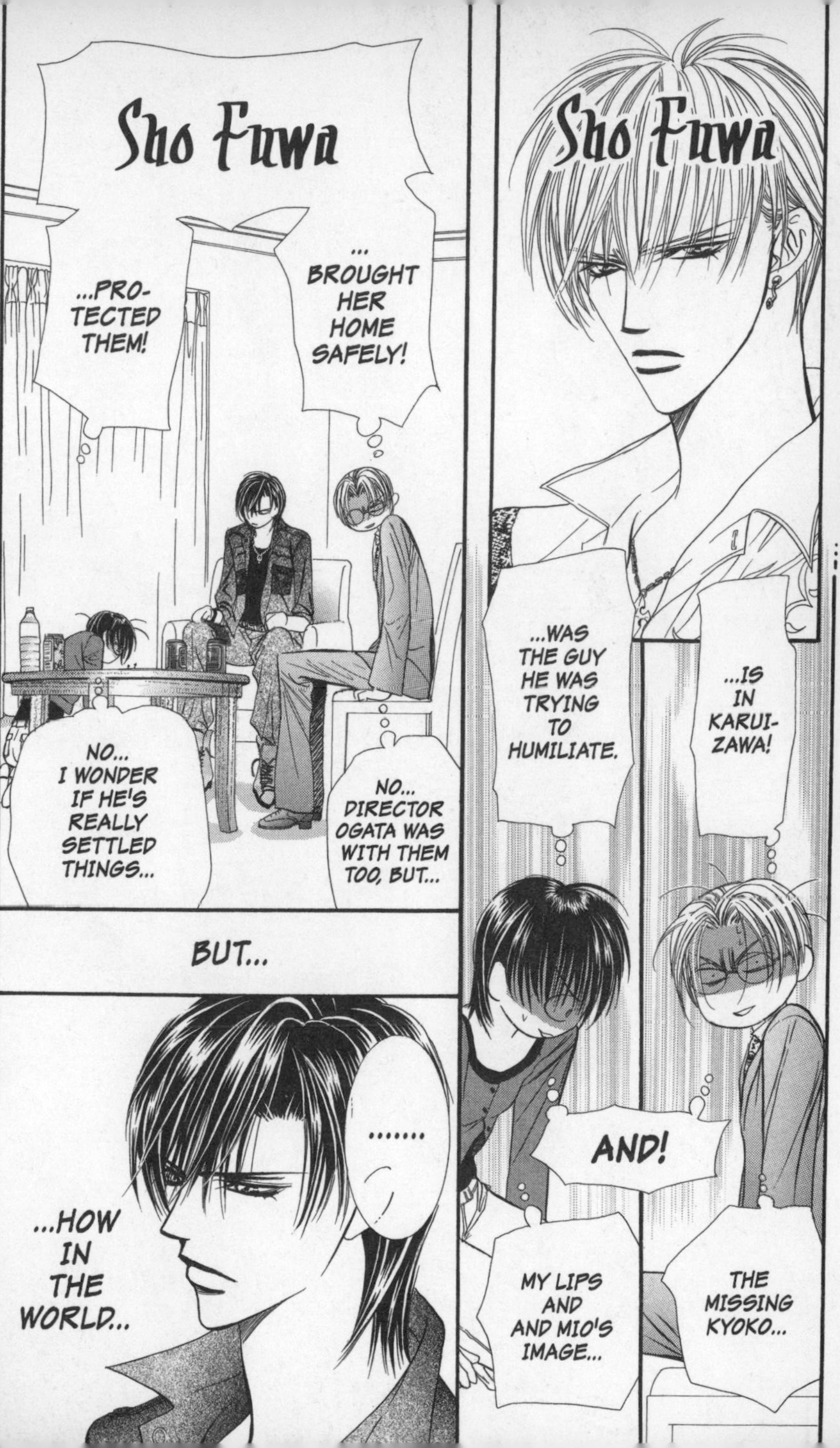
Sho Fuwa
...IS IN KARUI-ZAWA!
...WAS THE GUY HE WAS TRYING TO HUMILIATE.
THE MISSING KYOKO...
AND!
MY LIPS AND AND MIO'S IMAGE...
Sho Fuwa
... BROUGHT HER HOME SAFELY!
...PRO-TECTED THEM!
NO... DIRECTOR OGATA WAS WITH THEM TOO, BUT...
NO... I WONDER IF HE'S REALLY SETTLED THINGS...
BUT...
....
...HOW IN THE WORLD...

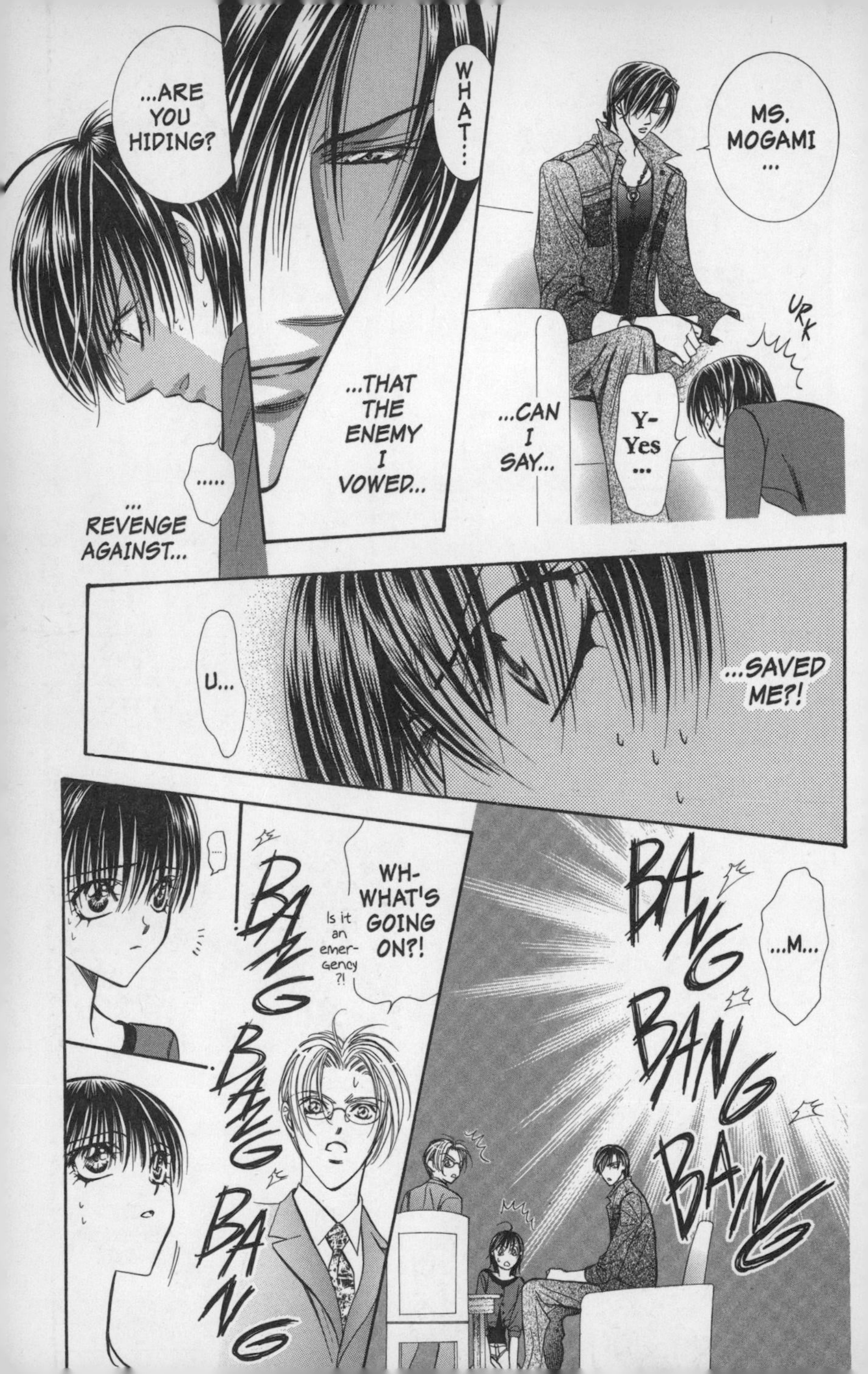
MS. MOGAMI ...
URK
Y-Yes ...
...ARE YOU HIDING?
.....
WHAT...
...CAN I SAY...
...THAT THE ENEMY I VOWED...
... REVENGE AGAINST...
...SAVED ME?!
U...
...M...
BANG BANG BANG BANG
WH-WHAT'S GOING ON?!
Is it an emer-gency?!
BANG BANG BANG
....

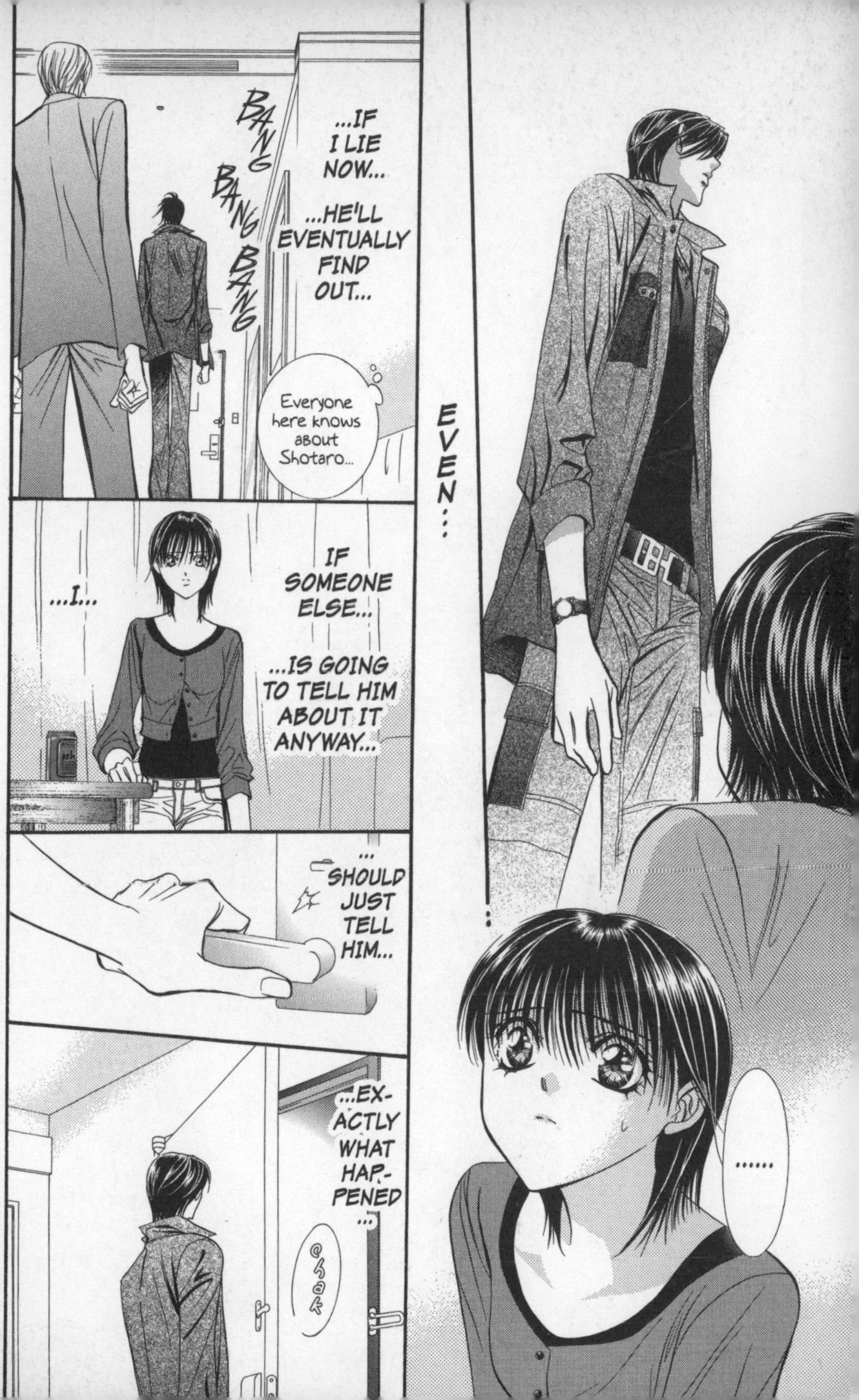

EVEN...
......
BANG
BANG
BANG
...IF I LIE NOW...
...HE'LL EVENTUALLY FIND OUT...
Everyone here knows about Shotaro...
...I...
IF SOMEONE ELSE...
...IS GOING TO TELL HIM ABOUT IT ANYWAY...
...SHOULD JUST TELL HIM...
...EX-ACTLY WHAT HAP-PENED...
Chak

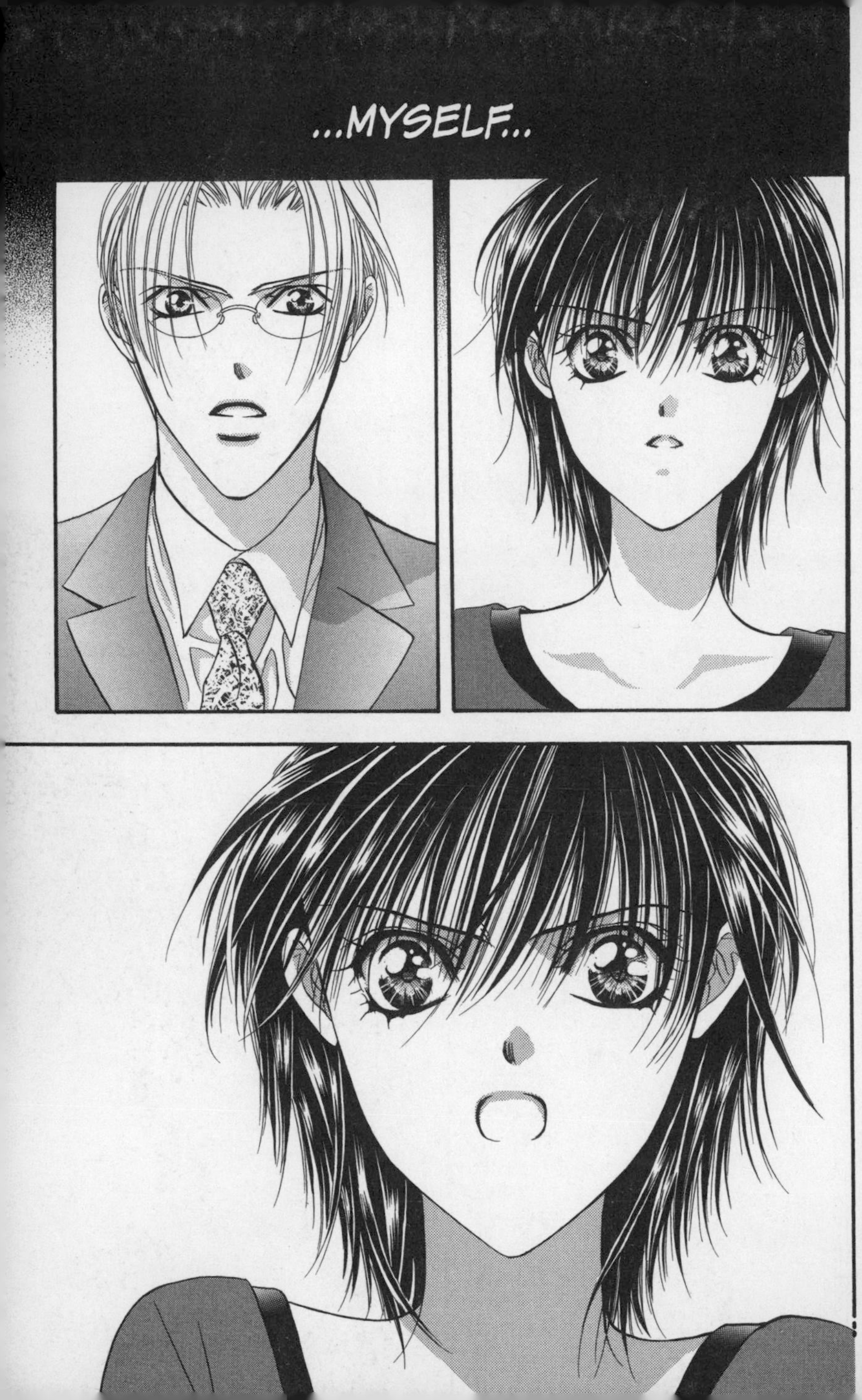
...MYSELF...

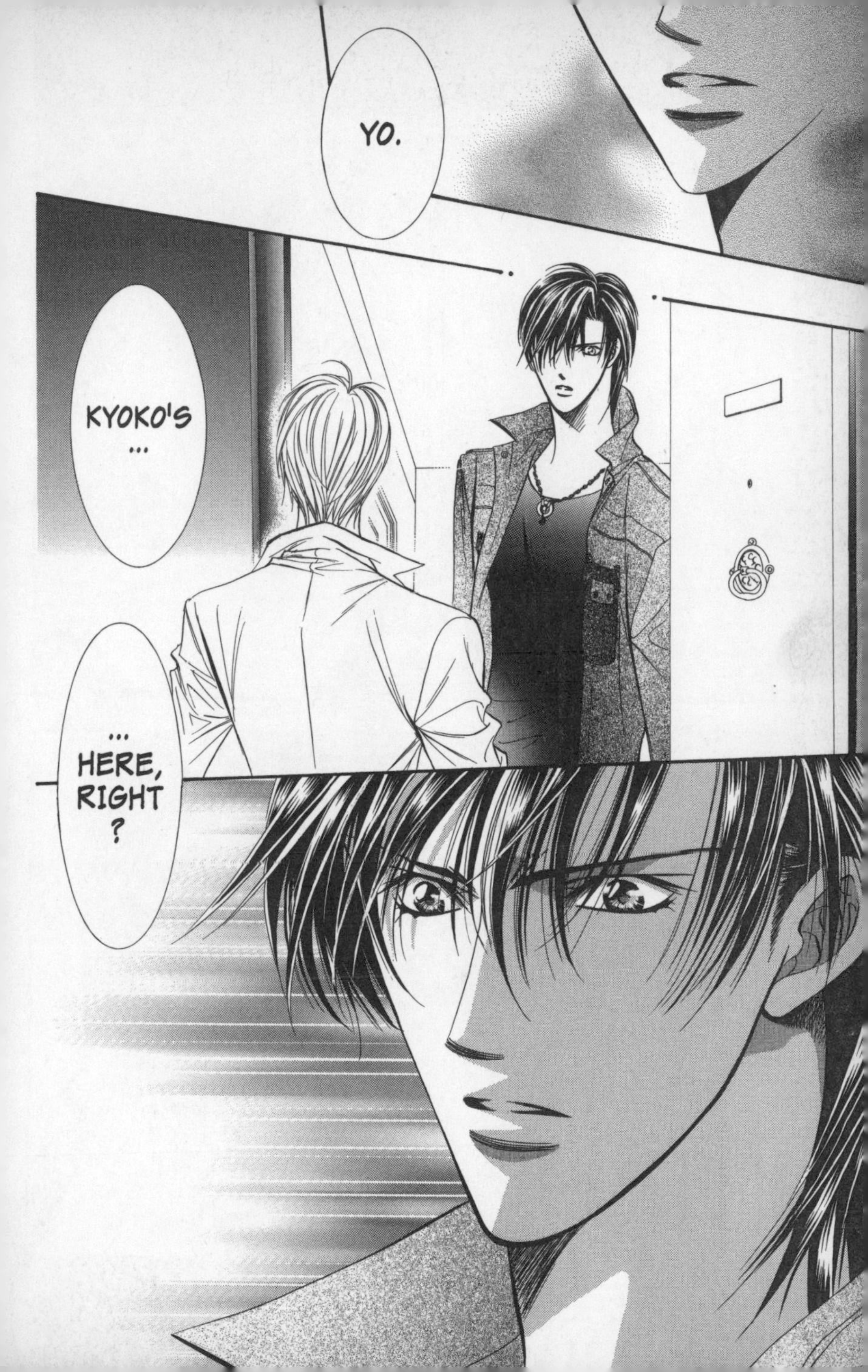
YO.
KYOKO'S ...
... HERE, RIGHT ?

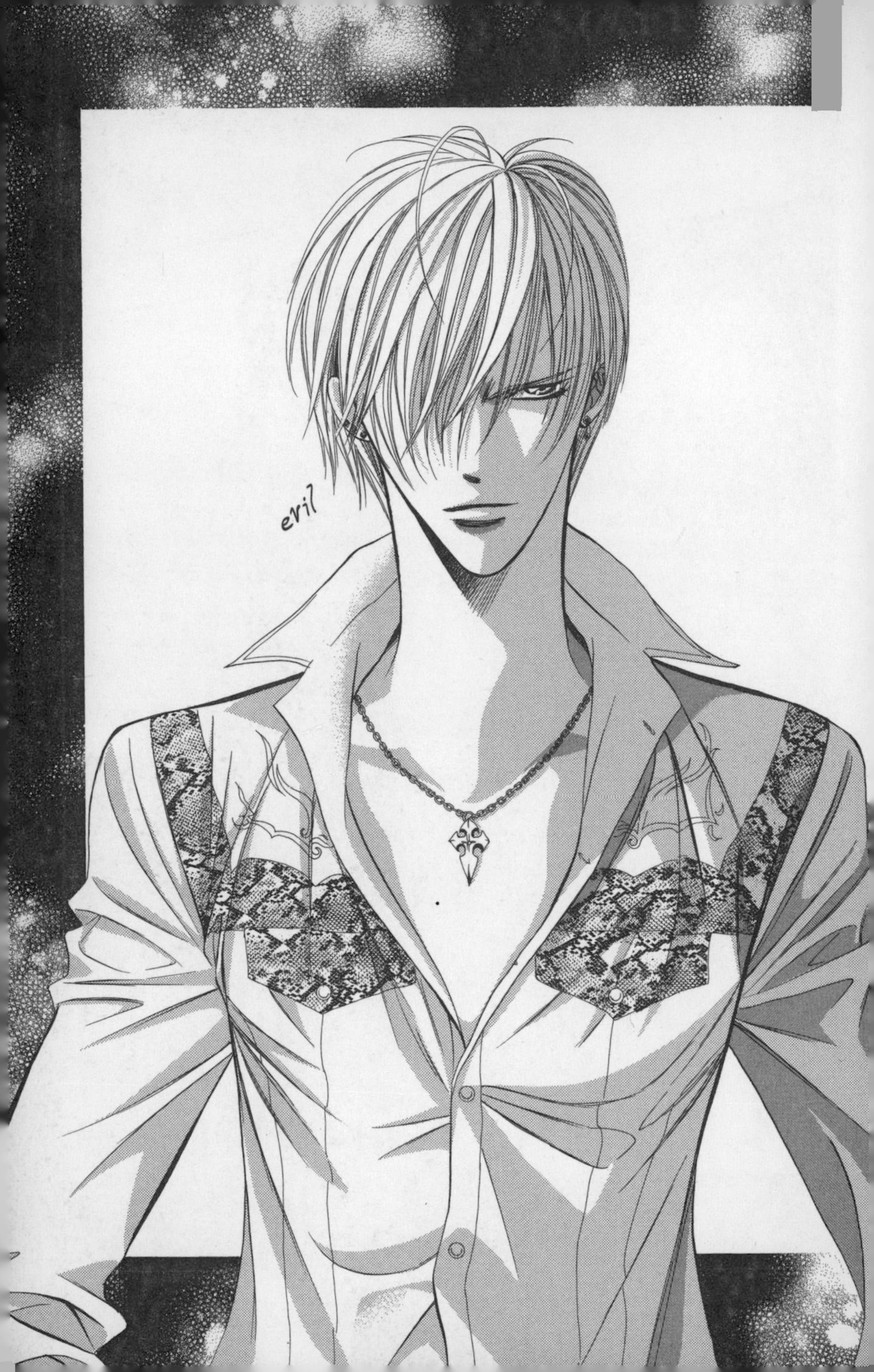
evil

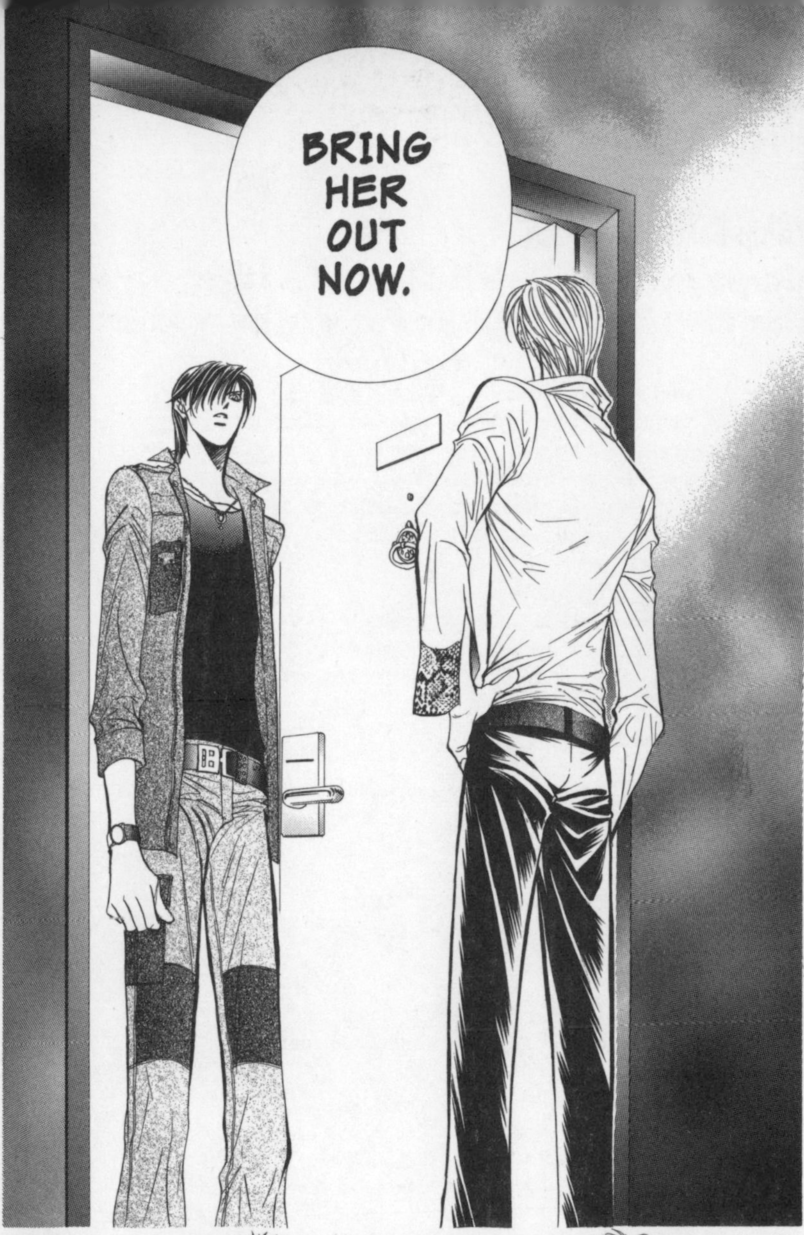
BRING HER OUT NOW.
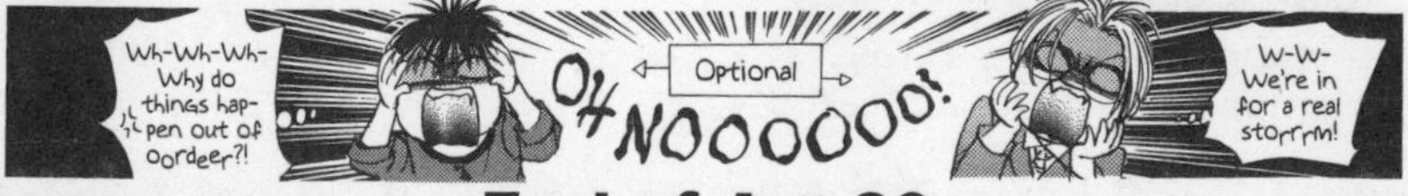
W-W-We're in for a real storrrm!
Optional
OH NOOOOOO!
Wh-Wh-Wh-Why do things happen out of oordeer?!

End of Act 90

Skip-Beat! End Notes
Everyone knows how to be a fan, but sometimes cool things
from other cultures need a little help crossing the language barrier.

Page 7, panel 2: Public baths
In Japan, public baths are not just found in resort settings. They are often
used on a regular basis by people whose living situations do not include a
bathtub, or by people who enjoy the communal aspect. Most public baths
include sex-segregated pools inside the larger bath complex, although there
are some bathhouses that have mixed bathing.

Page 21, panel 5: Yukata
Lightweight summer garments often worn by women and children to festivals
and fireworks displays. *Yukata* are also provided at traditional Japanese
inns that include a hot spring for customers to wear after bathing. The word
literally means "bath clothes."

Page 50, panel 3: Soft and firm tofu
Kinugoshi, or silken tofu, is a fine-grained tofu, with the softest texture.
Momen, or cotton tofu, has a firmer texture and is made by pressing the
excess liquid out of the tofu.

Page 76, panel 5: Visual kei
A style of Japanese rock that incorporates eccentric and fantastical costumes,
hairstyles, and make-up.

Page 137, panel 3: Crying yourself to sleep
The Japanese is *nakineiri*, and it means to let a matter drop without
protesting.

Page 158, panel 5: Haigorei
Haigorei means "spirits behind your back," and usually refers to evil spirits
that possess humans, although they could be spirits that protect or guide you.

Page 176, panel 4: Dogeza
The deepest, most formal type of bow. Kyoko often uses it to express her
regret and contrition when she feels words are inadequate.

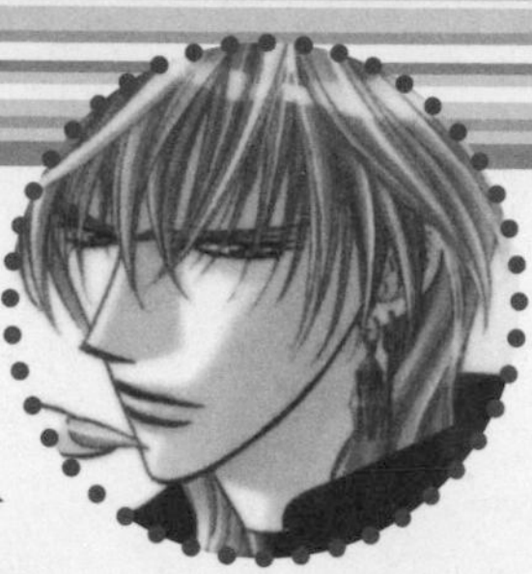

Yoshiki Nakamura is originally from Tokushima prefecture. She started drawing manga in elementary school, which eventually led to her 1993 debut of *Yume de Au yori Suteki* (Better than Seeing in a Dream) in *Hana to Yume* magazine. Her other works include the basketball series *Saint Love*, *MVP wa Yuzurenai* (Can't Give Up MVP), *Blue Wars*, and *Tokyo Crazy Paradise*, a series about a female bodyguard in 2020 Tokyo.

SKIP·BEAT!
Vol. 15
The Shojo Beat Manga Edition

STORY AND ART BY YOSHIKI NAKAMURA

English Translation & Adaptation/Tomo Kimura
Touch-up Art & Lettering/Sabrina Heep
Cover Design/Yukiko Whitley
Interior Design/Izumi Evers
Editor/Pancha Diaz

Editor in Chief, Books/Alvin Lu
Editor in Chief, Magazines/Marc Weidenbaum
VP, Publishing Licensing/Rika Inouye
VP, Sales and Product Marketing/Gonzalo Ferreyra
VP, Creative/Linda Espinosa
Publisher/Hyoe Narita

Printed in Canada

Published by VIZ Media, LLC
P.O. Box 77010
San Francisco, CA 94107

Shojo Beat Manga Edition
10 9 8 7 6 5 4 3 2 1
First printing, November 2008

store.viz.com

Tell us what about Shojo Beat Manga!

Our survey is now available online. Go to:

shojobeat.com/mangasurvey

Help us make our product offerings better!